MAKING ENGLAND WESTERN

MAKING ENGLAND WESTERN

Occidentalism, Race, and Imperial Culture

SAREE MAKDISI

THE UNIVERSITY OF CHICAGO PRESS

CHICAGO AND LONDON

SAREE MAKDISI is professor of English and comparative literature at the University of California, Los Angeles. He is the author of three books, including *William Blake and the Impossible History of the 1790s*, also published by the University of Chicago Press.

The University of Chicago Press, Chicago 60637
The University of Chicago Press, Ltd., London
© 2014 by The University of Chicago
All rights reserved. Published 2014.
Printed in the United States of America

23 22 21 20 19 18 17 16 15 14   1 2 3 4 5

ISBN-13: 978-0-226-92313-0 (cloth)
ISBN-13: 978-0-226-92314-7 (paper)
ISBN-13: 978-0-226-92315-4 (e-book)
DOI: 10.7208/chicago/9780226923154.001.0001

Library of Congress Cataloging-in-Publication Data

Makdisi, Saree.
    Making England western : occidentalism, race, and imperial culture / Saree Makdisi.
        pages cm
    Includes bibliographical references and index.
    ISBN 978-0-226-92313-0 (cloth : alk. paper) — ISBN 978-0-226-92314-7 (pbk. : alk. paper) — ISBN 978-0-226-92315-4 (e-book) 1. Great Britain—Colonies. 2. Civilization, Western. 3. Imperialism. 4. Great Britain—Foreign relations. 5. Great Britain—Ethnic relations. I. Title.
    JV1035.M35 2014
    303.48'241—dc23

                                                                2013014447

♾ This paper meets the requirements of ANSI/NISO Z39.48-1992 (Permanence of Paper).

FOR SAMIR AND MAISSA,

MY BEAUTIFUL

CHILDREN

Improvement makes strait roads, but the crooked roads
without Improvement, are roads of Genius.
—William Blake

CONTENTS

Preface   *ix*

Acknowledgments   *xxi*

Introduction: Occidentalism, Race, Imperial Culture   *1*

Part One: Preparing the Way

1. Making London Western   *39*

2. Civilizing the Ballad   *87*

Part Two: Episodes of Occidentalism

3. Domineering over Others: Occidentalism, Empire,
    Moral Virtue   *133*

4. Occidentalism and the Erotics of the Self   *151*

5. The Occidental Imperative   *174*

Part Three: Occidentalism in Crisis

6. "Irregular Modernization": Charles Dickens and
    the Crisis of Occidentalism   *195*

Conclusion   *233*

Notes   *243*

Index   *283*

PREFACE

England in the years around 1800 was not what would today be called a Western country, nor was it possible to neatly and cleanly distinguish it as a metropolitan space from the various colonial sites—both near and far—over which it sought to project political, economic, and cultural power. Those, at least, are the claims that mark this book's point of departure, and I'd like briefly to elaborate on each of them before more fully articulating my argument in the Introduction and in the chapters that follow.

To begin with, we too often take for granted just how settled the imperial metropolis was in the moment of revolutionary crisis and transition at the end of the eighteenth and the beginning of the nineteenth century, and hence how sharply England and the English could, at that time, be contrasted with spaces and populations subject to British colonial violence in a patchwork of territories stretching from Ireland and the Highlands of Scotland to the Caribbean, India, and southern Africa. For it's not as though England (and I want to emphasize that this book is specifically interested in England, rather than Britain more generally) were always already a metropolitan center in the fullest sense of that term; that is, a center of empire whose people and spaces could be uniformly distinguished as such from those of its peripheries (distinguished, for example, by virtue of a claim to greater civilization, advancement, progress, or to various forms of cultural, civilizational, or racial superiority).

Indeed, the Romantic period constituting the decades straddling the turn of the nineteenth century was the moment in which England really started to become a metropolitan center in a broadly consolidated social, economic, and cultural sense, on terms that would involve weaving together more and more people, and ultimately the national population, into a putatively homogeneous "we," a collectivity that could claim to possess—or rather, one whose proponents and champions claimed it possessed—cultural and racial homogeneity.[1] Extending over several decades well into the nineteenth century, this fraught process involved the decomposition and recomposition of a whole range of racial, national, and cultural logics, along with the emergence and development of an entirely new understanding of a national imagined community, one that was far more inclusive than earlier such understandings, even while it was also more specific in its acts of exclusion as well. Indeed, the simultaneity and reciprocity of these processes and acts of inclusion and of exclusion will be central to the story I want to tell in this book.[2]

As a result, nineteenth-century conceptions of nationalism in Britain (and particularly in England) were very different from their eighteenth-century predecessors: a difference marked in part by increasing literacy and the emergence of broad-based political participation beginning in the 1790s and persisting—despite various forms of government repression—through the tumult of 1819 and on through Chartism and beyond. (This is why many of the lessons we can derive from Suvir Kaul's meticulous and incisive readings of nationalist poetry from the eighteenth century can't so easily be extended into the later period.)[3]

To be more precise, these new conceptions of race and nation were made all the more necessary by two momentous and related developments. First, there was the appearance on the national stage of popular organizations speaking in the name of "the people" and demanding their political enfranchisement. This altogether altered the stakes of class relations on a national scale and made it quite impossible to take "the people" as much for granted as earlier eighteenth-century versions of nationalism had been able to do. For it is one thing to have made claims on behalf of the disenfranchised multitude when they were not yet speaking for themselves in an organized and sustained manner (that is, before the 1790s)—and quite another to do so in the wake of sustained popular challenges to the monopoly on both political and verbal representation claimed by the established elite.[4]

Second, there was a thickening of England's colonial relationships: an ever-greater interpenetration of peoples and spaces tying all the more closely the metropolis with the colonial realm, including the arrival in London of some fifteen thousand black soldiers who had fought with the British during the American war of independence, augmenting London's already considerable black population, as well as sailors, merchants, and various other travelers from the colonial realm, many of whom settled in London.[5] This in turn made it all the more urgent (for some) to begin to be able to differentiate spaces and peoples, to draw lines of distinction and separation distinguishing "us" from "them." This was especially true in a period in which, as Lauren Benton has argued, nations and empires "did not cover space evenly but composed a fabric that was full of holes, stitched together out of pieces, a tangle of strings," an unevenness that extended to the metropolis itself.[6] And it was all the more true given that, as Ian Baucom points out, "all the individuals born in the diverse places over which England claimed sovereignty" could, legally speaking, be "considered identically and interchangeably British."[7]

What I want to emphasize, however, is that the "us"/"them" distinction that began to emerge in the late eighteenth and early nineteenth century did not operate simply along native/foreigner or native/immigrant axes: it cut across and among native, indigenous English people as well, some of whom came to be seen from a certain privileged standpoint as culturally and racially separate and inferior, as not fit members of the race or nation, as alien and other (savage, Arab, both unsettled and unsettling) compared to an emergent notion of those of "us" who were seen to be more appropriately at home in England. Under such circumstances, distinguishing where exactly "our" domain and our population begin and end, and who exactly "we" are, became matters of both cultural and political urgency.

This raises the question of just how, in cultural and ideological terms, the formation of the metropolitan center was related to the opposing formation of the colonial realm: was the relationship one of more or less instantaneous binary opposition ("we" are "here" and "they" are "there")? Or was there a set of processes at work that took time to develop and work their way through a period of muddied confusion, as imperial and cultural dynamics changed in this period; as what Stuart Hall calls the articulated structure of race and class was comprehensively altered and recomposed; as the metropolitan center was itself also gradually brought under control; as what came to be called the civilizing process was carried out both overseas *and* at home in England?[8]

The latter line of inquiry is the one I follow in this book. I argue that for a considerable period the two spaces, the would-be metropolitan and the colonial, have to be thought in overlapping and intermixed relation, not in structural—much less binary—opposition, to one another, and that the dynamics at work in one sphere can also be seen at work in the other. The borders between "here" and "there," "us" and "them," were for some time rather more amorphous, even porous, than we might have imagined.

This brief account will, I hope, have given at least a sense of the first of the claims marking this book's point of departure, which will be elaborated at greater length in the chapters that follow. The second claim is that the process of transforming England into a metropolitan center of empire also involved the emergence and development of a new cultural and civilizational notion of a West, an Occident, to which England could claim to belong, in opposition to an Orient lying somewhere out there to the East (though where exactly remained an open question for much longer than we generally imagine). For England at the turn of the nineteenth century was not Western in two senses; first, in that the notion of the West as opposed to the East—as a cultural or civilizational opposition framed along a very specific moral and temporal or developmental matrix—was still very much in the process of formation (indeed, it is a notion that has never really stabilized, even though its incoherence as a category has never stopped it from being put to all kinds of cultural and political uses); and, second, in that, whatever one intends by the designation "Western," neither all of England nor all of the English (let alone the Welsh, the Irish, or the Highlanders of Scotland) would have been seen to conform to it at the turn of the nineteenth century.

This is an argument that I will develop more fully in the chapters to follow, but I'd like to anticipate a couple of points here. The idea of some kind of Western/Eastern opposition was of course not new at the turn of the nineteenth century, and in many ways the conceptualization that emerged in that moment involved drawing on and partially reframing earlier variants of such an opposition (for example, the Western vs. the Eastern Roman empire, Western vs. Eastern churches, Christendom vs. Islam). This reframing was inseparable from, really coextensive with, the transformation of an Orientalist discourse that was similarly drawing on an ancient lineage (going back to the classical period) even while transforming it, adapting it for new purposes and a new era into what Edward Said identifies as a specifically modern form of Orientalism.[9]

My account differs somewhat from Said's, however, in that I am more interested in the ways in which an emergent Orientalist discourse was directed against internal rather than primarily external targets: that is, sites or populations within the space of the nation that would be designated as other in specifically Oriental terms. Just as the radicalism of the 1790s had Orientalized the national aristocracy, seeing it as a foreign form of tyranny that needed to be expunged from the social body, other internal populations, which would later come to be considered white and English, were also Orientalized as the ideological ethos of 1790s radicalism—above all its obsessive, single-minded, almost pathological Orientalism[10]—took hold in the nineteenth century, among many conservatives as well as radicals themselves (with notable exceptions, to be sure).

The complication here is that, although from the 1790s onward, especially but not only in the work of radicalism, there emerged a very clear set of binary oppositions identifying a normative self (productive, modern, sober, unadorned, disciplined, rational, frank, fair-minded, moderate, regulated, democratic, hardworking, honest, natural, scientific, virtuous, manly, masculine, etc.) as opposed to a degenerate other (vain, retrograde, obsessed with appearances, irrational, unproductive, undisciplined, lazy, unnatural, licentious, capricious, deceitful, emotional, fanatical, tyrannical, violent, indulgent, voluptuous, sensual, feminine, effeminate, etc.), and although it was considered clear that the negative traits associated with the other were characteristically Oriental, the specifically Occidental nature of the self defined in opposition to the Oriental other remained implicit rather than explicit until somewhat later in the nineteenth century. That is, the idea of the West as the site of a culture or civilization defined specifically as democratic, modern, fair, progressive, scientific, secular, rational, productive and so on—an idea that began to be consolidated precisely in the moment to which this book is devoted—was at the turn of the nineteenth century still very much in process, not yet fully articulated, and certainly not named as such, even when it was articulated in opposition to a very specifically designated Orient. In designating the set of cultural and political discourses underlying and sustaining the emergence of this new conception of the West as Occidentalism, I am, as it were, filling in a blank, naming an absence.

In ways that will I hope become clearer in the Introduction and the chapters to follow, then, this book is interested in a particular moment, an episode in the formation of a civilizational category—the West—that has always been, and will always be, variable and unstable, even though it has also been deployed with such confidence, as though it could convey a transhistorical essence, by certain would-be authorities (Bernard Lewis comes to mind) right up to our own time.

What I will argue in this book is that the space that would eventually come to be established as the Occident had to be Occidentalized—that England, among other sites, had to be *made* Western. What I call Occidentalism was the set of discourses articulating the process that made England Western.

It ought to go without saying that I do not mean here to deny the specificity and violence of the work of empire overseas, or to say that binary oppositions such as Occident/Orient don't eventually come to function very powerfully, or that they can be undermined by simply trying to recover an in-between in the way that a magician pulls a rabbit out of his hat. Sometimes there really is no in-between, and Frantz Fanon was surely right to describe the colonial world persisting into our era as "a world cut in two," as the merest glance at our contemporary Jerusalem reminds us.[11] At the particular period (spanning the late eighteenth and much of the nineteenth century) in which I am interested in this book, however, a set of cultural, political and racial dynamics unfolded relationally *both* in England *and* in the colonial realm. This, for a while, allowed the two spaces (or parts of them) and their respective populations (or parts of them) to be thought of not merely in parallel or analogous terms, but actually in identical and interchangeable ones. Strategies and tactics of discipline, surveillance, and control were often shifted back and forth between explicitly colonial sites (such as Ireland and India) and domestic ones inside England, precisely because the targeted populations were thought of in the same terms—above all as being in need of discipline, surveillance, and control in the first place.[12] Thus, for instance, many of the practices that David Lloyd argues were designed to discipline Irish bodies, body parts, and organs, beginning with the mouth, were also mobilized in the regulation of certain English bodies, desires, and oral functions (including a thriving plebeian oral culture which was seen as just as subversively dangerous to the settled order of colonial modernity as various acts of resistance in Ireland itself).[13]

What all this meant was that, in the years around 1800, it was quite impossible to contrast "here" versus "there" or "us" versus "them" or Occident versus Orient in any clean or neat way—least of all along national lines—because "we," in this period, were not yet really all "we," and "our" space was not yet one that "we" could inhabit with an equal sense of homeliness or belonging. For there were sites within England that might as well have been in Arabia, and there were English people living there who, from a certain perspective, might as well have been Arabs, to whom the myth of the freeborn Englishman, or the narrative of racial Anglo-Saxonism explored by Laura Doyle, simply did not extend.[14]

I am not stretching the point. Let me give a quick couple of examples to help illustrate it and also rescue it from abstraction (though the fuller elaboration of these examples will have to wait until we get to the chapter from which I have borrowed them). "We have now a new term, that recognizes emphatically an evil too long ignored. I mean, 'The City Arabs,'" the Reverend James Pycroft recalls being told by a fellow church man in the second third of the nineteenth century. "This is one step towards realising the truth that a veritable heathen mission is as much wanted in the interior of London as in the interior of Africa. As to heathen ignorance," he adds, "in London we have a darkness that may be felt; as to the gross and debasing habits of the brutes that perish, we have hovels and savages not surpassed in Timbuctoo; and as to poisonous malaria, I can show you veritable patches of Sierra Leone no further off than Spitalfields."[15] As I discuss at length in chapter I, from the early nineteenth century on, it became quite common to speak of a whole segment of the population of London (again, people who would today be thought of as white and English) in terms of racial and civilizational otherness. And the point is that these wretched people were not merely being *compared* to other races and civilizations, as though really "we" knew all along that "they" were "our people," but rather that they really were *not* "our people;" they were not "us." The language of race here ceases to work simply on a comparative basis and becomes more genuinely descriptive: from a polite or refined perspective, these wretches are not merely being *compared* to savages; they *were* savages, pure and simple.

"Of all the dark and dismal thoroughfares in the parish of St. Giles's, or, indeed, in the great wilderness of London, few, we think, will compare with that known as Church Lane, which runs between High Street and New Oxford Street," writes Walter Thornbury several decades later, in the 1870s. "During the last half century, while the metropolis has been undergoing the pressure of progress consequent upon the quick march of civilisation, what remains of the Church Lane of our early days has been left with its little colony of Arabs as completely sequestered from London society as if it was part of *Arabia Petræa*. Few pass through Church Lane who are not members of its own select society. None else have any business there; and if they had, they would find it to their interest to get out of it as soon as possible. Its condition is a disgrace to the great city, and to the parish to which it belongs."[16] Under such circumstances, the sense of alienation that some English people felt toward others—and it is important to emphasize one last time that Thornbury is, like Pycroft, referring to people who would today be considered white and English whom he is Arabizing, not to real Arabs—was not any less profound than what they felt toward "real" foreigners.

And that is the point: who is the foreigner in such a situation? The real Arab or the City Arab? Or both? But how can an English "Arab" be a foreigner in her own land? Maybe, from a certain perspective, it wasn't really her land after all; maybe she did not belong there any more than the real Arab does, certainly not if one wants to imagine—as an increasing number of people at the time did—an Occident cleansed of the last traces of Oriental contamination. Given that, within the span of a few decades, around a hundred thousand such "Arabs" were forcibly displaced from their homes during the material reinvention—the Westernization, the Occidentalization—

of the space of London in the nineteenth century, as what Thornbury calls "the quick march of civilisation" was extended both inside England and outside it, this does not seem such a far-fetched proposition after all.

While the literary scholarship on the eighteenth century, Romantic, and Victorian periods has for some time embraced the exploration of the sense of otherness within Britain (particularly with reference to London, but also on a national scale),[17] part of what I want to propose in this book is that that sense of otherness was far more profound and more unsettling than has previously been allowed and also far more analytically challenging. Much of our understanding of the sense of otherness within Britain or England in this long period specifically rests on a contrast with what is taken to be an already stabilized national or racial sense of self. Indeed, some of the recent scholarly interest in the awareness or presence of cultural or racial others—Irish, West Indian, African, Arab, Indian, Chinese, so-called Lascars—within the imperial metropolis runs the risk of unintentionally reinforcing the very sense of normative sameness and identity that it seeks to decenter. For the underlying theme in some of that scholarship (to which I will return in the chapters that follow) is a recurring set of oppositions to an understanding of Englishness or whiteness whose status is taken for granted as defining a kind of norm, a stable standard of "self" in contrast to which otherness can be measured.

What I will be arguing in this book is that there was no dominant, secured, normative form—much less space—of racial and cultural identity in England in the years around 1800: rather, there was a struggle to locate and secure the space in which such an identity might be consolidated. Rather than being read against a normative sense of British or English or white or Occidental identity whose establishment and sense of self can be taken for granted, then, the sense of otherness that emerged in this period needs to be seen as posing far more of a challenge to the apparent security and normality of those identities. For that otherness and those forms of identity emerged together: it is in the same moment that, on the one hand, Africans, Arabs, Scottish Highlanders, and the wretched poor of London are reviled—in the same ways and with the same words—as being little better than beasts, while, on the other hand, a distinctly new English, white, Occidental form of identity begins to emerge. The kind of horror that gripped polite observers at the sight of the wretches of St. Giles's was, then, not quite the horror one feels in the face of otherness. Rather, it was the horror one feels in the face of that undifferentiated, amorphous, abject primal soup out of which the very self/other divide emerges in the first place. For it is only through the racial configuration of the other that the self becomes

racially defined in turn.[18] Such acts of configuration were slow and complicated, however, and at certain moments overlapped and intertwined with
other forms of configuration, including those of sexuality and class. This
helps explain why there is such mobility and fluidity of terms of reference
in describing encounters with otherness in this period: given the lack of familiar or reliable registers or discourses in which to frame the horror of such
encounters, certain categories that might otherwise (earlier or later) be kept
distinct are here collapsed into one another.

This collapse of categories helps us understand the highly charged, but
also highly unstable, relationship of race and class in this period. Even while
drawing our attention to the ways in which class and race categories were
deployed with or against each other in the early to mid-nineteenth century,
much of the recent scholarship has, perhaps inadvertently, taken for granted
the status of either or both of these categories. It has become quite common, for instance, to see scholarly references to the "racialization" of "the
working class" in late eighteenth- and early nineteenth-century England.
However, such readings not only assume the distinctness of race and class,
they invariably assert the ontological priority of the latter over the former:
first "they" are the working class, *then* they are racialized. In fact, class
structures were in enormous flux in this period, and "the working class," as
such (that is, as a class with its own internal sense of coherence and identity and a distinct set of relations to its exploitation by capital), did not yet
exist; not to mention that a whole range of occupations, from mudlarks and
costermongers to engravers and other artisans, could not precisely be made
to fit into the class structures—which is to say, the structural relations of
exploitation—of industrial capitalism.[19]

To this I would add not simply that racial categories were also in flux,
but that the point is that these structures were in flux in relationship to—
and, as Stuart Hall argues, as articulated with—one another. Hall's reading of Gramsci is especially productive in this context. He reminds us that
Gramsci refuses to think of class identities, and hence class relationships, in
a static or homogeneous way, and that he insists on thinking of the subject
as a composite amalgamation, a complex plurality of at times contradictory
identities rather than a unified force.[20] Hall uses Gramsci's insistence on
the amalgamated nature of identity to develop his own notion of the articulation of race and class: given the nonhomogeneous nature of the subject,
one can see multiple and overlapping elements of both racial and class formations within the subject and hence in relations between groups which
might assume the form of either class or race dynamics or both. Certainly
in the case of early to mid-nineteenth century London, the categories of

race and class were interpenetrating, bound up with each other, and to a certain extent inseparable, even indistinguishable, from one another. Forms of alienation or resentment that might at a later moment be expressed more specifically in class terms could at this moment be identified in vituperative racial terms, just as forms of racist exclusion or derogation might be driven by what might later be isolated more specifically as class dynamics. Forms of identity that it might be tempting to think of in class terms, in other words, also have racial logics immediately built into them.

It is for this reason that although those who were regarded (and came to regard themselves) as the "swinish multitude" were seen to be different from what was once called polite society in terms that either alternated between or simultaneously bound together the logics and languages of both race and class, it took much longer for the swinish multitude to be seen as having their own internal sense of homogeneity. Thus, for instance, what would today be regarded as mixed marriages between black and white people within what Douglas Lorimer calls the cosmopolitan world of the London poor in the early nineteenth century were not only not particularly unusual. They were, more importantly, not seen to be problematic in the way that they would come to be later on. Only in a later era would racial and class logics be somewhat more cleanly distinguished, allowing the emergence of, among other things, forms of working-class racism that would have been unthinkable in the years around 1800, as well as of the acts of racial exclusion to which Paul Gilroy has drawn our attention, which would ultimately enable a sense of differentiation all the more neatly preserving from racial and cultural contamination a putatively homogeneous "we," supposedly transcending class differences.[21] It was more difficult to mobilize such clean acts of separation earlier in the nineteenth century. The instability of racial and class categories can be seen at work, for example, in Carlyle's *Discourse on the Nigger Question*, in which he at times seeks to contrast "beautiful Blacks sitting there [in the West Indies] up to the ears in pumpkins" with "our own English labourers" who pay high sugar duties and are starving for want of work, while at other times collapsing the lazy blacks of the West Indies with the ought-to-be white underclass of England, "for they also have long sat Negro-like up to the ears in pumpkin, regardless of 'work,' and of a world going to waste for their idleness!"[22] At times, then, "our own English labourers" are truly ours; that is, members of what Carlyle identifies as a "Saxon British" race known for its "manfulness" and work ethic; at times, they are not "ours"—not "us"—at all.[23]

At a minimum, then, given the absence of a clearly identifiable set of terms to make such distinctions, "we" were not quite yet really "we" in a national sense in this period. In establishing such lines of demarcation, simply being English or British is not the point: what counts far more is being one of "us" in a racial or civilizational sense. In this context, it is, at best, misleading or confusing to speak of a single national culture, as some scholars of nationalism have done; or of a wider racial or civilizational identity that might locate all English people (never mind all Britons) on one side of a clearly delineated divide; or even simply to seek to disarticulate racism and nationalism, even with the best intentions.[24]

I want to emphasize that scholarly accounts of nationalism and national identity (whether English or British more generally) read in isolation from broader racial or civilizational dynamics cannot possibly provide an adequate framework for understanding the nature and the stakes of the political and cultural transformation that began to take place at the turn of the nineteenth century. Some parts of the English population could be captured or woven into the racial, the civilizational, the Occidental, or perhaps the national "us," and others simply had to go, be eliminated in one way or another, though in ways that I think also productively complicate Gilroy's account of the cultures of British racism.[25] Such acts of erasure or destruction remain invisible to some histories of British nationalism and imperialism, even if they are not seeking to deny the significance of race,[26] or to celebrate the empire, or to resort to unreconstructed forms of Orientalism themselves.[27] Moreover, the instability of these forms of identity was directly bound up with the instability, indeed, the absence, of a clear line separating the metropolitan from the colonial realm, the inside and the domestic from the foreign and the imperial.

It took decades for these lines to be established, in a process that was never seamless or straightforward. For it was consistently resisted, and, for all the texts that celebrate this process there were plenty of others that were far more ambivalent or adamantly critical. The chapters that follow will trace the arc of celebration, ambivalence, and criticism from the late 1790s through the middle of the nineteenth century to 1870, the year Dickens died, leaving his last novel, *The Mystery of Edwin Drood*, unfinished. *Edwin Drood*, as we will see in the final chapter of this book, offers a profound and highly critical meditation on the failure of the process and very logic of Occidentalism.

The book unfolds in three parts. The first part, comprising the first two chapters, develops the ground on which the rest of the book will build, in the first chapter by taking us to the extraordinary confrontation between the civilizing process and the unstable realities of late eighteenth- and early nineteenth-century London, which offers us a kind of palimpsest to sketch out some of the overall arguments the book will be proposing. We will then rewind, so to speak, and return in the second chapter to Wordsworth, and his own specific sense of ambivalence about the process of narrating and representing the transformation and "civilization of England."

The second part of the book consists of three relatively brief and localized discussions of particular episodes in the formation of Occidentalism: chapter 3 explores Jane Austen's sense of the continuity of the civilizing mission both at home and overseas; chapter 4 turns to the very different engagements with Occidentalism and Orientalism in the work of Byron and of Charlotte Dacre; and chapter 5 treats the bitter dispute between Southey and Macaulay at the end of the Romantic and the dawn of the Victorian age.

The final section of the book, comprising the chapter on Dickens, turns to the sense of a crisis in Occidentalism that we find in Dickens's last novel. What we will be left with, I hope, is a deeper appreciation not only of the relentless unfolding project of Occidentalism through the nineteenth century but also of the dogged resistance to it and the broader imperial logics of development, improvement, and triumphant moral virtue with which it was always bound up.

ACKNOWLEDGMENTS

It would have been impossible for me to write this book without the help and support of friends, colleagues, and my family.

Patrick Wolfe, Iain McCalman, David Bromwich, James Buzard, Pablo Mukherjee, Denise Gigante, Michael Hardt, and David Lloyd patiently read and offered invaluable comments and criticisms on drafts of sections or chapters; I am very grateful for their feedback. My colleagues at the University of California, Los Angeles, especially Jenny Sharpe, Felicity Nussbaum, Jonathan Grossman, and Anne Mellor, also read and commented extensively on chapter drafts. I am especially grateful to Helen Deutsch and Michael Meranze, who not only read chapters but also gracefully tolerated a stream of e-mailed paragraphs and sentences; they are the very models of collegiality.

Speaking of which, the sense of collegiality fostered by the English department at UCLA has been a major source of support over the years. In his capacity as department chair, Ali Behdad has always combined encouragement with judicious guidance, and in his capacity as friend and fellow scholar, he has helped me think through different approaches to the question of Occidentalism and its forms of representation.

The English department staff, past and present, make everything possible, and I am indebted to the support of Jeanette Gilkinson, Elizabeth Paray, Elizabeth Krown Spellman, Janet Bishop, Rick Fagin, Nora Elias, Lynda Tolly, Bronson Tran, Clinton Lam, Caleb Na, Nicole Liang, and Ivonne Nelson, to all of whom I am very thankful.

I must also acknowledge the students in my graduate seminars at UCLA over the past three years, who have helped me think through and articulate many of the readings and lines of argument that appear in this book. I am especially grateful to Katie Charles, Taylor Walle, Mike Nicholson,

Sina Rahmani, Kate Bergren, Alexandra Milsom, and Lauren Dembowitz for reading chapters and providing invaluable feedback and criticism. Ian Newman not only read chapters but offered many suggestions, tips, and leads as we sifted through many of the same archival sources, and his groundbreaking work on the spaces and texts of radical culture in the Romantic period will undoubtedly go on to inform other scholarship as much as it has my own.

I am also grateful to the scholars, colleagues, and friends new and old at universities around the world at which I have been fortunate to present versions of chapters or strands of the argument that runs through this book. These include the University of Warwick, the American University of Beirut, the University of Pennsylvania, the University of Essex, Brigham Young University, the University of Sydney, the University of Missouri at Columbia, the University of Chicago, the University of California at Berkeley, the University of Nottingham, the University of Michigan at Ann Arbor, the University of Roehampton, the University of Tennessee at Knoxville, Vanderbilt University, Rice University, Stanford University, and Cornell University. Among the many conversations that followed from those presentations, I would especially like to acknowledge those with Peter Hulme, Marjorie Levinson, Sean Silver, Helena Michie, and Alexander Regier, and a set of conversations with Walter Cohen, Salah Hassan, Fouad Makki, Barry Maxwell, Viranjini Munasinghe, Natalie Melas, and others at Cornell University that helped me tie up various loose strands of the argument.

Jon Mee and Kevin Gilmartin helped me shape this project, especially in its early stages, and I owe much not only to their judicious feedback and criticism but to their comradeship in the field of Romanticism.

David Theo Goldberg has been an invaluable source of assistance, especially on questions of race, and he too has been very patient in fielding endless phone calls and e-mail queries and helping me along.

I also want to acknowledge the friendship of Ghassan Hage and Cesare Casarino, with both of whom even a few minutes of conversation provide a long-burning source of inspiration; in particular, a series of long conversations with Cesare, going all the way back to our graduate school days, quite literally brought home to me a very different way of understanding what it means to be included or excluded from the category of the European, and in a sense this book, among other things, is a belated outcome of those formative conversations.

Alan Thomas at the University of Chicago Press has also helped me shape a bag of ideas into a book, and I am grateful to his keen editorial eye, as well as to Randolph Petilos, Erik Carlson, and Jo Ann Kiser for helping transform a manuscript into an actual book.

My parents, Samir and Jean Makdisi, and my brothers, Ussama and Karim, are always among my main sources of support and illumination, and I am lucky to be able to count on them for reading passages or chapters or talking through various arguments and approaches. Ussama in particular took the time to help me work through the overall argument and locate it in the world of historical scholarship. Wissam and Shermine Boustany have over the years provided me with the most welcoming and supportive base of operations in London that anyone could ever ask for, and I am very grateful to them for sustaining the indispensable logistical side of research.

More than anyone else, however, Christina and our children, Samir and Maissa, have had to endure the constant ebb and flow of work and pressure associated with this book; beyond thanking them, I can only hope that they think the final product worth the effort. I owe Samir and Maissa, in particular, much more than a backlog of bedtime stories and playtime with Daddy, and it is to them that I dedicate this book.

An earlier version of chapter 3 appeared as "Austen, Empire, and Moral Virtue" in *Recognizing the Romantic Novel*, edited by Jillian Heydt-Stevenson and Charlotte Sussman (Liverpool: Liverpool University Press, 2009).

Occidentalism, Race, Imperial Culture

I would like to introduce the broader stakes of the argument I will be making in the chapters that follow with a brief discussion of two important scholarly projects that have sought to define and explore the relationship between metropolis and empire, namely, Edward Said's *Culture and Imperialism* and Bernard Porter's *The Absent-Minded Imperialists*. What is significant in the juxtaposition of Said and Porter, and what has made the juxtaposition productive for the work in which I am presently engaged, is that, while each makes a vital contribution that is missed by the other—so that they in some sense complement and are necessary to each other—both also share in common a problematic taking-for-granted of a separation of the domestic from the imperial realm. In a sense, then, the point of departure for my own project can be located in a critical terrain that is overlooked by both Porter and Said and yet illuminated when they are brought into a common conversation.

The premise of Said's *Culture and Imperialism* is that the relationship between metropolitan and colonial spaces is primarily oppositional, based on a series of contrasts between scenes of imperial conquest and horror, on the one hand, and domestic settled quiet and order, on the other. Part of the point of his argument is that the settled quiet of "home" depends structurally on the brutality and violence of "empire," a point illustrated by his reading of the dependence, in *Mansfield Park*, of Bertram's great estate in England on his slave plantation in Antigua: no matter how repressed the knowledge of Antigua is in Austen's novel, the estate would not exist without it.[1]

The gap between metropolitan and imperial domains is what motivates Said's call for scholars to engage in what he calls a contrapuntal approach to literature, culture, and imperialism. "We must be able to think through and interpret together experiences that are discrepant, each with its particular agenda and pace of development, its own internal formations, its internal coherence and system of external relationships, all of them coexisting and interacting with others," he argues.[2] In principle—in the long run—I agree with this argument. But the devil is in the details. Just how much "internal coherence" do these discrepant experiences need to have? How clearly demarcated, how truly external, must those "external relationships" be? How much does the contrapuntal approach depend on a stable sense of "interior" and "exterior" that can be brought together in counterpoint only if they are each internally stabilized to begin with? If the discrepant experiences of empire are taken to be geographically separate, as Said argues (so that, as he says, we need to read Frantz Fanon and Aimé Césaire, from the outside, alongside *Mansfield Park* and *Jane Eyre*, from the inside, to establish a sense of counterpoint), where do London's City Arabs, as they were called, fit in? In the physical sense of geography, they were "here," but in imaginative geography (to use another of Said's terms), they were "there." Temporally, they were, as I suggested in the Preface and will show at greater length in chapter 1, thought to inhabit a "then," a zone of past-time, rather than sharing our "now-time" with "us." According to Johannes Fabian, Europeans deployed such a denial of coevalness to think through their relations with non-Europeans.[3] What happens if the Other is *also* European, though that throws open the meaning of what it means to be European in the first place? Dipesh Chakrabarty has provided a brilliant critique of the historicist claim that historical time can be seen "as a measure of the cultural distance (at least in institutional development) that was assumed to exist between the West and the non-West."[4] But the logics and claims of historical time were also deployed against populations and spaces within what would become— but was not quite yet—the West itself; against *internal* non-Western, or, more precisely, Orientalized, populations and spaces that were seen to be undesirably out of synch with the temporal requirements of modernity.

The ability to make clear distinctions between "here" and "there," "us" and "them," West and East, is important to those cultural and political formations that Said explores in his work, going back to *Orientalism* itself, where he first discusses imaginative geography. "A group of people living on a few acres of land will set up boundaries between their land and its immediate surroundings and the territory beyond, which they call 'the land of the barbarians,'" he writes. "In other words, this universal practice of designating in one's mind a familiar space which is 'ours' and an unfamiliar space beyond 'ours' which is 'theirs' is a way of making geographical distinctions that can be entirely arbitrary."[5] We can recognize this as Said's first step toward deconstructing the massive "ours" versus "theirs" of Occident and Orient as imaginative geographical constructs. Clearly, such constructs were assembled, nowhere more visibly than in the European nineteenth century.

The problem, though, is that if some of the would-be or ought-to-be "us" are Orientalized, and if some of what ought to be "our" space (even right in the very heart of London, like St. Giles's) is also Orientalized, then there is no possibility of instantly making these kinds of distinctions on a large scale. In the early nineteenth century, St. James's could perhaps be said to have been the "Occident" to St. Giles's "Orient"—and make no mistake that that particular pairing *was* described in such terms—but it would be impossible to make all of London, let alone all of England, instantly fit into a model Occident. It was not just that, as Sanjay Krishnan points out, the traces of the global empire can already be seen to be disrupting the space-time of London.[6] Rather, even without the pressure of the globalized dislocations to which Krishnan draws our attention—though they would surely be tied together—London was already far too mixed up with, and by, its own *internal* Oriental spaces and populations. It took time for these kinds of constructs to develop in a self-sustaining way, in other words, and for that to happen both population and space had to be configured and reconfigured, managed and manipulated, in order to eventually allow the self/other opposition to work on a large—racial or civilizational or even simply national—scale. An internal Occidentalism and an internal Occidentalization were the necessary correlates of an Orientalism and Orientalization that would eventually be exclusively directed to the outside, but only when the outside could be sufficiently distinguished from an Occidental inside—and that took time.[7] This internal Occidentalization was grounded in shifting social, cultural, political, and economic systems in the late eighteenth and early nineteenth centuries, and the transformations of societies that were only then beginning to think of themselves, without yet having a name for it, as somehow Western in the sense in which that term is often used today (for it was not exactly used at the time, though of course when it would be deployed it would be able to draw, as I pointed out in the Preface, on a whole legacy of similar oppositions, including ones between the Western and Eastern Roman empires, or between Christendom and Islam, civilization and barbarism, and so forth, with the major differentiation that this time the opposition was seen to be temporal and historical rather than merely religious or more narrowly cultural—which was of course due to the logic of capital and modernization itself).[8]

This complicates Said's argument in what I think are productive ways.

In the long run, what he says makes sense, but in the short run—especially in late eighteenth and early to mid-nineteenth century England—it's not quite as clear. Consider how Said develops his rich and suggestive appropriation of the musical term "counterpoint" in *Culture and Imperialism*. "Western cultural forms can be taken out of the autonomous enclosures in which they have been protected, and placed instead in the dynamic global environment created by imperialism, itself revised as an ongoing contest between north and south, metropolis and periphery, white and native," he writes. "As we look back at the cultural archive," he adds, "we begin to read it not univocally but contrapuntally, with a simultaneous awareness both of the metropolitan history that is narrated and of those other histories against which (and together with which) the dominating discourse acts."[9] He offers examples from British culture to illustrate his argument, arguing that "one may discover a consistency of concern in Spenser, Shakespeare, Defoe, and Austen that fixes socially desirable, empowered space in metropolitan England or Europe and connects it by design, motive, and development to distant or peripheral worlds (Ireland, Venice, Africa, Jamaica), conceived of as desirable but subordinate."[10]

I completely agree that cultural forms should be taken out of any autonomous enclosures and read in relation to one another. But running such an undisturbed line from Shakespeare to Austen sweeps aside major differences that we can't afford to lose sight of. It grants to Englishness a continuity of form and practice, a sense of security and consolidation, that it never actually enjoyed, as Ian Baucom reminds us in his exploration of the constructedness of Englishness in a later phase of imperial power.[11] As James Buzard has noted, viewing the metropolitan center as a more or less undifferentiated whole also overlooks the very specifically nineteenth-century cultural work in which the realist novel had to engage in order for it to project the air of superiority and confidence that Said detects in it.[12] There is a real difficulty, then, when one is considering cultural forms that were not yet so autonomously enclosed, even if they aspired to be; when one is reading work from a period where north and south, metropolis and periphery, white and native, to use Said's terms, were so much in flux that it was quite impossible to cleanly demarcate the line where one "enclosure" ends and its opposite begins.

The point, however, is that the Romantic period was the one in which these acts of demarcation began to take place in a systematic way, when it started to seem possible, or necessary, to systematically locate England—all of it if possible—as a socially desirable, empowered Occidental space and connect it to distant or peripheral worlds. It would take time, and a great deal of both cultural and political work, for this process to reach fruition sometime in the late nineteenth or early twentieth century. But for that cultural, economic, and political project to even begin taking place, the "distant" had first to be *distanced* from the center; the immediately rather than distantly "peripheral" had to be either assimilated or purged, in order for something eventually resembling or claiming to be an autonomous enclosure that could be defined in racial, civilizational, or national terms to be successfully consolidated. The "Arabs," in short, had to go, in order for England to become (or even claim to be) "English," "white," "Western" in any kind of recognizable way, in opposition to an external rather than an internal Orient, which Said's approach does not take into account.

This is where Bernard Porter's argument becomes important as a supplement to Said's. The problem with some of the scholarship that follows in the wake of Said, Porter argues, is that it tends to regard Britain as, "if not homogeneous exactly, nonetheless a single entity of a kind: complex, admittedly, and even contested, but still 'dominant' and 'national' and static over time."[13] And indeed British culture was far from homogeneous in this period. As Porter points out, it was usually the case at the time that "the various groups that made up what can really only very loosely be called British 'society' in this period went their separate ways. They had different material interests, different hopes and dreams, different gods. They did not—except in the ordinary business of daily living—meet." They were, he adds, "virtual foreigners to one another."[14] Not just that, Porter continues, but "there were millions of women and men [in Britain] who were as subjected and exploited by 'imperialists' as anyone in the colonies."[15] Throughout the period under discussion, for example, "when 'the British' are conventionally regarded as the imperialists and Australians, say—all of them—as colonial subjects, each of those populations in reality comprised mixes of both categories: the ruling classes in Britain lording it over their own lower classes in almost exactly the same way as they lorded over their colonial peoples."[16] Hence, he insists, "broad-brushing all nineteenth- and early twentieth-century Britons as necessarily on the same side of the colonial master-subject divide is clearly misleading. Only the imperial ruling class can be unequivocally located there."[17]

This last sentence, however, is where Porter oversteps the limits of the argument, and in ways that generate interesting problems that can productively be thought through. There are, as I see it, two main (and related) problems with where Porter ends up in his argument.

First, while I agree with him that British society was internally heterogeneous, and that forms of brutalization and exploitation took place within

Britain and even within England itself that mirrored to a certain extent (there were no large-scale massacres or attempts to exterminate entire populations within England, for instance) the brutalization and exploitation of people in Ireland or Asia or Africa or the Americas, I think it is a mistake to think of these forms of brutalization, especially in the earlier part of the nineteenth century, strictly in terms of class, as Porter does. This is partly because, as I explained in the Preface, class formations, especially at the lower end of the spectrum, were so much in flux at the time that class, in isolation, actually does not provide a very stable or useful framework for analysis.[18]

More importantly, though, relations between what Porter thinks of as higher and lower "classes" were actually framed as relations between the members of different ethnicities, civilizations, and races—as the case of London "City Arabs" illustrates so abundantly, and as I will elaborate at greater length in the following chapters, especially with reference to people whose occupations, such as they were, did not map onto modern class structures. And, moreover, the intellectuals and activists developing this racial and civilizational argument in the late eighteenth and early nineteenth centuries were distinctly *not* of "the ruling classes," as Porter has it, but rather those who can more productively be thought of as the ascendant middle class, or aspirants thereto, including many artisanal radicals during and after the 1790s who—as I argued in *William Blake and the Impossible History of the 1790s*—were as quick, or even quicker, to Orientalize their own ruling class as they were to Orientalize the Orient itself.

Were such forms of racial identity, differentiating one English population from another, artificial constructs? Certainly; but aren't they all? The "us"/"them" opposition between the "genuine" English and the Orientalized English "Arab" is no more and no less of a construct than the "us"/"them" opposition of Occident and Orient on a larger scale. The main difference is one of proximity: Orientalized English "Arabs" were seen to be swarming through the streets of London and inhabiting a different mode of space-time within the metropolis than that inhabited by the "genuine" English population; real Arabs were supposed to live in Arabia. The point, as we are reminded by the work of Paul Gilroy, Ann Stoler, and others, is that this dynamic has also to be thought through in racial terms, not solely class ones.[19] Or, rather, class and race have to be seen as articulated concepts, as Stuart Hall has suggested.[20]

The second, related, problem with Porter's argument is that, even when he argues that internal class relationships and antagonisms mirror external ones in the empire—even when he says that the term "imperialism" is often "used as a way of categorizing countries, when in fact it fits classes or other groups *within* countries better"[21]—"the empire" remains a purely external category for him. "When you are caught in the maelstrom—starving, striking, getting rich, struggling with new working conditions, agitating for reform, anticipating utopia, fearing the mob, bemused or exhilarated by all the profound social and moral changes that are going on around you— you do not have the time or need to look to the margins, unless they relate specifically to your concerns at home."[22] The "margins" here refers to geographical margins; that is, faraway, overseas places.

Indeed, much of Porter's book is an attempt to argue that "the empire" had little impact on the "stay-at-homes," as he puts it.[23] Since he thinks of empire as an external category, his approach is necessarily to separate it from the internal, to "look at the empire's impact on British society in context," thereby assuming and taking for granted the very thing he wants to claim that he aims to substantiate, namely, that there was a "British society" that was separate enough from "the empire" to gauge whether one had an impact on the other. And it's interesting to note that, while assessing the possible "impact" the empire had at "home," when it comes to the realm of thought and exciting new ideas, he wants to argue that the link "was mainly one-way: people applied lessons from home to abroad, rarely vice-versa."[24] (In fact, as I will point out in chapter 1, such thought-related matters as the first model of mass education were imported from India to England.)

These are not just semantic distinctions. Assuming the clean separation of inside and outside, "home" and "empire," leads Porter to also assume, for example, that "racism" is something that happens with respect to other, overseas, peoples, pitting the English "stay-at-home population" against "other races" out there in "the empire,"[25] or perhaps their constituents who, like De Quincey's Malay, come to England. He fails to recognize that racism is a constitutive feature of the modern state and completely bound up with its internal logic as well as its overseas investments.[26] This is severely problematic, and not only because, as Gilroy points out, "seeing racism as something peripheral, marginal to the essential patterns of social and political life can, in its worst manifestations, simply endorse the view of blacks as an external problem, an alien presence visited on Britain from the outside."[27] For this formulation also leaves Porter no way to account for internal racism directed against what would otherwise, in a later configuration, be counted as a "white" English population and hence no way to account for the fact that the best-known London reformer of the nineteenth century, Henry Mayhew, opens his classic *London Labour and the London Poor* by announcing that, "of the thousand millions of human beings that are said to constitute the population of the entire globe, there are—socially, morally, and perhaps even physically considered—but two distinct and broadly marked races, viz., the wanderers and the settlers—the vagabond and the citizen—the nomadic and the civilised tribes."

For according to Mayhew, even "here" in England, we can find not-yet-white, not-yet-Occidental English people, among whom there is, as he puts it, "a greater development of the animal than of the intellectual or moral nature of man," who are marked "for their use of a slang language—for their lax ideas of property—for their general improvidence—their repugnance to continuous labour—their disregard of female honour—their love of cruelty—their pugnacity—and their utter want of religion."[28] Thus Mayhew locates racial and other fault lines *within* the space of the would-be nation, among those who would eventually be considered members of the same race ("white") and nation (England or Britain), *not* between the nation conceived of as homogeneously "interior" and an Other space conceived of as "exterior" (see fig. 1). Though Gilroy is right to argue against Benedict Anderson's attempt to separate racism from nationalism as distinct phenomena—by pointing out that "the politics of 'race' in this country is fired by conceptions of national belonging and homogeneity which not only blur the distinction between 'race' and nation, but rely on that very ambiguity for their effect"—the sense of racial belonging is also at times more complicated than even Gilroy himself allows.[29]

What Porter shares with Said, then—and this is why I find the overlapping dissonance between them so productive—is an assumption of a clean separation of the domestic national space ("home") from the empire "out there." And it is in this critical conjuncture that I want to mark a point of disagreement. It is not possible to cleanly demarcate a racial or civilizational separation that operates along a neat internal/external axis between England, Britain, or even Europe and their various Others. The Others—the Arabs—were "here" among "us" as well. In order to sharpen the us/them dynamic on a global scale in the great age of empire in the later nineteenth century, separating Orient from Occident to the point where they could be recognized—as Lord Cromer would eventually put it, as "the poles asunder"[30]—the Occident had to be cleaned up, purged of any trace of Oriental contamination. Only then could it constitute one of Cromer's poles, in binary opposition to the East, to the point where he could safely say, "The Oriental generally acts, thinks and speaks in a manner exactly opposite to the European,"[31] a formulation that breaks down if Europeans—including the aristocracy and upper class, let alone the "swinish multitude"—are also Orientalized.

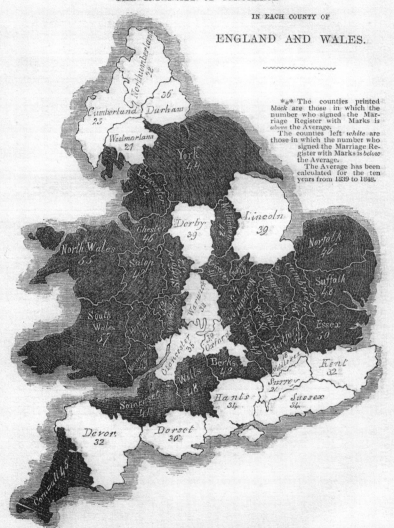

MAP

SHOWING THE NUMBER WHO SIGNED THE MARRIAGE REGISTER WITH MARKS IN EVERY 100 PERSONS MARRIED;

OR

THE INTENSITY OF IGNORANCE

IN EACH COUNTY OF

ENGLAND AND WALES.

*** The counties printed *black* are those in which the number who signed the Marriage Register with Marks is *above* the Average.
The counties left *white* are those in which the number who signed the Marriage Register with Marks is *below* the Average.
The Average has been calculated for the ten years from 1839 to 1848.

Fig. 1. "The Intensity of Ignorance," from Henry Mayhew, *London Labour and the London Poor*, vol. 4 (London, 1861).

What I will argue in succeeding chapters is that a domestic Occidental-ism was the necessary correlate of an eventually overseas-directed Oriental-ism: they were two sides of the same coin. By disregarding this, by insisting on seeing racism and the empire as external matters rather than structures of thought that crossed an altogether porous imaginary frontier and pene-trated England to its very core and helped to define and structure it from within, Porter comes to exactly the opposite conclusion than the one for which I argue in this book; for all his insistence that "imperial Britain was generally a *less* imperial society than is often assumed,"[32] it was actually a far *more* imperial society. Insofar as imperialism is concerned with rela-tions between a ruling power and its civilizational others, we can say that England was imperial to its very core. This also means we should reconsider the point that Simon Gikandi makes when he argues that "Englishness was itself a product of the colonial culture that it seemed to have created else-where."[33] For it was also a product of the colonial culture it created at home as well.

My contention in this book is that the logic of Occidentalism defined that imperial culture from within and must therefore be paired with the Orientalist logic that in the long run came to be exclusively projected over-seas. Occidentalism and Orientalism are not opposites, in other words, as they are often assumed to be by some of those who have appropriated the two terms. Rather, they operate on precisely the same continuum: the one is the extension and necessary continuation of the other. There is a caveat, however: not all versions of Orientalism are the same, and Occidentalism would emerge from, and come to be fused with, a particular version of Ori-entalism.

Here we must keep in mind the nature of the specific mode of Oriental-ism that emerged toward the turn of the nineteenth century and helped to inspire Romanticism, which was markedly different from the forms of Ori-entalism that had preceded it. It was increasingly concerned with knowledge of the Oriental other for the purposes of imperial administration: it was in-strumental, purposeful, and expedient. "Every accumulation of knowledge, and especially such as is obtained by social communication over whom we exercise a dominion founded on the right of conquest," wrote Warren Hastings, the governor-general of Bengal, in the preface to the first English translation (1785) of the *Bhagavad-Gita*, "is useful to the state."[34] Earlier eighteenth-century Orientalism seemed, by contrast, much more innocu-ous: it was concerned with moral instruction (of Britons, not Orientals), or, quite simply, with mere novelty and marketable entertainment value.[35]

Romantic-era Orientalism, then, differed from earlier eighteenth-century Orientalism partly because of the fact that (thanks to the work of Sir William Jones and others) it was based on a far greater knowledge of the East than had been available previously (which was essentially the *Arabian Nights* and its derivatives) and partly because it was—necessarily—much more heavily invested in Britain's imperial project than had been the case with earlier forms of Orientalism. For this form of Orientalism emerged as a by-product of the policy instituted by Warren Hastings to govern the East India Company's possessions in their own languages (or at least in those of their learned elites). As late as the 1750s, knowledge of Indian languages in the ranks of the East India Company was still very limited. But with the change in policy as ordered by Hastings, in the 1770s, the company systematically started using local languages in its government of India, which obviously entailed British officials' acquiring knowledge of those languages, in order, as Hastings put it, to "adapt our Regulations to the Manners and Understanding of the People, and Exigencies of the Country."[36] Hastings ordered the extraction and circulation of Oriental knowledge for the purposes of command, not mere entertainment. He encouraged the translation of classic texts into English as well as a process of acculturation that would enable Englishmen to study Indian languages and literatures in order to master Indian culture from within. As Javed Majeed points out, the urge "to draw 'orient knowledge from its fountains pure'" was applied both to the process of legal codification and to the process of generating imaginative works and works of fiction.[37] "Entertainment" itself, in this context, assumed an expressly political and administrative function, so that the cultural and the political were quite inseparable.

This was the period when the British began to produce an apparatus of knowledge: grammars, treatises, dictionaries (e.g., Jones's *Grammar of the Persian Language*, 1771)—and translations of more and more Oriental works, both legal (e.g., Halhed's *Gentoo Laws*, 1776) and literary or cultural (e.g., Charles Wilkins's translation of the *Bhagavad-Gita*). "Seen as a corpus, these texts signal the invasion of an epistemological space occupied by a great number of Indian scholars, intellectuals, teachers, scribes, priests, lawyers, officials, merchants, and bankers, whose knowledge as well as they themselves were to be converted into instruments of colonial rule," Bernard Cohn points out. "They were now to become part of the army of babus, clerks, interpreters, sub-inspectors, munshis, pandits, qazis, vakils, schoolmasters, amins, sharistadars, tahsildars, deshmukhs, darogahs, and mamlatdars who, under the scrutiny and supervision of the white sahibs, ran the everyday affairs of the Raj."[38] Thus, Cohn concludes, "the conquest of India was the conquest of knowledge." (This is also one of the central claims of Said's *Orientalism*, of course.)

However, the translations from Arabic, Persian, and Sanskrit, as well as the whole epistemological project of which they represented a crucial component, not only provided the textual materials for imperial rule—they would also inspire a whole generation of British writers. It was in this context that the work of Sir William Jones became so prominent. But while Jones (who worked as a judge in the East India Company) argued for the practical application of the knowledge obtained from this Oriental renaissance, he also insisted that the process of extracting all this knowledge served far more than a merely instrumental function. Europeans, he argued, would gain from this immense Oriental learning a cultural resource that they could go on to use for their own aesthetic purposes.[39] What Jones proposed, then, was to establish a cultural and literary parallel to the extraction of material wealth from the East and to transfer both sets of treasures back to Britain. Following Jones, the British interest in Orientalism (and hence the empire) quickly matured from being merely a passing fad to an essential component of the much broader process of cultural and political self-definition that was taking place at the turn of the nineteenth century.

The irony here is that that process of self-definition, though it was inspired by contact with other cultures, increasingly came to be more about the self being defined than about the cultural others, the fascination with whom had inspired self-awareness in the first place. For the process of gaining power over the other fundamentally required knowing not only what made the other "different" but also, in effect, what made the self the "same" (or in other words, collectively speaking, what made "us" who "we" are). The world of cultural difference that Jones proposed to explore thus both enabled and required a firmer sense of the identity from which it marked a departure; it helped inaugurate the process I am calling Occidentalism.

As I will argue at greater length in the chapters to follow, this investment in Occidental self-definition entailed the emergence of an altogether new, modern sense of imperial and national subjectivity, a sense of self that could be defined against the Asiatic others who were subjected to the empire. And on this very question it also introduced a fissure that runs through the various formulations of Orientalism that appear from the 1790s all the way through the 1830s (coming to a head in the work of Macaulay, and specifically in his denunciation of Southey, to which we will turn in chapter 5). On the one hand, there was what would quickly become the dominant form of Orientalism (which we can identify with Macaulay, for instance), which was heavily invested in legitimizing and authorizing the superiority of a Occidental sense of self as opposed to an Oriental other and hence was fused with what I am calling Occidentalism. On the other hand (Byron is the paradigmatic case here, as we will see in chapter 4), there were a last few, we might almost say residual, entanglements with the Orient that were interested in it as a site from which to resist or escape the stifling normalization of the emergent Western sense of self: a site in which to imagine, or on which to project, alternative modes of identity, subjectivity, and desire. This can then be thought of as offering a last-ditch Romantic effort to resist the normalizing pressures of Occidentalism.

In any case, insofar as the Orient became an obsession in the Romantic period, it was clearly in ways that, paradoxically, had increasingly little to do with the Orient itself and more and more to do with Britain's—and still more specifically England's—emerging sense of itself as Western. Because articulations of the sense of self (collective, social, national, imperial, and individual) were among the overriding concerns of the Romantic period, and because the sense of self that emerged during this period was so inextricably bound up with the circumstances of imperial rule, it should come as no surprise that the Orient was inevitably one of the period's focal points. This explains why an interest in—or at least the rhetorical deployment of—an Orientalist discourse recurs throughout the corpus of Romanticism, including in areas that at first glance ought to have nothing to do with the Orient at all: because the Orient had become essential to virtually every attempt to articulate a sense of selfhood or subjectivity. For the sense of self that was articulated through the 1790s and on into the nineteenth century was increasingly predicated on a sense of Occidental identity, a feeling of superiority over a supine and unmanly Eastern other. Hence an ongoing series of contrasts between the manly, honest, sober, virtuous Occidental self and the effeminate, luxurious, lazy, indulgent Eastern other permeates all forms of discourse in the Romantic period (with a few exceptions, such as Byron or Blake).

Apart from everything else, for instance, Wordsworth's project in the *Lyrical Ballads* (and how much more remote from the East can one possibly get?) was also, as he says, to rescue poetry from being merely a matter of those by then notoriously Oriental traits of "amusement and idle pleasure," "idleness and unmanly despair," and to affirm instead an explicitly "manly" style, one available to the "sound and vigorous mind" of the Occidental self. This involved creating a new kind of reader as well as a new kind of author. For if the genius of the poet represents "an advance, or a conquest," Wordsworth asks, "is it to be supposed that the reader can make

progress of this kind, like an Indian prince or general—stretched on his palanquin, and borne by his slaves? No; he is invigorated and inspirited by his
leader, in order that he may exert himself; for he cannot proceed in quies-
cence, he cannot be carried like a dead weight."[40] Only an Occidental reader,
obviously, is capable of the kind of self-discipline that Wordsworth insists
his poetry requires.

For the same reason, it is no coincidence that we see throughout the corpus of 1790s radicalism—in the work of John Thelwall, Tom Paine, and Mary
Wollstonecraft, among others—a conflation of the enemies of the radical
cause, the (real) aristocratic enemy and an (imaginary) Oriental enemy, in
which the faults of the former are rewritten in terms of the faults of the
latter, and the faults of both are gendered as feminine and/or effeminate. In
other words, the supposed characteristics of Oriental society and culture are
in radical writing projected on to the aristocracy ("the proud and polished,
the debauched, effeminate, and luxurious," as Thelwall put it),[41] while at the
same time the Orient becomes the topos of aristocratic degeneration and the
Oriental seraglio the dark cousin of the aristocratic palace, both oozing degeneration, corruption, and filth into the society at large. (As always, there is
a flip side to this, namely, the avowedly anti-bourgeois self-Orientalizations
of people like Byron and Beckford; indeed, as John Barrell points out, pseudo-
Oriental style continued to be enjoyed among the fashionable elite well into
the nineteenth century, even if as an "inoculating" gesture.)[42]

As I have argued at length in other contexts, the link between the aristocratic and the Oriental was taken to its most elaborate lengths in the work
of Mary Wollstonecraft.[43] But it was not unique to Wollstonecraft, of course.
A similar move is an essential component of Paine's attack on Burke's *Reflections on the Revolution in France* in *Rights of Man*.[44] In arguing that
Burke "is not affected by the reality of the distress touching his heart, but
by the showy resemblance of it striking his imagination," that Burke "pit-
ies the plumage, but forgets the dying bird," Paine is able to reconfigure his
opponent as a fawning servant of kings and priests, for whom "shew and
magnificence" constitute a kind of substitute reality, an imaginative world
to be accessed via hippogriffs and flying sentry-boxes. "Accustomed to kiss
the aristocratical hand that hath purloined him from himself," Paine writes
of Burke, "he degenerates into a composition of art, and the genuine soul
of nature forsakes him. His hero or his heroine must be a tragedy-victim
expiring in show, and not the real prisoner of misery, sliding into death in
the silence of a dungeon."[45] Here Paine prepares the way for the climactic
moment of his argument against Burke a few pages later, where he refuses
"to follow Mr Burke through a pathless wilderness of rhapsodies, and a sort

of descant upon governments, in which he asserts whatever he pleases, on the presumption of its being believed, without offering evidence or reasons for so doing." Paine insists that "before anything can be reasoned upon to a conclusion, certain facts, principles, or data, to reason from must be established, admitted, or denied," and that Burke's flowery, imaginative, and hence pseudo-Oriental discourse is not compatible with such reasoning.

For both Paine and Wollstonecraft the real problem with those "polished manners" that "render vice more dangerous, by concealing its deformity under gay ornamental drapery," is not merely a matter of morality. The problem with such false showiness is not simply that it substitutes the "plumage" for the "dying bird," the "showy resemblance" for the "reality of distress," the "tragedy-victim dying in show" for the "real victim of misery," a pretend reality (of "art," "show," and "tragedy") for genuine reality (the reality of "facts, principles, and data"). Rather, the problem is that artificiality and show corrupt the "genuine soul of nature" and allow an individual to be "purloined" from himself. "Vice" is rendered "more dangerous, by concealing its deformity under gay ornamental drapery," not just because it is more difficult for others to recognize in us, but above all because it is more difficult for us to recognize in ourselves. Showy style, elaborate forms of writing, excessive figuration, inflated phraseology—in short, the essential elements not just of Burke's *Reflections* as read by Paine and Wollstonecraft, but above all of Oriental and pseudo-Oriental style, the ultimate "pathless wilderness of rhapsodies"—are bad not just because they prevent us from engaging with "facts, principles, and data"; they are bad because they prevent genuine self-knowledge, self-awareness, and self-control. Art is to be distinguished from reality by the same mechanisms which allow us to distinguish excess from simplicity, idleness from vigor, unfounded assertion from reasoned argument, the artificial from the natural, the useless from the useful, the unmanly from the manly, and hence, ultimately, the East from the West: our others from our selves.

As I will discuss at greater length in chapter 5, it is no coincidence that we will see exactly this same line of argument—here being used by the 1790s radicals against Burke—deployed by Macaulay in his devastating attack on, and concomitant Orientalization of, Robert Southey some forty years later. The stabilization, the normalization, the rising to dominance, of this kind of thinking, this way of opposing a valorized Western self (regulated, rational, devoted to realities rather than appearances) against an Oriental other (irrational, emotional, devoted to beguiling and attractive, but misleading and dangerous, appearances) came to represent one of the core principles of a recurrent Occidentalism.

By the first third of the nineteenth century, then, the distinction between Occident and Orient, as well as the attendant distinction between
the Occidental self and the Oriental other had developed into a general principle. For a dwindling number of critics, of course, there would always be
something dangerous or worrying about the Western sense of self and the
supposedly rational self-control that had taken it to the point of nearly total
homogenization. When Blake complained, toward the end of his life, that
"Englishmen are all Intermeasurable One by Another," he was referring
in part to his sense that the rational, limited subjectivity essential to Occidentalist discourse was inherently suffocating and entrapping, not just
mind-numbingly homogenizing; he was also registering again his refusal to
participate in that form of discourse or the imperialist project from which it
was inseparable. For still others, there would always be something appealing about the Eastern self and its lack of standardization and self-control (it
is this sense of attraction to the East that would, for example, draw Byron to
it for most of his career and almost all of his best, and best-known, writing,
as we will see in chapter 4).

What we can distinguish as the form of Orientalism that would rise
to dominance at the turn of the nineteenth century is thus characterized
not merely by certain anxieties of empire, but by a set of philosophical and
political obsessions with a very particular conceptualization of subjectivity. Hence, to go back to what I was arguing earlier in this Introduction, the
convergence of this form of Orientalism and Occidentalism, which would
come to operate on a continuum—entwined with each other, extensions of
one another—such that the explosion through the Romantic period of writing on self-determination and the rights of the sovereign individual must be
recognized as simultaneously Occidentalist and Orientalist. This is why I
want to insist that at a certain point the logic of Occidentalism and that of
Orientalism converge, which is why they need to be read together. At the
moment of English culture and history with which this book is concerned,
a similar logic, a similar civilizing process, was being played out—or at
least projected, fantasized about—both at home and overseas; at home, in
order to purge the last traces of Oriental contamination from a putatively
Occidental space; and overseas, in order to begin the much more challenging process of converting Oriental difference into the universal culture of
Occidental modernity. Ann Stoler is quite right to ask why we have "treated
bourgeois 'civilizing missions' in metropole and colony as though they were
independent for so long."[46] That is a mistake. For it wasn't just Indians and
Arabs who were seen to be guilty of clinging to outmoded values and logics,
but also plenty of people inside England, at both the top of the social scale

(the landed gentry so scornfully disposed of by Jane Austen in *Mansfield Park* and *Persuasion*—think of Sir Walter Eliot obsessively staring at the one un-turning, un-changing page of the Baronetage and reading about his family lineage firmly ensconced in the past) and at the bottom (the coster-mongers of London and the City Arabs of St. Giles's as well as the vagrants and wanderers stumbling their way through *Lyrical Ballads*), and some-where in between as well, in the poets and writers themselves whose work I address here (it is no coincidence for example that Byron fled to the East to get away from the "tightness" of his Occidental self, or that Macaulay denounced Southey as essentially a "a bilious old nabob"). At this moment of crisis, then, in order to enable it to be distinguished more clearly from an Orient over which it claimed the right to rule, the Occident had to be cleansed of its own inner Orient.

However, it is one thing to use an Orientalist discourse to depict an Other out there in the East, but quite another—if Englishmen can also be Orientalized—to locate the putative West against which that East is being dialectically counterposed. Where was this West, if both the degenerate aris-tocracy and the teeming multitudes in England were infected with Oriental traits (indulgence, passion, rage, emotion, enthusiasm, lack of self-control, etc.)? Marking the Other is relatively easy, in other words, but designating the "we" who fit into the collective (in this case Western) self is not so easy. And finding a territory that is "ours" in that sense—in the sense in which everyone "here" is one of "us" as opposed to one of "them"—is more diffi-cult still. For, as I will later explain in greater detail, the "we" being desig-nated here is *not* the nationalist "we" of the sort captured in the work of, say, Benedict Anderson or Linda Colley, but rather a racial or a civilizational one, even though discussions of much narrower notions of national identity have dominated eighteenth-century and Romantic studies for some time now.[47] The "we" that I am talking about actually at certain moments ex-cludes large segments of the nation—patricians and plebeians both—while it could readily be extended to those beyond the nation (to those in America and France, for example). It is in fact a "we," this sense of affiliation with a West, that much of the recent work on nationalism has not sufficiently taken into account; it overlaps with the sense of the nation in some in-stances and transcends it in others. One reason it has not been taken into account is that it was, at the time, assumed rather than explicitly named as such: for all the exploding proliferation of frankly Orientalist discourses in this period, it is difficult, if not impossible, to locate an explicitly Occiden-talist discourse identifying itself as such. It was clear, then, that there was an East, out there somewhere, but its dialectical twin, the West, was not so readily named and geographically designated—at least not then. It was still very much in the process of formation and consolidation.

So England cannot be said, in and around 1800, to have been "Western" in the sense in which India could be said by English writers to be "Eastern." Strangely enough, it was far too Orientalized. And if by "Western" one means, for example, a liberal democracy and a market society "civilized" (to use Norbert Elias's term)[48] to a certain degree of social development, then England (let alone the rest of Britain) was certainly not Western in 1800. Indeed, although we tend to take for granted its economic development by referring to the industrial revolution of the late eighteenth century, England in and around 1800 cannot even be said to have been a market society at all. The single most important economic factor—labor power—was not yet comprehensively subject to market forces, and it is quite meaningless to speak of a market society without a labor market. "Not until 1834 was a competitive labor market established in England," as Karl Polanyi points out; "hence industrial capitalism as a social system cannot be said to have existed before that date."[49]

Indeed, it is no coincidence that the Romantic period is framed by the two pivotal decades of the 1790s and 1830s, which, between them, form the crux of Polanyi's account of what he calls "the great transformation." The former decade marks the introduction (1795) of the Speenhamland system, which, by guaranteeing parish support in aid of a worker's wages, sought to protect the paternalistic society dominated by landed gentry by shielding labor from the nascent market forces that were still gathering strength at the time (to be sure, this was done to preserve a different form of exploitation of rural labor—the form that benefited the rural gentry—rather than out of genuine altruism).[50] The latter decade marks the repeal of the Poor Law (1834)—the first great victory of the new class brought to power in the Reform Bill of 1832—and hence the opening of the floodgates to a market society in the full sense of that term, in which, as Polanyi so forcefully expresses it, society would ultimately become an adjunct of the market, rather than the other way around. Henceforth, in other words, instead of economic forces being embedded in and contained by social forces, social relations would come to be embedded in market forces—and society itself would be threatened with demolition as a result (a situation the consequences of which we contend with up to the present day).[51]

The formative transitional moment of Speenhamland, from the 1790s to the 1830s, happens to coincide more or less precisely with another major transitional period, this time in imperial policy, from the 1790s to the 1830s, by the end of which, in the age of Macaulay, Britain's imperial project would be transformed beyond recognition from what it had been in the age of William Jones and Warren Hastings (see chap. 5), as the ethos of empire went from the preservation and exploitation of difference to the eradication of difference. These giant transformations, both of which—no coincidence, this—span and frame the Romantic period, tell us why it is so disabling to try to collapse the Romantic period into a "long eighteenth century," which has been a recent trend in eighteenth-century studies.[52]

If 1834 marks the advent, in England, of market society and a recognizably "Western" social and economic system (building on the partial democratic expansion marked by the reforms of 1832), that is all the more reason to say that England before 1834 cannot be said to have been a Western country in any meaningful sense. It had to be made so—with catastrophic results in the short term, as the parish-based society dominated by the rural landlords was, to use Polanyi's terms, "smashed up" in order to free the individual bearers of labor power from its constraints. In the new, modern, social formation, individuals would be tied into a new web of interdependent relations with other individuals. "The establishment of the political state and the dissolution of civil society into independent individuals—whose relations with one another depend on law, just as the relations of men in the medieval system of estates and guilds depended on privilege," as Marx pointed out, "is accomplished by one and the same act."[53] Philip Corrigan and Derek Sayer argue that this process of "forming moral individuals of and from labouring persons, in the bourgeois image," and "'freeing' of individuals from feudal bonds to become the formally equal, abstractly human subjects of the bourgeois world-view" was one of the defining features of English state formation in this period.[54] "State formation and cultural regulation (the two are quite inextricably connected)," they write, "reach a frenzy during the years of what we can without exaggeration call the English terror, when the working class was hammered and machined into acceptable relations."[55]

This moral revolution required the transformation not only of the preexisting social order but also that of the personality structure of individual subjects. People had to learn, or be taught, the value of self-control, self-regulation, self-discipline, the rhetoric of all of which was, not coincidentally, so absolutely vital to the mainstream radical cause of the 1790s—from which Blake, for his part, would rebel for exactly this reason—and would be picked up anew by the reformers of the early nineteenth century (and by evangelicals like Hannah More who were, as Kevin Gilmartin has argued, trying to seize and control the same ideological terrain, albeit for different purposes).[56] Norbert Elias refers to the process by which the division of functions and of labor and its attendant web of interdependence are elaborated through a society as "the civilizing process." The drive to bring this kind of civilization (a term we have to use cautiously, and of course with Gandhi's famous joke in mind) to fruition in England, across shifting class and racial lines, in the years around 1800 was one of the main themes of literary as well as political works, and it reappears constantly from, say, Mary Wollstonecraft's 1791 *Original Stories from Real Life: with Conversations Calculated to Regulate the Affections, and Form the Mind to Truth and Goodness* to Jane Austen's *Mansfield Park* and *Persuasion* (see chap. 2). "Personality," as Major Cartwright put it, "is the sole foundation of the right of being represented."[57] Personality, of course, is not in this sense something that every person automatically possesses: it must be nurtured and developed in the cultural revolution elaborated by Corrigan and Sayer.

And from this standpoint, England (never mind Britain's Celtic periphery, which Michael Hechter discusses in his classic *Internal Colonialism*)[58] in and around 1800 was, again, for the most part, neither civilized nor "Western" in any meaningful sense of that relational term. It had to be made so, even as "Eastern" spaces had also to be redefined in terms of England's own emergent new understanding of itself, to await their own subsequent "civilization" later in the nineteenth century (see chap. 4).[59]

There should be no surprises here. "Savages" are precisely what a reasonably sophisticated middle-class Englishman (or woman) would expect to see when surveying the lower orders of his (or her) own country in the years around 1800, and in fact quite further into the nineteenth century as well. Susan Thorne reminds us of the extent to which native-born Englishmen—never mind Scottish Highlanders or the Irish, as Henchard reminds us, or the bardic nationalists whose work Katie Trumpener has so assiduously discussed[60]—could be thought of by their social superiors in exactly the same terms they used to think through their encounters with "savages" in Asia or Africa.[61] Much of England could be—and was—thought of as an uncivilized country. "I recollect the awkward gaze wherewith the people looked upon me, and the painful feelings of my heart when I retired to a little hovel from among them," writes the Reverend George Greatbatch after arriving in the village in Lancashire ("probably one of the most unenlightened and uncivilized parts of the kingdom") to which he had been sent as a church missionary in 1801. "I had little thought there was a station for me at home which so much resembled the ideas I had formed of an uncivilized heathen land."[62] Greatbatch was hardly unique; other missionaries found in England a "heathenism as dense as any in Polynesia or Central Africa" (as one put it); they found the population of England's rural towns and villages "as heathen and barbarian as the natives of darkest Africa" (as another noted).[63]

Indeed, such attitudes were not restricted to the clergy and were part of a consistent pattern whereby well-bred writers sought to distinguish themselves and their class "from the rude and uncultivated Vulgar, whose undisciplined passions, thro' indulgence, have more Ferocity than Beasts."[64] Even when it was not quite so aggressively put, it was quite normal for "polite" observers to deploy the discourse of barbarism and savagery with respect to the common people well into the nineteenth century. Engels, for example, quotes a preacher at Bethnal Green in London pointing out that "before the Bishop of London called attention to this most poverty-stricken parish, people at the West End knew as little of it as of the savages of Australia or the South Sea Isles."[65] And, as I mentioned in the Preface, there was the explosion, from the 1830s on, of a discourse of the "City Arab" to refer to the marginalized population (tens of thousands of men, women, and children) of Westernizing London.

One of the sites where the convergence of racial, civilizational, and proto-class terms becomes clear is in the discourses on language that proliferated in the second half of the eighteenth century and would continue to develop in the Romantic period interest in national culture—and, as we will see in chapter 2, would play a significant role in Wordsworth's poetry. John Barrell has thoroughly elaborated the deployment of language as a marker of class and national identity in the eighteenth century, and especially the growing distinction between, on the one hand, provincial and vulgar oral usage and, on the other hand, the language "properly so-called" (to use the period's own terms), which was addressed in Johnson's *Dictionary*.[66] Even if not framed explicitly in terms of conquest and occupation, this view of the project also had clear imperial overtones. Johnson's project in the *Dictionary* "alienated English from its contemporary speakers in ways not dissimilar to colonial linguistic practices," as Janet Sorenson points out. "As the *Dictionary* establishes a supraregional national standard, it refigures class and gender linguistic distinctions as cultural, ethnic, and, importantly, spatial differences, borrowing from the conventional marker of colonial difference," Sorenson argues. "The *Dictionary* makes English alien even to many of its 'native' speakers, and in this sense the position of colonial subjects and of national provincial, female, and labouring-class subjects would be aligned."[67]

The link between colonial elites at home and the range of otherness both at home and overseas marked out by the debates over "proper" and "vulgar" language was made explicit the other way around as well. As Barrell notes, for example, just as elite writers in Britain sought to defend what they perceived as *their* language from what the eighteenth-century grammarian Robert Nares distinguished as "vulgar or provincial barbarism," the radical writer Thomas Spence had in mind not only British plebeians but also "Negro slaves" and the inhabitants of India when developing his phonetic spelling system for English, which he designed precisely in order to empower and facilitate the literacy of populations pushed to the margins by the representatives of elite culture.[68] In both cases, it was clear that elite attitudes toward plebeian subcultures in England developed along the same lines as attitudes toward "barbarism" in Asia or Africa: the two sets of attitudes were necessary to each other. Alongside dictionaries for Persian, Arabic, and Sanskrit, dictionaries for English slang phrases, the canting language, "St. Giles's Greek," and the flash language—the *patois* commonly associated with the criminal subculture—were published all through the late eighteenth century into the nineteenth century, from Francis Grose's 1785 *Classical Dictionary of the Vulgar Tongue* (republished in the 1820s by Pierce Egan) to James Hardy Vaux's 1812 *Vocabulary of the Flash Language*.[69] That such a slang vocabulary persisted into the nineteenth century was precisely what led Mayhew to think of its users in racial terms: they spoke a different language, after all.

"It was not only the European exterior that was racialized by certain classes of Europeans: there was also a racialization of the interior," as Robert Miles points out.[70] "The task of civilization from above, a task in which the state was heavily involved alongside the emergent bourgeoisie, did not only have externally colonized subjects as its object," he explains. "The dominant class and the state were also confronted with the task of civilizing other categories of inferior Other, other 'savages' living within the boundary of the nation state."[71] Much of the work on the deployment of a racial discourse in the civilization of the European interior has focused on France: in Eugen Weber's classic *Peasants into Frenchmen*, for example, which reminds us of the extent to which such refined nineteenth-century writers as Balzac could think of their fellow countrymen as "savages" pure and simple;[72] or in Todorov's work on the late nineteenth-century racism of Renan or Le Bon. "The lowest strata of the European societies are homologous with the primitive men," Le Bon would claim; it is possible, then, "to see the superior grades of a population [in Europe] separated intellectually from the inferior grades by a distance as great as that which separates the white man from the negro, or even the negro from the monkey."[73] As Tom Holt has argued, the view that "the savage, the primitive, the yet to be civilized" could be "stig-

matized as underworked and oversexed, their material interests or drives un-
aroused while their libidos were out of control," could readily be extended to
"white" populations inside Europe.[74]

In Italy, this kind of attitude, expressed by some Italians toward others,
persisted well into the twentieth century, as we are reminded by Antonio
Gramsci's work on the Southern Question, and his illustration of the extent
to which northern Italians regarded the inhabitants of the Mezzogiorno as
culturally and even biologically inferior. "The ordinary man from Northern
Italy thought . . . that, if the Mezzogiorno made no progress after having been
liberated from the fetters which the Bourbon regime placed in the way of a
modern development, this meant that the causes of the poverty [in the south
of Italy] were not external, to be sought in objective economic and political
conditions, but internal, innate in the population of the South," Gramsci
argues. "There only remained one explanation—the organic incapacity of
the inhabitants, their barbarity, their biological inferiority."[75] Such attitudes
persist among certain northern Italian politicians to this day (those of the
Lombard League, for instance).[76]

As Susan Thorne reminds us, however, such attitudes were prevalent
in England as well, and at a period earlier than that generally covered by
the work on France and of course Gramsci's work on the Southern Question. This strongly reinforces Ann Stoler's contention that a racial discourse
played a key role in the formation of class identity—and middle-class identity in particular. "While social historians generally have assumed that
racial logics drew on the ready-made cultural disparagements honed to distinguish between middle-class virtues and the immorality of the poor, as
well as between the 'undeserving' and the 'respectable' poor among themselves, it may well be that such social etymologies make just as much sense
reversed," Stoler notes. "The racial lexicon of empire and the sexualized
images of it, in some cases, may have provided for a European language of
class as often as the other way around."[77] The language of race provided a
way for English writers—notably, in the years around 1800, those of the
rising middle class—to think about their social inferiors (and their social
superiors too, whom the middle-class radicals systematically Orientalized,
as I have argued elsewhere).[78] But the dynamic worked both ways because
of the ways in which race and class were bound up with each other in this
moment, given the composite nature of identities and subjects.[79]

Nor was the (selective) deployment of a racial language to represent the
common people of England restricted only to missionaries who sought to
evangelize among them, or to gentlemen like the one quoted by John Barrell
who, writing in 1794, is so pleased to see how far formerly the "barbarous

and savage" Kingswood colliers have improved since the middle of the eighteenth century, when "they were [such] a terror to the City of Bristol, which
they several times invaded" that "it was dangerous to go among them."[80]
For Kingswood was only one location among many others in England, a
place not yet incorporated, culturally, economically, and politically, into the
space-time of imperial modernity. "In many parts of England the formal
institutions of power were neither deeply rooted nor widely respected; the
populations of these places were partly withdrawn from, and sometimes resistant to, the exercise of 'lawful' authority," Robert Malcolmson argues.
"These, in short, were areas which had not been fully colonised by the nobility and gentry: official authority was weak, plebeian independence was
prominent and relatively unconstrained."[81] These were precisely the areas
that needed to be brought under control, and their inhabitants civilized, as
the missionaries were urging. As I will show in chapter 1, much of London
fell under this heading as well.

If we look at the opposite end of the political spectrum from that occupied by evangelical missionaries, however, we will find, for example in William Godwin's radical novel *Caleb Williams*, the elaboration of very much
the same racially inflected attitude toward plebeian culture. Consider the
description of Grimes, the tenant/servant of Tyrrel ("a common laboring
man," as Emily describes him, "who occupied a small farm, the property of
his confident").[82] "He was not precisely a lad of vicious propensities, but in
an inconceivable degree boorish and uncouth," we are told. "His complexion was scarcely human; his features were coarse, and strangely discordant
and disjointed from each other. His lips were thick, and the tone of his voice
broad and unmodulated. His legs were of equal size from one end to the
other, and his feet misshapen and clumsy. He had nothing spiteful or mali-
cious in his disposition, but he was a total stranger to tenderness; he could
not feel for those refinements in others, of which he had no experience in
himself." Such, then, was "the uncouth and half-civilized animal which the
industrious malice of Mr. Tyrrel fixed upon as most happily adapted to his
purpose."[83] It is worth adding that Grimes, unlike Caleb, speaks only heavily accented regional English.

To be sure, not all the novel's "common laboring men" are described
in this way, as half-civilized animals: the Hawkinses, for example, are exemplary characters, and they speak a markedly more standardized English
than Grimes. But when Godwin wants to convey a negative impression of
common people, his recourse is to a racial language of physical characteristics. The strange woman Caleb finds living with the gang of thieves, for
example, is described in exactly those terms. "The only person I saw within

[the thieves' lair] was a woman, rather advanced in life, and whose person had I know not what of extraordinary and loathsome," Caleb tells us. "Her eyes were red and blood-shot; her hair was pendent in matted and shaggy tresses about her shoulders; her complexion swarthy, and of the consistency of parchment; her form spare, and her whole body, her arms in particular, uncommonly vigorous and muscular. Not the milk of human kindness, but the feverous blood of savage ferocity, seemed to flow from her heart; and her whole figure suggested an idea of unmitigable energy, and an appetite gorged in malevolence."[84] This woman is English—whatever that means—but rendered as irredeemably, racially, Other.

What's interesting about Godwin's novel, in fact, is that while certain of its plebeian English characters are shown to be "not-white" or even in a sense "black" (here the marker has to do with civilizational attainment, not necessarily, or not always, as inflected in biological or physical terms as it is in *Caleb Williams*), certain others (again the Hawkinses come to mind, as does Caleb of course) are shown to be decent, articulate, honorable, in effect already "white," although they come from the same background and social context as their "black" fellows. "Blackness" and "whiteness" here are racial markers of location on the spectrum running from the savage to the civilized and by extension from the Orient to the Occident as well; the point is that one can find both "white" and "black," civilized and savage, Occidentalized and Orientalized English characters in the putative metropolitan center of empire. (Nor was Godwin by any means alone in this kind of construction: John Thelwall does much the same thing in *The Peripatetic*—referring, for example, to two "unfeeling" bird-catchers he encounters in the countryside outside London as clumsy and uncouth "barbarians," and Godwin and Thelwall are but examples of a much broader tendency.)[85] For *some* at least of these internal savages can be redeemed and incorporated into civilization, it turns out; they are capable of being drawn into what Ghassan Hage describes as modern society's mechanisms for the distribution, circulation, and exchange of hope, which were only then coming into play.[86] Caleb's self-appointed task when he flees from London to a remote village is, after all, to share "in the task of civilising the unpolished manners of the inhabitants."[87] In chapter 2, we will see Wordsworth treading the same line between savage and civilized English characters—those entitled to hope and those cut off from it—in his early poetry.

What one finds in portrayals of the interior of England in the years around 1800, then, is an unstable mixture of racial types, corresponding to different degrees of access to civilization and Westernization. What distinguishes the putative metropolitan center from the outer reaches of the empire at this stage is that, whereas the development and deployment of a racial language to depict overseas others—for example the Orientalization of the Orient—were, and would remain until the twentieth century, more or less comprehensive and all-encompassing,[88] the deployment of the same language in the domestic interior of England in the decades around 1800 was uneven and actually being dismantled as "civilization" and Occidentalism were spread: "they" out there in India or Africa or Arabia might be all the same, but "we" were not all yet really "we" in 1800. What distinguishes foreign from domestic space, in other words, was partly a matter of degree: "they" were completely uncivilized; "we" were at least partly civilized—and we were working on civilizing—recoding, implicitly reclassifying as "white" and ultimately "Western" or "Occidental"—the rest of our countrymen, or at least those who could be redeemed.

It is in this sense that the process of Occidentalism relates to that of Orientalism: it is about locating and clearing a space for a white, Western self who could be more effectively counterposed to the Orient out there. As David Theo Goldberg notes, the logic of race thus functions in two directions at once, both excluding (those who are permanently Other) and including (those who might yet be like "us").[89] The unevenness of the racial designations of the common people during the Romantic period in England is precisely an indication of the uneven incompleteness of the process of inclusion that was still taking place at home, as savage or Orientalized domestic populations were slowly being transformed into Occidentals, "whites" like "us." The two processes, of marking and re-marking racial identities and sites of location inside the metropolis and in the colonial realm "out there," Occident and Orient respectively, take place in an overlapping and mutually reinforcing manner.[90]

As I noted in passing in the Preface, this confusion of internal and external spaces and races poses a problem for some of the accounts of nationalism in this period as well, for the notions of a wider racial and geocultural or civilizational identity (the Occident) is not limited to the scale of the nation. "As even the briefest acquaintance with Great Britain will confirm, the Welsh, the Scottish and the English remain in many ways distinct peoples in cultural terms, just as all three countries continue to be conspicuously sub-divided into different regions," Linda Colley argues in *Britons*. "The sense of a common identity here did not come into being, then, because of an integration and homogenization of disparate cultures. Instead, Britishness was superimposed over an array of internal differences in response to contact with the Other, and above all in response to conflict with the Other."[91] The Other to which Colley refers is of course an exter-

nal one—France above all. Her account of nationalism does not really take
into account the range of internal forms of otherness, which are somewhat
stronger than the mere "differences" she alludes to, nor does it really take
sufficiently into account other forms of collective identity (other than religion). Perhaps this is because Colley is interested in British, rather than English, nationalism. Gerald Newman's account of English nationalism is in
this sense much more interesting for the purposes of my discussion, since it
is especially attuned to cultural, class, and racial tropes deployed throughout the eighteenth century: he elaborates a sense of a racially and culturally
identified English nationalism, privileging sincerity, innocence, honesty,
moral independence, frankness and originality.[92] But all in all I think that
nationalism in the narrow sense is not an especially useful formulation in
which to capture the far more profound cultural and political shifts that
I am trying to get at here. Ian Baucom's exploration of Englishness—in a
politico-cultural rather than strictly a narrowly nationalist sense—and in
particular his elaboration of the extent to which England must be seen as
being "continuously discontinuous with itself" is very helpful, and I will
return to it in later chapters.[93]

   Anticipating nineteenth-century developments, I don't mean to completely disagree with Victor Kiernan, who pointed out long ago that from
the vantage point of the dominant class in Europe a savage is a savage,
whether at home or overseas: "in innumerable ways his attitude to his own
'lower orders' was identical," Kiernan notes with respect to one who constitutes himself as superior, "with that of Europe to the 'lesser breeds.'"[94] The
lords of human kind (as Kiernan so aptly puts it) had the same disdain for
their inferiors, who were thought of in both civilizational and racial terms
whether inside England or outside it. "Discontented native in the colonies,
labour agitator in the mills, were the same serpent in alternative disguise,"
Kiernan notes. "Much of the talk about the barbarism or darkness of the
outer world, which it was Europe's mission to rout, was a transmuted fear of
the masses at home."[95] One problem with Kiernan's assessment, however,
is that it does not allow for the extent to which the language of race and
civilization can be mutable, changeable, malleable according to the circumstances: "we" and "they" are shifting categories, after all, not set in stone.

   The other—more serious—problem with Kiernan's summary of this situation is that the lordly attitude toward those perceived as civilizational
inferiors was not confined to the actual lords of human kind; that is, the politically dominant class. The Romantic period is so important as a moment
of transition precisely because the development and deployment of the discourse of race and civilization was especially prevalent *not* among those in

power—a parliament and government made up largely of the great landlords—but precisely among those who sought power and would be granted
it to a certain extent after 1832: not today's lords, in other words, but tomor-
row's (this is one of my reservations about Bernard Porter's account of imperial culture, as I argued earlier). There was even something of a convergence
between the still-emergent—and competing—radical and evangelical discourses of the common people in this period (which is why Godwin's text
can in certain respects look so much like the dispatches of the Reverend
Greatbatch): both radicals and evangelicals sought to civilize and enlighten—
en-whiten—the people of England, extend the circuits of social hope to include them, albeit in different ways and for different political purposes. They
both saw the same savagery that needed to be corrected and set straight—in
a word, civilized, made into an Occidental "us" that could function more
effectively in opposition to the "them" out there.

The point here is not only that a racial discourse has been used to signify populations subject to the power of the dominant (or ascendant) classes
within Europe—the kind of class racism also identified by Etienne Balibar[96]—but also that the concept of racial otherness is sufficiently mobile
that the same group of people can, as Goldberg notes, be alternatively defined as racially similar or as racially different as circumstances change.
"There has always been a multiplicity of Others," Miles argues, "with the
quality being attributed to different subjects in different contexts, often with
the result that the same population has functioned as Other and Us at different historical moments."[97] Whether undertaken by evangelicals or radical
reformers such as Francis Place, the task of the civilizing mission at home
was precisely to incorporate a population that had once been considered
Other into a still-developing "us." This is of course the central argument of
Norbert Elias's classic *The Civilizing Process*, on which Miles draws.

Tom Holt has suggested that class and racial identities are transposable
in this period. "It may be that the 'language' of class provided a vocabulary
for thinking about race, or vice versa," he argues. "It hardly matters; what is
important is the symmetry of the discourse, which perhaps intensified the
conviction that this vision of the world was just."[98] Craig Calhoun, however, argues that the language of class—in the nineteenth-century sense of
that term—may be a little misleading in this transitional context. Until
well into the Chartist period, he argues, workers' struggles were not the
result of their congregation in factories "but of the resistance of workers in
older trades to being subjected to the discipline of factory work and having
craft production itself subjected to the competition of factory (and more
generally capitalist) industry. Throughout the early phase of struggle, there-

fore, workers were not fighting for control of the industrial revolution as much as against that revolution itself."[99] Calhoun points out that in the late eighteenth and earlier nineteenth centuries, community and cultural tradition provided more important social bonds than class as such.[100] Given what I have referred to earlier as the articulation of race and class in this moment, the encounter between different classes was in this respect also an encounter between different cultures and different races, in which one side wielded disproportionate power over the other. Given the wide range of capital offenses, which meant that, as John Brewer and John Styles have argued, "the patrician elite, able to choose whether to prosecute, whether to provide character references for the accused and whether to ask that mercy be extended to the guilty, wielded a veritable sword of Damocles over plebeian Englishmen,"[101] power, including ultimately the power of life and death, was a key component of the relationship between elites and the people—one not altogether unrecognizable when transposed to a colonial context, in which a similar tension between cultures and a similar exercise of power held sway. Fielding comments in *Joseph Andrews* that the human species is divided "into two sorts of people, to-wit, *High* People and *Low* People," who, "so far from looking on each other as Brothers in the Christian Language . . . seem scarce to regard each other as members of the same Species." This, he adds, "the Terms *strange Persons, People one does not know, the Creature, Wretches, Beasts, Brutes,* and many other Appellations evidently demonstrates."[102] For all the irony of Fielding's comment, however, there is also a good deal of truth to it. Vic Gattrell notes, for instance, the stark limits of sympathy that extended to plebeian—rather than the rare cases of polite—victims of execution in the late eighteenth century by such well-cultured observers as Boswell.[103]

This takes us back to the question of race and racial identity, and in particular to Foucault's observation that racism is best thought of as a method of separating groups that exist within a biopolitical continuum. "When you have a normalizing society, you have a power which is, at least superficially, in the first instance, or in the first line a biopower, and racism is the indispensable precondition that allows someone to be killed, that allows others to be killed," he argues, with particular relevance here to the power of life and death that the English elites held over their plebeian counterparts. "Once the State functions in the biopower mode, racism alone can justify the murderous function of the State," Foucault adds. "If the power of normalization wished to exercise the old sovereign right to kill, it must become racist."[104] Foucault's point is that the logic of racism is completely bound up with and inseparable from the biopolitical state of the late eighteenth and early nineteenth centuries: it functioned equally with regard to both socially designated "others" within the domestic space and "others" in the zone of actual colonial contact. Nowhere is this racial logic of differentiation made more explicit in the period than in the caricatures of Gillray, which so consistently reduce plebeian characters to the visual equivalents of the racially distorted Other bodies we see in *Caleb Williams* (and it is important to note, of course, that Gillray was, politically speaking, the polar opposite of Godwin). This is especially true of Gillray's famous print of the London Corresponding Society (LCS) in a secret meeting (see fig. 2).

John Brewer has pointed out, in his study of the depiction of the representations of plebeian politics in eighteenth-century visual culture, that "in almost all the cartoons that portray common people, the plebs are depicted with ungracious, ill-formed features on a face whose conformation is exaggerated by a variety of crude expressions."[105] But he argues that a dramatic shift takes place in this kind of representation in the 1790s. "In the prints of the 1780s the plebeian politician is still a member of the species Homo sapiens; he may be reprehensible but he still belongs within the realms of ordinary experience," Brewer notes. "But Gillray's figures [of the LCS meeting, simian and grotesque], despite his use of the metonymic conventions to identify the butcher and the barber, do not belong to this earth: with the exception of the pipe-smoking butcher who resembles Gale Jones, the radical surgeon, they are all preternatural, monstrous creatures, skulking in the stygian gloom. Here is a picture of hell and its inhabitants."[106]

This allows us to add a further context and qualification to the important work that has been done on representations of plebeian subcultures, or representations of the urban or rural poor, in England during the Romantic period. Such forms of representation not only had striking equivalents in British representations of Africa or India during this period; they were driven by precisely the same imperial logic of surveillance and power/knowledge and were all too often structured by a "code of counter-insurgency," which Ranajit Guha has theorized with reference to British colonial writing in India, but which I would extend to forms of representation in England itself in the late eighteenth and early nineteenth centuries as well.[107] "Faced with a chronically restive plebeian sub-culture, from the 1790s onwards the British governing classes orchestrated a wide range of efforts to find out more about the 'character and condition' of the 'common people,' to organize this data on a systematic basis and to act, where possible, on its implications," David Solkin explains in his recent book on the depiction of ordinary life in British painting in the early nineteenth century. The period's visual and verbal texts have to be placed in that context, as one way of meeting the

Fig. 2. James Gillray, "London Corresponding Society, Alarm'd" (1798). Print Collection, Miriam and Ira D. Wallach Division of Art, Prints, and Photographs, The New York Public Library, Astor, Lenox, and Tilden Foundations.

demand "for the production of a certain kind of knowledge—not of the poor as a large, undifferentiated social mass, but in all their minute particularities as individuals."[108] This attitude, as it is exhibited in visual culture documented by Brewer and Solkin, among others, also has a very precise equivalent in literary representation, as well as in actual state policy making. Pablo Mukherjee has thoroughly elaborated the parallels between the surveillance and control of subaltern groups in England and in India. "The numerous descriptions of criminal India could be easily adapted from equally numerous descriptions of a lawless Britain," he points out, which suggests very clearly "the symbiotic nature of the colonialist and domestic discourses of power. It hints at the interest that the 'polite classes' had in the policing of both territories." Specific policies could be developed for the one context and then transposed wholesale to the other; practically all of the reforms Colquhoun proposes for London in *Police of the Metropolis* were adopted by colonialist writers in their depictions of India, for example. And later, in the era of Peel, "the rise of the 'new police' in Britain," Mukherjee writes, "had a palpable effect on the administration of India. If, at home, the improved network of surveillance resulted in the 'discovery' of a tide of criminality, the same technique was applied to represent the colony where allegedly rampant criminality could then serve to justify British presence there in the name of progress and reform."[109]

The reverse holds true as well, of course, as attitudes toward India were imported back into Britain. Thus the shifting attitude toward the poor so powerfully documented by John Barrell in *The Dark Side of the Landscape* can, in other words, be seen to be driven by an immediately imperial and racial logic, not just a class one.[110] In both cases, the colonial and the domestic, there is a similar degree of alienation of the observed and represented from the elite observer; in both, similar questions about the Other are registered; and in both there are similar anxieties about the status and activity of these Others—whether they are working or resting, whether they are happy or suffering; whether they are docile or threatening. The sense of a potentially threatening population that needs to be surveyed, known, controlled, improved—in a word, civilized—turns out to be not substantially different when constructed in an English setting than it is in an Indian one. (Indeed, the very fact that the term "subaltern" was adopted by modern Indian historians from Antonio Gramsci's use of it in terms specific to Italy and redeployed in a colonial situation in India is itself symptomatic of this convergence.)

What the two settings also have in common—and this is of crucial importance in understanding Wordsworth's poetry, as we will see in chapter

2—is the question of plebeian consciousness, which, precisely because of its ultimate unknowability, is often either displaced or negated in elite representations. Guha notes, for example, the tendency in counterinsurgent writing from the colonial period in India (and indeed in nationalist elitist historiography afterward as well) to refuse "to acknowledge the [subaltern] insurgent as the subject of his own history," for example, by denying the conscious agency of a subaltern rebel group, ascribing its rebellion to some transcendental consciousness. "In operative terms, this means denying a will to the mass of the rebels themselves and representing them merely as instruments of some other will," Guha argues. "If any consciousness is attributed at all to the rebels, it is only a few of their leaders—more often than not some individual members or small groups of the gentry—who are credited with it."[111] Much the same dynamic can be seen to be at work in representations of plebeian consciousness (or lack thereof) in England as well.

If nothing else, plebeian consciousness becomes one of the major questions (if not the major question) in visual and verbal culture in the Romantic period: not only whether it can be captured in visual terms or in print—as *Lyrical Ballads* purports to do—but whether it exists in the first place, and what kind of threat it poses if it does exist. The immense importance of the London Corresponding Society was that it seemed to represent or express—in articulate, persuasive, written form—the voice of a politically marginalized population previously totally excluded from the realm of written cultural as well as political representation. We go back, then, to the government's shocked reaction to the addresses and proclamations of the LCS: what was so traumatic for the elite was not merely the realization that there was a plebeian *organization* talking, reading, and writing about the rights of man, but that it was a *plebeian* organization to begin with: who knew they could read and write, or think about representation?!

For elite writers in the 1790s and after—and scholars ever since—the recurring question was quite similar to the one facing the twentieth-century Indian historians of the Subaltern Studies group, whose project aimed to recuperate and rescue from the prose of counterinsurgency the reality of the consciousness of the people as such.[112] As Pier Paolo Pasolini's discussion of free indirect discourse makes clear, the question of consciousness is bound up with and quite inseparable from the question of language itself. "The most odious and intolerable thing, even in the most innocent of bourgeois, is that of not knowing how to recognize life experiences other than his own: and of bringing all other life experiences back to a substantial analogy with his own," Pasolini argues. "It is a real offense that he gives to other men in different social and historical conditions. Even a noble, elevated

bourgeois writer, who doesn't know how to recognize the extreme characteristics of psychological diversity of a man whose life experiences differ
from his, and who, on the contrary, believes that he can make them his by
seeking substantial analogies—almost as if experiences other than his own
weren't conceivable—performs an act that is the first step toward certain
manifestations of the defense of his privileges and even toward racism. In
this sense," he adds, "he is no longer free but belongs to his class determin-
istically; there is no discontinuity between him and a police chief or an ex-
ecutioner in a concentration camp."[113] As we will see in chapter 2, Pasolini's
argument will prove indispensable for understanding Wordsworth's poetry
of the 1790s.

One elite response to the dilemma of the ultimate unknowability of the
plebeian among elite writers and artists was to mimic or caricature plebeian
consciousness—or rather what that consciousness was imagined to be—
precisely in order to defuse it as a potential threat: perhaps, by containing
plebeian consciousness in imaginary texts, its real life counterpart (assuming that it exists) could be contained as well. Surely this is part of what is at
stake in Hannah More's depiction of self-satisfied plebeian characters such
as Tom Hod in *Village Politics* or the title character of the *Shepherd of Salisbury Plain*: the fantasy that by representing a positive form of plebeian consciousness to a plebeian audience life could somehow be conjured to imitate
art. If nothing else, at least turning to mimicry and caricature can be used
to reassure an elite audience that all is still well with the common people,
as Barrell shows to be partly at stake in depictions of the rural poor in, say,
Gainsborough's work from his London period. By presenting the good and
deserving (i.e., not threatening) poor in scenes of pastoral innocence whose
time had passed in the 1780s, such works can, as Barrell argues, be seen as
attempts to deny or contest—or at least temporarily wish away—the emergence of a plebeian consciousness.[114]

A similar dynamic is in play in the humorous (but not really) paintings
of the "common vulgar" by David Wilkie. Solkin asks what it means that
Wilkie gives such attention to the caricature-like particularities of the plebeian characters in his paintings, something previously reserved generally
for polite subjects. "One reason why Wilkie employed this method, or so I
would suggest, was to reinforce the all-important separation between himself and his vulgar subjects, by presenting them as the objects of his (and of
course his audience's) amused and distanced observation," Solkin writes.
"Paradoxically, however, the same approach also extended to the lower
orders a presumption of familiarity that polite caricaturists had hitherto
tended to limit to their social equals—thus enabling Wilkie's viewers to

entertain the pleasing idea that they knew as much about the poor as they did about other members of their own class, albeit from a different and superior vantage point. But a third point is probably the most crucial of all: that to grant the poor the individualized character of bourgeois subjects was to deprive them of any distinct identity, or interests, of their own. While this tactic may have raised the risk of blurring all-important social distinctions, it was much to be preferred over the depiction of the masses as a coarse and undifferentiated mass."[115] Somehow, in other words, the threat of plebeian consciousness—or even the potential of that consciousness—seemed to be defused by translating it into bourgeois terms.

Certainly, more than merely translating, seeking to *transform* the Other into terms that can be understood and framed in terms of bourgeois discourse was a major component of the civilizing mission from the late eighteenth century onward. The most obvious work of the civilizing mission consisted in the many projects to school, evangelize, convert, improve, and instruct the common people of England, whether by evangelicals or radicals—hence the proliferation of, on the one hand, the Proclamation Society (founded 1787), Religious Tract Society (1799), Society for the Suppression of Vice (1801), British and Foreign Bible Society (1804), and, on the other hand, the Society for the Diffusion of Useful Knowledge, Mechanics' Institutes, Friendly Societies, Lancasterian day schools, and so on.

But there was also an extraordinarily important ideological counterpart of that kind of actual, engaged civilizing, and it is provided in much of the literary work of the period. In offering readers a multivalent, layered, and complex account of the common people—both like *us* and not—writers like Godwin, Thelwall, and Wordsworth helped their middle-class audiences see that some, at least, of those who might seem Other at home might actually be reclassified as, absorbed into, Us, under the appropriate circumstances. Ultimately, that is what allowed for a different kind of racial discourse at home and overseas: from a reformist point of view (whether evangelical or radical), English savages are not—could not possibly be—permanently classified as Other; there is—there has to be—hope for them. As Ghassan Hage argues, the discourse of hope itself becomes all-important in this context, and the question is to whom hope can be extended, who can be seen as eligible in obtaining even a little "share of hope."[116] From a reformist point of view, those savages had to be made into Englishmen, if not yet in real life, then in fiction and poetry, until such time as real life could catch up to the new ideal of a white Englishness, a new Occidentalism.

PART I

Preparing the Way

CHAPTER ONE

Making London Western

1. TIME AND HOPE

"The circumstances which it will be seen I have mentioned relative to the ignorance, the immorality, the grossness, the obscenity the drunkenness, the dirtiness, and depravity of the middling and even of a large portion of the better sort of tradesmen, the artisans, and the journeymen tradesmen of London in the days of my youth," notes the great nineteenth-century reformer Francis Place in the opening pages of his autobiography, "may excite the suspicion that the picture I have drawn is a caricature, the parts of which are out of keeping with [each other] and have no symmetry as a whole."[1] If there is a theme running through and tying together the immense accumulation of notes, clippings, testimonies, reports, and observations constituting Place's archive of plebeian London life in the late eighteenth and early nineteenth centuries, it is that a yawning abyss has opened between the ways and morals of the recent past—the past of Place's own London childhood—and those of the present in which he is writing. So large is this gap, Place keeps insisting throughout his archive, that the people of the present find it difficult or impossible to imagine the moral economy of the past.

"It will seem incredible that such songs should be allowed but it was so," he writes, for example, in the preface to his meticulously detailed manuscript notes on flash ballads and bawdy songs circulating through London in that previous era. "There is not one of them that I have not myself heard sung in the streets, as well as at Choir Clubs, Cock and Hen Clubs, & Free and Easy's." Although the obscene and politically subversive songs were eventually suppressed by a new police regime, he admits, such has been the shift in public morality that it would be unimaginable for them to make a return even if heavy-handed state and reactionary vigilante surveillance were ended. "I have no doubt at all that if ballad singers were now to be left at liberty by the police to sing those songs that the people in the streets would not permit the singing of them. Such songs, as even 35 years ago, produced applause, would now cause the singer to be rolld in the mud," he adds, whereas formerly, "not one of these songs even the most infamous was at all objected to. Servant maids used to stop in the markets, to hear them sung, and used to purchase them."[2]

And as with songs, so with other matters as well. The obscene prints the public display of which used to "offend the eye" not so long ago have now all but disappeared, he writes from the perspective of the 1820s and 1830s.[3] The behavior of "unfortunate females" in the streets today is not what it was even sixteen years previously, let alone in the eighteenth century.[4] Whereas in Place's childhood "the merits" of an outlaw like Mary Young (a.k.a. Jenny Diver) "were a constant theme and the subject of continual conversation," today "no one among decent people ever thinks of talking of an abandoned prostitute and thief" like her.[5] And although within Place's recollection a Tyburn hanging day "was to all intents and purposes a fair day," in which throngs of people gaily offered the condemned prisoners beer or gin to ease their passage to the gallows, "songs were sung and the ballads were sold at the corners of the streets, all along Holborn, St Giles's and Oxford Street," and pie men and pickpockets plied their trades, such public revelry at a scene of execution was by the 1820s unthinkable, according to Place.[6]

And, from the same early nineteenth-century vantage point, the "barbarous" pillory once installed at Charing Cross is beyond even memory or recollection, so remote a conception does it now seem. "So atrocious was the conduct of the mob when a man was 'pilloried,' so debased and cruel were they, that those who are now children, will scarcely be able, when grown up, to conceive the existence of such enormities, much less to believe they were promoted and encouraged by lawyers, judges and what are usually termed respectable people," Place notes. "Even the very populace better taught and more humane than their parents, will hear with incredulity the tales which may perchance be told of the Pillory."[7]

As Vic Gatrell has also pointed out, the constant theme of Place's writing is the running contrast between London's "then" of undignified, violent, obscene, gross, wasteful, and altogether barbarous activities both public and private and London's "now" of increasing respectability (not to mention its projected future when the past will be altogether unimaginable).[8] For Gatrell, although Place compares unfavorably with James Boswell in that he "was a clumsy, self-taught and not fully literate writer, and he lacked a sense of both irony and humour," he yet "monitored humble and middling-class London with an intensity that Boswell could never have attempted."[9] Although Gatrell acknowledges the importance of Place's project and the significance of its attention not merely to the improvement of the working people but to the fact that that their improvement was largely self-motivated rather than directed by benevolent bourgeois reformers or evangelical Sunday school teachers, he misreads the moral overtones of Place's work.[10] In itself this is not surprising, because Place enters Gatrell's narrative supposedly as a proto-Victorian opponent of the eighteenth-century satirical culture that Gatrell's book *City of Laughter* sets out to celebrate. "In repudiating past vulgarities, in distancing himself from the low world that he and his kind had outgrown, in his priggish humourlessness, earnestness and vanity about his own distinction," Gatrell argues, "he turned himself into another of the old laughter's enemies, speaking in this for many at aspirant middling levels, and announcing the coming of sober times."[11]

Place's attitude, however, is much more complex and ambivalent than Gatrell allows, largely because Gatrell overstates Place's interest in moralism and loses sight of what is far more important in Place's narrative. Take, for example, Place's account of his own father, to whom he frequently turns as a marker of the cultural logic of a bygone era:

> My father was a very bony muscular man about five feet six or seven inches in height dark complexion and very strong for his height. I have heard my mother say that he has carried two sacks of flour on his back at the same time. He was an elderly man from the earliest recollection I have of him, so he appeared to me, troubled with severe fits of Gout, yet when free from the disorder robust and active. He was a resolute daring straight forward sort of a man, governed almost wholly by his passions and animal sensations both of which were very strong, he was careless of reputation excepting in some particulars in which he seems to have thought he excelled. These were few, mostly relating to sturdiness and dissoluteness. Drinking, Whoring, Gaming, Fishing and Fighting, he was well acqua[i]nted with the principal boxers of his day; Slack and Broughton [mid-eighteenth century pugilists later celebrated by Pierce Egan in *Boxiana*][12] were his companions. Some of these desires and propensities never left him, though most of them became all but extinct with old age. He was always ready in certain cases to advise and to assist others, all who knew him placed the utmost reliance on his word, and as the habits

of all ranks then as compared with then as compared with the habits of each class of men now, were exceedingly dissolute, his conduct was not then obnoxious to the censure of others as such conduct would be now.[13]

Although Mary Thale and others, including Gatrell, have argued that Place was keen to denounce his father's barbarism—he would often beat his children with a stick until it broke—the sense we get of the older Place from the younger is rather more nuanced and sympathetic, not to say tinged with nostalgia for the resolution, daring, and straightforwardness demanded by a hard life of drinking, whoring, gaming, fishing, and fighting: a life whose attractions somehow seem to shine through Place's critical description of it.

The older Place may have had his investment in "animal sensations," but he also emerges from his son's description of him as a solid friend, ready to help those in need of his assistance: his reliability and dependability even end up weighing against, if not outweighing altogether, his interest in physical pleasures. Moreover, Place is eager to locate his father in his own time: what he did is what *everyone* did in those days, and placed in its own context, would not have been seen as objectionable. In fact, even in beating his children, he actually had their best interests at heart, according to Place himself:

> In his opinion coercion was the only [way] to eradicate faults, and by its terror to prevent their recurrence. These were common notions, and were carried into practice not only by the heads of families and the teachers of youth generally, but by the government itself and every man in authority under it, in the treatment of prisoners and the drilling of soldiers who were publicly beaten by the drill serjeants with a cane. Indiscriminating, sanguinary and cruel as our Statutes are, they as well as all the other practices alluded to, were much more so fifty years ago, and they were administered in a much more unfeeling and barbarous manner. The manners of all were much more gross then than now, what would now be thought intolerable cruelty towards inferiors was then practiced as mere matter of course. What would now be thought gross and brutal was then as little repugnant to common notions, to good sense and good teaching, as the more mild and efficacious modes now in use are thought to be by the present generation, however much room their [sic] still is for amendment.

The relationship of father to son, then, sums up and is bound up with the relationship of that older London to the present-day London in which

Place is writing; what matters is not what conditions were once like, but that they have changed in accordance with the flow of history.

In fact, Place was not all that interested in moralism as an end in itself, which is where Gatrell's reading of him as a prude takes us. He was interested in morals as markers of temporal modes: moral improvement was important for him not because he was invested in morality as such, in other words, but because it marks movement in time, and ultimately history. In short, Place was interested in a discourse of moral improvement because it offered him an index for the entry of working people into history—and that is what he is ultimately interested in. This is why Gatrell's reading of Place as prudish and judgmental is off mark; what excites Place about improvement is that he can look right through it to see the movement of time and ultimately history itself. He rarely mentions some past vulgarity without pointing out that things are now much improved.

Take drinking, for example. "Drunkenness is no longer the prevailing and conspicuous vice among workmen," Place argues in his 1829 tract *Improvement of the Working People*. "The very meanest and least informed being much more sober as a class, much more cleanly in their persons, than were those who in former times were far above them in respect to the amount of wages they received; whilst the most skilled and best paid are, as classes, more sober, more moral, and better informed, than were the generality of their employers at the time alluded to."[14] Taken at face value, this certainly seems moralistic and judgmental. But we have to follow Place's argument to see where it takes him. Why does a working man drink?

> Working, when he has work to do, from an early hour in the morning until late in the evening; excluded, as in most cases the working man is, from all rational enjoyment; during the days he is employed, shut out also, by the nature of his employment, from all reasonable conversation; doing the same thing, generally in the same place, always against his will and on compulsion; without hope of bettering his condition, and in a majority of cases with a conviction that it will become worse and worse as he grows older and his family increases, his thoughts are necessarily of a gloomy cast, his home is seldom comfortable: for be his wife ever so well disposed and industrious, she with spirits broken cannot even do those things for comfort which in former times she was wont to do, while in many cases her family occupies her whole attention and all her time, and the room and the husband as well as herself are neglected; and thus the man and the woman sink gradually, home becomes more and more comfortless, as he degenerates continually, neglects his

family, and at length becomes reckless and worthless. Such is the actual state of many, and especially among uneducated workmen and labourers, to whom none but the mere animal sensations are left; to these his enjoyments are limited, and even these are frequently reduced to two,—namely, sexual intercourse and drinking.[15]

Drinking is not a problem in itself; it is, instead, a marker of a certain conception of time. The workingman drinks because he feels, and is, trapped in time, caught in an endless present ("doing the same thing, generally in the same place") that threatens to, and actually does, swallow him and his family alive. Gradually he breaks down, losing not only his sense of agency but his very humanity, and he falls back instead on his "animal sensations" (and note the repetition of that phrase from his account of his father in his autobiography). Drink is thus not a sign of immorality as such; it is a sign of the sheer loss of humanity occasioned by a loss of time, literally timelessness, being stuck in time. "The uninformed man thinks only of sensual enjoyments," Place argues, because that is what he has been reduced to by social circumstances. "The better-informed man's thoughts," by contrast, "are occupied with the pleasures he has had, and those he anticipates;—from books, lectures, conversations, experiments, and ingenious mechanical contrivances."[16] He does not drink because he is aware of the flow of time from past through present to any number of possible futures—and his sense of agency is inextricable from his awareness of the flow of time.

Movement in time, for Place, is the very basis for hope, and hope in turn is the basis for politics. "Take away hope," he asks, "and what hold can you have of any man."[17] Without hope, the workingman will sink into despair; armed with hope, however, the better-informed workingman will seek to improve himself, and, Place notes, "such a man will frequently rise as the uninformed man sinks."[18] The sense of the working classes that one gets from Place's account is thus extremely uneven: a heterogeneous patchwork of rising and falling movement, and indeed, acceleration and deceleration, corresponding to the distribution of hope. Overall, the perspective he wants to convey is that the London of the 1820s and 1830s is a scene of temporal movement—and hence improvement—compared to what it was two or three decades previously, even if that movement is also at times so slow as to be imperceptible even to those propelled along by it.[19]

Even if in general there has been movement and hence improvement, however, there are also plenty of cases in Place's account where movement has not taken place, where people are sinking or standing still rather than rising. Place's map of his contemporary London thus consists of the spatialization of a heterogeneous and uneven distribution of time, speed, and hope, the point of which is to bring those sites and subjects that are falling behind into temporal, and hence political, alignment with those sites and subjects who have moved forward in time and into the flow of history. For, as Place's account of his father makes clear, history for him is the accumulation of individual movements in time, distributed through space.

2. TERRA INCOGNITA

In one of his many contributions to Charles Knight's monumental 1841–44 collection *London*, W. Weir provides a narrative map of the metropolis that supplements Place's account of its heterogeneous and uneven development and spatial distribution.[20] Early nineteenth-century London may still have its squalid and impoverished districts distributed among and between more stable and prosperous neighborhoods, Weir argues, but the situation a few decades previously was reversed, with a few well-off areas standing out from a more general background of poorly policed slums. "A mere glance at the comparatively large portion of the space then occupied by the city, over which this class of squalid dwellings extended, will supply the reader with some idea of the amount of this class of the population, over whose outcomings and ingoings it beho[o]ved the wretched police-staff to keep steady watch," he writes. He begins his depiction where Holborn and Fleet Street meet Farringdon Street (previously Fleet Market). "Turning from Fleet Ditch to the left along Holborn, after passing between the Scylla of Shoe Lane, and the Charybdis of Field Lane [the "emporium of petty larceny" close to Fagin's lair in *Oliver Twist*],[21] the passenger passed on the left Wheatstone Park [today's Whetstone Park], behind which were the environs of Lincoln's-Inn-Fields, in a very dilapidated condition, and the termination of the 'Hundreds of Drury' [a notorious region of coffee shops, taverns, and brothels off Drury Lane, in the even more notorious parish of St. Giles's and featuring in novels by Smollett and Fielding]." He continues, "From St. Giles's a chain of dilapidated streets extended down by Castle Street, behind Leicester Fields [later Square], and Hedge Lane, almost joining the Sanctuary of Westminster, for a notion of which the reader is referred to Fielding."[22] Having gone from the center to the far west of London,[23] he then resets his account from the Fleet valley to reveal an equally comprehensive survey of poverty and crime extending east to Wapping and south to the Mint. "This review of the resorts of the 'dangerous classes,'" Weir writes, "shows that although portions of their territory have since been occupied by the streets and dwellings of the more reputable and comfortable classes, they have not retaliated by taking up new quarters—they have rather shrunk like snails deeper into their shells at the approach of incompatible neighbors." Thus, he concludes, "the honest and opulent portions of society appear [in the eighteenth century] like small islands, encircled and separated by the ramifying arms of this sea of destitution and hunger for the goods of others."[24]

There was logic to this distribution of space. As Donald Low points out, "It was no coincidence that the most notorious of London's rookeries were located outside the City yet close enough to it for thieves to be able to steal from the centres of wealth and business there."[25] For example, "Fleet Street was close enough to the dingy sidestreets of Drury Lane and Covent Garden for any thief worth his salt to give pursuers the slip, and from there it was but a short step to sure sanctuary in the cellars and lodging houses of St. Giles: Buckeridge [Buckbridge] Street, Church Lane and Bainbridge Street [the worst part of St. Giles's, nestled between the church and Great Russell Street to the north] never saw City officers."[26] Similarly, Spitalfields and Whitechapel were just beyond the area patrolled by City officers, but conveniently close to the Bank and Royal Exchange and associated streets; Petticoat Lane was close to Leadenhall Street; Saffron Hill was close to the nucleus of the City, as were Bunhill Row and Grub Street (both disreputable areas); and Tothill Fields and Hedge Lane close to Westminster Abbey and the Houses of Parliament. In fact, the islands of prosperity throughout the metropolis were, as Low puts it, "ringed by thieves' kitchens, surrounded by ill-lit and unpatrolled criminal areas, into which those who stole were drilled from childhood to make their safe exits."[27] It was precisely this close proximity of fashionable and notorious districts that enabled the celebrated thief James Hardy Vaux to move so smoothly in between the jewelers' shops in Piccadilly or the Strand, where he would, assuming "the air of a Bond-street lounger," discreetly pilfer various objects, only to dispose of them subsequently—and in a different guise—at pawnbrokers' shops in the rougher districts near Covent Garden, where he would also indulge in his "fondness for flash-houses," in one of which (The Butcher's Arms, in Clement's Lane, near Clare Market) he would finally be arrested.[28]

Various improvements notwithstanding, the spatial unevenness depicted by Weir outlived the eighteenth century and lasted well into the nineteenth. Thus Engels, writing as the fastnesses of St. Giles's rookeries were about to be breached by developers in the 1840s, points out that the slum "is in the midst of the most populous part of the town, surrounded by broad, splendid avenues in which the gay world of London idles about, in the immediate neighborhood of Oxford Street, Regent Street, of Trafalgar Square and the Strand."[29] In an 1851 piece in *Household Words*, Dickens picks up where

Engels leaves off. "How many people may there be in London who, if we had brought them deviously and blindfold, to this street, fifty paces from the Station House, and within call of Saint Giles's church, would know it for a not remote part of the city in which their lives are passed?" he asks of the rookery. "How many, who amidst this compound of sickening smells, these heaps of filth, these tumbling houses, with all their vile contents, animate and inanimate, slimily overflowing into the black road, would believe that they breathe *this* air?"[30]

Partly this sense of heterogeneous compartmentalization was a consequence of London's lack of centralized planning and reliance instead on the kind of localized, ad hoc development schemes—such as Thomas Neale's Seven Dials, Henry Jermyn's plan for the area around St. James's Square, Richard Frith's project in what would become Soho, Thomas Bond's north of Piccadilly, Charles Cole's in Ely Place, or Jacob Leroux's in Somers Town—that, long before the nineteenth century, had gradually filled in some of what had been blank spaces on the urban map, albeit with the effect of turning the overall metropolitan space into what Burke would identify as "an endless addition of littleness to littleness, extending itself over a great tract of land."[31] As Burke himself knew, there was a political correlate to this. The great continental city radiated pomp and magnificence, Roy Porter points out; "with its grand boulevards, piazzas and obelisks, its vistas of cathedrals and citadels and other scenic climaxes, the baroque or neoclassical capital enshrined the aesthetics of absolutism: monumentality and wide open spaces bespoke power unopposed," Porter adds. "Nothing remotely like that appeared in London, at least not until the Prince Regent."[32] London's qualitative unevenness thus corresponded—though also unevenly—to its political decentralization and administrative heterogeneity.

As John Barrell points out, "London" was an elastic term in the eighteenth and nineteenth centuries, and it is impossible to say where Londoners themselves thought their city began or ended in spatial terms. More importantly, no matter how one imagined the contours and outer limits of the metropolitan space, it would have included several distinct political entities, not only Westminster and the City of London, but also outlying areas such as Clerkenwell and Lambeth (which were materially integrated into metropolitan London, although they remained legally separate), as well as areas swallowed up internally, such as St. Giles's (which, although it was now physically in the middle of London, was legally still in Middlesex).[33] And there were smaller spaces that also enjoyed various degrees of autonomy within the larger metropolitan space, such as the Liberty of the Savoy on the Strand (an outpost of the Duchy of Lancaster), or Ely Place just off Holborn (which was an outpost of Cambridgeshire), or the Middle and Inner Temples (which were autonomous extraparochial districts), in all of which the rule of law was different until the late nineteenth century, and even, in certain respects, until the twentieth. John Thelwall was able to carry on with his public lectures in Beaufort Buildings off the Strand, for example, despite legal attempts to shut him down by the reactionary Charles Reeves, precisely because the lectures were taking place not in "normal" London but in the exceptional space of the Liberty of the Savoy, and the Court Leet of the Manor and Liberty of the Savoy—which exercised jurisdiction over this tiny plot of land—refused to hear the case Reeves attempted to bring (it probably didn't hurt Thelwall that the radical antiquarian Joseph Ritson was a high bailiff of the Savoy at the time).[34]

As a result of all this administrative and legal heterogeneity, until the advent of Metropolitan Police in the 1830s, and despite the best efforts of Fielding's Bow Street Runners (established in the mid-eighteenth century), there was, and could have been, no systematic policing of the city, which was left to the ineffective and amateurish efforts of local beadles, parish constables, and dozing night watchmen—the comical Charleys whom Pierce Egan's Tom and Jerry take such delight in overturning inside their sentry boxes.[35] Hence came Patrick Colquhoun's repeated calls for a new institution of police at the end of the eighteenth century.[36] And, as with policing, so with all other administrative matters, such as lighting the streets (pedestrians often had to hire match boys to light their way home after dark), paving, cleaning, and so on. By the early nineteenth century, the City of London was relatively well run, but, as Donald Low points out, elsewhere, near chaos ruled. "The City alone enjoyed a common standard of administration, but only about one-tenth of the people of the metropolis now lived in the City," Low notes. "The rest, numbering about one million—approximately a tenth of the entire population of England and Wales—inhabited a kind of twilit administrative no-man's-land made up of over ninety parishes or precincts situated within the three counties of Middlesex, Surrey and Kent."[37] Practically speaking, what this meant is that London was not a smooth homogeneous space in the modern sense: it was deeply striated and contained all sorts of unevenly developed heterotopic pockets. Difference, as Simon Joyce has argued this point, was never just distant, but always also proximate, far closer than one might otherwise have imagined.[38]

This striation and unevenness is precisely what John Nash intended to address in his Regent Street project, which would turn out to be the first of many nineteenth-century schemes to plow through the messy "littleness" of central London and open up a new, smoother, and more rational kind of space (other such projects would include the transformation of Charing Cross into Trafalgar Square and the plowing of Shaftesbury Avenue and New Oxford Street through the slums in and around St. Giles's). For the point of Nash's plan, which was implemented between 1817 and 1823, was not merely to open up a wide boulevard running south to north between Carlton House and what would become Regent's Park, but also to demarcate the limit between one kind of space and another: between the systematic, rational order of Mayfair ("the Streets and Squares occupied by the Nobility and Gentry") and the irrational, haphazardly planned, seemingly overrun and out-of-control districts just to the east, beginning with Soho; or, in other words, as Nash himself put it, "a line of Separation between the inhabitants of the first classes of society, and those of the inferior classes."[39]

This social logic is manifest in the design and layout of the upper stretch of Regent Street, which arcs gracefully to the northwest when it reaches what would become Piccadilly Circus, rather than continuing the straight line established by lower Regent Street, which would have taken it right through Soho's Golden Square and on to Oxford Street. Had Nash taken the direct route through Golden Square, he would have left parts of bedraggled seventeenth-century Soho—which, sociologically speaking, extended to Swallow Street, a little to the west—on the wrong side of the new boulevard.[40] If, however, Regent Street curved to the west to follow the line of Swallow Street (and so demolishing it in the process), then, as Jerry White points out, it "would clearly mark the great divide—no less than 120 feet wide and with palatial six-storey shops and residences on both sides—between aristocratic London in the west and plebeian London in the east." And if Swallow Street went, White continues, "then so would its 'filthy labyrinthine environs' and 'dirty courts' filled with the poor."[41] Indeed, as would be the case with later urban renewal projects in London, thousands of poor people were displaced by the Regent Street project.

Regent Street may have helped consolidate a retrenched West End's sense of distinction and safe separation from regions to the east, but it still left intact large swathes of that uneven, heterogeneous, and unruly London between the West End and Westminster, on the one hand, and the City on the other. "To most members of both Houses of Parliament, and to many members of the politest classes residing in the West End, London east of Charing Cross [i.e., also east of Soho] must have been, if not exactly a *terra incognita*, yet largely unexplored except for the routes along the Strand, Oxford Street and Holborn to the shops, the City, the courts, the theaters, the Royal Academy," John Barrell notes. To such people, he adds, the knowledge "of the labyrinth of streets of the inner city—linked, as Caleb [Williams, in Godwin's novel] describes them, by 'narrow lanes and alleys, with intricate insertions and sudden turnings,' must have seemed impossible to acquire; the geography must have seemed, by contrast with the broad streets and squares of St. James's, St. George's, Marylebone, almost designed to frustrate the acquisition of that knowledge."[42] For Don Manuel Alvarez Espriella, the fictional narrator of Robert Southey's 1808 *Letters from England*, it is indeed "impossible ever to become thoroughly acquainted with such an endless labyrinth of streets" that separate the parts of London so comprehensively that, as he reports, "they who live at one end know little or nothing of the other."[43]

Espriella's adventures, like those of countless other characters in literary texts set in London in the eighteenth and nineteenth centuries, take him along the Strand, which merges with Fleet Street at Temple Bar to form the southernmost of the two streams of traffic connecting the West End to the City. The northern stream took passengers along Holborn, which even in the nineteenth century involved dealing with certain nuisances, such as the Scylla and Charybdis (as Weir puts it) of Shoe Lane and Field Lane at the eastern end of Holborn, not to mention the rough edge of St. Giles's at the western end. This was also once the route taken by the procession of condemned men and women on their way from Newgate to Tyburn (the sordid details of which were discussed by Francis Place). Not until the opening up of New Oxford Street, the eastward extension of Oxford Street that was plowed through part of the St. Giles's slum in the 1840s, and the even later (1869) opening of the Holborn Viaduct—which, with neighboring works along Farringdon Road and the opening up of the warren of streets in Saffron Hill, involved similarly extensive demolitions and displacements of tens of thousands of people—would the northern passage be relatively more secure for "polite" travelers, and the effort to further secure it would continue through the nineteenth century until the opening of Shaftesbury Avenue in 1886 enabled direct communication along wide boulevards between Piccadilly and the City via Holborn (a mere forty-minute walk).[44] Hence the importance of the Strand earlier in the period, as the primary means of communication and traffic between the West End and the City.

Until well into the middle of the nineteenth century, then, the considerable expanse of apparently (for some) unnavigable space between the West End and the City (that is, the area in between Holborn and the Strand or Fleet Street in the very heart of the metropolitan space) was, at best, a racy area of theaters, coffee houses, taverns and brothels, if not altogether a no-go zone for any person of reputation or property—its status as such is precisely what drew Pierce Egan to send Tom and Jerry into it in *Life in London*. This

area, which appears quite blank on a map of the city from the period show-
ing the holdings of the great estates—including that of the Crown—among
which the western and northern districts are parceled out,[45] was dominated
in the collective imagination of the polite classes by the dismal threatening
slum of St. Giles's, "of the pristine condition of which the Rookery is at this
day a living monument," Weir notes as late as 1841.[46] Into this rookery, as
Barrell notes, literary narratives from the period rarely ventured (a notable
exception, to which I will later return, is Hannah More's *Betty Brown, the
St. Giles's Orange Girl*).[47]

When *The Dens of London Exposed* was published in 1835, offering
readers what it claimed was the first accurate exploration of "that frater-
nity called 'Cadgers,'"[48] and of their principal base of operations in the St.
Giles's rookery, it was greeted in Leigh Hunt's *London Journal* as a novelty,
"for our living writers (with rare and qualified exceptions) do not deal with
these regions, as their predecessors did in the last century."[49] There were indeed exceptions: Egan's *Life in London* came close (though not specifically
into the rookery), and Dickens's sketch of Seven Dials (which was originally
published in 1835 before being included in *Sketches by Boz* in 1836, along
with his piece on Monmouth Street, which, until it was broadened into
what would become Shaftesbury Avenue, would run right into the rookery)[50] would come closer still, since Seven Dials was a stone's throw from
the rookery and was part of the same notorious parish of St. Giles's. (It's
worth pointing out that Leigh Hunt's own *Saunter through the West End*,
which skirts along the edges of St. Giles's, makes only a couple of passing
mentions of the poverty there, while his account of London in *The Town*
doesn't mention it at all).[51]

Admittedly, *The Complete Modern London Spy*, which appeared in
1781, offered its readers a full account of bagnios, night-houses, and other
insalubrious destinations with corresponding "scenes of Midnight Entertainment and curious Adventures in high, low and middling life," but it
went out of its way to avoid the "infamous" parish of St. Giles's, which
contains "the lowest of rogues, the lowest of harlots, and, in a word, the
worst of mankind." If we had chosen to enter the region, the narrative continues, "we might have been witnesses to scenes degrading human nature,
and leveling it with the brute creation;—but we were not so inclined."[52] The
narrative of the *New London Spy* of 1771 had, however, already penetrated
deeper into St. Giles's, making its way to the rookery from Covent Garden
via Seven Dials. Having already witnessed on the way scenes "representing
human nature in a more abject, deplorable state than the brute creation,"
the narrator and his companions then head toward "a mansion celebrated

for its infamy, where the very mask of decency is thrown off, and the greatest blackguard claims ascendancy: it is the university of slang, a nursery for
the gallows, a picture of the dark side of human nature, and a contrast to
whatever is decent, sober or reasonable." The narrator himself enters the
region of the rookery "with as much glee as a countryman does a booth in
Bartholomew fair; every step we made presented to our view some odd figure
or other, that looked as if the infernal fiend had effaced their natural countenance, and had infused a diabolical spirit into their corrupt carcas[s]es,
for *all hell* appeared in every feature; theft, whoredom, homicide and blas-
phemy were legible in every face; lying, misery and impudence were depicted in every countenance."[53] But this account was exceptional, and in
any case clearly imposes its own interpretive code (the infernal language)
on what could not otherwise be interpreted or understood. When, decades
later, the *Dens of London* returns the polite reader to St. Giles's, and to the
fullest account yet offered of both cadgers and the common lodging house at
the heart of the rookery, it is right to note that "it certainly appears strange
that those two subjects, which offer such an abundance of original matter
to writers and other observers of mankind, should have remained so long
without any other notice than merely that they were known to exist."[54]

What *Dens of London* is expressing here is the extent to which London
retained, well into the first half of the nineteenth century, the same uneven
patchwork of spaces that Weir, in Knight's *London*, had also detected in
eighteenth-century London. An archipelago of relatively prosperous islands
still stood out from a sea of squalor, even if certain of the islands had grown
and parts of the uncharted, unexplored sea had retreated somewhat in certain places over the previous decades. After all, Weir himself had said that
the St. Giles's rookery was a *living* monument of the previous state of much
of the rest of the parish (up to Drury Lane in the east). And when Engels visited it still later, in the mid-1840s, as it was about to be plowed through and
torn down, he found exactly the same squalor as the authors of the *London
Spy* books had found decades previously:

> It is a disorderly collection of tall, three or four-storied houses, with nar-
> row, crooked, filthy streets, in which there is quite as much life as in the
> great thoroughfares of the town, except that, here, people of the working
> class only are to be seen. A vegetable market is held in the street, bas-
> kets with vegetables and fruits, naturally all bad and hardly fit to use,
> obstruct the sidewalk still further, and from those, as well as from the
> fish-dealers' stalls, arises a horrible smell. The houses are occupied from
> cellar to garret, filthy within and without, and their appearance is such

that no human being could possibly wish to live in them. But all this is nothing in comparison with the dwellings in the narrow courts and alleys between the streets, entered by covered passages between the houses, in which the filth and tottering ruin surpass all description. Scarcely a whole window-pane can be found, the walls are crumbling, door-posts and window-frames loose and broken, doors of old boards nailed together, or altogether wanting in this thieves' quarter, where no doors are needed, there being nothing to steal. Heaps of garbage and ashes lie in all directions, and the foul liquids emptied before the doors gather in stinking pools. Here live the poorest of the poor, the worst paid workers with thieves and the victims of prostitution indiscriminately huddled together, the majority Irish, or of Irish extraction, and those who have not yet sunk in the whirlpool of moral ruin which surrounds them, sinking daily deeper, losing daily more and more of their power to resist the demoralizing influence of want, filth, and evil surroundings.[55]

In fact, St. Giles's may have been the most notorious slum in London, but despite its relative antiquity it was not unique: the relationship of our metaphoric islands and sea was not at all stable in this period. "Overcrowding was not new in London," Francis Sheppard points out. "The rookeries at St. Giles in the Fields, or the valley of the Fleet, or Saffron Hill, or Whitecross Street, or Houndsditch, or in Spitalfields and Whitechapel, were already old at the beginning of the nineteenth century. But all these concentrations were either within the City itself or near to its boundaries." What was new in the nineteenth century, he adds, "was the great extension of overcrowding (though not always in such acute form as the word rookery suggests) to parts of Bethnal Green, St. George's in the East, Bermondsey, Rotherhithe and Southwark, and even to Westminster (particularly around the Abbey), and to such outlying points as Lisson Grove in St. Marylebone or Jennings Buildings in Kensington High Street."[56] Early to mid-nineteenth century London still consisted, then, of a shifting pattern of areas visited and areas avoided, areas known and areas as yet unknown, and even if, as the author of *Dens of London* puts it, the latter "were known to exist," they still by and large constituted a terra incognita.

So far, my account of London has been broadly consistent with the arguments elaborated by others, including White, Barrell, Joyce, Porter, Low, and Sheppard, to whom I am clearly indebted. But to connect this spatial account of London with what Francis Place says about time and hope, it is necessary to rethink the striated heterogeneity of the city, and in particular to conceive it not just in terms of space, which is how most of the extant

scholarship approaches the question, but also in temporal terms. The spatial unevenness of London in the Romantic and early to mid-Victorian periods corresponds, in other words, to a temporal unevenness, and, moreover,
to an unevenness in the distribution of movement and speed—and hence
also the forms of hope to which Francis Place appeals. Time, it turns out, is
of the essence here.

3. TEMPUS INCOGNITUM

In 1691, Thomas Neale drafted a plan for a new project at the edge of the
built-up area of London on the Cock and Pye fields: open ground (named
after a nearby tavern) that had until recently been used as pasture. Neale's
plan featured a circle with several streets elegantly radiating from it. He
commissioned the well-known sculptor Edward Pierce to construct a Doric
pillar at the center of the circle, with sundials on it: six dials, to be precise,
each facing in a different direction. This has led to some confusion, because
from the time it was built until the present, the area has been known as
the Seven Dials (see figs. 3 and 4), and visitors didn't (and don't) know how
to square the problem of the pillar's *six* dials with the area's name and the
seven streets that actually radiate from the circle. One explanation that
has been proposed is that the pillar itself formed the seventh dial, and in
our own time people often assume that the seven dials refer to the seven
streets themselves (perhaps because the central pillar was removed in the
eighteenth century and a replica only recently reinstalled, making the reference to "dials" all the more inscrutable for most of the twentieth century).

But it turns out that Neale's original plan, as submitted to Sir Christopher Wren (the metropolitan plan checker), actually did set a circle with six
streets radiating from it in the figure of a star, on the basis of which Pierce
designed his sundial pillar in 1693, with one dial facing toward each radiating street in a graceful and symmetrical balancing of space and time.[57] Only
after work on the project commenced was a seventh street retroactively
added, too late to modify the sundial pillar. William Baer suggests that the
last-minute change was made for financial reasons: adding a seventh street
yielded 10 percent more street frontage and hence higher returns for the
project.[58] In terms of time, though, this was all very awkward, because, spatially, the seven streets no longer neatly corresponded to the six faces of the
sundial; and, chronologically speaking, seven does not correspond evenly
with the twenty-four-hour day in the way that the original six does.

However, there is something magical about the fact that the Seven Dials
had six sundials that offered rapidly urbanizing and modernizing eighteenth-

Fig. 3. The area around Seven Dials, from Horwood's 1799 Map of London.
Courtesy of Motco Enterprises Limited/www.motco.com.

century London a totally outmoded way of measuring *time*, in a layout that
is *spatially* totally out of synch, given the seven streets unevenly radiating
from its center. Because shortly after Neale's plan was laid out and first developed in the early eighteenth century, the area of the Seven Dials became
a byword for a broken-down and nondeveloping urban space, in very close
proximity to the heart of the infamous St. Giles's rookery, which lay only
a few minutes' walk to the north, in the area around St. Giles's church,
and with which it eventually merged in the urban imaginary (see figs. 3
and 4). And time and temporality—a sense of chronological and historical
dissonance strangely mapping onto spatial unevenness—have long offered

Fig. 4. Seven Dials (detail of fig. 3), from Horwood's 1799 Map of London. Courtesy of Motco Enterprises Limited/www.motco.com.

critics the means with which to express their view of the place. "Here to sev'n Streets, seven [sic] Dials count the Day," writes John Gay in *Trivia*; "And from each other catch the circling Ray: / Here oft the peasant, with enquiring Face, / Bewilder'd, trudges on from Place to Place; / He dwells on every Sign with stupid Gaze, / Enters the narrow Alley's doubtful Maze, / Tries ev'ry winding Court and Street in vain, / And doubles o'er his weary Steps again."[59] In fact, even after the pillar with the dials was taken down and removed in 1773 (in a vain attempt to help clear the area of the "undesirables" who gathered around it; see fig. 5),[60] the area has retained a sense of spatiotemporal dissonance not merely because there is confusion as to whether the "dials" refer to time or space, but also because, as we shall see, time—and stalled time in particular—has repeatedly offered a way to think of this area, as well as St. Giles's, in relation to the surrounding districts of London. And I want now to focus on the region of the Seven Dials and St. Giles's precisely because they offer us an exemplary—though not unique— spatiotemporal convergence with which to think through the larger questions in which I am interested.

"Look at the construction of the place," writes Dickens of the Seven Dials in the 1830s. "The gordian knot was all very well in its way: so was the maze of Hampton Court: so is the maze at the Beulah Spa: so were the ties of stiff white neckcloths, when the difficulty of getting one on, was only to be equaled by the apparent difficulty of ever getting it off again. But what involutions can compare with those of Seven Dials? Where is there such another maze of streets, courts, lanes, and alleys?"[61] Writing a few years later about the St. Giles's rookery just to the north of Seven Dials, Weir also uses the spatial language deployed by Dickens (which can be traced back to Gay). Approaching "the genuine unsophisticated St. Giles's," the limits of which are so imprecisely defined that "its squalor fades into the cleanness of the more civilised districts in its vicinity, by insensible degrees, like the hues of the rainbow," he also finds "one great maze of narrow crooked paths crossing and intersecting in labyrinthine convolutions, as if the houses had been originally one great block of stone eaten by slugs into innumerable small chambers and connecting passages."[62] More than three decades later still, Walter Thornbury also finds "a maze of buildings" in the vicinity of the Seven Dials.[63]

What is important, however, is not just that the language of spatial disorientation (mazes, labyrinths) is so consistently used to describe this part of London all through this period, but that, almost inevitably, a discourse of temporal dislocation also accompanies it. "The stranger who finds himself in 'The Dials' for the first time, and stands Belzoni-like, at the entrance of

Fig. 5. "Seven Dials," from Walter Thornbury, *Old and New London* (London, 1893).

seven obscure passages, uncertain which to take, will see enough around him to keep his curiosity and attention awake for no inconsiderable time," writes Dickens in his Seven Dials piece. Suspended in time, the visitor to this district is thus compared with the well-known Italian explorer—and hence the district itself to Belzoni's Egypt: actually entering into it is like traveling back in time, and to an altogether foreign space at that.[64]

This sense of suspension in time is extended from Seven Dials to the surrounding neighborhood. Dickens writes, for example, that Monmouth Street is "venerable from its antiquity" (though he is referring not to today's Monmouth Street, which radiates directly from Seven Dials, but the street slightly to the north that would be absorbed and demolished in the construction of Shaftesbury Avenue in the way that Swallow Street was absorbed and demolished by Regent Street).[65] "It is the times that have changed, not Monmouth-street," he adds.[66] Similarly, Weir contrasts St. Giles's, whose character seems "ineradicably burned into it," with other parts of London, which have undergone development and transformation. "St. James's, which was also originally a lazar-house, has become a kingly residence, and Tyburn too has in its day been the shambles or sacrificial altar (which you will) of the law," he notes; "all traces, however, of the disagreeable associations which clung to the one locality, and are still conjured up by the name of the other, have vanished. But St. Giles's combined within itself what was repulsive about both, and accordingly St. Giles's remains true to itself, 'unchanged, unchangeable.'"[67] (It is worth pointing out that although Peter Ackroyd offers a more sympathetic portrait of contemporary St. Giles's, he too makes the point that, given the number of vagrants and beggars there today, "the place of transients in the life of St. Giles's has never faded").[68]

This view of St. Giles's as permanently stuck in some uncivilized past, even as the rest of London moves on in the flow of time associated with the civilizing process, receives its fullest elaboration in Thomas Beames's 1851 investigative account, *Rookeries of London: Past, Present and Prospective*. From Beames's reformist perspective, the problem with St. Giles's and areas like it (including the rookery near Westminster) is not merely that they are "plague spots" housing "the very refuse of the population," nor even that the rookery of St. Giles's has grown to such an extent that "it is well nigh a penal settlement, a pauper metropolis in itself."[69] Rather, the problem is one of time. "A change has come over us," he writes. "The rich have room, have air, have houses endeared to them by every comfort civilisation can minister." But, he adds, "the poor still remain sad heralds of the past, alone bearing the iniquities and inheriting the curse of their fathers; with them Time has stopped, if it have not gone back."[70] Beames here is echoing Southey's sense that, whereas "the gentry of the land are better lodged, better accommodated, better educated than their ancestors," the poor man "lives in as poor a dwelling as his forefathers did when they were slaves of the soil, works as hard, is worse fed, and not better taught." Or, to be precise, Beames is spatializing Southey's contention that "the improvements of society never reach the poor: they have been stationary, while the higher classes were progressive."[71]

Little wonder, then, that according to Beames the poor live in "strongholds of corrupt antiquity" that prove so impervious to improvement.[72] "Rookeries still survive by their very isolation, by their retention of past anomalies,—possessing still the errors, and handing down the discomforts of our ancestors,—and memorials of the past," he argues.[73] "Improvement has swept on in mighty strides," he adds; "pity that there should still remain the monuments of this olden time in the Rookeries of London,—that the close alley, the undrained court, the narrow window, the unpaved footpath, the distant pump, the typhus or the Irish fever should still remind us of what London was once to all—what it still is to the poor."[74] On this view, then, those who venture into the strongholds of the poor (figs. 6 and 7) are indeed,

Figs. 6, 7. "Views in the Rookery, St. Giles's," from Walter Thornbury, *Old and New London* (London, 1893).

to go back to Dickens, Belzoni-like time travelers: social status, race, and temporality map on to each other. And when, at midcentury, Dickens accompanies Inspector Field on a police raid into St. Giles's, it should come as no surprise that, throughout the narrative, the sound of the clock outside the rookery serves as a kind of lifeline back to that other, more civilized, London: its tones intermittently punctuate the piece, from 9:00 p.m., when the raid is being prepared, through 10:30, 11:00, 11:30, and so on.[75] Time may have been suspended in St. Giles's, in other words, but it is reassuringly moving forward in the rest of London.

But it is not just that time has stopped in St. Giles's, for the frenetic movement so characteristic of the rest of London also slows down and grinds to a halt here as well. Surely the "maze" of narrow crooked streets that isolate the area help sets this up, but it is not only a matter of the street layout. "On entering this region of sin, we, of course, had the usual difficulties of foot-passengers to encounter," writes the author of *Dens of London*, "in picking and choosing our way among the small but rich dung heaps—the flowing channels and those pitfalls, the cellers [sic], which lie gaping open, like so many man-traps, ready to catch the unwary traveller."[76] The air itself seems to slow down as it filters through into the dense mass of streets near the Seven Dials and deeper into St. Giles's. The streets and courts here "are lost in the unwholesome vapour which hangs over the house-tops, and renders the dirty perspective uncertain and confined," Dickens writes; "and lounging at every corner, as if they came there to take a few gasps of such fresh air as has found its way so far, but is much too exhausted already, to be enabled to force itself into the narrow alleys around, are groups of people, whose appearance and dwellings would fill any mind but a regular Londoner's with astonishment."[77] If the air itself is so enervated—and it is worth bearing in mind that people then still thought, until John Snow proved otherwise, that the miasma of foul, stale air could harbor diseases like cholera[78]—it is hardly any wonder that the people themselves are lethargic as well. According to Dickens their idleness is expressed in endless leaning on posts, to the extent that "every post in the open space has its occupant, who leans against it for hours, with listless perseverance."[79] Weir notices this too; the women hang around the doors, but "the men lean against the wall or lounge listlessly about;" it is, he says, "a land of utter idleness."[80]

We are left, then, with the sense that this part of London is cut off from the movement (both circulating and developing movement) defining the rest of the urban space. This theme is most fully elaborated in Weir's

account of St. Giles's, which contrasts "airy thoroughfares" like Holborn
and Oxford Street, "along which no small portion of the ease and affluence
of London is daily rolled in cab, 'bus, or in their own private vehicles," with
the squalor of "'the back settlements,' as they are poetically named by the
natives."[81] And even amid the squalor of St. Giles's, there are differences
between bad areas and worse ones, that is, between areas in which "there
is still thought, and hope, and exertion," and others where "all these seem
dead in the human bodies which move mechanically about amid its pesti-
lential effluvia."[82] Weir eventually develops a useful aquatic metaphor in
working through this contrast between the London of movement and the
London of varying degrees of stagnation. In most of London, he says, life is
like a powerful stream, but there are parts cut off from the current and flow,
to a greater or lesser extent. "The feeblest eddy on the outer edge of the
ever-foaming torrent of London life, it may be, with just enough of motion
to enable us to distinguish between it and the dull moisture which keeps
out the ooze alongshore as torpid as itself," he writes of the less bad part
of St. Giles's, "but still there is life in it; and unspeakable is the difference
between life, however faint, and utter apathy."[83] We have, then, a city of
linear movements and flows , as well as deeply embedded shallows and eddies where time—and with it life itself—slowly spins down and ultimately
comes to a halt.

4. EDDIES OF TIME

Nowhere are London's temporal contrasts and dissonances more fully elaborated than in the literary output of the period from the 1790s through the
first half of the nineteenth century. What emerges from this work is a recurring contrast between different approaches to the question of how to relate
narrative to time; that is, the question of how to narrate the different—and
dissonant—modes of temporality that are mapped out in London's heterogeneous spaces. At some point, London as a spatiotemporal problematic is
confronted as a generic question: what genre is most appropriate for engaging a space that is both spatially and temporally heterogeneous, or is there
a need for a new genre? On this score, it is all too tempting to think of the
contrast between different ways of thinking space-time in London in terms
of an opposition between different genres. Vic Gatrell follows this line of
reasoning in developing his contrast between the people he repeatedly refers
to as "the poets," with their (apparent) moral indignation, and the makers of
satirical prints, who (he says) refuse to take anything seriously.[84] In *Capital*

Offenses, Simon Joyce develops another version of this argument, contrasting, on the one hand, "the impulse in romantic poetry," when "faced with a potential dissolution of self" in urban space, to "seek recourse in a redemptive aesthetics of nature" and "in ritualistic denunciations of the city," with, on the other hand, "a countertendency within romanticism which consciously championed an urban experience and aesthetics to the pastoral preferences of the Lakeland poets."[85] Whether intentionally or not, however, this inevitably slides into an opposition between poetry (Wordsworth) and prose (Lamb, Hazlitt, Hunt, De Quincey), one of the effects of which is the exclusion of urban poetry that does not fit the binary; as a result, the most consummately urban poet of the period, Blake, drops out of Joyce's otherwise very compelling discussion.

Nevertheless, the question of genre does become increasingly prominent in this period. The contrast is not, however, between poetry and prose (or prints), or between a natural- as opposed to a civic-oriented aesthetic, but rather between different modes of aligning narrative and time into a form appropriate to the increasingly homogeneous—flattened, smoothed out, linear—space-time of modernity, as well as the forms of subjectivity appropriate to it; or refusing to align them, and hence stubbornly returning to temporal, narrative and ontological modes that can't be made to accommodate the requirements and exigencies of modernity, ones that are more interested in the eddies than in the main flow of the current of time. One can locate both poetry and prose on either side of the argument, though in general it is the case in this period that poetry tends to end up on the more critical side of things, whereas prose, and the novel in particular, would increasingly turn to this mode toward the end of the nineteenth century, and especially in modernism (though, as we shall see in the last chapter, Dickens himself furnishes us with many earlier examples, especially in *Edwin Drood*, from considerably earlier).

One of the ways the spatiotemporal dissonance of London is elaborated in the writing of the period has to do with a recurring alternation or opposition between flickers and flashes, on the one hand, and sustained narratives on the other. There is nothing generically particular about flickers and flashes: we can see them at work both in poetry and in prose. They convey meaning in the form of a discontinuous sequence of the kind that we see, for example, in Mary Robinson's "January, 1795," with its sequence of stanzas offering contrasting different (indeed, opposing) views of the city: "Pavement slipp'ry, people sneezing, / Lords in ermine, beggars freezing; / Titled gluttons dainties carving, / Genius in a garret starving."[86] Much the same logic is at work in Robinson's "London's Summer Morning," with its sequence of images and sounds working together to constitute a recurring "now."[87]

We see a similar mode—not quite as critical perhaps, but similarly discontinuous—at work in the prose of Charles Lamb whenever he tries to convey his love for London. "Streets, streets, streets, markets, theatres, churches, Covent Gardens, shops sparkling with pretty faces of industrious milliners, neat seamstresses, ladies cheapening, gentlemen behind counters lying, authors in the street with spectacles, George Dyers (you may know them by their gait), lamps lit at night, pastry-cooks' and silver-smiths' shops, beautiful Quakers of Pentonville, noise of coaches, drowsy cry of mechanic watchman at night, with bucks reeling home drunk; if you happen to wake at midnight, cries of Fire and Stop thief; inns of court, with their learned air, and halls, and butteries, just like Cambridge colleges; old book-stalls, Jeremy Taylors, Burtons on Melancholy, and Religio Medicis on every stall," he writes breathlessly. "These are thy pleasures, O London with-the-many-sins. For these may Keswick and her giant brood go hang!"[88] For Lamb, this is invariably the only way to narrate—to write—London, which is why his letters and other prose so readily slide into this discontinuous imagistic mode when he attempts to do so. Lamb's London cannot be told in a straightforward linear narrative.

And discontinuous flickers and flashes inevitably leave much uncaptured, outside or beyond narration. They are, in fact, structurally at odds with sustained, progressive, developmental narrative: flickers and flashes can't be strung into a single coherent thread. The attempts to engage London in writing, whether poetry or prose, inevitably return to this question of inclusion and exclusion, and to the attendant problematic of narrating the space-time of modernity—or refusing to do so, cutting across it, or simply refusing assimilation into its modal requirements, seeking out discrete moments rather than overall flows. Thus both Wordsworth and Southey, both in poetry and in prose, seek a location from which to question, if not to interrupt or escape, the pressing flow of time and hence of narrative. "On each side of the way there were two uninterrupted streams of people, one going east, the other west," writes Southey's fictional narrator from the City of London. "At first I thought some extraordinary occasion must have collected such a concourse; but I soon perceived it was only the usual course of business. They moved on in two regular counter-currents, and the rapidity with which they moved was as remarkable as their numbers."[89] Repeatedly, the narrator stops to try to interrupt his own narrative as flow, to seek out eddies, as it were, in the main stream.

There are many moments of such interruption in Southey's prose narrative, most strikingly when the narrator encounters a beggar who has scrawled a petition on the sidewalk in colored chalk: the petition is not actually rendered in prose, as words, but rather as impressionistic colors, the moment where words turn to images marking a departure from narrative into some other form of expression.[90] But in *The Prelude* the search for calms and leeward backwaters is even more prominent. Here again there is a running contrast between zones of movement, flow, and speed—the Strand, for example—and areas that are becalmed, where time, and hence the narrative of flow and speed, slows down or stops altogether, precisely in anticipation of Weir's and Beames's accounts of St. Giles's. What Wordsworth seeks is some shelter from flow and speed, from the stream of "Streets without end, and churches numberless," from "the quick dance / Of colours, lights and forms, the Babel din; / The endless stream of men, and moving things," and "the rash speed / Of coaches travelling far, whirled on with horn / Loud blowing."[91]

He finds just such an eddy of time when, "Escaped as from an enemy, we turn / Abruptly into some sequestered nook, / Still as a sheltered place when winds blow hard! / At leisure, thence, through tracts of thin resort, / And sights and sounds that come at intervals, / We take our way."[92] In such moments, the roar of speed and time slow down and stops and we encounter a spot of time in the fullest sense, where, for example, "Following the tide that slackens by degrees, / Some half-frequented scene, where wider streets / Bring straggling breezes of suburban air,"[93] Wordsworth is able to pause or suspend the flow. What his text consistently marks, then, is the lack of narrative, even the lack of narration: we hear "some female vendor's scream, belike / The very shrillest of all London cries,"[94] and, "single and alone, / An English ballad-singer,"[95] but those sounds are not verbalized; we see signs, symbols, "files of ballads dangl[ing] from dead walls,"[96] even fronts of houses "like a title page / With letters huge inscribed from top to toe,"[97] but none of those texts are actually rendered verbally as parts of the narrative. Encounters like the famous one with the blind beggar open up further spots of time, further interruptions to the flow and current imposed by the "endless stream" and "rash speed" of London.

What we encounter in such texts, in other words, is narrative reluctance, an unwillingness to flow with the stream of time, and a contrary desire to seek out not only a space-time of refuge but a place from which to contest and resist narrative altogether, to stand out from the flow rather than be absorbed into it. Critics (including myself, in the discussion of Wordsworth's London in *Romantic Imperialism*)[98] have often read this as an attempt to escape from a space where subjectivity cannot be formed—this is precisely Simon Joyce's contention as well—but I now think this sense of crisis in Wordsworth's London is more productively read not simply in terms of subjectivity but rather as an attempt to contest the form of time imposed by unilinear narrative, by locating the kind of sparkling stillness we find for example in the sonnet "Composed upon Westminster Bridge," where, from a critical distance, Wordsworth is finally able to slow down and halt the immense energy of London, to see that "all that mighty heart is lying still."[99] Even the poem's title conveys that sense of the moment—the moment of composition (of the image of stillness) rather than of the poem itself.

This actually brings Wordsworth quite strangely close to Blake, who ought to be his antithesis both in terms of the question of individual subjectivity (in which Blake has zero investment) and in terms of the urban space of London, of which Blake, unlike Wordsworth, was a native son. But we do indeed find in Blake a reluctance to embrace flow and linear narrative, though the alternative is not a search for stillness but rather for a disruption of flow, a resistance to it of the kind that we see, for example, in "Holy Thursday" of *Songs of Innocence*, where the charity children possess an uncontainable energy that constantly overflows and threatens to overwhelm the narrow linear circuit—conveyed so strikingly in visual terms in the plate's design—of "two & two in red & blue & green," into which they have been formed and channeled by "grey headed beadles."[100] Blake's resistance to rationalizing unilinearity is even more striking in "London." That song is often read as a dark and depressing piece (a reading quite at odds with the visual component of the plate), but it is important to note that the narrator wanders *through* "each charter'd street, / Near where the charter'd Thames does flow."[101] That is, he cuts across, he defies, he is not bound by, both the commercial and spatial chart(er)ing that otherwise seeks to control and define the space-time of the city, though its failure to do so is marked not only by the narrator's own defiance (I wander, I meet, I hear, I mark) but also by the constant slippage away from the unilinear verbal flow into aurality, visuality, texture, and touch: the chimney sweeper's cry, the soldier's blood, the blight that blasts the newborn infant's tear.

In this context the innovation of Hannah More's story, *Betty Brown, the St. Giles's Orange Girl*, is all the more unusual. For, unlike the texts of Southey, Lamb, Robinson, Wordsworth, and Blake, all of which are resistant to unilinear narrative flow in one way or another, More produces here a text that is, on the contrary, all about intervening in the pretextual, the prenarrational, the pretemporal—in a part of London almost completely neglected by other writers of fiction at the time—and drawing them out into the stream of narrative time and into a developmental narrative. In a nutshell, Betty Brown of St. Giles's, unlike other denizens of that part of London, is not idle and is keen on developing and improving herself. She is set up as a costermonger by a woman who lends her a shilling at an extortionate rate of interest but so disguised that Betty is naively unaware of it. She works hard and does well, but her winnings are always absorbed by the flow of payments to the crooked Mrs. Sponge, the moneylender. In a word, she is stuck, but without realizing it. Finally a charitable proper lady (from a better part of town, obviously) explains the extent of her trapped, circular exploitation to Betty and helps her to break the cycle and escape into a kind of fiscal freedom and independence, owning her own cart, and ultimately future success as the owner of a sausage shop near the Seven Dials.

The point, though, is that this story unfolds at two levels: first, as a story of accelerating economic development and improvement; and, second, as a story narrating the shift from stalled time to the time of development. For Betty Brown "was born nobody knows where, and bred nobody knows how,"[102] that is, outside or before narrative and even history, essentially untranslatable into the idiom of unilinear narrative time. And through the course of the story we see her enter narrative time, we see her progress from being a preyed-upon simpleton to becoming her own independent mistress, and we see her held out as a model for other people—the text's "common" readers—to emulate and reproduce into the future. Betty Brown, in short, becomes *Betty Brown*, a narrative, a prototype for replication, complete with a set of "RULES FOR RETAIL DEALERS" toward the end of the story which hold out the morals that readers are presumably to obtain from having read the story and carry over into their own lives and conduct ("Resist every temptation to cheat," etc.).[103] The key to the story, though, is that it takes the outside genteel lady's direct intervention into the cycle of stalled time and repetitive exploitation to break the cycle and launch Betty into developmental time. Once that intervention takes place, time can suddenly move forward, we can skip or fast forward—as the story does—months into the future, and even when the story formally ends, it is with a pointer toward some still more distant future off in the distance, toward which the narrative points in ending. "How Betty, by industry and piety, rose in the world, till at length she came to keep that handsome Sausage-shop near the Seven Dials, and was married to an honest Hackney-Coachman, may be told at some future time, in a Second Part," promises More in ending the story: a promise she would keep when she later wrote a ballad called "The Hackney Coachman," which begins with a reference back to the aforementioned sausage shop and the coachman's happy married life.[104]

Betty Brown is thus rescued from a background of indistinct indiffer-
ence and immobility—temporal stasis combined with ignorance in every
sense of the term (she "was born nobody knows where, and bred nobody
knows how")—and propelled forward into a narrative of development that
launches her into a future of success and prosperity. What is fundamental to
this rescue is that it involves the redemption of a single individual—*as an
individual*—and that it takes place in linear, progressive time, the time of
narrative. (I say "progressive" even though More is famously a conservative
authority, but she shares this notion of linear, developmental time with her
erstwhile radical or progressive adversaries, men such as Francis Place, to
whom we will shortly return, in a way that is fundamentally distinct from
the interest in time elaborated by both the increasingly conservative Wordsworth and Southey, and the far more radical Blake.) What More helps establish in the story, then, is the confluence of a certain conception of individual
subjectivity, a certain notion of temporality, and a certain understanding of
urban space as open to intervention, based, More says, on her own "inti-
mate acquaintance with the night-cellars and other places of polite resort in
the metropolis."[105] In *Betty Brown*, then, the time of narrative and the time
of character are linked to the time of the modern urban fabric; and movement or development of places, times, and subjects that are stalled or stuck
fundamentally require outside intervention.

5. DENSITY

For the problem with urban neighborhoods such as St. Giles's or Seven
Dials, from an early to mid-nineteenth century reforming perspective—
whether radical or evangelical—is precisely that they seem to preclude the
possibility of individual distinction or temporal movement. That time has
stalled there means not only that movement of any kind is rendered difficult or impossible (think of all those listless idlers in Dickens's or Weirs's
accounts of Seven Dials and St. Giles's) but also, correspondingly, that individuation is impossible. Nowhere is this clearer than in the rookery of
St. Giles's. The term "rookery" itself says it all: originally used to refer to a
place of animal habitation (rooks or birds of any kind, later seals and other
marine mammals), it acquired its urban connotation, referring to a "dense
aggregation" or a "dense collection of housing, esp. in a slum area," only
in the period I am discussing here.[106] A rookery is a place where people essentially become animals by virtue of a kind of density that absolutely precludes individual distinction, never mind improvement along the stream of
time. "Rookeries they are," argues Beames, referring to the rambling build-

ings in the worst parts of St. Giles's, "if rooks build high and lie thick together, young and old in one nest, and colonies are wedged up, not so much
because of connection between families as by common wants and a common nature, and yet with their fierce discord and occasional combats."[107]

Rendered in animal terms, the urban space, the streets and structures defining it, and the inhabitants residing in it all lack distinction and merge together into an unwieldy and ultimately unknowable density (Hannah More's
"nobody knows"). Entering St. Giles's, we encounter "one dense mass of
houses, 'so olde they only seemen not to falle,' through which narrow tor-
turous lanes curve and wind, from which again diverge close courts innumerable, all communicating with those nearest them," writes Weir in his
account. "There is no privacy here for any of the over-crowded population;
every apartment in the place is accessible from every other by a dozen different approaches."[108] The space itself comes to express the animal nature
of its inhabitants. "The peculiar character of these streets, and the close
resemblance each one bears to its neighbour, by no means tends to decrease
the bewilderment in which the unexperienced wayfarer through 'the Dials'
finds himself involved," writes Dickens in his Seven Dials piece. "He tra-
verses streets of dirty, straggling houses, with now and then an unexpected
court composed of buildings as ill-proportioned and deformed as the half-
naked children that wallow in the kennels."[109] It is impossible to imagine
individual agency emerging from a context like this: the urban fabric itself
precludes the possibility of forming a developing, progressive, individual
subjectivity. All residents are reduced to "common wants and a common
nature," as Beames puts it, so that just as the space itself disables discrete
compartmentalization (because people are living on top of and almost literally through each other, lacking any kind of private zone into which they
might withdraw as individuals), the people themselves lack individuation;
it is impossible to become individual when one is stuck in a massified, common, animal existence.

In fact, in most of these accounts, what such a massified indiscrete space
produces instead of the individual is the perversion of the individual: the
fraud. The fraud in this instance is not exactly the opposite of the genuine
individual, however, but rather the apparition of the individual: part of a
mass that seems to assume an individual identity but that, when the need no
longer presses, or when enough income has been generated for a day by selling that fraud to an unwary public, gives up that identity and slinks or crawls
back to St. Giles's to resume the mass, common, animal existence of its warren of interlocking garrets and night cellars. There the mass was packed,
as Dens of London notes, in houses with a hundred beds each, "distributed

three and six in a room; the single ones are fourpence, and the double ones sixpence."[110] And that is for those who could afford (shared) beds, never mind those whom Dickens finds, "ten, twenty, thirty—who can count them! Men, women, children, for the most part naked, heaped upon the floor like maggots in a cheese."[111] Night alone, as Beames points out, "witnesses the real condition of our Rookeries." For it is then that "the swarm of beggars, who have driven their profitable trade, return to their lair; trampers come in for a night's lodging; the beggars' operas, as they were wont to be called, then open their doors, to those whom necessity has made skulkers or outcasts."[112]

Dens of London goes out of its way to denounce the "thousands and tens of thousands" whose trade, it says, is imposture. It complains,

> The flash letter-writer and the crawling supplicant; the pretended tradesmen, who live luxuriously on the tales of others, and the real claimant of charity, whose honest shame will hardly allow him to beg for sufficient to procure the hard comforts of a bed of straw; the match seller and the ballad-singer, whose convenient profession unite the four lucrative callings of begging, selling, singing, and stealing; gangs of shipwrecked sailors, or rather, fellows whose iron constitutions enable them for the sake of sympathy, to endure the most inclement weather, in almost a state of nudity, and among them only one perhaps ever heard the roar of the ocean; jugglers, coiners, tramps (mechanics seeking work), strolling players, with all the hangers-on of fairs, races, assizes, stable-yards; besides the hosts of Irish who yearly migrate from sweet Erin to happy England, to beg, labour and steal.

"Here then, is a wide field for speculation, a vast common in life, where a character may almost be picked up at every step—mines of vice and misery as yet unexplored."[113] We can speak, then, of kennels and swarms, rooks and maggots, dozens and scores, a "vast common in life," but not discrete individuals: individuality is for the constituents of this multitude merely a guise to wear, a character to "pick up" and throw off as circumstances require, only to return to the common—the common lodging house, the common room, the common kitchen, the common life, the common form of being to which these miscreant creatures really belong.

We can speak, in other words, of a not-quite-human form of being, of an animal existence of some kind. In St. Giles's, "poverty hides its head through shame, and crime lurks concealed through fear," writes George Reynolds in his midcentury *Mysteries of London;* "there everything that is squalid, hideous, debauched and immoral, makes its dwelling;—there woman is as far removed from the angel as Satan is from the Godhead, and man is as closely allied to the brute as the idiot is to the baboon."[114] Such a deployment of a language of physical, intellectual, and moral ruin to describe this part of London is nothing new (after all, the London *Spy* books used a similar language decades previously), but the emergence in the late eighteenth and early nineteenth centuries of a more clearly articulated biological and racial language is. Already in the 1790s Mary Wollstonecraft's Maria had confessed, "in viewing the squalid inhabitants of some of the lanes and back streets of the metropolis," to feeling "mortified at being compelled to consider them as my fellow-creatures, as if an ape had claimed kindred with me."[115] This use of a racial and biological language becomes deeper and more extensive in the first part of the nineteenth century, and deeper and more extensive still later on—though it is already abundantly evident in Gillray's well-known print of the London Corresponding Society meeting in one of the city's dingy cellar taverns, which depicts the LCS members in racially caricatured—if not altogether animalized, simianized—terms (see fig. 2 in Introduction, above).

It was, of course, often the case that London's "back settlements," as Weir calls them, were partly inhabited by east or southeast Asian seamen ("Lascars") or African immigrants (including those referred to as "St. Giles's blackbirds"), of whom there were up to twenty thousand in London by the turn of the nineteenth century: enough for a Committee for the Relief of the Black [i.e., Asian and African] Poor to be set up in 1786, not to mention the development of schemes to deport some of these people to Sierra Leone. There was also a very considerable Irish population in London—enough packed into the area around St. Giles's for it to be referred to as the Holy Land. But the use of a racial discourse was by no means restricted to Asian, African, or Irish people; it was readily extended also to English plebeians as well (as we will also see in the next chapter's discussion of Wordsworth).

After all, in the opening pages of his monumental 1851 *London Labour and the London Poor*, Henry Mayhew announces that there are only two races in the world, and a neat "white" vs. "black" line doesn't figure in his demarcation. "Of the thousand millions of human beings that are said to constitute the population of the entire globe, there are—socially, morally, and perhaps even physically considered—but two distinct and broadly marked races," argues Mayhew; "viz., the wanderers and the settlers—the vagabond and the citizen—the nomadic and the civilised tribes."[116] The nomadic tribes, according to Mayhew, share certain moral and physical characteristics in common no matter what land they inhabit and which settled people they prey upon or terrorize, as, he says, the Kafirs of South Africa and the Fellahs of Arabia and the Finns are tormented by, respectively, Sonquas,

Bedouin, and Lapps (I am using Mayhew's terms of course: the term "fel-lah" simply means "farmer" in Arabic, for example, rather than denoting an ethnic community of some kind, as he seems to assume).

Mayhew's contention is that the same division between the settled and the nomadic, or the civilized and the restless, can be extended to England. "That we, like the Kafirs, Fellahs, and Finns, are surrounded by wander-ing hordes—the 'Sonquas' and the 'Fingoes' of this country—paupers, beg-gars, and outcasts, possessing nothing but what they acquire by depredation from the industrious, provident, and civilised portion of the community," he writes; "that the heads of these nomads are remarkable for the greater development of the jaws and cheekbones rather than those of the head;—and that they have a secret language of their own—an English 'cuze-cat' or 'slang' as it is called [i.e., the "flash language" of London addressed in the many slang dictionaries suddenly appearing at around this time, includ-ing the one James Hardy Vaux appended to his memoir as a thief]—for the concealment of their designs: these," he continues, "are points of coinci-dence so striking that, when placed before the mind, make us marvel that the analogy should have remained thus long unnoticed." But, he concludes, this comparison "becomes of great service in enabling us to use the moral characteristics of the nomad races of other countries, as a means of com-prehending the more readily those of the vagabonds and outcasts of our own."[117] The "we" here is markedly more limited and circumscribed than a national "we" in the broader sense: it is a civilizational "we," and it clearly excludes, at least until their entry into civilization—if such a thing is pos-sible—a significant portion of those who might otherwise be thought of as members of the nation.

"We," clearly, are not quite yet really "we" in a national sense. In estab-lishing such lines of demarcation, simply being English or British is not the point: what counts far more is being one of "us" in a racial or civilizational sense—being what would become white, or Occidental (and hence also separate from and superior to those other settled peoples who are preyed upon by their own wanderers and vagabonds). In this case, the racial and civilizational categories excluded a considerable portion of the national population not merely way out "there" in the hinterland (the wandering vagabonds populating *Lyrical Ballads*), but right "here" in the very heart of London (see figs. 8 and 9). For here too one can, as Mayhew shows, find not-yet-white, not-yet-Occidental English people, among whom there is, as he puts it, "a greater development of the animal than of the intellectual or moral nature of man" (does this not remind us of Francis Place's account of

THE LONDON COSTERMONGER.

"Here Pertaters! Kearots and Turnups! fine Brockello-o-o!"

[From a Daguerreotype by BEARD.]

Fig. 8. "The London Costermonger," from Henry Mayhew, *London Labour and the London Poor*, vol. 1 (London, 1861).

THE COSTER-GIRL.

"Apples! An 'aypenny a lot, Apples!"

[*From a Daguerreotype by* BEARD.]

Fig. 9. "The Coster-Girl," from Henry Mayhew, *London Labour and the London Poor,* vol. 1 (London, 1861).

his father, or of the man who drinks?), who are marked "for their use of a slang language—for their lax ideas of property—for their general improvidence—their repugnance to continuous labour—their disregard of female honour—their love of cruelty—their pugnacity—and their utter want of religion."[118]

This gap between a national sense of self and a racial or civilizational one—a gap not at all adequately addressed in the ample body of work on nationalism in this period, much of which remains quite blind to it—perfectly captures the sense of cultural crisis in the Romantic and early to mid-Victorian period. There are, among those internal "others," those who can be salvaged and incorporated into a reconsolidated sense of self, made into people like "us." That is precisely the point of a story like *Betty Brown*: one can be born "nobody knows where" and raised "nobody knows how," that is, in such stalled, degenerate and othered spaces as Seven Dials or St. Giles's more generally, and then—though only as an individual, never as a member of an animalized collective—be gradually drawn into civilization, rescued from the eddies of time and drawn into the mainstream of historical and cultural and indeed individual development.

In this sense, we can anticipate a gradual alignment of national with racial or civilizational development, a process that would extend well into the twentieth century and would culminate in what Ian Baucom identifies as a shift from place to race as the central organizing principle of identity, which would become especially explicit in the racist language of the New Right in Britain. As Baucom points out, that language was merely the culmination of "a species of racial nationalism long present in the discourses of Englishness and empire."[119] If the end point of this racial-national discourse would be the twentieth-century consolidation of such racism, or what Ghassan Hage calls paranoid nationalism, which we can see in the line running from Enoch Powell to Margaret Thatcher (and directed primarily against black British or new South Asian or Afro-Caribbean immigrants to Britain), its origins in the early nineteenth century are much more confused and were directed as much at the varieties of autochthonous Englishness that (as Mayhew makes so clear) did not fit the desirable national racial type as they were at the threat of African or Oriental contamination brought to England on the winds of imperial trade.[120]

In other words, pending the more explicit alignment of national and racial or civilizational identities in the twentieth century, the nation remained in the nineteenth century a category still to be filled in. For, just as there are some, like Betty Brown, who prove capable of assimilation into the stream of development, there are also those others—not merely Irish or

African or Asian others but also English ones—within the national space who are seen as not so capable of assimilation, whose otherness therefore now requires an even stronger or clearer or starker language of racial or civilizational distinction, one capable of separating "them" more clearly from "us," whether in order to evangelize among them and attempt to civilize them to whatever degree might be possible or appropriate for them or simply to root them out and subject them to what can really best be thought of in terms of ethnic cleansing.

Hence the explosion of a racial and civilizational language to map out the interior spaces of London, particularly those in areas like St. Giles's and Seven Dials, which seemed to be exceptional in the terms in which I have been describing them so far in this chapter. "A few years ago it was a fashion to visit the 'Rookery' of St. Giles's, and wonder at the peculiarities of that strange land," writes George Godwin in 1854. And despite the kinds of transformation to which such areas had already been subject by then, he explains that they remain dangerous. "To investigate the condition of the houses of the very poor in this great metropolis is a task of no small danger and difficulty: it is necessary to brave the risks of fever and other injuries to health, and the contact of men and women often as lawless as the Arab or the Kaffir," he writes. "In addition to these obstacles, there is amongst the very poor a strong feeling against intrusion. Few persons venture into these haunts besides the regular inhabitants, the London missionaries, the parish surgeon, and the police, and thus the extent of this great evil is imperfectly understood."[121] In Godwin, at least, the comparison of poor English with Arabs or Africans is just that: a comparison. Quite consistently from the second third of the nineteenth century on, however, the comparative framework would be dropped and certain segments of the English poor—street children in particular—would be transformed, as it were, into Arabs.

And not only children were so transformed. "Of all the dark and dismal thoroughfares in the parish of St. Giles's, or, indeed, in the great wilderness of London, few, we think, will compare with that known as Church Lane, which runs between High Street and New Oxford Street," complains Thornbury. "During the last half century, while the metropolis has been undergoing the pressure of progress consequent upon the quick march of civilisation, what remains of the Church Lane of our early days has been left with its little colony of Arabs as completely sequestered from London society as if it was part of *Arabia Petræa*. Few pass through Church Lane who are not members of its own select society. None else have any business there; and if they had, they would find it to their interest to get out of it as soon as possible. Its condition is a disgrace to the great city, and to the parish to which it belongs."[122] The neighborhood itself has been figuratively shifted to Arabia, and its inhabitants transformed into Arabs. This new imaginative cartography of London now marks those heterotopic spaces, or spaces of otherness, much more clearly and comprehensively as geographically foreign, exterior. And such acts of geographical exclusion within the metropolis, by figuratively demarcating the internal "Arab" presence, reinforce the growing sense of normative Occidentalism that is being consolidated all through the century.

Thornbury was writing in the late 1870s, but the proliferation of a language of foreignness, referring specifically to an English population Orientalized as Arabs, was in place already by the 1830s and 1840s. Thomas Guthrie, in his campaign to establish the so-called Ragged Schools for urban children, complained that "these Arabs of the city are as wild as those of the desert."[123] In a speech in Parliament advocating the transplantation of London street children to Australia, Lord Shaftesbury (he of the Avenue) declared that these "city Arabs . . . are like tribes of lawless freebooters, bound by no obligations, and utterly ignorant or utterly regardless of social duties."[124] And so it goes up and down the century. "Observe the vast number of the 'city Arabs,' to be encountered in a walk from Cheapside to the Angel at Islington," writes James Greenwood in the 1860s; Dickens, writing in the same decade, with a nod to the "wild tribes of London or City Arabs" running around, points out the "London Hassaracs or Abdallahs, in laced boots and velveteen jackets" who seem to pop out of nowhere.[125]

This interest in the street or city Arab would become somewhat obsessive in the final decades of the century, as Lydia Murdoch points out. "By the late nineteenth century, the 'street arab' had become a popular subject for photographs and drawings, and also a well known literary type," she argues, pointing to texts such as *The Little London Arabs* (1870), *Little Scrigget, the Street Arab* (1878), and *Mahomet, A.J.: From Street Arab to Evangelist* (1885), to which we might add such theatrical references as *The Street Arab, or, Adrift on the World* (1871).[126] What is interesting about the deployment of this Orientalizing discourse of the urban Arab in Occidentalizing London, though, is that it always seems to have a kind of double edge to it. On the one hand, it clearly marks out both spaces and populations, however territorially indigenous—English—they may happen to be, as culturally, racially and civilizationally foreign and hence exterior to the space of the nation. On the other hand, this kind of exteriorization of interior populations and spaces—mobilizing knowledge of an exotic population, just as Mayhew had called for, in order to understand a population interior to the national space—inevitably also takes us back to the question of what can be done about them: can they be salvaged, or must such populations be expunged and their spaces reclaimed for other purposes, just as Regent Street had reclaimed Swallow Street, Trafalgar Square Charing Cross, and Shaftesbury Avenue Monmouth Street?

Thus there remains a kind of ambiguity around the figure of Arabized, Orientalized English others and the animalized spaces to which they correspond. "The urban 'street Arab' was neither fully foreign nor fully irredeemable," argues Lydia Murdoch. "Reformers could categorize poor children as a race separate from the English and yet at the same time suggest that with intervention and assistance these urban youths, unlike their parents, could eventually evolve into English citizens."[127] Clearly this was part of the mission of Guthrie's Ragged Schools. It was also the point of those missionary societies that were established to send missions not into the metaphorical darkness of Africa or India but into that of London itself. "We have now a new term, that recognizes emphatically an evil too long ignored. I mean, 'The City Arabs,'" the Reverend James Pycroft recounts a fellow churchman telling him in the 1840s. "This is one step towards realising the truth that a veritable heathen mission is as much wanted in the interior of London as in the interior of Africa. As to heathen ignorance," he adds, "in London we have a darkness that may be felt; as to the gross and debasing habits of the brutes that perish, we have hovels and savages not surpassed in Timbuctoo; and as to poisonous malaria, I can show you veritable patches of Sierra Leone no further off than Spitalfields. As to hunger and thirst, I can say with Smollett, that a man without money may starve in Leadenhall Market as well as in the wilds of Arabia; and clean wholesome water to the weak and sickly is as inaccessible in some parts of London as in the sandy desert."[128] Even the Surrey side of London Bridge, he says, "wants the same sort of Mission as the interior or Africa or Chinese Tartary."[129] This was the mentality that had led to the establishment of the London City Mission in 1835. As Susan Thorne has argued at length, there was extensive missionary activity in London and elsewhere in England, precisely paralleling the missions sent to Asia and Africa.[130]

One way or another, such indigestible foreignness in the very heart of London fundamentally seemed to require action—just the kind of outside intervention to simultaneously and inseparably instill a sense of individuality and a corresponding sense of temporal mobility that we see at work in *Betty Brown*. However, such interventions were never restricted solely to populations; the spaces themselves were also at stake. That is, the rookeries and other slum areas needed to be opened up, integrated into the outside space of movement, flow, speed; they needed to be brought into time; in a

word, they needed to be *civilized*. For the point was never merely to evangelize among the population, but also to civilize their spaces by drawing them
into the flow-time of modernity: the same triangulation of people, time and
space that had elaborated by Hannah More in *Betty Brown* was now being
thought through not simply metaphorically but also quite literally and materially in relation to the urban fabric of London. The civilization of people
meant also the civilization of space, drawing both into the mainstream of
historical time, the time of development.

6. SETTLING LONDON

"The impression naturally produced upon men's minds by such a state of
things," writes Weir with reference to the feelings of the settled and respectable population of London toward the "dangerous classes" that surrounded
and impinged upon them, "was, that they were living in the presence of an
enemy against whom they must defend themselves. Or rather, perhaps,"
he adds, "they looked upon the worshipful community of thieves much in
the same way that settlers in a new country regard the wild beasts prowling
in the forests around them."[131] Eighteenth-century London may have been
a wilderness that was still being settled, but it was clearly the case that
nineteenth-century London still retained its pockets of savagery—reservations that needed to be dealt with in one way or another in order for the
city to be declared truly settled once and for all. It is not that such attempts
were not made in the past, but they failed for one reason or another. The
Seven Dials, Weir points out in his piece on St. Giles's, "are an evidence of
an attempt to civilise the neighbourhood by introducing respectable houses
into it."[132] Clearly, such piecemeal efforts could never work in a space as resistant to improvement as "unchanged, unchangeable" St. Giles's.[133] Much
stronger and more comprehensive action would be required to overcome the
resistance of what Beames identifies as "strongholds of corrupt antiquity"
and their swarms of residents who still hold out against what Thornbury
calls "the quick march of civilisation."[134]

Beames himself was quite clear on this point. It is not just that "the habits
Rookeries generate must be eradicated," but that the spaces themselves must
be eradicated in turn.[135] Rookeries are our "plague-spots," Beames argues,
where "our convicts [are] nursed—the men whom our distant colonies re-
ject; for whom there is our vast array of penitentiaries, prison-ships, hulks,
penal settlements, and the like."[136] In closing his book, he eagerly anticipates
the day when the rookeries will be remembered "not by what they are, but
as the dungeons of an ancient castle, whose horrors tradition records, custom

has long superseded, like monoliths and cromlechs, relics of an elder age."[137] That is to say, there is no room in the present for the spaces of the past; they must physically be eliminated and wiped clean in order to confirm that they now well and truly belong to the past and do not linger on into the present.

The cleansing and settling—the civilizing—of London was thus simultaneously a spatial process and a temporal one. To be precise, the space needed to be reorganized in order to secure the temporal and historical process that was ultimately at stake: the process that smooths time clearly and neatly into a flow leading from past to present and on into the future. This conception of time was central to the imperial projects of the modern age, according to which, as Johannes Fabian argues in *Time and the Other*, "all living societies were irrevocably placed on a temporal slope, a stream of Time—some upstream, others downstream. Civilization, evolution, development, acculturation, modernization (and their cousins, industrialization, urbanization) are all terms whose conceptual content derives, in ways that can be specified, from evolutionary Time."[138] Spaces like Seven Dials and St. Giles's had to go, or be cleaned up, because they represented disruptions in this smooth flow, kinks and distortions in the smooth space-time of modernity.

This is exactly why opening them up was never simply about the spaces on their own; it was always about linking them to the broader space of circulation, flow, and temporal development that marked the rest of the city. "The 'inrailed column' with its seven dials has been removed, but the seven streets still open into the place where it stood, and perplex the stranger in their maze-like appearance," writes the organ of the Society for the Diffusion of Useful Knowledge about Seven Dials. "A filthy, gin-drinking and obnoxious-looking neighborhood it is; fit companion for the purlieus of St. Giles's, but an unseemly contrast with the not very distant magnificence of the West-end. Monmouth Street, that ancient storehouse of old clothes and old shoes, is in the immediate neighborhood of the Seven Dials. If St. Martin's Lane, which runs up from Charing Cross, were extended, it would be carried right through the Seven Dials; it is a pity but that projects often talked about could be carried into execution, and that the nests of the Seven Dials and St. Giles's were plowed up to make room for broad, spacious streets."[139] That was in 1837, and the pity did not have to last long.

It was not St. Martin's Lane that was bulldozed through the area from the south, however, but New Oxford Street, and later Shaftesbury Avenue, from the west. Even after the New Oxford Street project was completed, Thornbury complains in the 1870s that "there are still streets [in the western part of St. Giles's, i.e., in the vicinity of New Oxford Street] which demand to be swept away in the interest of health and cleanliness."[140] And he identifies parts of the eastern sector of the parish that similarly "should without delay be removed to 'fresh fields and pastures new,' and a thoroughfare opened up through this crowded district."[141] This would complete the logic articulated by Weir decades earlier in identifying, for example, Oxford Street as "an airy thoroughfare," in contrast to the stifling, dead, backwaters of St. Giles's. But even Weir had pointed out the argument that wide streets and handsome storefronts, by themselves, "are of little avail, so long as close and noisome lanes and courts are allowed to remain in their rottenness behind, only hidden by those whitened sepulchers." Therefore, he continues, "it is proposed to apply, to 'the Rookery' in particular, a more thorough-going cure," namely, the development of New Oxford Street to Holborn, "where the Rookery now stands, sweeping the offensive mass away bodily."[142]

The point, though, is that the material movement of traffic and air represent also the movement of time. To allow the circuits and movements of traffic and time to penetrate the obscure darkness of St. Giles's, Shoe Lane, Field Lane, the especially dilapidated parts of Soho, and so on, was to open those areas up and connect them to the flow of history and civilization, in precisely the same way that India was also (according to people like James and John Stuart Mill, or, as we will see in chap. 5, Macaulay) being opened up and connected to the flow of history and civilization.[143] In other words, it was not just India that had, according to improvers like Mill, stopped developing and that needed to be helped on its "progress towards the high attainments of a civilised life."[144] Parts of England—even parts of London itself—were also locked in the past, outside of time and history, and simultaneously in need of precisely the same kind of developmental civilization. Pablo Mukherjee has pointed out the symbiotic nature, in this period, of discourses of power and surveillance both at home in England and in the explicitly colonial realm in India.[145] To his astute reading of these two sites of control, we need to add that this was not just a matter of policing criminality and lawlessness—so that, as he points out, specific policies that were developed for one context could be seamlessly transposed to the other—but also of development and improvement more generally.

It wasn't just that India and the inner districts of London had to be policed more effectively, in other words: it was that they were both in need of the same kind of development, the same kind of linkage to the flow of time and history—in a word, the same civilizing process. For, as Uday Mehta points out, the conceptualization of linear, progressive time "requires an identification of those whose past and present did not align themselves with the expectations of that view of progress—that is, those who were deemed

to be 'backward'—and consequently the need and justification of a power
to bring about such a progressive alignment."[146] Mehta's critique of liberal
thought concerns its attitudes toward empire, but the point I am making
here is that precisely the same thinking was going on with reference to domestic spaces as well. In identifying "the tutorial and pedagogic obsession
of the empire and especially of the liberal imperialists" as "all part of the
effort to move societies along the ascending gradient of historical progress,"
Mehta is also putting his finger on (without acknowledging it, for it falls
outside the scope of his study) a logic at work in England as well. If, as he
puts it, the empire comes to be thought of as "an engine that tows societies stalled in their past into contemporary time and history," the engine
was at work at home in England as well, and not just in India and places
further afield.[147] More than that: the empire is an engine tying together a
process that was unfolding relationally—binding the two spaces together—
both abroad and at home. The hidden flaw in Mehta's brilliant book, then, is
that it takes too much for granted (as do other works focused exclusively on
the empire) a certain set of rhetorical assumptions about the civilizational
development of the center of empire in England itself. What I want to insist
on is that the two domains need to be thought of together—as many were
doing in the period under discussion here.

Hence, for example, it is all too appropriate that the first model of mass
education in Britain (the so-called monitorial system) was actually adapted
from a method developed to teach orphan children in Madras and imported
in order to teach "the lower orders" or "the inferior classes" at home, beginning with the school opened by Joseph Lancaster on the Borough Road,
which was inspired by Andrew Bell's book on his experience in India.[148]
"Dr. Andrew Bell had published in 1797 a pamphlet describing the 'Madras
System' of setting the children to teach each other," Graham Wallas notes.
"This system Lancaster copied or reinvented, and soon formed vague plans
of covering all England with schools, in each of which a thousand children should be taught in squads of ten by a hundred monitors."[149] Competing schemes to propagate this method in England, especially in London,
developed through the early nineteenth century, involving individuals and
organizations as varied as Patrick Colquhoun and the Church of England
on the one hand, and, on the other, reformers like James Mill, the brothers
Bentham, Robert Owen, David Ricardo, and Francis Place. Among Place's
papers in the British Library, for instance, are extensive notes and clippings
detailing his involvement in the ill-fated West London Lancasterian Association in 1813 and a later scheme in 1817 to establish a day school for

children modeled on Bentham's panopticon, with hundreds of kids under "central inspection."[150]

The ultimate objective of these plans varied to a certain extent. Colquhoun being Colquhoun, for instance, his educational scheme was highly moralistic, and it aimed to prevent "those calamities which lead to idleness and crimes, and produce poverty and misery, by guiding and properly directing the early conduct of the lower orders of the community, and by giving a right bias to their minds."[151] For the more radical advocates of the Lancasterian method, such as Place, however, the point of education was broader and should include reading, writing, mathematics, mineralogy, botany, zoology, physics and chemistry, as well as more applied fields such as husbandry, gardening, manufacturing, mining and domestic economy.[152] Wallas points out that Place's greatest fear, in his involvement in such schooling, "was that the Lancasterian method might become instruments of social oppression by being connected with the idea of 'charity.'"[153] In both cases, though, there was a common sense that the objects of the educational mission, that is, the urban poor, needed to be helped, as the British and Foreign School Society (into which the Lancasterian Society had morphed in 1814) put it, to "rise in the scale of civilization."[154] Or, as Mehta so aptly expresses the same point, they needed to be towed into contemporary time and history.

The civilization and Occidentalization of London thus took place in two tracks at once: reform of those who could be reformed and displacement, removal, and erasure of those who could not. For we know from Gareth Stedman Jones's classic *Outcast London* that there was a heavy price to be paid for this view of development—and we know who paid it. Projects to rehabilitate the space of London by clearing away slums and rookeries, broadening streets, converting residential districts into commercial ones, developing dock areas, and eventually making room for railroad networks necessarily involved the displacement of thousands of people at a time, without making provision for their accommodation elsewhere. The extension of New Oxford Street, for example, forced five thousand people from their homes, however squalid they may have been; development north of the Strand to make room for the new law courts displaced six thousand people; the demolition of Crown Street and the cutting up of St. Giles's by the development of Shaftesbury Avenue and Charing Cross Road unhoused another six thousand people; work on Southwark Street and the railway extension across the Thames into Ludgate Hill also displaced six thousand people; the great clearances around the Farringdon Road forced the removal of an estimated forty thousand people. Altogether, according to Stedman Jones, the aeration of London enabled by such street clearances "accounted for the displacement of not far short of 100,000 persons between 1830 and 1880."[155]

Given that the people thus forced from their homes were in some cases black or Irish, or, when they were not, were racially configured as "Kaffirs" or "Arabs," was this not an act of ethnic cleansing recapitulating those of the seventeenth and eighteenth centuries (in Ireland or the Americas) and anticipating those of the twentieth century (in such places as Palestine and the Balkans)? Would it have been so easy to displace tens of thousands of people without their prior classification as members of a racial and civilizational other?

Of course, we should not lapse into a misplaced nostalgia: the circumstances of life for those who were thus displaced were abysmal. The intense overcrowding, unsanitary conditions, poor diet, and so on took its toll; as Boyd Hilton notes, mid-nineteenth-century slum life was appalling: mechanics, servants, and laborers condemned to it had a life expectancy of just fifteen years.[156] Vast improvements were made through this period in social infrastructure, transportation, education, and public health, all of which, as Michelle Allen argues, made London a much cleaner and healthier place to live at the end of the nineteenth century than it had been at the beginning.[157] But, as Allen also points out, for all the innovations and the material improvements inspired by investigators like John Snow or reformers like Chadwick, there was always also a price to be paid, principally by those "human beings who live amidst—and are swept aside with—the old rubbish."[158]

On this note, however, we return again to the ambivalent duality of the project to civilize London, and with it the ambivalent duality of national and civilizational identity in the earliest stages of making England Western. What had to be purged from central London was, to use Weir's phrase, "the offensive mass," the Orientalized, Arabized multitude, or in other words, that depersonalized, common, animalized form of being that was deemed to be both spatially and temporally out of synch with modernity. What had to be allowed back in, or allowed to remain, were the individual modes of being that could be salvaged from the offensive mass as redeemed individuals, "Free-Born Englishmen," to use the ideological term that I think requires much further unpacking than its frequent uncritical deployment, even by as great a historian as E. P. Thompson, generally allows.[159] In other words, the process of excluding one form of identity was the inseparable flip side of the process of including the other, recreating the urban space for (in theory at least) the habitation of new, white, properly Occidental individuals. The spatiotemporal project of civilizing London, making it Western, went hand in glove with the biopolitical one.

What was clear in all of the work from the period was the sense that space and population mirror each other. If Weir, Dickens, Beames, and Thornbury were right to see in the urban fabric of St. Giles's or other sites of suspended development in London the appropriate habitation for the animalized, Orientalized mass that lived there, changing the people fundamentally meant changing the space itself. "Of the condition of the greater part of these people it is difficult to convey anything like a just idea," writes George Godwin of the residents of the rookeries, for example. "It is a certain and melancholy fact that this dangerous, and to the State, expensive class of persons is alarmingly increasing in London and other large towns," he adds. "It is, however, certain that one important and leading cause of this degradation is the condition of the dwellings in which thousands of these outcasts are born, and in which they live and die. Improving *these* would do much towards improving *them*."[160] Godwin explains this mirroring of space and population. "If there were no courts and blind alleys, there would be less immorality and physical suffering," he argues. "The means of escaping from public view which they afford, generate evil habits; and, even when this is not the case, render personal efforts for improvement unlikely. We would have such cleared away, therefore."[161] Even though he admits the necessity of rehousing those who are removed, he thinks of the removed people and the "cleared away" space in the same terms. With reference to a rookery in Berwick Street, Soho (the site of Richard "Citizen" Lee's British Tree of Liberty in the 1790s), he writes, for instance, that "the houses destroyed were abominable, and the inhabitants most difficult material to deal with. Several very desperate characters had lived there, and only those who had seen the houses previously can form a just estimate of the benefit of their removal."[162] The people themselves have become material to work with.

The sense that a certain spatiotemporal layout produces a certain kind of population, which is drawn to it in turn, was echoed all through this period. "There were districts in London through which no great thoroughfares passed, and which were wholly occupied by a dense population composed of the lowest class of persons who being entirely secluded from the observation and influence of better educated neighbors, exhibited a state of moral degradation deeply to be deplored," notes a Select Committee report in 1838. "The moral condition of those poorer occupants would necessarily be improved by communication with more respectable inhabitants," it adds, pointing out also that "the introduction at the same time of improved habits and a freer circulation of air would tend materially to extirpate those prevalent diseases which not only ravaged the poorer districts in question, but were also dangerous to the adjacent localities."[163] The point was never simply to drive big boulevards through these districts, however, but to reform them by also parceling out their spaces, finally, into individuated units that could mirror, and thus help generate, the individual subjects that would eventually live there. "Let nuisances, Rookeries, fever courts, *et hoc genus omne*, die the death," writes Beames; "let them be replaced, not by shops for the tradesman, but by dwellings for the working man; let the number of inmates for each house be fixed, the due supply of water regulated by some provision which shall bring Water Companies to their senses; let each family have a sitting-room and at least two bed-rooms."[164] What is necessary, in other words, is the replacement of massified, anonymizing, indistinct, unnavigable, mysterious spaces by space discretely parceled out into simultaneously individual and individualizing packets, appropriate for the habitation of discrete individuals and nuclear families, headed by Free-Born Englishmen, whose very mode of existence is compatible with the flow of civilized, modern, time—and a truly Western England.

CHAPTER TWO

Civilizing the Ballad

B y exploring the relationship between Wordsworth's turn to the ballad and his representations of the common people in his poetry, this chapter aims to connect Wordsworth to the larger sets of questions involved in asking who "we" English are in the late eighteenth and early nineteenth centuries, and how, whether, or to what extent "we" constitute a collectivity with a coherent racial and civilizational identity. I will argue that there are racial and civilizational dynamics at play in the relationship, repeatedly explored by Wordsworth, between a narrating self and represented others. Even if that relationship does not always explicitly turn on an Occidental/Oriental axis (the Occident/Orient binary is merely a variation on the more general self/other theme, after all), there are, I will argue, subtle Occidentalizing forces at work in his work, certain strands of which I have already discussed in other contexts.[1] Moreover, the racially inflected tensions between self and other in Wordsworth's work operate at a material and a formal, even a generic, level, rather than strictly a representational one. This is especially so in the case of *Lyrical Ballads* and the poems connected in one way or another to that volume, some of which, including the Salisbury Plain poems, span Wordsworth's entire career from the 1790s to the 1840s.

Even to approach these poems and the *Lyrical Ballads* project requires us to consider the social, cultural, political, and civilizational status of the ballad by the early nineteenth century. We have to ask what it might mean to approach the ballad—which would be captured by Henry Mayhew in *London Labour and the London Poor* as "the rude uncultivated verse in which the popular tale of the times is recorded"[2]—with the intention of representing the common people, not to themselves, but rather to their emerging social superiors, albeit in a form that was at the time increasingly coming to be associated with plebeian culture in certain loaded (and largely negative) respects. The act of representing the other is here also the act of re-claiming the literary form of the other—*depopulating* it, to borrow the term that Nigel Leask and Philip Connell quite rightly propose for this operation (though probably not with the same emphasis in mind that I intend here)[3]—for a new set of social and political as well as aesthetic purposes.

For although *Lyrical Ballads* was never intended for a plebeian audience, it appeared at a time when various social forces were struggling to sepa-rate written from oral culture and polite from plebeian culture: a struggle complicated by the fact that the boundaries separating such apparently bi-nary opposites—a terrain squarely occupied by the ballad—were actually remarkably porous, crossed repeatedly from one direction or stratum to the other, as Ian Newman has recently documented.[4] In asking what it might mean to seek to make the ballad lyrical (a question that, as Newman re-minds us, is far more complicated, both aesthetically and politically, than scholars have long taken it to be),[5] I want to keep a particular focus on the drive to consolidate an Occidentalized sense of self, a project that required aesthetic engineering and acts of aesthetic reclamation just as much as it did the kinds of social engineering and spatial reclamation—or ethnic cleans-ing—described in my chapter on London. In particular it seemed to generate a pressing need for the articulation and safeguarding of new generic forms seen to be appropriate to a new, self-regulating Occidental subject: generic forms that were in certain cases both the same as and different from—that is, translations of—earlier literary forms in which the polite and the plebe-ian, the written and the spoken, print culture and oral culture, had once seemed much more entangled.

1. TRANSLATING THE VOICE OF THE OTHER

To open up the complicated question of the relationship of self to other, and in particular of a narrating poetical self to a represented plebeian other, it is worth noting that one of the most remarkable characteristics of Words-worth's poems of the 1790s, especially of the poems in or connected to *Lyri-cal Ballads*, is that they oscillate between denying plebeian characters a voice and providing them with that voice—and hence lifting them out of the strange distance from ourselves that the poetry attempts to depict. Let me provide one brief example, from a poem Wordsworth worked on and re-vised over the length of his entire career, from the mid-1790s to the mid-1840s, constantly treading the very fine line between granting and denying speech and self-representation to plebeian characters.

"The Female Vagrant" appeared in the first edition of *Lyrical Ballads*.

From the first stanza, it appears to—and in a sense it does—give the vagrant a voice:

> By Derwent's side my Father's cottage stood,
> (The Woman thus her artless story told)
> One field, a flock, and what the neighboring flood
> Supplied, to him were more than mines of gold.
> Light was my sleep; my days in transport roll'd:
> With thoughtless joy I stretch'd along the shore
> My father's nets, or watched, when from the fold
> High o'er the cliffs I led my fleecy store,
> A dizzy depth below! His boat and twinkling oar.

Here, the woman herself plainly speaks, and Wordsworth risks the pedantry of a parenthesis to tell us so. However, the poem also undermines its granting of a voice to the Female Vagrant. In the first line, her speech is not marked off by quotation marks, so in a sense she might be seen as the narrator, and the poem seems to announce itself as the tragic life story of a hapless plebeian woman, told in her own voice (which would be unique in *Lyrical Ballads*). But a second voice intervenes in the very next line, to draw attention to the mediation taking place between the Vagrant's original story and the reader of the poem, reminding us that there is actually a process of translation at work between the "artlessness" of her oral tale and the written work of art on the printed page before us. The woman is thus not really the poem's narrator as such: the story can become art only insofar as it is translated into a medium over which she has no control, a medium where her raw experience, conveyed to an intermediary authority in speech, can enter written narrative. Many of Wordsworth's poems force us to attend to the distinction between plebeian experience (fictional or otherwise) and the translation of that experience out of speech and into poetry in both representational and formal or material ways: a distinction that was particularly fraught at a moment when the limits or ongoing contacts between speech and writing were increasingly subject to political surveillance and interdiction.

2. MAPPING THE BALLAD

We will return to our reading of "The Female Vagrant" a little later in the chapter, but for now, in order to set up that later and fuller discussion of the poetry, I want to take a detour to describe in greater detail some sense

of what was at stake in turning to the question of the translation of plebeian experience into a peculiar work of art, which reviewers immediately
recognized as coming dangerously close, and at times crossing over into,
the low and vulgar. They saw this in the attempt to emulate a vulgar literary form ("none but savages have submitted to eating acorns after corn
was found," complains Charles Burney in his critique of *Lyrical Ballads* for
the *Monthly Review*, damning the ballads' attempt to "degrade" poetry by
emulating "barbarous and uncouth" predecessors)[6], and they also saw it in
the process of translating oral expression into a written form ("the language
of *conversation*, and that too of the *lower classes*, can never be considered
as the language of poetry," chides the *New London Review* in its piece on
Lyrical Ballads).[7]

Yet in the *Lyrical Ballads* project Wordsworth is not simply conveying
the stories of the wanderers, vagrants, and nomads who would, as we saw
in the Introduction and in the previous chapter, gradually come to be seen,
beginning in the 1790s, as racially distinct from England's settled population and hence necessarily at some social distance from the narrator and
the reader of the text. For he is also intervening in and in effect cutting off
from itself a literary form that at the time was being assigned unmistakable
social connotations and associations, as earlier continuities between polite
and plebeian culture were being obscured or overwritten. These works offer,
in other words, both a representational and a formal intervention in the
stories and cultural forms of people increasingly taken to be socially and
indeed racially different from a putatively settled "us." The very process of
mediating and translating the world of the vagrant to the polite and settled
world of letters helps establish who "we" are in the first place, at a time
when—as I hope the previous chapter has already begun to make clear—
that question was anything but obvious. Wordsworth's own response to it
was, as we will see, politically complex, ambivalent, and even to a certain
extent paradoxical or self-contradictory.

Scholars have long situated *Lyrical Ballads* at the tail end of a wide range
of literary and political projects in the last third or so of the eighteenth century to investigate, rummage through, borrow from, and emulate popular
culture, whether as gestures of political solidarity or as somewhat less al-
truistic entrepreneurial ventures. As Nigel Leask, Philip Connell, and Ian
Newman, among others, have argued, much was at stake in these interventions into the shifting force field that would eventually be identified as
popular culture. Connell reminds us that there was an unstable fault line
separating "popular" from "polite" culture in this period and that a great
deal was invested in maintaining various distinctions between them.[8] For

example, although we tend to associate political ballads with plebeian culture in this period, there was, as Newman has shown, a thriving tradition of political balladry and associated drinking songs in elite Whig circles as well, and it took considerable effort—beginning precisely at the cultural moment when Wordsworth was making his intervention into balladry—to try to distinguish a literary hierarchy more or less claiming correspondence to social hierarchies as well.[9]

The best-known venture into what might otherwise have been seen as the literature of a lower social stratum in order to reclaim it for new purposes was the work of Thomas Percy, who produced in his 1765 *Reliques of Ancient English Poetry* cleaned-up and carefully edited appropriations from England's popular traditions, expressly for consumption by the polite and lettered elites.[10] However, although he is for us the best-known figure of the so-called ballad revival of the late eighteenth century, Percy was far from the only one interested in reviving an interest in English literary traditions (whether real or invented). Dianne Dugaw observes that the ballad revival flourished at a popular as well as at an elite level, and indeed that there was a great deal of circulation between these levels, which, other things being equal, ought to have rendered them indistinct. Thus, for all his claims to the originality of his discoveries, Percy himself drew on materials that had already enjoyed considerable circulation on the lower tiers of the eighteenth-century literary marketplace. Dugaw's primary example is the London-based chapbook and ballad empire of William and Cluer Dicey, which catered primarily to a lowbrow audience. She points out that at least a third of the 180 pieces in Percy's collection were already circulating on broadsides churned out by the Diceys' Cheapside headquarters at the time the first edition of the *Reliques* was published in 1765. Many of these are known to have been purchased by Percy from the Diceys themselves, though his intention was to refurbish and repackage them for sale to a more sophisticated audience—and, naturally, at a higher price.[11]

In his now-classic reading of the *Lyrical Ballads*, Robert Mayo points out that, given the proliferation of the kinds of texts circulated by the Diceys among others, the poems gathered together in that volume would hardly have offered surprising new themes for a contemporary reader in 1798, particularly a reader of journals and magazines and more lowbrow publications. "Most of the objects of sympathy in the volume belong to an order of beings familiar to every reader of magazine poetry—namely, bereaved mothers and deserted females, mad women and distracted creatures, beggars, convicts and prisoners, and old people of the depressed classes, particularly peasants," Mayo argues. "For nearly every character, portrait, or figure [in *Lyrical Ballads*], there is some seasoned counterpart in contemporary poetry."[12] In fact, he adds, "the more one reads the popular poetry of the last quarter of the eighteenth century, the more he is likely to feel that the really surprising feature of these poems in the *Lyrical Ballads* (as well as many of the others)—apart from sheer literary excellence—is their intense fulfill-ment of an already stale convention, and not their discovery of an interest in rivers, valleys, groves, lakes, and mountains, flowers and budding trees, the changing seasons, sunsets, the freshness of the morning and the songs of birds."[13]

So far, so good. But there was far more at stake than simply thematic ap-propriation in Wordsworth's turn to popular literature and in particular the question of the ballad: a form with so loose and baggy a set of definitions by the turn of the nineteenth century that it actually comes to defy definition in strictly literary or generic terms (in terms of a particular metrical struc-ture or rhyme scheme, for example) and ends up suggesting rather more allusively popular literary expressions straddling or repeatedly crossing the line between oral and written culture. In seeming to align his work with the unsettled world of the plebeian and the popular, then, Wordsworth was also coming dangerously close to the world of broadsides, chapbooks, and ballads directed for sale to a more plebeian audience—including many with ribald themes or politically subversive content—which continued to flourish all through the late eighteenth century and well into the nineteenth, even as they were also increasingly seen to be problematic or dangerous.

Moreover, the dangers lurking in this world involved far more than lit-erary or aesthetic disgrace, which ought to prompt us to think through all the more clearly what it would have meant for Wordsworth to have delved into—or even skated close to—this world in a formal sense even while also turning to representations of the very kind of people who used to constitute one of the primary markets for this kind of literature, which was consis-tently scorned by polite circles not only on aesthetic grounds but on moral and political grounds as well. "30,000 Hawkers are maintain'd by this dis-solute Traffic," Hannah More complained to Hester Piozzi about the circu-lation of popular ballads and songs at around the same time as Wordsworth was turning to the ballad form, "and Boat loads of it are sent away from the Trading towns to infect the villages."[14] The Bishop of London was equally alarmed at the extent of the spread of these wares. "There is a central set of booksellers, that are to the soil as mischievous as your hawkers, pedlers [*sic*] and match-women, in vending the vilest penny-pamphlets to the poor people," he wrote to More. "I am told it is incredible what fortunes they raise by this sort of traffic, and what multitudes of the lowest rabble flock to their shops to purchase their execrable tracts."[15]

Although provincial towns had their own local producers of ballads and broadsides, the "central set of booksellers" to whom the bishop refers were largely based in London, whose ballad warehouses, as Leask and Connell point out, "dominated the nation's popular print industry."[16] And by the early to mid-nineteenth century—the peak of the Occidentalization of London discussed in the previous chapter—the center of ballad production was none other than the Seven Dials (an area with whose connotations we should by now be familiar), and in particular the rival lowbrow publishing empires of James Catnach and John Pitts (see figs. 10 and 11).[17] "Seven Dials! the region of song and poetry—first effusions, and last dying speeches," writes Dickens in his piece on the district in *Sketches by Boz*. "Hallowed by the names of Catnach and Pitts—names that will entwine themselves with costermongers, and barrel-organs, when penny magazines shall have superseded penny yards of song, and capital punishment be unknown!"[18] Dickens was far from the only one who saw popular song and poetry, especially (loosely conceived) ballads, as entwined or entangled with costermongers and what were taken to be (by polite observers) the very worst and most dangerous aspects of plebeian culture: a culture that was seen to be sure to be outmoded by continuing historical progress. Little wonder, then, that the *Dens of London*, as we saw in the previous chapter, thinks of ballad-singing as a kind of amalgamation of begging, selling, singing, and stealing by the very dregs of society.[19]

Long before Dickens and the *Dens of London*, however, in the magisterial 1797 *Treatise on the Police of the Metropolis*, Patrick Colquhoun includes 1,500 "Strolling Minstrels, Ballad Singers, Show Men, Trumpeters and Gipsies" in the "shocking catalogue of Human Depravity" that, according to him, assails passersby in the streets of London.[20] This adds much needed context to Wordsworth's sighting of "files of ballads dangl[ing] from dead walls" in book 7 of *The Prelude*, dating from the era of Colquhoun.[21] The printing, hanging, selling, and singing of ballads are specifically categorized among the types of degenerate and criminal activities that would be brought under stricter surveillance and control in the new system of police advocated by Colquhoun. "Since it has never been possible, under the existing Laws, to suppress the herd of Ballad-Singers which are to be found in such multitudes in every part of the Metropolis, and, indeed, in all the large Towns in the Kingdom: and which at present are under the controul [*sic*] of a very feeble Police, which does not, and indeed cannot, restrain effectually

LONG-SONG SELLER.

"Two under fifty for a fardy!"

[From a Daguerreotype by BEARD.]

Fig. 10. "Long-Song Seller," from Henry Mayhew, *London Labour and the London Poor*, vol. 1 (London, 1861).

THE STREET-STATIONER.

[From a Daguerreotype by BEARD.]

Fig. 11. "The Street-Stationer," from Henry Mayhew, *London Labour and the London Poor*, vol. 1 (London, 1861).

the immoral and often seditious tendency of the Songs sung to the listening multitude," Colquhoun asks, "why might not this lowest cast of amusement be turned to good purposes, tending to counteract and prevent the corruption of Morals, which are at present generated through this Medium?"[22]

Precisely such an attempt to counteract and prevent moral and political corruption was at the heart of the project to which Hannah More had already turned by the mid-1790s. However, judging at least by the prosperity of Catnach, it was to little avail: Mayhew estimates that he amassed a fortune of £10,000 through the sale, often by the yard, of the penny ballads produced by the so-called "seven bards of Seven Dials" who churned out lines of verse for him.[23] For Mayhew in the 1850s as for Colquhoun in the 1790s, ballads, ballad singers, and anyone connected to "the rude uncultivated verse in which the popular tale of the times is recorded," was far closer to the world of costermongers than even Dickens playfully suggests in *Sketches by Boz.*

Moreover, to be connected to the world of the costermongers is, as we saw in the discussion of London in the previous chapter, to be connected to a racial order fundamentally different from "our" own: to those who "for the most part, are allowed to remain in nearly the same primitive and brutish state as the savage—creatures with nothing but their appetites, instincts, and passions to move them, and made up of the same crude combination of virtue and vice—the same generosity combined with the same predatory tendencies as the Bedouins of the desert—the same love of revenge and disregard of pain, and often the same gratitude and susceptibility to kindness as the Red Indian—and, furthermore, the same insensibility to female honour and abuse of female weakness, and the same utter ignorance of the Divine nature of the Godhead as marks either Bosjesman, Carib, or Thug," as Mayhew characteristically reminds us in introducing his chapter on "patterers" and the street sellers of ballads and other literature.[24]

Not just that, but, as Mayhew argues, whereas it is impossible to blame the costermongers for their degraded state because they "are mostly hereditary wanderers—having been as it were born to frequent the public thoroughfares," the more educated "patterers" and scribblers or hawkers of verse "have for the most part neither been born and bred nor driven to a street life—but have rather taken to it from a natural love of what they call 'roving.'"[25] This propensity to lapse "from a civilized to a nomad state—to pass from a settler into a wanderer—is a peculiar characteristic of the pattering tribe," Mayhew continues. "The tendency however is by no means extraordinary; for ethnology teaches us, that whereas many abandon the habits of civilized life to adopt those of a nomadic state of existence, but few of the

wandering tribes give up vagabondizing and betake themselves to settled occupations."[26] For Mayhew, clearly, to affiliate oneself with the rude and uncultivated and their degraded literature—which resides at the very limit,
the contact zone between oral and written culture—is not only to endorse
nomadism; it is also to lapse from a civilized to a nomad state, really to "go
native" in every sense of that expression, to cross a racial line.

3. GOING NATIVE

As such racial lines were charted out and then deepened and hardened all
through this period—a process in which Wordsworth played an ambiguous
role—crossing such a line, dabbling in popular culture with anything other
than an evangelical sense of missionary conversion designed to save that culture from itself, would come to mean almost inevitably dabbling in the potentially radical politics with which that culture had become associated by
1798, especially as the memory of a rather more polite form of the political
ballads faded (or was driven) into memory.[27] Even when it was undertaken
by relatively educated and sophisticated intellectuals, after all, much of the
popular antiquarianism of the 1780s and 1790s assumed an expressly radical political cast. Many of the leading antiquarians of the period—such as
John Brand, Francis Grose, and Francis Douce—combined an interest in and
sympathy for popular culture with varying degrees of commitment to radical
politics.[28] And in one of the most famous literary controversies of the period
it is ultimately impossible to distinguish aesthetic from political considerations: this was the fiercely contentious debate between Thomas Percy and
the self-declared *sans culottes* sympathizer, Joseph Ritson, who assembled
several collections of popular songs and ballads expressly intended to challenge Percy's grip on polite literary culture. These included *Pieces of Ancient
Popular Poetry* (1791), *Robin Hood* (1795), and the earlier *Select Collection
of English Songs* (1783), which was published by the great radical publisher
Joseph Johnson (who would go on to publish Wordsworth's *An Evening Walk*
and *Descriptive Sketches* in 1793) and illustrated with engravings by William Blake.

Expressed in aesthetic terms, the difference between Ritson and Percy
was evident in their editing styles. "Percy strove to present the songs and
ballads of his collections in a polite form," Jon Mee points out; "Ritson, on
the other hand, delighted in the 'vulgar' qualities of the material he published."[29] But of course—especially in the 1790s—such a preference for the
vulgarity of the "swinish multitude" also took on immediately political
implications as well. This is probably nowhere more evident than in the

way in which Ritson seeks to correct Percy's misrepresentation of the figure
of the English minstrel. Whereas Percy invokes an image of the minstrel as
playing in the homes of the high and mighty in Norman England, Ritson
turns this image on its head. "That there were men in those times, as there
are in the present, who gained a livelihood by going about from place to
place, singing and playing to the illiterate vulgar, is doubtless true," Ritson
argues, "but that they were received into the castles of the nobility, sung
at their tables, and were rewarded like the French minstrels, does not any
where appear, nor is it at all credible."[30]

The point of Ritson's challenge to Percy is not simply to question the
authenticity and accuracy of the latter's claims (though he does that in exhaustive detail): it is to undermine what he saw as Percy's ambition to clean
up popular literature and repackage it as the literature of a bygone elite, or
in other words to alienate popular literature from the people themselves.
But polite reviewers in the 1790s were clearly perfectly happy with Percy's
cleaned-up ballads—despite their evident lack of authenticity—and indeed
preferred them to the "real thing" as presented by Ritson. Percy's rendition
of a two-penny ballad like "Adam Bell," the *Monthly Review* insists in its
1792 evaluation of Ritson's critique, whose accuracy it grants, "is preferable
to the *true* one, and should therefore remain undisturbed."[31] The author of
an article in a 1795 issue of the *Critical Review* was not so generous—and
the class and political nature of his rejection of Ritson's *Pieces of Ancient
Popular Poetry* is that much more obvious. With perhaps one or two exceptions, he writes, "there is not one piece in this collection which a man of
sense would not be ashamed to publish, or even to say that he had read; so
puerile, so childish are these old rhymes." While many of the classics, he
continues, "have been published in this country in a slovenly manner, it is
with pain we observe that this collection of trash is printed in a superior
style."[32]

Ritson was not only interested in popular culture; he was also close to
many of the leading radicals of the 1790s. In addition to Godwin and Holcroft, Ritson knew quite well the radical organizer, orator, and writer John
Thelwall of the London Corresponding Society; in fact, according to Bertrand Bronson, it was through Ritson that Thelwall would have paid the
rent for Beaufort Buildings off the Strand, in which he gave the political
lectures that earned him a place on the government's watch list—and gave
it further excuses to pass the repressive legislation of 1795, one clause of
which was specifically aimed at public lecturers such as Thelwall.[33] Ritson also knew the agrarian communist and journalist Thomas Spence and
also Daniel Isaac Eaton, and he supplied the latter with ballads of antiquar-

ian—but also political—interest for Eaton's journal *Politics for the People*: a publication that earned Eaton several arrests and spells in prison through the 1790s.

In fact, poetry of the very kind into which *Lyrical Ballads* marks a kind of intervention was an integral component of publications such as Spence's *Pigs' Meat* and Eaton's *Politics for the People*. Partly with Ritson's help, some three dozen songs—many in ballad form—were published in the latter, including such specimens as "The Tyrants' Downfall: A New Song," "An Occasional Song for 1794," "Song Written for the 14th of July, 1793," and "A New Song" to be sung to the tune of "God Save the King." "To Daniel Isaac Eaton [on the occasion of his acquittal in February 1794]," among many other examples, is structured on the traditional four-line ballad form (e.g., "Swear our taxes are but trifles, / And the nation's debt a joke; / That Pitt the public never rifles, / Nor his promise ever broke").[34] So is "A New Song," to be sung to the tune of "Mrs Casey," which goes, "But join your hands, resist, be free, / And quickly claim possession / Of your lost Rights and Liberty, / And overthrow Oppression."[35] Spence's *Pigs' Meat* also abounds with songs—many, again, in classic ballad form—including one to be sung to the tune of "Rule, Britannia," that begins, "When BRITAIN first impelled by pride, / Usurp'd dominion o'er the main, / Blest peace, she vainly threw aside, / And gave her sons the galling chain."[36] Some also incorporate elements of the ballad (including ballad stanzas) into other, less conventional forms, such as, for example, "The Americans Happy," which weaves four-line ballad stanzas in between rhyming couplets (e.g., "There liberty is law, / And joy o'erspreads each cheek, / No more 'tis 'vive le roi!' / But 'vive la REPUBLIQUE!'").[37] Both *Pigs' Meat* and *Politics for the People* also carried other songs and poems that were not formally structured as ballads (bearing in mind, again, the lack of a really stable definition of the ballad in this period).

What is distinctive about the political infusion of the ballad in the 1790s is that it came to be associated with a particular form of radicalism, especially as the memory of that older tradition of elite political ballads and songs was gradually erased from memory at the same time.[38] Increasingly, it came to stand for the racial politics of the swinish multitude: internationalist, fiercely communalist if not downright communist (as in Spence's *Pigs' Meat*), enthusiastic, unrestrained, and singularly uninterested in the highly regulated rights of the individual subject who would come to define the very cornerstone of an Occidentalist political imagination; in a word, much closer to the spirit (if not the aesthetic standards) of Blake than to what I refer to in my book on Blake as the hegemonic form of radicalism of the 1790s, which was far more invested specifically in the rights of the self-regulating Occidental subject, in which Blake had no interest.[39] The notion of what I am calling the racial politics of the swinish multitude is important here because one component of Occidentalism involved developing political logics that could be clearly distinguished from, on the one hand, the residual class and social hierarchies of the aristocracy and landed gentry and, on the other, the potential of an emergent politics associated (also in racial terms) with the multitude. The latter not only refused the demands of the tightly regulated Occidental subject but also conceived of the collective itself in terms that did not at all necessarily line up with the racial, national, or civilizational containments of Occidentalism—seeking, for example, to make common cause with non-European peoples struggling for freedom from slavery and colonial tyranny in a variety of sites around the world. As it developed, Occidentalism had to contain the threat posed by such political desires, actively seeking to limit the scope of rights to self-regulating individuals (rather than collectives) and to further refine the logic of such rights so that they would come to be seen as appropriate only to individuals from certain racial or civilizational configurations and not others; or, rather (as such an argument reaches its inevitable conclusion in the mind of someone like John Stuart Mill) to races and civilizations that were seen to be capable of enabling and fostering the spirit of individual liberty. I will return to this point in later chapters (see especially chapters 5 and 6), but for now I want at least to flag the significance of the potential affiliation of the ballad with the racial politics of the swinish multitude.

There were so many of these kinds of ballads and other publications in circulation by the middle of the decade that Hannah More amassed a considerable collection of them as she was mulling over how best to counteract them. "I should be much gratified with the sight of those invaluable original productions, both in prose and verse, which you have collected together from your friends the village hawkers and peddlers," the bishop of London wrote her. "They would form the best *sans culotte* library in Europe, and will, I dare say, some day or other be visited by travellers, as we now do the Vatican or the Museum."[40] What both the bishop and More intended, of course, was to relegate these specimens to museum status by forcing them off the streets.

The bishop and Hannah More were not alone in looking for ways to counteract the "*sans culotte* library" of seditious songs and ballads appealing to the worst instincts of the swinish multitude. As the radical organizer Francis Place points out, the Association for Preserving Liberty and Property from Republicans and Levellers was extraordinarily active in the project to flood the marketplace with countersubversive ballads and songs. One volume of the association's tracts, published in 1793, includes one loyal song after another printed for distribution that year. One verse in "The Happy Man: A New Song," for example, goes, "When my day's work is done, to the alehouse I fly, / And there I hear all the fine chatter, / A deal about Freedom, and Equality, / And such like nonsensical matter; / Tom Paine's Rights of Man! What are those Rights to me? / To do what is right, I am sure I am free; / I want to hurt no man, no man can hurt me, / Neighbors, mind this, and be quiet."[41] Admittedly, such songs don't quite have the panache of the radical ones, but what they lack in quality they make up for in sheer quantity. "Let that Reformer *Payne* / Know that his vile arts are vain," exhorts a verse in "A New Loyal Song" from January 1793; "Britain is Free! / Confound his Politicks / Frustrate his Knavish Tricks / With Equal Laws we Mix / True Liberty!"[42] Appended to certain copies of the widely distributed 1793 print "THE CONTRAST" opposing English liberty (religion, morality, loyalty, property, industry, etc.) to French liberty (atheism, treason, rebellion, perjury, anarchy, murder, equality, etc.) is "A New Song" to be sung to the tune of "Hearts of Oak." One verse gloats, "No Religion or laws the vile Jacobins Own / Their God they deny, their King they dethrone; / To Gain their own ends the poor people they cheat / Then leave them, too, not a morsel to eat!"[43]

The best-known countersubversive songs and ballads were of course those published by Hannah More in the Cheap Repository Tracts, many of them in stand-alone broadsheet format mimicking the radical or obscene songs against which they were directed. Even when they are identified as ballads, they frequently depart from the traditional four-line stanza or the alternating rhyme scheme typically associated with the ballad. "The Roguish Miller; or, Nothing Got by Cheating: A True Ballad," for example, has six-line stanzas with rhyming couplets. Reminding us how unstable the definition and usage of "ballad" were in the period, however, "The Sorrows of Hannah: A Ballad," uses eight-line stanzas with only the thinnest rhyme scheme.

The specific literary form of the conservative responses to radical songs and ballads was not really the issue, however; what mattered, as Kevin Gilmartin points out, was the urgent need, from a conservative standpoint, to flood the literary marketplace with alternatives.[44] The bishop of London spoke of this quite frankly as a kind of counterinsurgency operation. After complaining to Hannah More about the numerous booksellers trafficking in songs, ballads, broadsheets, and penny pamphlets intended for "the lowest rabble," the bishop suggests that they can perhaps be turned around as

the scheme of the Cheap Repository unfolds. "If we gain any of these mis-
creants to our side," he suggests, "we shall have a most respectable set of
booksellers to dispose of our works in town and country, from the most eminent dealer in small wares in Paternoster Row, to the vendor of cards and
matches at Cowslip Green. It would," he adds, "be a most edifying spectacle
to see this ragged regiment all drawn up there together, and chanting forth
our admirable compositions to the astonished villagers, with their ballads
and last dying words."[45]

Little wonder that conservatives found the seditious songs and ballads
so alarming and in need of a counterinsurgent response. *The Life, Death,
and Wonderful Atchievements* [sic] *of Edmund Burke: A New Ballad*, published in 1792, for example, mocks that statesman in classic ballad form
(e.g., "Far different arms did he employ / Than those our soldiers wield /
His dagger was an argument / And sophistry his shield").[46] John Thelwall
wrote *John Gilpin's Ghost; or, the Warning Voice of King Chanticleer: An
Historical Ballad*, while still in Beaufort Buildings, and published it in 1795,
on the occasion of the (third) acquittal of Daniel Isaac Eaton on a charge of
sedition, for having, among other things, published a speech by Thelwall
himself. It also sticks to a four-line form (e.g., "'Twas at the solemn hour of
night, / When all lay still in bed;—/ Except the Swinish Multitude, / Who
grunt for lack of bread").[47] The anonymous *Ballad of the French Revolution*,
to be sung to the tune of "Ça Ira" and published on Bastille Day 1791, also
uses a four-line form (e.g., "The soldiers to a man forsook / The tyrant's
cause, and changing station / With fellow citizens partook / The joy of a de-
livered nation," and "The king and queen were still too lofty / To stomach
any degradation; / And laid a plan to scamper off to / Metz, and rebel against
the nation").[48] Many of the radical songs and ballads from the 1790s are de-
posited today in the United Kingdom National Archives, having been collected by spies working for the government or prosecutors preparing legal
cases against radicals.

Many of the London radicals—especially those at the lower end of the
social spectrum—were as interested in transgressing literary and aesthetic
formulas and boundaries as they were in challenging political ones, and often
for the same reasons. They did this precisely by drawing on popular cultural
traditions and giving them renewed political currency, as well as by appropriating themes from what might otherwise have remained an elite preserve
of literary meditation. Poetry was, in other words, an essential component of
the radical political culture of the 1790s. Thelwall himself contributed various pieces to LCS gatherings and publications, in addition to composing and
publishing his own independent work, which thus embodied a link between

popular culture and popular politics on the one hand, and a somewhat more sophisticated audience on the other, driven by a very different set of motivations than those driving Percy. Thelwall's work, and in particular *The Peripatetic*—which appeared five years before *Lyrical Ballads*, at a time when Thelwall was still very heavily involved in radical politics—was not only a major influence on Wordsworth. As a self-declared experiment itself, *The Peripatetic* offered a valuable example of the ways in which a literary work could genuinely, even passionately, seek to engage the concerns of the common people without necessarily seeking to take advantage of them—and to repackage them as aesthetic objects in the way that Percy did. Thelwall's work was thus a potent reminder that Ritson was hardly the only one in the 1790s to see the vital possibilities inherent in an engagement with what some regarded as unpleasantly—or perhaps even dangerously—"vulgar," even though Thelwall was more invested in individual rights than someone like Spence and hence closer to the imperatives of Occidentalism.

Clearly, in the politically charged atmosphere of the 1790s, anyone with a penchant for the genuinely low and vulgar would have preferred Ritson's collections to Percy's. And no matter how disingenuous they might actually have been, Wordsworth's apologies to "readers of superior judgment" and his excuses for having "descended too low" need to be read in the context of that atmosphere. Although Wordsworth would later—once his political apostasy had been confirmed—express his preference for Percy, his protestations in the 1798 Advertisement to *Lyrical Ballads* could certainly be seen to place him on the side of Ritson, the low, and the vulgar. This is especially notable given the fact that Wordsworth moved in many of the same circles as Ritson all the way through the 1790s, sharing with him a common publisher in Joseph Johnson, common friends or at least common associates in Southey and Coleridge—as well as John Thelwall—and of course common interests in the common people, not to mention radical politics. Moreover, Wordsworth owned at least three copies of Ritson's works: the 1791 edition of *Pieces of Ancient Popular Poetry*; the 1790 edition of *Ancient Songs, From the Time of King Henry the Third to the Revolution*, inscribed by Ritson on the title page; and the 1783 edition of *A Select Collection of English Songs* (the one with the illustrations by Blake) published by Joseph Johnson, also inscribed by Ritson himself.[49] So although he may have complained about the "trash infesting the magazines," Wordsworth knew full well that to some readers *Lyrical Ballads* might look like more of the kind of material that Ritson was interested in, for political as well as aesthetic purposes, if not the kind of material that had been circulating at political meetings or in journals such as Spence's *Pigs' Meat*, and some of the early reviewers did not hesitate to point this out, chiding him, for instance, for copying "the rudest effusions of our vulgar ballads."[50]

Moreover, just as Ritson's challenge to Percy was at once political and aesthetic, Wordsworth's claim that *Lyrical Ballads* seeks to challenge what he calls, elsewhere in the 1798 Advertisement, the "pre-established codes of decision" of the late eighteenth century involves a racial and civilizational as well as a political and an aesthetic claim—and hence it is in these terms that it must be understood. After all, in claiming to descend from the elevated heights of the lyric to the conversational language of the lower classes and the ballads of "our elder writers," *Lyrical Ballads* claims, or seems, to cross the shifting and not yet stabilized racial line between the settled and the wanderers.[51] Such a project also had unmistakable political implications in the late 1790s, as the government crackdown on radical activity (and in particular on any possible alliances between educated and uneducated reformers) was reaching its inevitable conclusion, for example, with the final suppression of the London Corresponding Society in 1798–99.

It was not a coincidence that that crackdown had also been directed at ballads, not just at political activity in the narrower sense of that term. The ballad form was beginning to carry with it not only "vulgar" cultural associations but also a deepening association with one strand of radical politics. Indeed, suppressing that strand of radicalism came to mean suppressing that "vulgar" culture as well: the one went with the other. In his unpublished notes on popular balladry in late eighteenth-century London, Francis Place (of the LCS) points out the heady mixture of obscenity, celebration of criminal activity, and political subversion conveyed in these ballads, and he gives plenty of examples. "The following songs and specimens of songs, are all of them from ballads, bawld [*sic*] about the streets, and hung against the walls. It will seem incredible that such songs should be allowed but it was so," he adds. "There was not one of them that I have not myself heard sung in the streets, as well as at Choir Clubs, Cock & Hen Clubs & Free & Easy's."[52] Among many other samples, he offers an example from the popular obscene song "Morgan Rattler," which goes, "First, he niggled her, then he tiggled her / Then with his two balls he began for to batter her / At every thrust, I thought she'd have burst / With the terrible size of his Morgan Rattler."[53] As morality came to serve as a marker not merely of political respectability but also of racial identity, a line begins to develop from the 1790s through the first half of the nineteenth century, ending up in Mayhew's understanding of the ballad as a reflection of "the same insensibility to female honour and abuse of female weakness, and the same utter ignorance of the Divine nature of the Godhead as marks either Bosjesman, Carib, or Thug."[54] This developing moral, political, and racial understanding of the plebeian ballad involved locating it on the wrong side of gradually settling class and racial fault lines.

Given this, it was hardly any surprise that ballads were frequently attacked by the spokesmen of respectable society all through this period. Place quotes, for example, the Bishop of London complaining about "the infamous and obscene songs and ballads that are openly sung in our public streets, to the great uneasiness of all modest virtuous persons who are passing by, to the great corruption and depravity of our servants and children and to the total discouragement of virtue among the common people in general."[55] Place notes that, from the early 1790s on, popular ballads started coming under intense political pressure from above—not merely for their obscenity but also for their political content—and were ultimately severely curtailed. "The causes of their being discontinued to be sung are various, among them, a more active Police," notes Place. "The Association against Republicans and Levelers also contributed to their end," he adds. "The Association printed a large number of what they called Loyal songs, and gave them to the ballad singers; if any one was found singing any but loyal songs, he or she was carried before a magistrate who admonished him or her, and they were then told they might have loyal songs for nothing, and that they would not be molested while singing them. Thus the bawdy songs and those in praise of thieving and getting drunk were pushed out of existence."[56]

Increasingly, songs—ballads in particular—were being monitored by the government during the surveillance and crackdown on radical activities in the 1790s; in the treason trials of the mid-1790s they counted as evidence of potentially seditious behavior as well. In the cross-examination of Lorriman Goddard—a member of the London Corresponding Society—during the trial for high treason of the LCS Secretary Thomas Hardy, the prosecution was especially interested in the role of songs at LCS meetings. Goddard was repeatedly asked about a song called "God Save the Rights of Man," and another with the chorus, "Plant, plant the tree, fair freedom's tree." He was also asked about the songs of John Thelwall—three of which were printed on one sheet and distributed around the country—which Goddard admitted he owned. "I have them all, and never thought there was any harm in them," Goddard answered. "Do you mean to swear that you thought there was no harm in Thelwall's songs; be so good as to tell us the name of some of them?" replied the prosecutor. After being further pressed, asked to identify song titles, lines, and so on, Goddard retorts, "I am no ballad singer."[57]

4. WORDSWORTH AND THE COMMON

These, then, were the circumstances in which Wordsworth decided to approach the ballad, even as it was beginning to acquire the cultural, political, moral, and racial baggage that the coming century would impose on it. How, then, are we to evaluate Wordsworth's attitude toward the common people of England, of whom he is often taken to be a champion? His attitude may not be exactly what it seems to be at face value. It is true, of course, that much of his poetry, especially the early poetry (notably *Lyrical Ballads*, but also the early variants of the Salisbury Plain poems dating from the mid-1790s), develops a very positive and sympathetic portrait of the common people. And there are various notes and prefaces—most famously the Fenwick notes—in which he also indicates sympathy for marginalized people (such as the Old Cumberland Beggar). We know that, wherever they lived, the Wordsworths were constantly exposed to a stream of beggars and vagrants, who were, as Mary Moorman points out, "a source of interest and often compassion for the Wordsworths; Dorothy's descriptions of them in her Journal were not infrequently used by Wordsworth as the material for a poem."[58] No doubt there were, as Moorman suggests, real-life inspirations for the Old Cumberland Beggar, the Female Vagrant, the Leech-Gatherer, the discharged soldier of *The Prelude*, and so on. I don't doubt the sincerity of Wordsworth's sympathies for the human detritus of the era of post-Speenhamland industrialization and global warfare so elaborated in, for example, David Simpson's recent book on Wordsworth.[59]

However, the question here is not the sincerity of Wordsworth's feelings for the people but rather the structures and conditions of possibility for his encounters with them as an aspiring, educated—"civilized"—middle-class poet and writer: as someone who tended to give them voice in poetry. It is interesting, in fact, that Wordsworth's depictions of the common people are found predominantly in his poetry (and various appended notes and prefaces), rather than in other forms of writing, which tend to be remarkably silent on the question of the people—or at least silent in comparison with the profound visibility and importance of the common people in the poetry he was writing at the same time. Based on what one finds in *Lyrical Ballads*, one would expect to find Wordsworth's other writings brimming with concern for the common people, but that is not exactly the case.

With William Mathews he considered at one point in the mid-1790s launching a monthly magazine, *The Philanthropist*, the principal focus of which, Wordsworth said, ought to be "life and manners," in order "to make our publication a vehicle of sound and exalted Morality."[60] Manners and morals and instruction to "the people" formed a major part of Wordsworth's conception of the magazine, which he hoped would help offset the extent to which "the multitude walk in darkness."[61] The magazine project was never realized, however, and the language of Wordsworth's depictions of "the people" in these letters, as a formless mass to be instructed and illuminated, suggests a very different Wordsworth—a more "conventional" radical from the period (there is no such thing of course, but I mean in general one closer to the reforming spirit of Thelwall, Hone, Carlile, and Place)—than the one who actually developed.

In the end, Wordsworth chose not to take the well-trodden path of the radical reformer, which, for all its difficulties, was open to him in the early to mid-1790s, when what he would later refer to as "the jacobinical pathos" was still upon him.[62] He restricted his representations of the common people to poetry which was never intended for them to read, and in his poetry—as literary characters speaking what Connell and Leask identify, via Jon Klancher, as a deterritorialized lower-class vernacular, "removed from the actual vernacular of rural Britain, while at the same time 'all but inaccessible to the middle-class mind'"[63]—they became objects of greater sentiment and affection than were afforded to them in real life, just as the Scottish Highlanders got more sympathy in the pages of *Waverley* than in the hills and glens of their homeland itself.[64]

In "Michael," Wordsworth writes in a letter to Thomas Poole, "I have attempted to give a picture of a man, of strong mind and lively sensibility, agitated by two of the most powerful affections of the human heart; the parental affection, and the love of property, *landed* property, including the feelings of inheritance, home, and personal and family independence."[65] The poem, he adds, "has, I know, drawn tears from the eyes of more than one, persons well acquainted with the manners of the 'Statesmen, as they are called, of this country; and, moreover, persons who never wept, in reading verse, before." The character of Michael turns out not to be all that common in the end, in Wordsworth's imagination of him, as he was partly modeled on Poole himself, who, as a wealthy merchant, was hardly one of the common people.[66] In any case, in the period after the publication of *Lyrical Ballads*, Wordsworth's references in his letters to the common people tend actually to be references to the characters inhabiting his volume, rather than to the people themselves: the characters come to stand in for and to replace their actual counterparts.

And in combing through the thick volume of Wordsworth's letters from

1770 through the period of the composition of *Lyrical Ballads*, I found only
one explicit reference to the common people—and not a very sympathetic
one at that. "We are now at Racedown and both as happy as people can be
who live in perfect solitude," Wordsworth wrote to Mathews in October
1795. "We do not see a soul. Now and then we meet a miserable peasant
in the road or an accidental traveller. The country people here are wretch-
edly poor; ignorant and overwhelmed with every vice that usually attends
ignorance in that class, viz—lying and picking and stealing &c &c."[67] Dorothy's assessment was not dissimilar. "The peasants are miserably poor; their
cottages are shapeless structures (I may almost say) of wood and clay," she
writes to Mrs. John Marshall in November 1795; "indeed they are not at all
beyond what might be expected in savage life."[68]

As I pointed out in the Introduction and in chapter 1, "savages" are precisely what a reasonably sophisticated middle-class English writer would
expect to see when surveying the lower orders of his (or her) own country in
the late eighteenth or early nineteenth century. Just as in other work from
the period, such as Godwin's *Caleb Williams* (which I discussed in the Introduction), we can see plebeian characters distributed across a wide racial
spectrum, so that sometimes the plebeian characters inhabiting Wordsworth's poetry from the 1790s—especially, but not only, *Lyrical Ballads*—
are identifiably like "us," and at other times they are permanently other:
unassimilable into Occidentalizing modernity, almost impervious to conversational interaction, if not totally oblivious to the very presence of the
narrating self. And sometimes, as we will see in the next section of this
chapter, those characters go through changes, moving along this racial spectrum, as Wordsworth revised his poetry in later years.

Wordsworth's attitude to the common people of England and their cultural and political forms was (however sympathetic it may have been) on
the same wavelength as the Orientalist's attitude toward his Oriental objects of representation (Orientalists could also be sympathetic to Orientals).
But the kind of cultural and political work in which Wordsworth was engaged was also essential to the formation of a sense of metropolitan Occidentalism—locating a Western space for "us"—against which the unruly
spaces of the Orient could be more effectively juxtaposed. On the one hand,
in other words, Wordsworth treats the common people as though they were
cultural and racial Others; on the other hand, he participates in the project
that, by ultimately serving to defuse the sense of radical alterity at home—
incorporating plebeian England into a Western "us"—would make Africans,
Arabs, Indians, and Muslims all the more Other to England. This reminds
us of the extent to which Occidentalism and Orientalism were necessary to

each other, they reinforce each other and must be understood together, not separately, as has so far been done.

5. OTHER CONSCIOUSNESS

With all this contextualization in place, it is now time to return to the poetry. I will get back to the "Female Vagrant" shortly, but first I want to consider another piece, a poem that first appeared in the 1798 edition of *Lyrical Ballads* as "Old Man Travelling; Animal Tranquillity and Decay, a Sketch":

> The little hedge-row birds,
> That peck along the road, regard him not.
> He travels on, and in his face, his step,
> His gait, is one expression; every limb,
> His look and bending figure, all bespeak
> A man who does not move with pain, but moves
> With thought—He is insensibly subdued
> To settled quiet: he is one by whom
> Long patience has such mild composure given,
> That patience now doth seem a thing, of which
> He hath no need. He is by nature led
> To peace so perfect, that the young behold
> With envy, what the old man hardly feels.
> —I asked him whither he was bound, and what
> The object of his journey; he replied
> "Sir! I am going many miles to take
> A last leave of my son, a mariner,
> Who from a sea-fight has been brought to Falmouth,
> And there is dying in an hospital."

In the first few lines, the old man is really more of an object than a subject, so pushed into the landscape that the transfer of agency to the birds and away from the human object seems naturalized—even the birds themselves have no regard for him. Once communication begins, it is conducted not in a verbal register but rather in a visual one, and in terms of object appearances: the expression is not in the man's speech but rather in his look; there is no speaking but rather "bespeaking," speaking of or for, which is done not by the man himself but by the look of his gait, limbs, and figure. The old man's meanings are not internal, in what he speaks, in other words,

but rather external, in what can be said about him, how he can be read—by
us. If he does not move with pain, but rather with thought, that is because
really he is not the one moving: he merely enables the movement of others
(it is in thinking of him that *we* are moved).

Even in emotional terms the old man has no agency: he has been sub-
dued insensibly, or without any conscious effort on his part; if he is composed, it is not because of his own will but because long patience—itself
abstracted from the man and endowed with its own autonomous agency—
has composed him. Such movement as he is capable of making is not of his
own motivation but rather that of the nature by which he is merely *led*.
And to underscore the extent to which the visual field has here supplanted
the verbal—this is "a sketch," after all—lines 12 and 13 remind us that
this is a poem all about looking and seeing the other: the young *behold*
what the old man hardly feels. David Bromwich suggests that the young
see in the old man "the image of a tranquillity that may have nothing to do
with his experience of himself."[69] There's another way of putting this contradiction, however: they see and register visually the pain that is so hard
("*hardly* feels," like the "hardly paining" of "An Evening Walk"; that is, the
hardship and pain are palpable) that the old man hardly *feels* it; again, he
does not move with pain, but rather with thought, because thinking of and
visually recognizing the pain of which he remains insensible moves others;
what consciousness is at work here is in the viewing subjects (the speaker,
the audience), not the object viewed (the old man).

The poem's ending reveals that our reading of the visual cues provided
by the old man's body is actually a misreading: the false narrative of composure, patience, and a perfect peace is supplanted by the verbalization of suffering, sorrow, and a very imperfect war. Thus the intrusion of the old man's
voice contradicts and disrupts the narrative that the speaker has, with our
complicity, imposed on him. And in that self-interpellating gesture, the old
man resolves the contradiction between viewing subject and viewed object
and removes himself from the realm of the objectified and naturalized Other,
thrusting himself into a commonality with us, his middle-class readers: he is
capable of speech, after all—and not just vulgar plebeian speech, but clean,
proper, polite, English.[70] So complete is the integration between old man and
audience at the end that a reply on the part of the speaker would be altogether redundant: having been absorbed into the scene of his suffering, what
response could possibly be appropriate, other than contemplative silence?
The mediating speaker disappears, in fact, leaving us, the audience, alone
with the old man, who is now addressing us directly, speaking out of the
pages of the volume: the "Sir!" bypassing the absent narrator and aimed di-

rectly at the reader. And it is in that awkward directness that we realize the total misreading of the previous fourteen lines with which we had unwittingly gone along. The reason why the old man departs from the impervious shell of otherness is that he is able to resist the narrative that had been imposed on him by providing a counternarrative that demonstrates consciousness. Lack of contradiction by the other—because the other does not speak at all—is here a condition of possibility for that very otherness: by talking back, the other loses his constitutive otherness. In speaking, he is indeed no longer other after all.

As Wordsworth revised the poem over successive editions, he gradually reversed the narrative and political energy of the 1798 version of "Old Man Travelling," and the self-reflection that it enables, first by removing the old man's direct speech and absorbing it into the speaker's own—so that what the old man says is mediated by the speaker—and then by eliminating it altogether. The version of the poem included in the 1800 edition of *Lyrical Ballads* is retitled "Animal Tranquillity and Decay, a Sketch," the title retained by all later editions:

> The little hedge-row birds,
> That peck along the road, regard him not.
> He travels on, and in his face, his step,
> His gait, is one expression; every limb,
> His look and bending figure, all bespeak
> A man who does not move with pain, but moves
> With thought—He is insensibly subdued
> To settled quiet: he is one by whom
> Long patience has such mild composure given,
> That patience now doth seem a thing, of which
> He hath no need. He is by nature led
> To peace so perfect, that the young behold
> With envy, what the old man hardly feels.
> —I asked him whither he was bound, and what
> The object of his journey; he replied
> That he was going many miles to take
> A last leave of his son, a mariner,
> Who from a sea-fight had been brought to Falmouth,
> And there was lying in an hospital.

Here, the directness of the old man's speech is contained: its paraphrasing in the speaker's words breaks the immediacy of the link enabled by the end

of the 1798 version between his speech and the momentarily stunned audience that is left to digest what it is forced to acknowledge as its incapacity for knowing the Other and the awkwardness of the fact of having been
taken in and gone along for the sentimental ride (in the previous fourteen
lines), of the misreading of the "bespeaking" enabled by the old man's appearance. Nevertheless, even if it is mediated, the final six lines still serve
to abruptly correct the misreading of the previous fourteen.

In the final state of the poem, from 1815 on, however, Wordsworth removed the old man's speech altogether:

> The little hedge-row birds,
> That peck along the road, regard him not.
> He travels on, and in his face, his step,
> His gait, is one expression; every limb,
> His look and bending figure, all bespeak
> A man who does not move with pain, but moves
> With thought—He is insensibly subdued
> To settled quiet: he is one by whom
> Long patience hath such mild composure given,
> That patience now doth seem a thing, of which
> He hath no need. He is by nature led
> To peace so perfect, that the young behold
> With envy, what the Old Man hardly feels.

Removing the old man's corrective, whether contained in paraphrase or
spoken directly, prevents him from breaking out of his otherness. What is
revealed to be a misreading of the old man's bespeaking in the previous versions of the poem goes without correction in this version. His consciousness—if that is even what it is—is now quite impermeable, sealed off and
inaccessible to us. The other notable change in this state of the poem is the
capitalization of Old Man, which serves to reinforce the imperviousness of
his consciousness: that "old man" had gone uncapitalized in the previous
states of the poem had actually made him seem more accessible somehow:
he is just an old man.

The combination of his silence in the final state of the poem, together
with the capitals, makes him seem that much more iconic and hence de-
individualized. He is more a representative of a certain state than he is an
individual human being with a discrete consciousness. And he is inscrutable, unreadable; or rather he can be read, and meanings can be projected
on to him, without any risk of correction and awkwardness should the read-

ing turn out to be false after all. Thus, if in the earlier state of the poem the concluding lines resolve the tension between what the young observe and what the man hardly feels, in the final state not only is there is no such resolution, there is even the sense that the Old Man may feel nothing at all because to feel is to have consciousness, and it's not clear that that is something he possesses or is capable of. Or if he does possess it, it is a form of consciousness that necessarily remains cut off from us.

In this final state, the Old Man merges much more fully with the Old Cumberland Beggar, with whom he had once been associated (the two poems were first drafted at around the same time in the mid-1790s and may have been thought of as parts of a larger whole; "Old Cumberland Beggar" would appear in the second volume of the 1800 edition of *Lyrical Ballads*).[71] The Beggar is completely impervious to us; to the extent that he has an interiority at all—which is doubtful at best—it is glimpsed only in outward gestures, and hence it remains something that is imposed on his body from the outside, rather than derived the other way around, as the outer manifestation of an inner consciousness. When we first encounter him, he is sitting by the roadside:

> The aged man
> Had placed his staff across the broad smooth stone
> That overlays the pile, and from a bag
> All white with flour, the dole of village dames,
> He drew his scraps and fragments, one by one,
> And scann'd them with a fix'd and serious look
> Of idle computation.

Juxtaposed in this way, the "fix'd and serious" and "idle," which represent the opposite poles of the same spectrum, cancel each other out: the possibility of inner consciousness is negated as surely as it is raised as a possibility. As he shuffles along the road,

> On the ground
> His eyes are turn'd, and, as he moves along,
> *They* move along the ground; and evermore,
> Instead of common and habitual sight
> Of fields with rural works, of hill and dale,
> And the blue sky, one little span of earth
> Is all his prospect. Thus, from day to day.
> Bowbent, his eyes for ever on the ground,

He plies his weary journey, seeing still,
And never knowing that he sees, some straw,
Some scatter'd leaf, or marks which, in one track,
The nails of cart or chariot wheel have left
Impress'd on the white road, in the same line,
At distance still the same.

Not only does the Beggar seem not to have any control of his body (here,
his eyes seem, so to speak, to have a mind of their own; in an earlier passage, his "palsied hand," rather than he himself, is "baffled" in its—rather
than his—attempt to keep half his meal from falling on the ground). He
is at once cut off from the common sights of our shared world and from
our temporality (Roman chariot and eighteenth-century cart are much the
same for him)—indeed from the possibility of coevalness which is necessary
to communication among equals.[72] At no point does anyone actually enter
into conversation with the Beggar; the locals see in him what they want
to, which has nothing to do with his own agency—"the Villagers in him /
Behold a record which together binds / Past deeds and offices of charity /
Else unremembered") just as the young see in the Old Man Travelling what
he may himself be utterly oblivious to. "Most of the poem's readers will be
alert, articulate, and sociable; the beggar is none of these," David Simpson
observes. "Nothing in the beggar as a person *in himself* reflects or validates
our images of ourselves. He has no inner life—or none that is apparent to
the observer."[73] He is "a silent monitor," in the same way that a mirror is,
involuntarily reflecting back to you what you project into it. Insofar as he
has any consciousness at all (which is doubtful), it's certainly not a form of
consciousness that can be translated into the modern idiom with which the
readers of the poem are familiar and comfortable.

Dipesh Chakrabarty sees a similar tension recurring in the historiography of colonial India. One of the dilemmas noted by Chakrabarty has to do
with the question of how to convey subaltern rebels' own understanding of
their own relationship to the historical events in which they participate.
How, for instance, can one reconcile the fact that a rebel group might ascribe agency for their rebellion to a god with, on the other hand, the historian's desire to represent the rebels as historical agents in their own right? "A
narrative strategy that is rationally defensible in the modern understanding of what constitutes public life—and the historians speak in the public
sphere—cannot be based on a relationship that allows the divine or the
supernatural a direct hand in the affairs of the world," Chakrabarty argues.
"Historians will grant the supernatural a place in somebody's belief system

or ritual practices, but to ascribe to it any real agency in historical events will be [to] go against the rules of evidence that gives historical discourse procedures for settling disputes about the past."[74] Such subaltern pasts, as Chakrabarty calls them, cannot really be translated into conventional academic history.[75]

A similar dilemma occurs throughout Wordsworth's poetry of the 1790s, though the desire there is not to convey plebeian pasts into academic history but instead the desire to convey plebeian consciousness (or what seems to be that consciousness) into poetic modernity. This incommensurability and at least partial untranslatability comes up most explicitly in "Old Man Travelling," "The Old Cumberland Beggar," and "The Female Vagrant," but it is also there in poems such as "Lines Left Upon a Yew-Tree," "The Thorn," and "We Are Seven," where the frustrated narrator realizes that "'Twas throwing words away" to try to persuade the little girl that there is a difference between counting the living and the dead, and that there is therefore a fundamental irreconcilable difference between her irrational way of accounting for her siblings and his way of doing so.

One of the most interesting versions of this occurs in "Simon Lee," where, having given the prehistory of Simon Lee and his wife Ruth, the narrator interrupts himself:

My gentle reader, I perceive
How patiently you've waited,
And I'm afraid that you expect
Some tale will be related.

O reader! had you in your mind
Such stores as silent thought can bring,
O gentle reader! you would find
A tale in every thing.
What more I have to say is short,
I hope you'll kindly take it;
It is no tale; but should you think,
Perhaps a tale you'll make it.

The mediation here explicitly enlists the reader as well as narrative voice of the poem itself. The raw experience goes through two layers of translation, one from oral expression into narrative poetry and a second when that poetry is turned into a tale by conscripting the efforts of the reader herself. A mere experience is not a poem; a mere poem is not a tale—it has to be

made into a tale by the intervention of the reader. Just as the plebeian character offers the raw experience to the narrator, the narrator in turn offers the
poem to the reader: "I hope you'll kindly take it," the "kindly take" functioning like the "hardly feels" of Old Man Travelling: take it *kindly*; take
it kindly. The effect of all this is to reinforce the distinction between plebeian experience and the textualization of that experience in poetry or tales.
There is a kind of structural causality at work here: plebeian experience is
not a text, not a narrative, but, as an absent cause, it is inaccessible to us
except in textual form, and our approach to it necessarily passes through its
prior textualization, its narrativization.[76]

"The Female Vagrant," in particular, conveys the gap between plebeian
experience and its narrativization in poetry in a formal dimension as well
as in a thematic one, emphasizing the gap even further. It is the only poem
in the 1798 *Lyrical Ballads* that appears in Spenserian stanzas, a form not
at all typically associated with Wordsworth (though it would be adopted
by later Romantic poets, notably Keats, Byron, and Shelley). So the stanza
form associated with Spenser's great epic of British state formation and imperial power in *The Faerie Queene* is here deployed to convey the travails
of a forsaken and broken woman who is, like others of her class, paying
the price for the expansion of the very same empire whose emergence is
celebrated by Spenser. On the one hand this represents Wordsworth's brilliantly ironic subversion of one of the grand forms of imperial epic in Britain; on the other hand, though, as I said, it actually pushes the Female Vagrant further into the background of her own story, adding yet another layer
of poetic mediation between her experience and its appearance in textual
form apprehensible to a middle-class reading audience. So while, unlike
the Old Cumberland Beggar or the final version of the Old Man Travelling,
the Female Vagrant does get to speak, any possible sense of authenticity is
dashed not only by the high poetic language she uses ("finny flood," "fleecy
store," etc.) but by the layers of formal intermediation in which it is contained. Her story may once have been "artless," but it is available to us only
in the refined language and the high poetic formalism of a work of art into
which it has been translated.

Such a contradiction is addressed at length in Pier Paolo Pasolini's essay
on free indirect discourse, where he argues that the question of consciousness is bound up with and quite inseparable from the question of language
itself.[77] How, for example, can an author writing in a "high" literary language depict the consciousness and inner thoughts of a character from a
"low" cultural background? This dilemma is especially obvious in the Ital-

ian context, of course, with its distinction between dialect and the national language (itself also internally stratified), or Arabic, with its sharp distinction between written and spoken forms, but it is entirely relevant in English as well.

What makes this more interesting still is that "The Female Vagrant" as it appears in *Lyrical Ballads* is but an excerpt from a much longer poem which started out in manuscript form in 1793–94 as "Salisbury Plain" and, continually revised over the intervening years—via an intermediate manuscript state from 1795–99 called "Adventures on Salisbury Plain"—would finally be published in 1843 as "Guilt and Sorrow; or Incidents Upon Salisbury Plain."[78] In those longer works, the story of the Female Vagrant is woven into a longer narrative—also written in Spenserian stanzas—involving a vagrant man, who becomes, in the later versions of the poem, an ex-soldier, returned from colonial service and guilty of committing a terrible crime, though under extenuating circumstances (having been driven to it by social and political circumstances, above all his neglect at the hands of the government he had recently served). In those longer poems, when the Female Vagrant begins her own narrative (line 226 of "Salisbury Plain" and line 199 of "Guilt and Sorrow"), her speech is directed toward the vagrant man, so that it has an audience within the frame of the larger poem itself. When it is transposed to a stand-alone poem as "The Female Vagrant," that internal referencing gets cut off, of course.

So there's a kind of substitution, among and between versions of the poem, of the audience for her narrative: sometimes she is talking to a fellow vagrant, and sometimes directly to the middle-class reader (albeit with the mediation I have already pointed out). This raises the question not only of whether the plebeian can speak, but whether she can hear as well, and whether there is a difference—for Wordsworth, for this is of course unavailable to the reader who lacks access to all the versions of the poem—between her telling her story to one of her own kind, so to speak, and telling it to a middle-class reading audience. That the plebeian *can* hear is in fact one of the themes of the larger poems, especially "Guilt and Sorrow," where there are several tellings and re-tellings among the plebeian characters. But the other thing that happens in the transposition from the larger frame poem to the stand-alone version of "The Female Vagrant" is that the quotation is cut off—the whole shorter poem *is* a quotation contained by a longer poem, after all—and with it the quotation marks. In "Salisbury Plain," her narrative begins "'By Derwent's side my father's cottage stood,' / The mourner thus her artless story told." In "Guilt and Sorrow," her speech is framed in

the previous stanza ("The Woman thus retraced her own untoward fate")
and her speech begins a new stanza, "By Derwent's side my father dwelt—a
man / Of virtuous life, by pious parents bred."

In presenting her speech to the reader of *Lyrical Ballads*, then, Wordsworth even further complicates the question of who possesses and controls
the narrative and that of to whom it is directed, given the substitution of a
real middle-class reading audience for the fictional plebeian audience in the
longer versions of the poem. A similar substitution takes place among the
characters of the longer poem. After a kind of reflective preface, the narrative opens with a weary traveler—an old vagrant bearing a distinct resemblance to Old Man Travelling and the Old Cumberland Beggar—crossing
Salisbury Plain: "O'er Sarum's plain the traveller with a sigh / Measured
each painful step, the distant spire / That fixed at every turn his backward
eye." In the intermediary manuscript version of 1795–99, however, the traveler we encounter at the beginning is not the old vagrant, but a middle-class
man (some version of Wordsworth perhaps, given that the poem was partly
inspired by his own forced walk across Salisbury Plain in 1793 after an ac-
cident disabled the carriage in which he had been traveling with his friend
Calvert, who then took off with the horse, leaving Wordsworth to cross the
plain accompanied only by "his firm Friends, a pair of stout legs"):[79]

> A Traveller on the skirt of Sarum's Plain
> O'ertook an aged Man with feet half bare;
> Propp'd on a trembling staff he crept with pain,
> His legs from slow disease distended were;
> His temples just betrayed their silver hair
> Beneath a kerchief's edge, that wrapp'd his head
> To fence from off his face the breathing air,
> Stuck miserably o'er with patch and shred
> His ragged coat scarce showed the Soldier's faded red
>
> "And dost thou hope across this Plain to trail
> That frame o'ercome with years and malady,
> Those feet that scarcely can outcrawl the snail,
> These withered arms of thine, that faltering knee?
> Come, I am strong and stout, come lean on me."
> The old man's a wintry lustre dart,
> And so sustained he faced the open lea.
> But short the joy that touched his melting heart,
> For ere a mile be gone his friend and he must part.

In the final, published version of "Guilt and Sorrow," however, the young healthy interlocutor is again removed, and the "Traveller" with whom the scene opens is once again the old vagrant, without a companion again.

> A Traveller on the skirt of Sarum's Plain
> Pursued his vagrant way, with feet half bare;
> Stooping his gait, but not as if to gain
> Help from the staff he bore; for mien and air
> Were hardy, though his cheek seemed worn with care
> Both of the time to come, and time long fled:
> Down fell in straggling locks his thin grey hair;
> A coat he wore of military red
> But faded, and stuck o'er with many a patch and shred.

The striking thing about these modifications to the poem is not simply the substitution of the position of the Traveller on the plain, who, in different versions of the poem is either the old vagrant or a distinctly more privileged voyager—as I said, quite possibly a stand-in for Wordsworth himself—who encounters the old vagrant, but the fact that that substitution registers again the question that Wordsworth is so consistently concerned with in his early poetry, namely, encounters with plebeian experience.[80] This also frames the stand-alone version of "The Female Vagrant" and circles back to the question of whether the plebeian can speak, and, if so, to whom, and under what circumstances and forms of mediation.

In all these cases, unlike "Old Cumberland Beggar" or the later versions of "Old Man Travelling" (i.e., "Animal Tranquillity and Decay"), an encounter takes place between two different forms of subjectivity, and we seem to gain access to a plebeian experience—but at the price of having that experience mediated, and, indeed, of having that mediation call attention to itself, itself become one of the themes of the poetry, even take over the poetry.

This is important because what *Lyrical Ballads* and the poems connected to it (including the Salisbury Plain poems) consistently return to is the idea that the condition of possibility for accessing plebeian experience is that it cannot be rendered on its own terms: it has to be translated into more familiar, more refined terms: the vulgar ballad transformed into—or at least merged with—the ode and the Spenserian epic. The common or vulgar characters that we encounter in these poems can't be represented on their own terms, in other words; they have to be translated into modern, civilized terms; they can speak, but on condition that their collective experience is translated into individual terms. In giving these plebeian characters voice and agency, then—in conveying the trauma of the loss of the collectively structured life-world to which they had all once belonged—Wordsworth is at the same time canceling out the very otherness that he seems to be merely representing. In order for us to be able to identify with these characters who express the violent loss, the forcible destruction of a former social system—and is that not what ties together the plebeian characters of *Lyrical Ballads*?—they have to be not only assimilable to modern terms of reference: they actually have to be like "us," civilized Occidental individuals, not a savage collective.

So while, on the one hand, *Lyrical Ballads* seeks to contest and to resist "the multitude of causes unknown to former times"[81] that were, in the years around 1800, wreaking havoc on whatever still remained of a recognizably precapitalist culture in which individuals were bound together and given identity in a rooted collective existence, on the other hand, the volume and its associated poems participate in the very same process of transformation: in order to be able to record the loss, they have to perpetuate it. In just this sense they replicate the forcible extraction of individual from collective identity that was central to that transformation and to that loss: it was in many ways its defining feature. "To separate labor from other activities of life and to subject it to the laws of the market was to annihilate all organic forms of existence and to replace them by a different type of organization, an atomistic and individualistic one," Polanyi argues. "Now what the white man may still occasionally practice in remote regions today [1940], namely, the smashing up of social structures in order to extract the element of labor from them, was done in the eighteenth century to white populations by white men for similar purposes."[82] The new social system based on the principle of the self-regulating individual could only brought about by the destruction of the previous social system, in order, as Polanyi puts it, to release the individual from its grip and subject him or her, as the bearer of labor power, to a new economy of punishment and incentive. In presenting plebeian characters who can speak only on condition that they speak as recognizably civilized individual subjects, Wordsworth may in one sense be mourning the trauma and loss that led to the individual's release from the grip of an older social system, but at the same time, by privileging individual experience, he is necessarily validating the destruction that led to that traumatic loss in the first place.

It is worth recalling Norbert Elias's point that what he calls the civilizing process crucially involved the transformation not merely of large-scale social and economic systems but also, more intimately, of individual personality structures.[83] When we see a "savage" in *Lyrical Ballads*, it is often a savage already civilized or Occidentalized; or else, like the final "Old Man Travelling" or "Old Cumberland Beggar," it is a savage who is marked as unassimilable into Occidental civilization, permanently Other, its consciousness structurally unavailable to us. The original, 1793, version of "Salisbury Plain," from which "The Female Vagrant" would be extracted for inclusion in *Lyrical Ballads*, actually opens with a meditation on savage life, part of the point of which is to indicate how far England has come from the days when "The hungry savage, 'mid deep forests, roused / By storms, lies down at night on unknown plains / And lifts his head in fear," but the other part of the point of introducing the long narrative poem with a mediation on savage life is that that life persists into Wordsworth's own time. The houseless vagrants we see fearfully encountering each other in a terrific storm on the wild plain are not, in the end, that very different from the "unhouzed" savage of those "unknown plains" after all. This very point comes up in a somewhat different way in Alan Bewell's insightful reading of the anthropological dimension of Wordsworth's early poetry, but whereas Bewell argues that "'savage peoples' generally enter Wordsworth's poetry through displacement and naturalization,"[84] I would argue that that is not necessarily the case, especially not in *Lyrical Ballads*. After all, there we have, mixed in without comment among a series of poems about the degradation of plebeian life in England, "The Complaint of a Forsaken Indian Woman," and she too is given voice in the same terms as the Female Vagrant. "The Complaint" is among the least discussed of Wordsworth's poems, but its very inclusion in the volume—where it otherwise might seem so totally out of place—reconfirms that this is in fact a book all about savage life. We might even say that the ultimate concern of the volume, and of the poems connected to it, is in fact the civilization of savagery.

6. FORMING THE SAVAGE

Ultimately, however, the content of *Lyrical Ballads* can really only be understood with reference to form. "The majority of the following poems are to be considered as experiments," Wordsworth writes in the Advertisement to the volume. "They were written chiefly with a view to ascertain how far the language of conversation in the middle and lower classes of society is adapted to the purposes of poetic pleasure. Readers accustomed to the gaudiness and inane phraseology of many modern writers, if they persist in reading this book to its conclusion, will perhaps frequently have to struggle with feelings of strangeness and aukwardness [*sic*]: they will look round for poetry, and will be induced to enquire by what species of courtesy these attempts can be permitted to assume that title."

Although four decades have passed since E. P. Thompson thought that he could announce the demise of the critical stereotype that "Wordsworth the poet begins at the moment when Wordsworth the politically committed man ends,"[85] I think it's still fair to say that the general perception of *Lyrical Ballads* among historically minded scholars is that it marks the beginning— if not quite the end—of Wordsworth's definitive turn away from politics and into poetry: an expression of what has been taken as his political apostasy.[86] David Bromwich's readings of "Tintern Abbey," "The Old Cumberland Beggar," and other poems offer a sensitive and compelling reconsideration of the depth of Wordsworth's traumatic reappraisal of his own political commitments in the 1790s. David Simpson's recent book *Wordsworth, Commodification and Social Concern* adds further depth to our sense of Wordsworth's continuing engagement with radical and oppositional politics in the 1790s and the poet's "effort to oppose the coming modernity."[87]

In her discussion of *Lyrical Ballads* in her book *Lyric and Labour in the Romantic Tradition*, Anne Janowitz offers a compelling account of the ways in which Wordsworth negotiates the seemingly contradictory relationship between ballad and lyric, which hinges in part on the political affiliations of those forms in the Romantic period, as exemplified by the ways in which the volume's title "emphasizes the closeness and the ineradicable distance between the elite and the popular, traditional and voluntaristic, embedded and unencumbered selves."[88] I want to take the exploration of the relationship between politics and form in a different direction from the one taken by Janowitz, however. And while this chapter has already taken us back to the questions of social concern as registered by Bromwich and Simpson, it will nevertheless take us to a very different conclusion concerning the relationship of Wordsworth's political stance to the new imperial and racial politics unfolding in—and helping to define—the early Romantic period.

A long line of scholarship—going back to the 1950s at least—has sought to discount the experimental claims of *Lyrical Ballads* as a literary venture (that is, its claim to challenge the dominant tastes of its own time) by revealing the extent of its involvement with popular (or at least non-elite) culture, especially with the popular ballad revival of the late eighteenth century. But whereas some of the more explicitly political and historical scholarship on *Lyrical Ballads* has not taken sufficient notice of the poetry's formal and literary affiliations, it seems to me that much of the scholarship on the volume's literary affiliations is insufficiently aware of the political resonance and depth of the very connections that it has so assiduously worked to uncover.

"When first-generation Romantic poets are picked off for individual study," Marilyn Butler warns, "they are removed from their exceptional environment" and hence many of their vital connections to that environment are either oddly foreshortened or cut at the roots.[89] Butler is right: in abstracting Wordsworth's work from its historical and intellectual context, too many modern scholars (including myself) have taken Wordsworth's word at face value when assessing the claims of the 1798 Advertisement to *Lyrical Ballads*, especially the claim that it makes a clean break with the "gaudy and inane" writing of its own time (as Robert Mayo reminds us).

Indeed, in view of the strong affinities between *Lyrical Ballads* and contemporary poetry, Wordsworth's claims for the volume's novelty have been seen by some scholars as a kind of self-serving feint. Alan Boehm points out, for example, that Wordsworth and Coleridge decided to proceed with *Lyrical Ballads*, rather than one of the various other projects they had discussed with the publisher Joseph Cottle in 1797–98, precisely because they thought they would be able to count on its potential marketability and strong sales.[90] Other scholars, however, have downplayed the extent of the overlap between the *Lyrical Ballads* and contemporary middlebrow or popular culture. Mary Jacobus observes that Wordsworth used to complain about "the trash infesting the magazines" and points out that he is unlikely to have tried to emulate them. Despite superficial resemblances, Jacobus argues, the poems of *Lyrical Ballads* "have little but their themes in common with the poetry of the magazines, drawing instead on a more substantial tradition of humane and identified writing."[91]

At this stage of my argument, I don't think that it matters much whether Wordsworth was trying simply to emulate or somehow to go beyond the popular poetry of the 1790s; what matters, rather, is that *Lyrical Ballads* needs to be seen in some kind of relation to those "lower" traditions which were at the time beginning to pick up the kinds of social, political, and racial associations I mentioned earlier, from which Wordsworth had to be careful to distance himself, even while acknowledging how close he was coming to those traditions. "Readers of superior judgment may disapprove of the style in which many of these pieces are executed," Wordsworth writes in the Advertisement. "It must be expected that many lines and phrases will not exactly suit their taste," he continues. "It will perhaps appear to them, that wishing to avoid the prevalent fault of the day, the author has sometimes descended too low, and that many of his expressions are too familiar, and not of sufficient dignity." Whether it descended too low, or just low enough, it ought to be clear that the volume seeks its inspiration from "below," rather than from the literary elite "above."

7. SETTLING THE COMMON

What's most compelling about the context surrounding the origins of *Lyrical Ballads* is that at precisely the moment that Wordsworth has come to be understood by most critics as turning away from politics and into poetry, he chose to turn to a literary form and to cultural pursuits that were themselves coming to be saturated with political, civilizational, and racial significance: hardly a refuge from politics as such, especially for someone who had only shortly earlier declared himself "of that odious class of men called democrats."[92] It seems to me that to publish this kind of material, in this kind of packaging, in this kind of atmosphere, cannot possibly be considered a gesture of political withdrawal.

What is at stake in the politics of the *Lyrical Ballads*, then, is something somewhat more complicated than is captured by Kenneth Johnston's suggestion that Wordsworth's sudden turn to the ballad was as surprising as it would have been had Beethoven, at a similar point in his career, suddenly decided to abandon symphonies and turn to songs and bagatelles; or by E. P. Thompson's suggestion that the volume is the product of political disenchantment rather than of out-and-out defeatism, the kind of apostasy that Coleridge, for his part, would signal with his announcement that "I have snapped my squeaking baby-trumpet of Sedition & the fragments lie scattered in the lumber-room of Penitence. I wish to be a good man & a Christian—but I am no Whig, no Reformist, no Republican."[93]

For, at the very moment at which, by all accounts, Wordsworth was supposed to be reassessing his political commitments, if not withdrawing from them altogether, he turned to this increasingly politically and racially charged literary form and put it to new political and aesthetic uses, or, rather, to an aesthetic use that subsumed and reconfigured politics, including his own prior political commitments.

Here, however, we must attend to various important complications to this argument. For one thing, it is essential to pin down in greater detail the exact nature of the relationship between *Lyrical Ballads* and its contemporary literary environment, including the very material which Wordsworth himself once dismissed as "the trash infesting the magazines." I mentioned earlier that various scholars, including Mary Jacobus, have argued that *Lyrical Ballads* has little in common with that kind of material, which they say Wordsworth would never have been likely to emulate. Linda Venis, however, argues that Wordsworth's ambition was not exactly to imitate, but rather to *reform*, the popular poetry of his day. Noting Wordsworth's long-standing interest in popular ballads (pointing out, for example, that the narrator of *The Prelude* encounters "an English ballad-singer" and "files of ballads" as he winds his way through the streets of London in book 7), Venis quotes from a letter from Wordsworth to Francis Wrangham in which Wordsworth explains his own attitude toward that kind of material. Referring specifically to street poetry, Wordsworth writes, "I have so much felt the influence of these straggling papers, that I have many a time wished that I had talents to produce songs, poems, and little histories, that might circulate among other good things in this way, supplanting partly the bad; flowers and useful herbs to take the place of weeds. Indeed some of the Poems which I have published were composed not without a hope that at some time or other they might answer this purpose."[94] The letter from which Venis quotes is from 1808, a decade after the first publication of *Lyrical Ballads*, by which time Wordsworth's political and literary ambitions had certainly undergone significant further transformations. Even allowing for a certain degree of retrospective embellishment, however, Venis's point that Wordsworth sought to replace popular "weeds" with his own "flowers" is compelling. But whereas Venis reads Wordsworth's retrospective claim in narrowly literary terms, there is a great deal of political significance to the claim as well.

After all, Hannah More's ambition was similarly to supplant plebeian "weeds" with evangelical "flowers" through her own—expressly political—intervention into the popular street literature of the 1790s. For the intention of her Cheap Repository Tracts was to challenge the "infidelity" of the tracts, songs, ballads, broadsides, and chapbooks circulating among the lower orders in the 1790s: precisely the kinds of material in which antiquarians like Ritson were interested—and the kinds of material to which the 1798 Advertisement to *Lyrical Ballads* explicitly invites comparison. "Vulgar and indecent penny books were always common," Hannah More notes in a 1796 letter to Zacharay Macaulay; "but speculative infidelity, brought down to the pockets and capacities of the poor, forms a new era in our history."[95] The peculiar intention of More's scheme, as G. H. Spinney points out, "was that it was designed to meet the enemy on his own ground by the production of tracts and broadsides, in outward appearance as nearly as possible resembling the chapman's wares, at a competitive price." The principal aim of the Cheap Repository Tracts, in other words, "was to compete with, and if possible, to outsell, the street ballad."[96] More's endeavor was spectacularly successful: over two million tracts were sold during the first year of their production alone.[97]

Hannah More's project was, of course, driven by sharply reactionary—rather than politically radical—motivations. In churning out fake street poetry as a form of political warfare, she really transformed poetry into (if I may abuse von Clausewitz's memorable phrase) the continuation of politics by other means. More's ballads were simultaneously and immediately political and literary; they fused aesthetics and politics inseparably together. Especially given all the contextual considerations that I have already elaborated, it seems inevitable that when Wordsworth and Coleridge ushered *Lyrical Ballads* into this highly politically charged arena in the late 1790s, they too were engaging in a form of political warfare. In a literary and ideological terrain that was dominated by the Cheap Repository Tracts, *Lyrical Ballads* might almost be seen as a mission behind enemy lines. There was, however, one major difference between the two projects: More's tracts were aimed directly at a plebeian audience; *Lyrical Ballads* was not.

In arguing that there is an essential distinction between apostasy and disenchantment, that the creative impulse that emerges out of the conflict between the two would fade away once genuine withdrawal had taken place, and that *Lyrical Ballads* is the product of that tension, E. P. Thompson pushes us to see the collection as a sign of the realignment of Wordsworth's political commitments, rather than their abandonment altogether. Such a realignment indicates, according to Thompson, "a move away from the *déraciné* Godwinian intelligentsia but toward the common people."[98] The question now is what it means, in the context of the 1790s, for a volume meant to express a commitment to the common people, not to be aimed at the common people themselves—who were, after all, already exposed to materials from which *Lyrical Ballads* sought a kind of inspiration, and among which it sought to mark a kind of intervention—but rather to an altogether different audience.

"It is absurd to suppose," Francis Jeffrey would write in his assessment of the attempt, in *Lyrical Ballads*, to descend to the "low," "mean," and "vulgar," "that an author would make use of the language of the vulgar, to express the sentiments of the refined."[99] Jeffrey was, of course, signaling the reality that, for all its expressions of concern for and interest in "low and rustic life," *Lyrical Ballads* was hardly directed at a "low and rustic" audience. Indeed, quite apart from its strictly literary ambitions, the volume was never intended to be simply a radical version of the Cheap Repository Tracts, doing battle with an ideological enemy on the very terrain that that enemy already dominated. Rather than taking on that enemy on the terrain that it already controlled, then, *Lyrical Ballads* sought to seize a different set of ideological, and cultural-political, landmarks: those associated with a different, but politically no less important, class of readers.

Scott McEathron argues in an important article that Wordsworth's relationship to low and rustic life—and to so-called peasant poetry in particular—was one of appropriation and displacement. "Although we are accustomed to thinking of Wordsworth as breaching the fortress of elite literature," McEathron argues, "it is important to consider that he also breached the implicit class boundaries of literature in the other direction. In appropriating lowly rustic voices and literary forms, he could be seen as invading the demographic domain of peasant writers, occupying the class-specific territory from which they derived their tenuous (and perhaps only) artistic authority."[100] Challenging Jon Klancher's assertion that the secret ambition of *Lyrical Ballads* is "to represent the rural poor to themselves," McEathron insists that "these poems do in fact represent the rural poor, but not so much to *themselves* as in relation to those who would seek to make poetry about them."[101]

McEathron's point is a good one, but again it is intended to address the volume's ambitions in a rather narrowly literary dimension (and hence to see it as an attempt "to subsume or displace the historical presence of peasant poetry").[102] The question now, in view of everything I've said so far, is whether this narrowly literary approach also has a political correlate, and, clearly, I think that it does. In aiming to interpose itself between the common people and a more "elevated" audience, *Lyrical Ballads* aimed to subsume the politics of the common people and to redirect them to a presumably well-intentioned bourgeois, increasingly Occidentalized audience that by 1798 had largely abandoned whatever common cause may have been made across shifting lines of race and class earlier in the decade: precisely the common cause that it had long been one of the government's explicit intentions to tear asunder. The volume thus drew on the combined cultural, literary, and political legacy already tapped into and redefined by interventions like those of Ritson or those of Thelwall, Eaton, and Spence. For a new era had begun, one in which Jacobin, revolutionary, radical and merely reformist desires were finally being extirpated by a revanchist government and its closest political allies and affiliates (such as Hannah More, or the Association for the Preservation of Liberty and Property against Republicans and Levellers), and the ballad, in particular, was developing the kind of reputation that would culminate with its treatment in Mayhew's *London Labour*.

But such transmutations are not so easy, of course; nor do they come without a price. In the case of the *Lyrical Ballads*, the price might seem obvious: it's suggested, for example, in M. H. Abrams' furious insistence, against what he calls the joyless and monochromatic political readings of *Lyrical Ballads,* that an "open" reader of "Tintern Abbey," for example, will find "that it speaks now, as it has spoken for almost two centuries, and will continue to speak."[103] If I disagree with Abrams, however, it's not because I am against reading poetry for the sake of poetry, nor is it because I believe that poetry is never really written entirely for its own sake: it's because such an approach to poetry—in cutting off and terminating what Edward Said would have identified as its own *worldliness,* not to mention our own—actually diminishes, rather than enhances, its enduring value.[104] That is especially true for the class of poetry that seeks to challenge and resist the dominant tendencies of its own time.

On the other hand, in reading *Lyrical Ballads* as a kind of resistance poetry, we should be wary not to re-Romanticize it all over again. For something else is at stake in interposing between the producers of a certain kind of poetry—a certain kind of politics—and the class of readers from which those producers would henceforth find themselves cut off by the very intervention designed in some way to preserve them; there is another, different price to be paid. This is captured most powerfully, I think, in the volume's very title. For what, after all, is a lyrical ballad?

By the end of the eighteenth century, it is true, almost any kind of narrative poem could be classed as a ballad. So is a lyrical ballad merely a narrative poem packaged with the kind of meter more typically associated with lyric? This is certainly Robert Mayo's contention, and he argues, moreover, that Wordsworth was not the only one combining lyrical meter with narrative poetry. "The more one reads the minor poetry of the magazines from 1788 to 1798," Mayo argues, "the more it is impossible to escape the impression that the concept of the 'lyrical ballad' does not represent a significant innovation in 1798, nor as a term is it particularly appropriate to the contents of this volume of poems." Perhaps, he adds, "the title was chosen casually. Perhaps it was designed to be nondescript—uniting poems of diverse subjects and kinds. Perhaps it was meant to suggest that the poems might be popular, and promised that they would eschew the recherché and the ultra-refined. Certainly as titles went in the years before 1798, this one was likely to surprise nobody."[105]

I take Mayo's point, but I also suspect that more is at stake in the volume's remarkable title than narrowly literary considerations, let alone mere happenstance. For his approach loses sight of another way of classifying different kinds of poetry, one not dependent on only technical differentiations. By the late 1790s, after all, the ballad was beginning to acquire unmistakably popular, "vulgar," even dangerous associations and connotations, as a range of authorities across the ideological spectrum running from Joseph Ritson to Hannah More made perfectly clear. Lyric, however, is more typically associated not only with a totally different class of poetry—elevated, distinguished, introspective—but also, by the late eighteenth century, with an altogether different form of subjectivity and political and racial subjectivity, increasingly compatible with the developing values of a still-emerging Occidentalism.[106] Making the ballad *lyrical* can thus be seen to involve not merely yoking together two otherwise incompatible *literary* forms (as scholars including Mayo and Janowitz have pointed out) but also merging a *low* cultural form, with all of its political associations, and a *high* cultural form, a form not previously politicized (or at least not to the same degree). In a sense, then, what's involved in the process of making the ballad *lyrical* is the incorporation and indeed the subsumption of the lower literary form into the higher one, translating "vulgar" politics into "polite" ones.

Thus the lyrical ballad can be thought of as an attempt to Occidentalize and settle the restless, itinerant, and nomadic in a generic form appropriate to modernity and a new Occidental subject, confirming its new location firmly on one side of the oral/written, plebeian/elite, self/other, us/them divides which had hitherto been more amenable to border crossings and incursions back and forth; really, to colonize and settle a literary form, alongside territory and space that were also being reclaimed, settled, civilized, Occidentalized.

For, by turning to and breathing new life into the popular ballad form at the very time when it was (according to Francis Place at least) being pushed "out of existence," by lyricizing it—infusing it with the culturally and politically opposed, essentially "high art" form of the lyric—Wordsworth was defusing and containing what had been the danger of a not-yet-Occidental plebeian cultural and political radicalism, translating it into the modern in a way compatible with—rather than potentially subversive of—modernity. This is not exactly a turning away from radicalism, but rather a way for Wordsworth simultaneously to preserve his radical commitments and to cancel them out.

This claim needs to be qualified somewhat and made more precise. In privileging individual experience as transmitted in a modern linguistic idiom, Wordsworth is, as Pasolini suggests in a different (but not unrelated) context, effectively colonizing the consciousness of the racial other. He is translating a disappearing social and cultural order into a new form. The closest relatives of this kind of work, then, were not Thelwall's rural effusions or Charlotte Smith's sonnets (to which Wordsworth's rural poetry has often

been compared)[107] but rather the texts emerging from the late eighteenth-
and early nineteenth-century Orientalist press (Beckford's *Vathek*, Southey's *Thalaba*, Moore's *Lalla Rookh*, Landor's *Gebir*, and so on). And this
translation of pre-Occidental England has the effect of confirming the very
process of Occidentalization and civilization, the advent of which it also
simultaneously mourns. In the process, a new kind of Englishness emerges.
When Simon Gikandi writes that "English identities are constituted in the
spaces of imperial alterity," what he has in mind are the spaces of cultural
difference in Africa, the Caribbean, and elsewhere.[108] What I have been trying to argue in this chapter is that the struggles around the constitution of
English identities do indeed take place in the spaces of cultural difference,
but that those sites begin in England itself.

PART 2

Episodes of Occidentalism

Domineering over Others:
Occidentalism, Empire, Moral Virtue

Much of the recent scholarship on Jane Austen has been gripped by a controversy concerning the relationship between Austen and imperialism, especially in *Mansfield Park*. Some critics have worked to retrieve and elaborate the subtle cues that link the quiet, settled order of Austen's domestic setting with the drama of imperial conquest, while others have read the novel as a critique of British imperialism, and Austen herself as a sister and friend to the wretched of the earth. Building on the arguments elaborated in the previous two chapters, what I want to propose in this one is that *Mansfield Park*'s engagement with the cultural politics of imperialism is at once less straightforward and more profound than has been suggested so far, but that that engagement can only be understood in relation to the novel's treatment of questions seemingly far removed from the blood and sweat of imperial conquest, to which they are, however, inexorably tied. For in *Mansfield Park*, we can see Austen articulating—precisely in connection with Britain's changing national and imperial project and the emerging civilizing process—some of the key cultural and political concerns underlying the emergent culture of Occidentalism, above all the vital new role of individual self-regulation rather than external, almost theatrical, regulation as the key to the subject who would form the core of Occidental culture, as well as the new role for women as the ideological guarantors of that self-regulation. In many ways, this makes *Mansfield Park* one of the key texts for understanding the profound cultural, political and psycho-affective transformations of Occidentalization that took place all through the Romantic period and that have continued to play a role in an age of conflict extending into our own time.

What makes Austen's novel interesting from the geoaesthetic perspective elaborated by Edward Said in his book *Culture and Imperialism* (whose chapter on *Mansfield Park* ignited the recent controversy) is the way it links together the space of the Bertram slave plantation in Antigua with the domestic estate at Mansfield.[1] Said argues that although the two spaces (domestic and imperial) are structurally essential to each other, representationally they are utterly separate. Some of Said's critics have, however, drawn attention to the novel's expression of moral revulsion against the slave trade, and, arguing against Said's reading of *Mansfield Park* as an essentially imperialist novel, they see this moral outrage as an indicator of what they take to be the novel's critique of imperialism.[2] Now, it could be argued that one shortcoming of Said's reading of the novel, to which I will return shortly, is that its privileging of geoaesthetic questions ends up understating the complexity of Austen's interest in empire (which was, I would argue, not simply geoaesthetic in nature). Some of his critics, however, have overcompensated for this shortcoming, and they have done so not simply by overstating the novel's expression of moral outrage but rather by taking it at face value and hence misreading it altogether, conflating slavery and imperialism and thus treating a critique of the one necessarily as a critique of the other.

Slavery and imperialism have not shared an entirely continuous history, however, and the late eighteenth and early nineteenth centuries marked a significant divergence between them. Indeed, Austen was working precisely at a moment when it wasn't just well-meaning novelists and poets who were writing against the slave trade or slavery itself. We have to remember that all around the period of her novel's publication, the transforming British empire itself was starting to work to jettison slavery and turn toward other, more productive and efficient modes of imperial rule. As C. L. R. James points out, especially when the British realized that the empire of their enemies the French was far more dependent on the slave trade than was their own, the abolitionist cause was embraced by the advocates of a new form of imperial power, one centered on free trade more than slavery and also on a shift in the center of gravity of the empire, from the Western hemisphere to the exploitation of colonial possessions in Asia, tied to growing industrialization at home. "The British colonies had enough slaves for all the trade they were ever likely to do," James notes in *The Black Jacobins*. "With the tears rolling down their cheeks for the poor suffering blacks, those British bourgeois who had no West Indian interests set up a great howl for the abolition of the slave trade."[3]

Part of the point here is that the critique of the slave trade was carried out by the advocates of a form of imperial power tied to the emergent middle class rather than the residual landed gentry and their West Indian plantations. The critique of the slave trade was in other words tied inevitably to a domestic, English, process of cultural and political realignment, the "great transformation" described by Polanyi (see Introduction). There was a seamless continuity of logic here. Thus, if we follow Claudia Johnson's lead and read *Mansfield Park* as Austen's attempt to "turn conservative myth sour," we can see that the critique of the slave trade was essential to the novel's more general critique of the outmoded forms of power and obedience tied to the landed gentry in England, which, as Johnson argues, Austen parodies in the novel.[4]

By the time of *Mansfield Park's* publication, then, a critique of either the slave trade or slavery as such would not merely have been irrelevant to a critique of imperialism. It would have fit seamlessly into ongoing efforts to strengthen and revitalize the British empire; that is, efforts to shore up the empire's moral resources and to prepare it for what was at the time an entirely new preoccupation of imperial politics, namely, a civilizing mission against individual decadence and idleness, against inefficiency, against barbarism, against individual moral failing and unregulated desire: all the threats that the lingering aristocracy and its West Indian extensions posed to an as yet unconsolidated logic of Occidental self-regulation, especially at home in England—which is to say that the new, self-regulating kind of logic endorsed by the novel was just as tied to a new logic of imperial power. The key to all this, however, is that Austen develops her critique of those outmoded forms of power not primarily at an institutional or social level— as a critique of the great estate or the plantation economy, say—but rather at the level of the individual subject: a terrain vital to the process of Occidentalism.

Thus, the first point I want to register here is that readings of the novel that take its moral stance with regard to slavery at face value will be unable to engage with its historical and political complexity. The second point, however, essentially the flip side of the first, is that any investigation of the novel's political and historical complexity, especially its relationship to empire, must take into account its moral dimension, especially as that develops at the level of the individual subject. For in *Mansfield Park*, moral critique serves as the expression of an underlying political stance, precisely because of the politicization of individual morality in Jane Austen's lifetime, its mobilization in a civilizing mission that was seen to be unfolding not just overseas but, more importantly, at home in England, where it was the key to a broader Occidentalist logic.

It is essential to bear in mind that imperialism really became a moral issue only during the lifetime of Jane Austen. The transition toward a form of imperial domination in which moral questions, and the imposition of new and specifically modern institutions, manners, morals, virtues, and ways of life on other cultures—in other words, the attempt to bring civilization to supposed barbarism, a process whose bankruptcy would receive perhaps its most scathing condemnation (albeit for the wrong reasons) in Conrad's *Heart of Darkness* at the other end of the nineteenth century—took place all through the decades around 1800. One of the key signs of this transition was the trial of Warren Hastings, who was accused of having been corrupted by the lusts and passions of Oriental despotism, rather than upholding supposedly true British values in confrontation with the moral degradations of the East.

Once it had successfully jettisoned slavery (thanks in no small part to the ferocious resistance put up by slaves themselves, of course), the new British empire would use individually located moral virtues as the spearhead of new imperial adventures, which lends credence to Blake's furious assertion that "The Moral Virtues are continual Accusers of Sin & promote Eternal Wars & Domineering over others."[5] For it was precisely in the name of individual, internal virtue such as Austen's novel celebrates in Fanny Price that the new British empire would ransack the world, at home as well as overseas, looking for the sources of "barbarism" in order to extirpate them, crush them, stamp and burn them out, and replace them with sober, productive, efficient—and above all respectably proper—prosperity, just as we see when Sir Thomas goes through his estate after his return from Antigua, organizing, computing, calculating, and moralizing, burning every copy of the play *Lovers' Vows* that he could find and erasing every trace of the aborted performance staged by his children and their friends.

Ironically, then, moral critique at the individual level was hardly a weapon to be used against empire, for it defined the sharpest cutting edge of the new imperialism that was emerging in Austen's time. At the same time, morality—or, more precisely, a certain conception of moral virtue—was also, however, essential to an emergent understanding of individual subjectivity that was simultaneously taking on new significance as the cornerstone of a new and properly Occidental cultural, political and psychoaffective order at home. As I have argued in other contexts, this new conception of subjectivity was inseparable from the new understanding of Britain's national and imperial destiny. Individual, self-regulating moral virtue therefore offers the key to understanding Occidentalist subjectivity. What all this raises in turn, then, is the all-important question of how morality and the cultural politics of subjectivity itself would come to serve the needs of a growing empire.

What I am saying here builds on Claudia Johnson's reading of *Mansfield Park* as a parody of outmoded conservative values; that is, the values tied to the landed gentry. "Conservative apologists pitched their flag on the claim that the patriarchal family nurtured moral sentiments, and that the same affections that make us dutiful children and feeling siblings make us obedient subjects and responsible members of our neighborhoods," Johnson argues.[6] On her reading, *Mansfield Park* demystifies the conservative ideology of collective moral regulation tied to patriarchal values in which women were systematically kept subordinate through a logic of manners to which they were all supposed to subscribe. "The system of female manners is supposed to eliminate the need for the nakedness of coercion, and the embarrassment this entails," Johnson notes, "by rendering women so quiescent and tractable that they sweetly serve in the designs of fathers or guardians without wishing to resist and without noting that they have no choice."[7] The limitation of this code of propriety, which Austen strips bare in the novel, however, is that it depends on an external logic: it works as long as everyone believes in it and subscribes to its authority and the patriarchal power standing behind it. It depends above all on the silencing of individual subjects—women in particular—and denial of their agency.[8] This makes it hollow and ultimately ineffective, operating at a surface level perhaps but not really deeper within the subject, therefore requiring the restoration of order by the use of overt coercion and the use of force (not unlike a slave plantation). By exposing the discrepancies between the pretenses and the substance of this conservative myth, Johnson argues, Austen questions the moral efficacy that it was supposed to produce.[9] This critical mode is made all the more effective, as Jill Heydt-Stevenson points out, by Austen's deployment of a profoundly subversive and sexualized as well as humorous critique of patriarchal repression.[10]

So far, so good. But Austen's novel does not just parody and strip bare and slyly subvert the conservative cultural and social logic of slavery or the landed gentry. Jane Austen was not an anarchist, in other words: her text also proposes an alternative model of regulation, one founded on the mobilization of individual agency as the key to a logic of self-control. Thus *Mansfield Park* anticipates the new role of the empire as a machine for the production of a new form of subjectivity, one appropriate to its needs both at home and abroad, needs that cannot be understood simply in terms of national interest and national identity, let alone geopolitical organization. The Occident is vital to this form of thought not as a geopolitical site as such, but rather as a locus of a certain form of individual subjectivity, a model that can also (eventually) be exported beyond the West.

In this sense, what is perhaps most remarkable about the novel's treatment of imperialism is that it demonstrates the extent to which a certain disciplinary logic, namely, the logic animating the self-regulating subject, must operate seamlessly *across* the empire's domain, unifying rather than separating domestic and imperial space. In the project to replace the outmoded logic of slavery (in other words, discipline enforced by external brutality) with a disciplinary regime based on self-regulation—a far more efficient mode of governmentality—the subject would become one of the key sites for the intensification of imperial activity. Strangely enough (though not really), Austen is here anticipating the work of John Stuart Mill, for whom slavery was not so much a political or economic status but rather a state of mind. "A slave, properly so called, is a being who has not learnt to help himself," Mill writes in *On Representative Government*. "It is the characteristic of *born* slaves to be incapable of conforming their conduct to a rule, or a law. They can only do what they are ordered, and only when they are ordered to do it. If a man whom they fear is standing over them and threatening them with punishment, they obey; but when the back is turned, the work remains undone."[11] In a word, the slave has "to be taught self-government."[12] Austen's novel narrates the progress, at the scale of the family and its constituent individuals, of the progress from a regime of slavery to one of self-government. In other words, what was at stake in the new imperialism was not merely the subjectivity of the slave but the subjectivity of the master, and perhaps above all the subjectivity of the mistress herself, all bound together in the civilizing process, which, in the domestic arena, took the form of Occidentalism.

My claim here, then, is essentially the opposite of the one proposed by Katie Trumpener in her reading of Austen in *Bardic Nationalism*.[13] For rather than tracing what Trumpener calls the "long reach" of the plantation system into the heart of Britain, I would argue that *Mansfield Park* traces the development of an entirely new form of imperialism, reaching out from the empire's heart to tie masters and slaves, colonizers and colonized, all the more thoroughly—however unequally and brutally—together, not just geopolitically but in terms of the logic of an unfolding civilizing mission. In this sense, however, what I am suggesting is also quite different from the argument put forward by Said; for if *Mansfield Park* is an imperialist novel—which I believe it to be—its imperialism is one that is comprehensive and indeed potentially universal, rather than being geopolitically restricted to distant settlements beyond the scope of narrative and representation. In fact I would say that what we are dealing with in *Mansfield Park* is the articulation ahead of time of a kind of imperialism whose intensities exceed the actually existing geotemporal scale of empire itself. For there is nothing limiting the civilizing mission to the Occidental domestic sphere.

In order to assess the ways in which Austen's novel integrates, rather than separates, the imperial and the domestic, consider, for example, the way in which Sir Thomas's return to Mansfield Park following his stay in Antigua is staged, in grossly and hence rather satirically exaggerated terms, as something of an imperial counterinsurgency—or search-and-destroy—operation. For during Sir Thomas's absence from Mansfield, things had clearly got out of hand. When he returns, he restores order to the estate's material well-being ("he had to reinstate himself in all the wonted concerns of his Mansfield life, to see his steward and his bailiff—to examine and compute— and, in the intervals of business, to walk into his stables and his garden, and nearest plantations").[14] But above all he restores the estate's moral well-being, especially in the wake of the abortive attempt to perform the scandalous play *Lovers' Vows*.

The narrator of *Mansfield Park* tells us that the preparations for the play, by allowing a certain degree of moral looseness, had threatened the material well-being of the estate, which Sir Thomas also has to put to order upon his return ("The scene painter was gone, having spoilt only the floor of one room, ruined all the coachman's sponges, and made five of the under-servants idle and dissatisfied; and Sir Thomas was in hopes that another day or two would suffice to wipe away every outward memento of what had been, even to the destruction of every unbound copy of 'Lovers' Vows' in the house, for he was burning all that met his eye.")[15] Sir Thomas's return then precipitates a series of crises, the end result of which is that all those bad, undisciplined, unproductive, wasteful, frivolous, inappropriate, indulgent, pleasure-seeking, degenerate characters associated with the *Lovers' Vows* performance—the unfortunate Maria and Julia as well as the Crawfords and the aiding and abetting Aunt Norris—are essentially purged, leaving us with a revitalized Sir Thomas, his wife, and their still-recovering (and hence somewhat negligible) eldest son, and, of course, an ultimately happily married Fanny and Edmund. This of course is the point of Johnson's reading of the novel: Austen is revealing the extent to which an externally based morality requires continual reinforcement.

The key feature of the novel's ending is that Fanny and Edmund now dominate the representational space of Mansfield Park, though—crucially— they don't actually own the estate itself, and indeed on the contrary find themselves happily squeezed into the confines of Thornton Lacey. For the master of the property in England as well as in Antigua—that is, Sir Thomas— the story's denouement offers a lesson in something far more profound than

mere property management. By the end of the novel, he learns, and we presumably learn with him, that moral well-being and material well-being at
the individual rather than simply the family or collective level are inseparable. In other words, the real lesson that Sir Thomas learns is that Occidental self-discipline counts far more than a mere show of obedience to an
overlord, a system of external regulation, such as Sir Thomas had demanded
both from his slaves and from his children. For, at the end of the novel, Sir
Thomas, "poor Sir Thomas, a parent, and conscious of errors in his own
conduct as a parent," recognizes his earlier "grievous mismanagement; but,
bad as it was, he gradually grew to feel that it had not been the most dire-
ful mistake in his plan of education. Some thing must have been wanting
within, or time would have worn away much of its ill effect. He feared that
principle, active principle, had been wanting, that they had never been properly taught to govern their inclinations and tempers, by that sense of duty
which can alone suffice. They had been instructed theoretically in their
religion, but never required to bring it into daily practice. . . . He had meant
them to be good, but his cares had been directed to the understanding and
manners, not the disposition; and of the necessity of self-denial and humility, he feared they had never heard from any lips that could profit them. Bitterly did he deplore a deficiency which now he could scarcely comprehend
to have been possible."[16]

What was "wanting within" the four Bertram children, then, is the very
sense of principle and moral virtue that Edmund only learns by the end of
the novel (from Fanny)—but that Fanny, of course, had known all along. For
it is precisely on the basis of her principles, which she—unlike Maria, Julia,
and Tom—had learned from an early age because she received such strict
disciplinary treatment at Mansfield, that Fanny learns to govern her incli-
nation and temper, "by that sense of duty which can alone suffice." It is, in
other words, precisely thanks to her strict governance that Fanny learns "the
necessity of self-denial and humility," and all of the other principles which
are so lacking in Crawford, because of which she rejects him. For Fanny
sees right away that all these moral virtues are lacking in him. Sir Thomas
is angered at Fanny's rejection of Crawford only because he (Sir Thomas)
had been deceived and was not as aware of Crawford's moral failings as
Fanny had been all along: otherwise, he would surely have agreed with her
judgment of him (as in fact he does in the end, almost, but not quite, too
late). Clearly, if Fanny is such an admirable character in the novel's terms
(even though, as Marilyn Butler argues, as a flatly unidimensional character
she also represents the weakest moment of Austen's novel from a technical
and aesthetic point of view),[17] it is because she, unlike the others, learns

to internalize self-regulatory discipline; for which, presumably, she can be thankful for her harsh treatment at the hands of Aunt Norris.

Far from a critique of authority in general (rather than specifically a conservative mode of authority), far from a celebration of human freedom and women's liberation, what the final pages of Austen's novel yield to is a celebration of the virtues of discipline and moral virtue generally: hard work, self-denial, and above all the internalization (that is, the rendering far more efficient) of the policing mechanisms which for the other children had been merely external signs and hence not really taken seriously. For it turns out that the real enemies here are indulgence, pleasure, luxury, excess, idleness, and the host of quasi-Oriental corruptions that they give rise to; whereas the principles vindicated by the end of *Mansfield Park* are sobriety, self-discipline, self-denial, frugality, composure, and so on, which Sir Thomas so happily acknowledges in Fanny, and which enable her to marry an appropriately reformed Edmund. Of course, part of the point here is that Sir Thomas learns this lesson a little too late for the benefit of his children; thus what the novel narrates is the passing of the torch of Occidental moral virtue to the next generation, to Fanny and Edmund.

Indeed, the union of Fanny and Edmund expresses the affirmation of a new form of marriage, a new form of family, or, as Clara Tuite puts it, "the tight and reluctant squeeze of the aristocratic family . . . into the smaller, narrower space . . . of the bourgeois-identified nuclear family."[18] Hence, according to Tuite, *Mansfield Park* narrates not so much "the qualified rise of the bourgeoisie as [the] tight squeeze of the aristocracy into the confines of the bourgeois ideology of domesticity."[19] And this emergent ideology of Occidental domesticity centered on the affirmation of a new role for women in a domestic sphere which, as Linda Colley argues, was paradoxically understood to be both separate from the sphere of politics, nation, and empire and yet at the same time absolutely essential to its survival and prosperity.[20] It falls, of course, to Fanny—rather than to any of the dissipated and indulgent Bertram women—to play this new role called for by the emergent ideology of what Colley calls "womanpower." For Fanny sees, long before the narrator explicitly admits it to us, that Crawford was "ruined by early independence and bad domestic example," that he "indulged in the freaks of a cold-blooded vanity a little too long."[21]

The emphasis of the novel's end, then, is not so much on Sir Thomas's contrition as it is on the positive role that Fanny plays in securing the happy ending. As Clara Tuite argues, the "domestic improvements" that Mansfield undergoes are specifically middle-class and are effected "by the specifically feminine-gendered agency of Fanny Price."[22] Maaja Stewart points out that by the end of the novel the drooping and sentimental Fanny has replaced the dazzling, witty, and independent-minded Mary Crawford, in a process that Stewart says itself "involves a redefinition of 'feminine' character and a radical increase of male authority," whose institutions (e.g., the church, the Royal Navy) Mary Crawford refuses to idolize and even makes fun of, whereas Fanny reveres them through her love for Edmund and her brother William.[23] But by the end, as Stewart says, Fanny has also replaced the daughters of the house "as the one who will sustain the Mansfield values into the next generation." Again, I think Marilyn Butler is right to argue that it is when the novel is bluntest in the expression of ideological commitments—as in the ending—that it is least interesting in aesthetic terms; for by the end Fanny ceases to be a genuinely believable character and becomes more a flattened-out marker of an ideological position.[24] Even if we agree with Jill Heydt-Stevenson that there is a kind of subversive energy at work in the novel, I would argue that what is subverted is the conservative structure of externally enforced morality rather than the bourgeois values operating at the level of the individual subject that are affirmed at the end.[25]

Although I agree with Stewart that "class formation in *Mansfield Park* occurs at the expense of kinship relations,"[26] it's important to bear in mind here that the class whose formation we witness in these pages, in which merit is privileged over inheritance, in which discipline and self-denial are privileged over idleness and luxury, and in which hard work is privileged over privilege itself, is identifiably Occidental in nature, replacing at once the values of the slave plantation and those of the landed gentry with the values of a new class and a new way of life—that is, a new form of exploitation—in whose reproduction and regulation women would play a central ideological role, and in which, as Gary Kelley has argued, "a certain figure of 'woman' was constructed to represent a professional middle-class discourse of subjectivity."[27] Thus by the time of the novel's ending the values of bourgeois—rather than aristocratic—marriage have been affirmed, as critics including Tuite, Butler, and others have argued, even if as a result of the adaptation or compression of elements connected to the former aristocracy into a new role, rather than as a result of the autochthonous emergence of a full-fledged Occidental bourgeoisie.

This is surely the first of the links between Mansfield itself and the estate in Antigua, and indeed the whole question of empire. Said argues that "what assures the domestic tranquility and attractive harmony of one is the productivity and regulated discipline of the other."[28] But the problem with this reading is that in *both* cases, at home and abroad, tranquility and discipline are shown to be essential, and in this sense the imperial pressure in the novel is far more extreme than it is revealed to be in such an account. Yes, this is a novel saturated with the discourse of empire, not only in the ways that Said discusses, and in the presence of goods and property derived from unequal exchange, and in the perpetual celebration of Fanny's brother William, his promotion and successful career in the armed services of the British Empire, but also in a few other things—Fanny's own obsession with the colonial estate in Antigua, or the fact that at one point we discover her reading Lord Macartney's account of his 1793 colonial expedition to China. Of all the characters, Fanny and William are not only the ones rendered in the most positive light: they are also the ones who are most closely aligned with the interests of the new empire and the imperial quest for moral virtue in aid of the civilizing mission.

One point that I would like to emphasize, then, is that the operations of empire here involve not only the subjugation and exploitation of distant colonial possessions but also the ever more efficient and productive exploitation of property and possessions—people and capital—in the domestic sphere, and more than that the ever more efficient regulation of subjectivity itself, in a recognizably Occidentalist mode. We might even say that the real enemy that is hunted down and destroyed in *Mansfield Park* is pleasure for its own sake, that is, unproductive pleasure. By the time of the novel's ending, we are presented with the triumph of the ideology of duty, self-denial, humility, internalized self-regulating discipline, frugality, and above all the relentless productivity and nourishment of property consummated in the marriage of Fanny and Edmund, whose greatest enemy is pleasure for its own sake, that is, the kind of momentary gratification henceforth taken to be typical of degraded Orientals suffering from all the worst excesses of femininity, effeminacy, licentiousness, ungoverned sexuality, and moral corruption, and who are thus all the more in need of the civilizing mission, the weaning and tutelage, that it would fall to a morally virtuous empire to so reluctantly provide to subjects both at home and overseas.

This in turn reinforces the second point I want to emphasize, which is that this new imperial discourse is also intimately concerned with the production and regulation of subjectivity. In fact one of the most remarkable things about this conclusion is that Austen's elaboration of subjectivity is most readily aligned not with a putative conservatism (with which she is often misleadingly identified) but rather with the so-called English Jacobins of the 1790s. I don't mean to understate the very real differences between Austen and 1790s radicalism, but on the other hand it is hardly a coincidence that the regulation of subjectivity was an essential component of a dominant strand of radicalism in the 1790s. What Claudia Johnson identi-

fies as the novel's "progressive, though muted, social criticism" can be tied
to the legacy of radicalism as it developed from the 1790s into the early
nineteenth century.[29] Most of the English radicals of the 1790s would have
been as keen as Jane Austen to distance themselves from the excess and indulgence of the Crawfords or the Bertram children. For most of the radicals
of the 1790s—with the notable exception of Blake—individual self-control
was the key to Liberty.[30] We can be free, they argued, only when we are free
to exercise control over ourselves, rather than having that control imposed
on us by a tyrannical government. "Let us exert over our own hearts a virtuous despotism," the radical Coleridge writes, "and lead our own Passions in
triumph, and then we shall want neither Monarch nor General."[31]

In fact, it is in a radical position like Coleridge's that we can best see the
link between the discourse of subjectivity and the Occidentalist discourse of
governmentality in a broader sense in the years around 1800. For Coleridge,
the self-regulation offered by what he calls Liberty is not an antidote to despotism; it is, on the contrary, an extension and intensification of the logic
of despotism, through its internalization. Liberty, or at least this kind of liberty—the liberty of the self-regulating subject—represents, in other words,
not the opposite of despotism, but rather its purification, rendering it morally virtuous (hence "virtuous despotism"). Despotism becomes virtuous,
then, when it becomes self-regulating rather than externally imposed; just
as the empire becomes virtuous when it moves from the logic of whips and
chains to the logic of self-regulated good behavior.

The key to such good behavior is of course a proper education, and Austen's interest in education, and particularly the education of women, provides another link to 1790s radicalism, in which this was one of the major
concerns. Various critics have, for example, pointed out the centrality of
the abortive *Lovers' Vows* performance in *Mansfield Park*, which ties Austen's novel to Elizabeth Inchbald's adaptation of one of those "sickly and
stupid German tragedies" derided by Wordsworth in the Preface to *Lyrical
Ballads*. Even more interesting, however, is *Mansfield Park's* relationship
to Inchbald's 1791 novel *A Simple Story*. Paula Byrne argues that what Austen offers in effect is a kind of rewriting both of *Lovers' Vows* and *A Simple
Story*, in both of which we see a charming, but dangerously miseducated,
coquette fall in love with an erstwhile clergyman. Byrne suggests that that
theme is replayed in *Mansfield Park* with the transition from the abortive
Mary Crawford/Edmund relationship—interestingly played out through
their roles in the *Lovers' Vows* performance—to the Fanny/Edmund relationship.[32] With the failure of the former and the successful consummation
of the latter, it is no longer the witty and dangerous coquette who wins the

clergyman's heart but rather the morally virtuous (though admittedly some-what boring) woman, who has her stern education to thank for her moral propriety and, ultimately, her material prosperity. A similar move happens in Inchbald's *Simple Story*, where the operative contrast is between the flighty and ill-educated but nevertheless attractive Miss Milner, whose life ends in failure (following her husband's voyage to tend to *his* West Indian estate), and her daughter Matilda, who, thanks to her harsh upbringing at her tutor's hands, learns to regulate her subjectivity appropriately, and who, after a difficult period of alienation from her moody and tyrannical father, ends up succeeding in life and romance (with her self-regulated and submissive male equivalent, Rushbrook), thanks, in the novel's famous last line, to a "proper education."[33]

What goes for "education" here, as in much of the 1790s, has little to do with pedagogical content and much to do with form; for here education means learning—as we are reminded by the subtitle of Mary Wollstone-craft's *Original Stories from Real Life*, a children's training manual—how to "regulate the affections and form the mind to truth and goodness."[34] Matilda and Rushbrook are so successful at learning how to regulate them-selves that the tyrannical Lord Elmwood revokes many of the rules he has devised to keep them in check, but then, as Eleanor Ty points out, "Matilda and Rushbrook have so thoroughly internalized the Law of the Father that they will police themselves."[35] For with such self-regulating virtuous des-potism in place, there is no longer any need for an external despotism, though Ty also points out that in her novel Inchbald kills off the vital threat to patriarchal power represented by the vivacious Miss Milner just in case. It is interesting, in fact, to note that Mary Wollstonecraft, who reviewed *A Simple Story*, wrote approvingly of the novel's lessons for "thought-less and unprincipled minds" but lamented that Mrs. Inchbald did not re-inforce it by even more sharply contrasting the "vain, giddy miss Milner" and Matilda, who, "educated in adversity," should "have learned (to prove that a cultivated mind is a real advantage) how to bear, nay, rise above her misfortunes."[36] After all, for Wollstonecraft as much as for Coleridge, the key to success in life is the kind of self-regulation that we see perfected in the characters of Matilda and Rushbrook—which would resurface in Fanny Price and Edmund Bertram.

A similar pattern unfolds in Austen's *Persuasion*, which tells two stories at once. On the one hand, there is, paralleling the development mapped out in *Mansfield Park*, a narrative of transition from the landed gentry and the increasingly empty and broken-down mode of theatrical, appearance-driven morality that was essential to that class, to the emergent, professionalized middle class. On the other hand, there is the increasingly consolidated realization on Anne's part that one must look to one's own internal sense of moral judgment—which teaches her to disregard the external advice that had led to the initial breakup of her engagement to Captain Wentworth and to re-attach herself to him again—rather than relying on the completely broken-down moral system of the landed gentry, which would, had she followed it, have paired her with the vicious Mr. Walter Eliot, who appears on the outside to be eminently suitable but is in fact internally a monster.

Even more than in *Mansfield Park*, the narrative of *Persuasion* maps the shift in morality from an external regime of appearances to an internal one of self-regulation: the attainment of the civilizing mission. The primary representatives of the old order are Sir Walter Eliot and his eldest daughter, Elizabeth, both of whom are obsessed with appearances and neither of whom is capable of judging or assessing morality at an individual level precisely because they are so blinded by appearances in precisely the manner by then—following over a decade of radical Orientalism—commonly associated with Orientals. It is especially significant that their moral blindness is tied to their class disposition (again, a relationship Austen inherited willy-nilly from 1790s radicalism). Sir Walter is so invested in maintaining the appearance of a country gentleman—reinforced through his compulsive consultation of the *Baronetage*—and so careless of the material basis of that appearance that he and his daughter drive their estate into the ground through mismanagement. "While Lady Elliot lived, there had been method, moderation and economy, which had just kept him within his income," after all, "but with her had died all such right-mindedness, and from that period he had been constantly exceeding it."[37] If the old patriarchal system of external moral codes that had once sustained the members of his class is no longer functioning, Sir Walter is no better placed to judge the individuated moral code of the emergent professional class, represented here by navy officers, which he despises "first, as being the means of bringing persons of obscure birth into undue distinction, and raising men to honours of which their fathers and grandfathers never dreamt of," as Sir Walter puts it; "and secondly, as it cuts up a man's youth and vigour most horribly; a sailor grows old sooner than any other man."[38] Again, the misleading investment in appearances blinds him to what are shown to be the much more important, valuable, and durable moral characteristics produced by the self-regulating individual agent, of whom Mrs. Croft is an ideal example.

Such self-regulation is the moral terrain dominated by Anne, who, like Fanny in *Mansfield Park*, learns it by having her own desires denied and thus attenuated. Part of what is interesting about this is that the people who matter the most in the new way of thinking things are the perfect "no-bodies" according to the outmoded moral economy of the gentry. Anne herself, "with an elegance of mind and sweetness of character, which must have placed her high with any people of real understanding, was nobody with either father or sister," we learn at the beginning of the novel, for example; Sir Walter refers to Mr. Wentworth as "nobody, I remember; quite unconnected; nothing to do with the Strafford family."[39] Someone who is "somebody" has that status because of the moral regime that operates externally and by way of enhancement in the visual field; the privileging of "nobodies" comes with the retracting of moral judgment into an interior process appropriate to the self-regulating individual subject. Lady Russell, for all her merit, "had a cultivated mind, and was, generally speaking, rational and consistent—but she had prejudices on the side of ancestry; she had a value for rank and consequence, which blinded her a little to the faults of those who possessed them."[40] Her flaw, that is, has to do with the visible—she is blinded by appearances. Anne, on the other hand, is quickly bored with the "elegant stupidity of private parties,"[41] and she focuses her energy on developing her interiorized moral compass, revealing her to be a self-regulating, civilized, Occidentalized woman.

After all, for most of the radicals of the 1790s (Blake is a notable exception), the self-restraint exhibited by Anne is the main feature differentiating a putatively Occidental culture from the barbarous excesses of European aristocrats and Oriental despots.[42] Saturated to its very core this strand of Orientalist discourse, in fact, 1790s radicalism consistently deployed the image of the Orient as the ultimate locus of the culture of excess (despotic, enthusiastic, exotic, erotic) that it also identified with the aristocratic European regimes, or the landed gentry like Sir Walter Eliot, whose legitimacy it had set out to challenge. This Occidentalist logic cut both ways, however; for if, on the one hand, the Orient could serve as an imaginary representation of all the bad features of the ancien régime (despotism, patronage, ritual, corruption) that the radicals sought to overturn, it could also serve—and indeed it did—as a very real sphere for European intervention and modernization, a site for the extension of the civilizing mission that was also at work at home in Europe. It is, in other words, hardly a coincidence that Volney's *Ruins* served as one of the key texts for both Romantic radicalism and European imperialism, beginning with Napoleon, who carried Volney's works with him to Egypt as handbooks for imperial conquest.[43] Decades later, in Egypt, in India, in Palestine, in Arabia, Cromer, Balfour, and Lawrence would justify their own imperialism in terms of bringing order and systematization to the East: an argument that has its origins in Romantic period radicalism and its zeal for self-regulation. For, after all, the proclaimed mission of European imperialism was precisely to teach non-Europeans how to regulate themselves. "You may look through the whole history of the Orientals in what is called, broadly speaking, the East," wrote Lord Balfour (author of the notorious 1917 declaration that carries his name), "and you never find traces of self-government . . . conqueror has succeeded conqueror; one domination has followed another; but never in all the revolutions of fate and fortune have you seen one of those nations of its own motion establish what we, from a Western point of view, call self-government."[44] Balfour's point, however, is that Orientals are incapable of self-government at the collective or the national level exactly because they are incapable of self-government at an individual level, at the level of the (Occidental) subject.

If it was a zeal for self-regulation that would align the interests of 1790s radicalism with the new imperial project that began to emerge in the Romantic period, it can hardly be a coincidence that it was precisely in its relationship to self-regulation that the logic of virtuous despotism here articulated by the 1790s radicals would be seized on by the advocates of British imperialism early in the nineteenth century. I already suggested that *Mansfield Park* anticipates the new role of the British empire as a machine for the production of a new form of subjectivity. Lest we forget how essential the question of subjectivity would become to British imperialism in the nineteenth century, it is worth recalling Macaulay's dictum that, in view of the practical difficulty of ruling hundreds of millions of Indians with a relatively small number of colonial administrators, "We must at present do our best to form a class who may be interpreters between us and the millions whom we govern; a class of persons, Indian in blood and colour, but English in taste, in opinions, in morals, and in intellect."[45] It's no coincidence that Macaulay's articulation of a new imperial mission in the *Minute on Indian Education* took place exactly when slavery itself (and not merely the slave trade) was finally being abolished throughout the British empire, that is, in the mid-1830s. Clearly, in the new empire only just coming into being as slavery was finally being done away with, imperial power would operate not merely on the battlefield and on the high seas; its most important zone of operations would be the newly discovered terrain of moral, manners, and intellect, that is, in the manufacture and regulation of individual subjectivities (whose traumas and neuroses Frantz Fanon would so clearly document in *Black Skin, White Masks*).[46] And in thus announcing the centrality of the question of subjectivity to the new imperial mission, Macaulay was drawing on the logic of Paine, Wollstonecraft, Coleridge, Volney, and the other radicals of the 1790s for whom self-regulation was of such profound importance. It is in Macaulay then—to whom we will return in chapter 5—that we see the extent to which not only morally virtuous abolitionism but moral virtue itself in the years around 1800 laid the foundations for a new kind of empire which would now begin its extraordinary expansion, by the end of which it would control a quarter of the globe, an empire tied to the consolidation of an Occidental logic in the metropolis itself. (I am not saying that the abolition of slavery necessarily led to the intensification of empire; I am just saying that the form that abolitionism took in alliance with moral virtue contributed to this outcome; there were of course far more radical articulations of the cause of freedom, but they were pushed to the margins.)

Mansfield Park, published in 1814, is situated exactly halfway between the radical discourse of subjectivity in the 1790s and the new imperial and more overtly Occidentalist discourse of the 1830s that I am exploring in this book. It came to light at a moment in which the prerogatives of imperialism—the torch of the imperial mission—was passing in fact from what had been a radical position in favor of progress, efficiency, and the moral virtue of the self-regulating subject to an entirely new brand of colonial administrators. We can trace this transmission in the work of various radicals, in the networks linking together old 1790s activists like Francis Place with the new voices of Thomas Malthus, James Mill, and Thomas Macaulay. We can also trace it in terms of the evolution of a newfound role for women as the guarantors of social order. Linda Colley argues that the consolidation of a separate-spheres ideology actually (though to us it may seem contradictory) implied a major role for women in the nation, as the centralizing source of domestic virtue. On the uses to which women put their influence, according to Hannah More, "will depend, in no low degree, the well-being" of the state, "nay perhaps the very existence of . . . society" itself.[47] According to Colley, "This (to us) contradictory set of arguments, an insistence that women must stay within the private sphere, while at the same time exerting moral influence outside it, dominated though it did not exhaust discussion of female rights in Great Britain in the first half of the nineteenth century."[48] Moreover, as Moira Ferguson points out, while "the historical intersection of a feminist impulse with anti-slavery agitation helped secure white British women's political self-empowerment," it did so by the development of a particular racial logic, so that, as Ferguson argues, "anti-slavery colonial discourse . . . played a significant role in generating and consolidating nineteenth-century British imperialist and 'domestic-racist' ideology."[49]

In fact, the development of early English feminism, as Deirdre Coleman has cautioned, at times anticipated and at times replicated some of the central axioms of a new imperialist ideology.[50]

Given all the new cultural, ideological, and political work being expressed in the pages of Austen's novel, it would therefore be misleading, as Claudia Johnson, Jill Heydt-Stevenson, and others have pointed out, to identify *Mansfield Park*, or Austen herself, with something called "conservatism," especially with regard to the novel's position on empire. For, precisely on the question of empire, we see an older form of conservatism (namely, Burke's) dropping away, to be replaced by a remarkable political and intellectual convergence—Occidentalism—in which it is virtually impossible to distinguish putatively conservative from would-be radical voices. In the early nineteenth century, then, the civilizing mission of empire would become almost universal, as England sought to become Western and as the discourse of self-regulating moral virtue took hold in Britain and was simultaneously directed overseas. Even later on in the century, the voices of dissent—for example, the organized women's movement, the trades-union movement—explicitly shared in the imperialist vision in their bid for respectability and centrality, a role in the consensus constitutive of the culture of Occidentalism as we have come to understand it.

CHAPTER FOUR

Occidentalism and the Erotics of the Self

In this chapter I want to continue the previous chapter's discussion of the so-called civilizing process that came to be seen to lie at the heart of the project to make England Western, in order to connect it more fully to a certain economy of desire, and a certain related mode or logic of subjectivity, with which it affiliated itself. The previous discussion of *Mansfield Park* allowed us to get a sense of the extent to which the treatment of desire within England came, by the early nineteenth century, to be increasingly situated in a global frame and seen as comprehensively bound up with shifts in the logics and patterns of empire. I now want to continue to elaborate this connection, but specifically with regard to the Orient, which from the 1790s on emerged as the primary locus of alternative economies of desire and of subjectivity, ones threatening to the emergent Occidental subject and the productive libidinal order with which that subject gradually came to be bound up.

The more the Orient came to be seen as the other to the emergent Western sense of self, the more it also came to attract the attention not only of those interested in stamping out resistance to the logic of Occidental selfhood but also of those interested in developing critiques of—or alternatives to—that sense of self and the economies of sexuality and desire associated with it. This of course ought to make it all the more surprising that questions of race and empire have played such a relatively minor role in so much (though not all) of the considerable body of scholarship on gender and sexuality in the Romantic period; or that the racial, civilizational, and imperial or proto-imperial affiliations of certain modes of gender discourse in the period (above all, from Mary Wollstonecraft onward, in critiques of Orientalized femininity and effeminacy in the name of a proto-Occidental, rational, virtuous masculinity) should have received as little notice as they have; or, for that matter, that it should ever have seemed possible to think of gender and sexual desire in this period strictly in domestic terms, as though the domestic existed in isolation from the global and the imperial, and as though the discourses of gender and sexuality in the period were not completely saturated with references to the non-European, and specifically the Oriental. By the turn of the nineteenth century, to think through these matters was almost inevitably to think in racial and civilizational terms, as an emergent Occidentalism sought to differentiate itself from an Oriental other.

This chapter will begin with a discussion of Byron, whose Eastern tales— and in particular *The Giaour*—opened up an aesthetic space for imagining other modes of desire and being, which were seen to be incompatible with the structures and requirements of Occidentalism. We will then turn to Charlotte Dacre's little-read novel *Zofloya*, in which the discourse of Orientalism also features very prominently, only, I would argue, with a very different sense of the stakes for desire and subjectivity than that which drew Byron to the East. For all the differences between Byron and Dacre, however, what the juxtaposition of their two texts will allow us to see is the extent to which the East/West opposition built into Occidentalism was ultimately concerned not with geography as such, or even with what Said calls imaginative geography, but with the consolidation of a specific mode of subjectivity and, eventually, with the impetus to either colonize (to civilize) or to eradicate various alternatives to it, at home in Westernizing England as much as in England's far-flung colonial possessions.

1. BYRON AND EASTERN DESIRE

It is all too tempting to imagine a form of imperial cosmopolitanism in bourgeois terms, that is, in terms of a self who can come and go unfettered and feel, or claim to feel, at home anywhere, even while actually being contained in a bubble that prevents much actual contact with other peoples and cultures. Byron and his characters have often been thought of in these terms, as projections of a stable and contained Western self across different cultural spaces, particularly in the Orient. What I want to propose here is that Byron's Eastern tales are grounded not in such autonomous forms of agency—consumers of eroticized scenes of cultural difference—but rather in an almost utopian effort to imagine eroticism as a force to open up and explode the contours and limits of Occidentalist individualism. Far from being autonomous agents who project an internalized logic of power and desire onto external others, the heroes of Byron's Eastern tales are more productively read in terms of Byron's interest in imagining alternative forms of desire, of temporality, and of being than those sanctioned by the Occidentalist project.

When the hero of Byron's 1814 poem *Lara* returns from parts unknown (though presumably, given its associations, somewhere in the East), his servants and others are unable to read him. He no longer belongs to their settled, established, conventional Occidental world, but stands a being apart:

> There was in him a vital scorn of all:
> As if the worst had fall'n which could befall,
> He stood a stranger in this breathing world,
> An erring spirit from another hurled;
> A thing of dark imaginings, that shaped
> By choice the perils he by chance escaped;
> But 'scaped in vain, for in their memory yet
> His mind would half exult and half regret.[1]

Lara has in fact become quite literally inscrutable to them:

> In him inexplicably mix'd appeared
> Much to be loved and hated, sought and feared;
> Opinion varying o'er his hidden lot,
> In praise or railing ne'er his name forgot;
> His silence formed a theme for others' prate—
> They guess'd—they gazed—they fain would know his fate.
> What had he been? what was he, thus unknown,
> Who walked their world, his lineage only known?
> A hater of his kind?[2]

Lara seems, in short, a man lifted out of—perhaps liberated from—national customs and cultures, someone who can cross borders apparently in the manner advocated about twenty years previously by Kant in his theorization of the "cosmopolitan right" of the citizen of the world.[3] The same might be said of all of the heroes of Byron's Eastern tales, except that what we might be tempted to consider their cosmopolitan nature turns out to hinge not so much on their being at home and feeling a sense of belonging anywhere, but rather on the exact opposite: what unites them is their lack of belonging, their sense of dislocation, their feeling at home *nowhere*. Far from being free and at ease anywhere their journeys take them, they are haunted and hunted, outcasts, misfits, and renegades. Of Conrad, in *The Corsair*, "That man of loneliness and mystery, / Scarce seen to smile, and seldom heard to sigh," we read:

> He knew himself a villain—but he deem'd
> The rest no better than the thing he seem'd;
> And scorn'd the best as hypocrites who hid
> Those deeds the bolder spirit plainly did.
> He knew himself detested, but he knew
> The hearts that loath'd him, crouch'd and dreaded too.
> Lone, wild, and strange, he stood alike exempt
> From all affection and from all contempt[4].

Alp, the hero of *The Siege of Corinth*, is also described as a loner and a renegade, fighting against his own people:

> From Venice—once a race of worth
> His gentle sires—he drew his birth;
> But late an exile from her shore,
> Against his countrymen he bore
> The arms they taught to bear; and now
> The turban girt his shaven brow.[5]

And, perhaps most famously, the unnamed hero of *The Giaour* is also described as a man out of place, of unknown origin and with no sense of attachment or even identity, picked out as "yon lone caloyer" from among the inmates of a monastery:

> 'Tis twice three years at summer tide
> Since first among our freres he came;
> And here it soothes him to abide
> For some dark deed he will not name.
> But never at our vesper prayer,
> Nor e'er before confession chair
> Kneels he, nor recks he when arise
> Incense or anthem to the skies,
> But broods within his cell alone,
> His faith and race alike unknown.
> The sea from Paynim land he crost,
> And here ascended from the coast;
> Yet seems he not of Othman race,

But only Christian in his face;
I'd judge him some stray renegade,
Repentant of the change he made.[6]

At home nowhere, the heroes of Byron's Eastern tales emerge from the erotically charged contact zone between Orient and Occident to which Byron himself was sufficiently drawn as to ultimately sacrifice his life there. As Andrew Elfenbein points out, it has become something of a critical commonplace to see the heroes of the Eastern tales as Byron's projections of himself.[7] And although Elfenbein also quite rightly pushes us to ask more self-critically how this consensus came to emerge, there is no doubt that it is all too tempting to read in Byron's heroes his own sense of exile and dislocation, his separation at once from an Occident in which he no longer felt at home and from a Levantine life-world which he found immensely attractive but to which he knew he could never truly belong. Abigail Keenan, for example, argues that this contact zone offered Byron a space in which to express his "othered self and voice," and in particular a space in which to work out his own complex sexual identity through his explorations of what she identifies as "sexual outlaws" like the Giaour. "What we find throughout these tales are men isolated, displaced and left without a country and without meaningful relationships," writes Keenan. "They reflect a poetics of estrangement" that she identifies with Byron's own.[8] Louis Crompton argues that this sense of estrangement had to do with Byron's own sexuality, especially in the context of what he calls the "homophobic witch hunts" that characterized Georgian England.[9]

Whatever position one takes on the relationship between Byron and his heroes, many scholars have also jumped from reading the extent to which Byron's heroes' sense of displacement mirrored his own to claiming that this represents a subversion of Orientalism—and in particular an undermining, if not an outright negation, of the thesis advanced by Edward Said in his work of that title. In their nuanced and insightful readings of Byron's Eastern tales, both Alan Richardson and Nigel Leask have proposed versions of such an argument, even if only in passing. Leask, for example, writes that although Said is right to assert the links between representations of the East and the institutions of colonial power, "the internal and external pressures determining and undermining such representations are more various than Said's thesis will allow."[10] Peter Cochran makes a similar argument, albeit in less productive and more strident terms, in an article that aims to clear Byron of the charge of Orientalism partly by developing a gratuitously crude *ad hominem* attack on Said himself.[11]

The assumption underlying such an attempt to use Byron to develop a critique of Said's thesis is that Byron's ability to insert himself into the gap between East and West proves that Said exaggerates the extent of the binary opposition between Occident and Orient and the ways in which it was developed by Orientalist discourses and institutions. Such an assumption represents both a misapprehension of Said's thesis and a misunderstanding of the dynamic relationship between Orientalism and imperialism in the Romantic period. I am not as interested in dwelling on the former point as I am in developing the latter.

In developing the ambiguous cultural and political terrain of the Eastern tales, Byron was—far from negating the powerful Orientalist discourses and institutions discussed by Said—taking advantage of them. If it's true, in other words, that Byron is interested in cultural ambiguity, a sense of displacement between East and West, that move relies for its own coherence on the whole range of assumptions and stereotypes generated and sustained by Orientalism itself. His gesture toward the culturally ambiguous, the in-between, would be meaningless—it would fall flat—without the presence of an Orientalism which it therefore affirms rather than subverts. The irony of claiming that Byron sought to subvert Orientalism is that virtually everyone who makes that claim also knows and quotes those celebrated lines in which Byron advises Thomas Moore to "stick to the east" as the "only poetical policy." The North, South, and West "have all been exhausted; but from the East we have nothing but [Southey's] unsaleables," Byron famously wrote. "The little I have done in that way is merely a 'voice in the wilderness' for you; and, if it has had any success, that also will prove that the public are now orientalizing and pave the path for you."[12] As Leask points out, Byron is here speaking "like a Levantine or East India merchant who has tapped a lucrative source of raw materials in a newly opened up Orient, which he feels will make a splash on the home market."[13]

The market for cultural Orientalism was not, however, quite as bare as Byron made it sound in that well-known letter to Moore. Marilyn Butler has argued that Byron's Eastern tales were a direct response to Southey's *Curse of Kehama* (1810) and that *The Giaour* launched a series of liberal poems on the topic of empire at least in part to counter Southey's espousal of the evangelical cause in India. "Written in the year when Parliament was brought to allow 'missionizing' in India, it [*The Giaour*] questions the claims to progressiveness of proselytizing Christians. Instead of finding Christian morality necessarily advanced, it likens its backward, despotic tendencies to those of Islam, the other current imperial religion." Butler cautions, however, that Byron's own "policies for empire in the East, insofar as his works imply them, appear feudal, nostalgic, and just as surely constructed in the interests of one class within Western society as the policy to Christianise was. It's not clear in the light of history (if indeed it is a light) that Byron had overall the better of his political argument with Southey."[14]

Southey's position was not, however, quite as unambiguous as Butler makes it seem. As I argued in *Romantic Imperialism* (and this is a point to which I will return in the next chapter as well), both Orientalist discourse and British imperial policy were undergoing momentous changes in the transition from the late eighteenth to the early nineteenth century. We can now understand these changes as taking place alongside the emergence of the Occidentalist mode of thought that I have been describing in this book. One point that it is essential to bear in mind here, then, is that the differences between Southey and Macaulay (and William Jones, Warren Hastings, James Mill, Charles Grant, and countless others) demonstrate not that Orientalism does not exist as a coherent system of thought, but that it underwent a momentous shift in the Romantic period, emerging in a new and much more fully and systematically Occidentalized form by the 1830s and ending up in a continuum with Occidentalism itself, as I suggested in the Introduction and elsewhere in this volume.[15] What I now want to argue is that, for all his investment in a certain mode of Orientalism, Byron refused the Occidentalist imperative that emerged and began to transform Orientalist thought in his own lifetime.

Even if Byron felt himself to be, like Lara, "a stranger in this breathing world," and if he used characters like Lara, Conrad, Lap, and the unnamed Giaour to project his own sense of displacement between cultures, that does not mean that his work should be seen to undermine the opposition between Orient and Occident or mobilized as evidence in the critique of the discourse of Orientalism in general. Even in those moments when Byron seems to go out of his way to deny the difference between East and West, he is often also subtly reinforcing it. "I see not much difference between us and the Turks," he wrote in a letter to Henry Drury from his cabin on a thirty-six-gun Royal Navy frigate in the Dardanelles (lest we forget all the machinery of empire that actually enabled his trip to Turkey), "save that we have foreskins and they none, that they have long dresses and we short, and that we talk much and they little.—In England the vices in fashion are whoring & drinking, in Turkey Sodomy & smoking, we prefer a girl and a bottle, they a pipe and a pathic."[16] So:on the one hand there may not be many substantive differences between us and them (i.e., one man's girl is another man's pathic); on the other hand, all those Oriental stereotypes really are true.

The point that I am trying to make here is not that Byron's individual trajectory could not on its own undermine the much larger institutionalized discourses of Orientalism that both frame and contain his work; it is that he took advantage of a certain mode of Orientalism for his own purposes, and hence, far from undoing or challenging that mode of Orientalism, he reinforced it, in order to be able to insert his narratives and characters (and perhaps himself, though we must keep Elfenbein's caution in mind) into what he imagined to be the gap between West and East.

Byron frequently expressed a desire to get away from England and, once away, never to return, or to return only to attend to such business transactions as demanded his physical presence there. "It neither suits me—nor I it," he wrote of England in a letter to Douglas Kinnaird. "If I could manage to arrange my pecuniary concerns in England—so as to pay my debts—& leave me what would be here [Venice] a very fair income—(though nothing remarkable at home) you might consider me as posthumous—for I would never willingly dwell in the 'tight little Island' [Britain]."[17] Not exactly the Orient, then, but rather what Byron thought of as the cultural and political no-man's-land between East and West, including Venice, offered him the opportunity to generate characters who could also seemingly embody his own desire to live as a perpetual stranger.

Caroline Franklin suggests that Byron took advantage of his estranged characters and the culturally and politically ambiguous world through which they traveled to criticize the normative sexual politics of Regency England, though she points out that Byron's critique of chivalry in particular is both antifeminist (offering a libertine "voice of opposition to [the] bourgeois, protestant ideology of [British] femininity") and emancipatory, critical of the period's emergent sexual and political ideologies.[18] Elfenbein argues, similarly, that we need to read Byron's behavior in the context of the fact that "aristocrats in Regency society reinforced their class solidarity by tolerating behavior that flouted norms associated with Victorian 'household morality' as set out in the work of writers such as Hannah More, Maria Edgeworth and Jane Taylor."[19] And Leask develops a similar line of thought, suggesting that "Byron in 'renegado form' embraced Thomas Thornton's critique of chivalry as the marker of Western superiority over 'orientals,' a fact which strongly inflected his attitude to the question of Greece."[20] Alan Richardson also argues that Byron was able to make use of his characters' "cultural transvestism" to sustain a critique of British cultural and political norms, including what Richardson refers to as the "phallic imperialism" of the era. Richardson adds that "in his pursuit of sexual and cultural difference Byron is more engaged in a (however risky) 'imperialism of the imagination' . . . , attempting to figure a transcendent self against a proliferating series of possible 'other' selves, than in disrupting the master code of Western self-fashioning."[21]

I am not so sure about this last claim, however. What I want to argue here, in fact, is that Byron's refusal of the Occidentalist imperative is actually contained in his treatment of the heroes of the Eastern tales themselves and their refusal—rather than embodiment—of the logic of a transcendent self transposed against an other. In other words, Byron's engagement with Occidentalism is tied to the erotically charged nature of the characters he produces in the tales: if they don't fit in, that is because they refuse and cannot thrive in, or even perhaps continue to exist in, the Occidental space which demands of them that they conform to its emergent norms, the normative structures it makes available for sexuality and subjectivity. Which is exactly why, unlike the period's more conventional figures, as Elfenbein points out, "Byron's heroes had neither the sincere earnestness nor the melodramatic wickedness that readers had come to expect. As Francis Jeffrey noted, Byron's works presented 'no very enlightened or equitable principles of morality,' and Henry Crabb Robinson thought his poetry lacked 'the recommendation of teaching any moral truth.' For readers used to moral instruction, Byron's heroes were a puzzle."[22] Byron's plots, Elfenbein adds, "never resolve the ambiguities of his hero. No moment of ultimate judgment arrives, and Byron neither unmasks him as truly evil nor lets him grow into an ideal."[23] A culturally and politically ambiguous space, in other words, afforded Byron the opportunity to flesh out morally ambiguous characters which it would have been much more difficult so situate somewhere amid the immediately legible, readily identifiable, and class- and race-specific spaces of Occidentalizing England itself.

That desire expresses, however, a very specific understanding of the relationship between personal and cultural identity, on the one hand, and place, on the other: an understanding that Byron would have shared to a certain extent with Southey, and, whether he liked it or not, even somewhat with Wordsworth and Burke as well. On this view—the later nineteenth-century ramifications of which Ian Baucom has explored at length[24]—individual identities and whole cultures emerge in inextricable association with particular places. A shift in place enables, perhaps even generates, a shift in identity. As we will see in the next chapter, Southey's Orientalist epics rely on this stable association of identity and place: he can move from location to location and create narratives that pertain to and reflect the underlying nature of their site of origin. Individuals and whole cultures are generated by the locations they inhabit; even if there are universal currents that all cultures share in common, they do so according to the specificities of their own location. If the location is altered in nature, so are the individuals who inhabit and hence embody its values. Byron, for his part, was more interested in the gaps between discrete locations than in those locations themselves, but a similar logic drives his poetry.

One way of reading the culturally ambiguous—we might even say the culturally androgynous—characters of Byron's Eastern tales, then, is in terms of the sense that they can be seen to reflect the culturally ambiguous space from which they emerge, which in turn, as I have already said, takes for granted the binary opposition between East and West generated by an Orientalist discourse that Byron's work affirms rather than challenges. Such an essentially Romantic position would be changed forever with the emergence and development of the notion that individual identities—and, through them, from the ground up, whole cultural identities—can be divorced from the specificities of their spatial locations, an idea expressed in Macaulay's argument (to which we will return in the next chapter) that Indians could be turned into virtual Englishmen and, indeed, in the general idea that the empire should be thought of as a machine for generating new individual identities (as we saw in the chapter on Austen). Unlike either Southey or Macaulay, however—or Shelley for that matter—Byron did not want those other cultures to be transformed. And this was for a simple reason: if the whole world were to be transformed into a kind of global West, there would no longer be anywhere to escape to, and culturally ambiguous spaces would be threatened with eradication..

In attempting to break and disrupt the logic tying Orientalism to Occidentalism as one continuous process, Byron's work might be seen as an exception helping to prove the rule whose formation I have been exploring in this book. But that is because his understanding of the Orient, and his conception of Orientalism, is at odds—out of synch—with the emergent Occidentalism of his own time and more closely affiliated with a particular Orientalist logic that the turn into the nineteenth century had increasingly made to seem impossible. Part of what is at stake here is the experimentation with other modes of identity, desire, and eroticism and with other modes of thinking of time that the Eastern tales afforded Byron, and it is to this connection that I would now like to turn, via a reading that I want to ground specifically in the most complex and most formally ambitious of Byron's Eastern tales, *The Giaour*, which I take to be at odds with the racial and cultural logic of Occidentalism.

To see this, we must be careful in reading the heroes of Byron's Eastern tales as the products of the culturally ambiguous space out of which they are generated. It is all too tempting to read them as autonomous agents, versions of the self-regulating individual subject, or the transcendent self, that emerged from the 1790s on as one of the central organizing principles of Occidentalism. Such an approach would lead us to see the heroes as individualistic, even hedonistic, consumers of the scene out of which they emerge (as indeed they, and Byron, have often been read).

At this stage of my argument, I want to propose another way of thinking through Byron's Eastern heroes, suggesting that we see them not as autonomous individual subjects or agents, but rather as existing within—as bound up with—the multidimensional spatiotemporal force field, charged by affect and desire, where the competing realities of Occident and Orient (themselves also understood to be in a process of formation) make contact, overlap, and struggle. In this field, an individual being exists not as a predetermined autonomous enclosure but rather as a complex of affective relations that emerges and is caught up with the surrounding field. Remove such a being from that force field, and his being diminishes—he fades into inscrutable shapes and shadows, precisely as we see with Lara ("a thing of dark imaginings") or Conrad: "Lone, wild, and strange, he stood alike / From all affection and from all contempt"; that is, cut off from social being exactly to the extent that he is cut off from the affective field of desire. What we see activated in Byron's Eastern heroes, then, is an ontology of desire, which strangely places him much more comprehensively in the camp of Blake than we might at first have imagined.[25] There is more at stake in this ontological process, which I would now like to explore via my reading of *The Giaour*.

Normally, to offer a plot summary of a narrative poem is to do the work a disservice. In this case, however, what drives the poem is not the plot but rather the discordant and contradictory frames through which we access it. The hero is a young Venetian (Venice, you may recall, held sway over parts of what would become Ottoman-held Greece until the very end of the eighteenth century) who has no name and is identified only (and tellingly) as "the Giaour," a word which is an English corruption of a Turkish corruption of the Arabic word for "infidel." (Indeed, that the hero is identified solely by the designation applied to him by his antagonists already tells you almost everything you need to know about the poem in a nutshell.) The story is set somewhere at the fringes of the Ottoman Empire, where Occident shades over into Orient. The Giaour has an affair with Leila, one of the harem girls of the local Ottoman commander, Hassan. Their affair is discovered, Leila is captured and drowned in "typical" Oriental manner (albeit a circumstance "now less common in the East than formerly," the Advertisement hastens to reassure us), and the Giaour achieves vengeance over Hassan when the

latter, in pursuit of him, falls into his ambush and is killed in battle. The
Giaour then withdraws from society and ends his days on a remote monastic island, where the Christian monks want nothing to do with him, regarding him as not one of their own, though they also recognize that "seems he
not of Othman race" either.[26]

As I said, the frames are what matter here, and the plot, such as it is,
is visited and revisited in a fragmentary and disjointed manner as we sift
through a whole range of different narrative voices, including both Ottoman
Muslim narrators and Christian ones, as well as at one point the voice of
the Giaour himself. Much of the story is relayed in the voice of a Muslim
fisherman who had been minding his own business when he was pressed
into service in order to take Leila out on the water so she could be drowned.
He also sees the Giaour galloping past on the way to set the ambush for Hassan or perhaps in flight afterward. In either case, he understands the stake of
the battle and then recognizes the Giaour years afterward when he sees him
again on the monastic island: "How name ye yon lone Caloyer," he asks the
monks; "His features I have scann'd before / In mine own land—'tis many a
year, / Since, dashing by the lonely shore, / I saw him urge as fleet a steed /
As ever serv'd a horseman's need. / But once I saw that face—yet then / It
was so mark'd with inward pain / I could not pass it by again; / It breathes
the same dark spirit now, / As death were stamped upon his brow."[27]

It is worth noting that although I say the fisherman recognizes the
Giaour, in fact in their encounters recognition is always a lack of recognition: "Who thundering comes on blackest steed?"[28] he asks at the first
sighting; "who and what art thou / Of foreign garb and fearful brow?"[29] he
asks later, and then finally, "How name ye yon lone Caloyer?" To recognize
the Giaour is to grapple with an absence rather than a presence—hence his
"name" which is not a name, an individual designation, but rather a derivation from three different languages intended precisely to deny the individuality of the other. The absence of marking turns into a mark; the lack
of identity is what identity turns out to be.

In addition to the variety of voices, which are difficult to identify, there
is a series of flashbacks and forward leaps, all of which are also quite difficult and at times impossible to piece together, and the narrative voice
changes over several times as we move back and forth through time. The
last thing to add in terms of general description of the poem is that when the
narrative is spoken in a Muslim voice, the attendant references and imagery
refer to Oriental themes ("Rhamazani's sun," "Bairam's feast," "Sultana
of the Nightingale," "the jewel of Giamschid," etc.) and when it is spoken
in something approximating a European or what we might cautiously call

a Western voice, the imagery is of a very different variety ("his rounde-lay," "say, is not this Thermopylae?" etc.). The one exception to this rule is the Giaour himself, who invokes both a Christian imaginary and a Muslim one and sometimes freely mixes both. "The very name of Nazarene / Was wormwood to his Paynim spleen,"[30] he says in explaining Hassan to the monk, albeit referring to Christianity as "thy creed"; but shortly afterward he explains love as "light from heaven— / A spark of that immortal fire / With angels shar'd—by Alla given, / To lift from earth our low desire."[31]

The Giaour was published in a series of seven editions over a spread of several months in the summer and fall of 1813, each of which added new lines or sections of text, taking the poem from 407 lines in the first edi-tion of July to over thirteen hundred lines in the last, of November. The work's somewhat misleading subtitle is "A Fragment of a Turkish Tale"— misleading because it does not consist of a single fragment, but rather of a series of jarring and discordant fragments, whose dissonance was greatly amplified by the lines and sections gradually added during the period of re-vision. "All the 'fragments' in the poem," William Marshall argues in his 1961 essay on the poem, "representing the result of accretion with occa-sional verbal alteration and no more than trivial deletion, do not constitute a whole that can be pieced together. Any consideration of the structure or imagery of 'The Giaour,'" he adds, "should begin with this proposition."[32] Robert Gleckner, in his classic *Byron and the Ruins of Paradise*, disagrees with Marshall. "The basic plot is extraordinarily simple: it is all contained in the original 'sketch' of the poem. Byron's main interest, however, was not in the plot," Gleckner continues, "but rather in the conflicting points of view from which that plot could be viewed. The sketch is, as it were, a piece of sculpture around which the viewer walks in order to see it in dif-ferent lights and shadows, the eye building up a structure of fragmentary apperceptions, disjointed by virtue of their temporal and spatial disconti-nuity, but all tending toward a unified imaginative perception of the whole and its 'meaning.'"[33]

Here I would like to push Gleckner's argument a little further. Whereas he argues that the plot offers a single stabilized core which is then seen from a variety of different perspectives, what I want to suggest is that what the poem gives us access to is not a single reality as seen from a series of per-spectives, but, rather, a series of multiple realities. What Byron is pushing us to think about, then, is not the clash over perspectives on, or represen-tations of, a single reality, but rather the encounter and struggle between altogether different realities.[34] It is the discordant clash between these reali-ties, each of which is, moreover, internally unstable, that generates the eroticized force field which animates and gives life to the characters. What seems to be merely each individual's perspective, in other words, actually turns out to be the expression of the charged and contested reality to which it corresponds—charged and contested because it is under threat and facing dissolution—rather than merely a take on a fixed reality.

This turn toward a multiplicity of realities rather than a variety of perspectives on a single shared reality is what makes *The Giaour* both so difficult and so rich a text. It also explains the decentering of individual characters in the work, for, as I mentioned earlier, it is best to see the characters not as autonomous agents but rather as caught up with, inseparable from, perhaps even expressions or manifestations of, the realities to which they correspond and the charged force field constituted by the overlapping tension between these realities.

Take, for example, the clash between the Giaour and Hassan. The most straightforward reading of their relationship in conventional terms is that they form, together with Leila, one of those homoerotic love triangles discussed by Eve Sedgwick in *Between Men*, in which, as she argues (via René Girard), "the bond that links the two rivals is as intense and potent as the bond that links either of the rivals to the beloved" and hence that "the bonds of 'rivalry' and 'love,' differently as they are expressed, are equally powerful and in many senses equivalent."[35] And indeed the homoerotic bond of simultaneous rivalry and attraction between the Giaour and Hassan can be seen exactly in such terms. Their battle is erotically charged to the point where it might as well have been described as a sexual encounter *tout court*: "But Love itself could never pant / For all that Beauty sighs to grant, / With half the fervor Hate bestows / Upon the last embrace of foes, / When grappling in the fight they fold / Those arms that ne'er shall lose their hold; / Friends meet to part—Love laughs at faith;—/ True foes, once met, are joined til death."[36] The homoerotic bond here, even of hate, is far stronger and more durable than that of conventional love, a true union "'til death do us part," which is why it should come as no surprise that when the survivor of the ambush returns to inform Hassan's mother of her son's death, he tells her, "Lady, a fearful bride thy Son has wed."[37]

The limitation of such a reading, however, is that it is necessarily bound and limited to the plot. The dissonant, contradictory, and fragmentary nature of the text, however, keeps pulling us away from the plot narrowly conceived and hence away from the individual characters seen as autonomous agents to the force field composed of conflicting realities of which they are parts. Reading the characters as autonomous agents, lovers or haters in a conventional sense, misses the point that their very identities are not independent to begin with: quite literally, the Giaour could not be himself—the Giaour, the infidel—without Hassan; he is the self who is also other. These dynamics of attraction and accretion emerge out of the force field constituting the larger encounter between realities to which the text is always insistently drawing our attention. And if we shift our frame of reference away from the characters and the plot and toward the frame, we can understand eroticism as part of the force field of affective relations generated by the jarring overlap between multiple realities, to which the poem also keeps drawing our attention as narrative voice succeeds narrative voice, and flashbacks take turns with narrative based in the present or reflections on the future.

Time, indeed, is of the essence in *The Giaour*. The opening section (which was added in bits and pieces in the second, third, and fifth editions of the poem)[38] reflects the decline from a mythical golden age into an unstable present. And one of the refrains of the poem is that we are as cut off from a future as we are from the past—set adrift in the present. One of the operations of the poem, then, is to break down the very logic of unilinear, progressive time which was (and is) so essential to the logic and discourses of Occidentalism. The jarring and discordant flow of different temporal locations (present, past, future, flashback, memory, anticipation), combined with an alternation back and forth between specific instants ("'Twas but an instant," "'Twas but a moment," "in that instant," "in that drop of time")[39] and a larger temporal structure of an eternity ("infinite as boundless space")[40] which we can never access, insistently breaks down the very possibility of smooth linear time. And in terms of time, the Giaour shares Hassan's fate: just as the latter is doomed not to have a future ("But ne'er shall Hassan's Age repose / Along the brink at Twilight's close—/ The stream that filled that font is fled—/ The blood that warmed his heart is shed!"),[41] so too do we find the former cut adrift in time, cut off from a past to which he can never return and a future to which he is denied access.

What we are left with, then, is a sense of a discordant and heterogeneous present, generated by the struggle not between two characters but between two realities, each of which carries its own distinct structures of linear time (the Muslim as against the Christian, the proto-Western against the quasi-Eastern). If the poem's shattered form keeps dragging us back to the present, that is in part to reinforce the sense that this present is only made possible by the fact that one reality has not yet attained victory over the other. The key for Byron—hence his resistance to, his refusal of the dictates of Occidentalism—consists in making sure that the two realities remain intact and unbridged.

Byron could see that the process of Occidentalization could never stop simply with the civilizing of the West; having Westernized the West, it would have to go on to Westernize the East as well, to "civilize" it and extend to it the same set of cultural and social practices that had already transformed—or perhaps were in the process of transforming—the Occident. What we can detect in Byron, in other words, is the same Romantic spirit of resistance to modernization that we also detect in figures such as Blake and Southey, for different kinds of reasons and manifested in all kinds of ways, both ultraradical (Blake) and ultraconservative (Southey). What unites them is a particular sense of temporality, a refusal of the progressivist notion of linear time, of an unfolding and ultimately universal history to be imposed across different cultural locations and populations, and an embracing instead of a sense of time and space as profoundly uneven and fractured, dissonant.

In the case of Blake, as I argued in *William Blake and the Impossible History of the 1790s*, the refusal of the Occidentalist imperative was tied expressly to a refusal of the temporal logic of modernity and the modes of restricted, self-regulating subjectivity that emerged with that temporal logic.[42] Byron's refusal of the Occidentalist imperative involves an investment in ontological and libidinal forces that cannot be assimilated into a highly regulated ("tight") Occidentalist logic. The Romantic spirit of resistance that links Blake to Byron is best thought of not in transcendent terms, but rather in immanent and highly variable ones. And by no means does it encompass and contain all forms of writing or of thought in the Romantic period. The other point to make here is to recall that neither this Romantic refusal of Occidentalism nor its opposite is necessarily tied to a particular form of politics; the radical Shelley could embrace Occidentalism while the radical Blake could refuse it. This period of uneven contradictions could easily generate both trajectories, and they need to be read alongside one another, dare I say contrapuntally.

2. CHARLOTTE DACRE'S ORIENT

If the Orient seemed to offer Byron a site from which to think about questioning or resisting the imperatives of Occidentalism, it plays a very different role in Charlotte Dacre's seemingly little-read 1807 novel *Zofloya; or, The Moor*. Rather than dreading the colonization of the world and the homogenization of its cultural spaces in the Occidental project—Byron's worst nighmare—*Zofloya* anticipates and embraces both.

Like much of Byron's poetry, Dacre's novel is set in Venice. Its heroine is a young woman named Victoria de Loredani. She and her brother Leonardo are raised in an aristocratic family, but both children are spoiled by not being taught to regulate their affections and desires (as the narrator reminds us at least a dozen times, if not more, through the course of the novel). Victoria, for example, is described as "beautiful and accomplished as an angel . . . proud, haughty, and self-sufficient—of a wild, ardent, and irrepressible spirit, indifferent to reproof, careless of censure—of an implacable, revengeful and cruel nature, and bent upon gaining the ascendancy in whatever she engaged." She is like a nasty, rather than merely self-destructively self-obsessed, version of Elizabeth Eliot in Austen's *Persuasion*.

When Victoria is fifteen, her mother abandons what had been a happy (but conventional) marriage and precipitates the destruction of the Loredani family by running off with the dangerous German rake Count Ardolph, who then, to add injury to insult, kills Victoria's father in a duel. This disaster past, and now in the care of her mother and her German lover, Victoria soon falls in love with Count Berenza, a match that her mother and Ardolph seek to sabotage by basically imprisoning her, but to no avail. Soon enough Victoria has seduced Berenza into marrying her (against his own original plan—and it is important to note that the woman is in the driving seat in this, as in almost all the sexual relationships in the novel). But Victoria soon tires of the "refined" and "delicate" Berenza, who, we are told, lacks both the mind and the body to be "a true voluptuary" and never satisfies her sexually or otherwise.

By way of variety, the sexually aggressive Victoria latches onto Berenza's somewhat more masculine (but not really any more virile) Hispanophile brother Henriquez. The latter, however, is committed (though not yet married) to Lilla, "an unformed wisp of girlish virtue," as one critic (James Dunn) puts it, who is "seen rather than heard."[43] Blonde, innocent, virginal, utterly vacuous, a marker of "feminine emptiness," Lilla is, in short, "the epitome of an emerging British domestic ideology transplanted rather clumsily to fifteenth-century Italy," as Diane Hoeveler puts it.[44] And she is the diametrical opposite of the dark, aggressive, assertive, sexually voracious Victoria.

What happens next is all too predictable, perhaps (and I trust that the hasty plot summary offered here will be excused, given the somewhat obscure nature of the novel). Victoria jettisons the hapless Berenza by poisoning him; and she stabs Lilla to shreds and throws her body off a cliff. Her counselor and assistant in these crimes is none other than Satan, who appears to her in the guise of the Moorish servant Zofloya (the original Zofloya, whom we meet only in passing, and even then about halfway into the novel whose title bears his name, had been murdered by a jealous Italian servant). Ultimately, Satan exults in having captured the mind, body, and presumably the soul of Victoria, and he dashes her off a cliff, thus bringing to a close one of the Romantic period's most interesting literary exercises in drugs, sex, and violence.

There has been surprisingly little scholarship on *Zofloya*. Most of what exists centers on a reading of the novel's gender dynamics. In her article on the novel, for example, Anne Mellor points out that one of the main themes of the novel is the frustration of female sexual desire and an accompanying sense of male impotence.[45] Indeed, the critical consensus on *Zofloya* is that Dacre develops a devastating critique of the emerging ideology of bourgeois domesticity and its attendant sexual norms and values, which privilege masculine agency and feminine modesty—and that the character of Victoria represents a dire threat to that ideology because of her irrepressible sexual desires and her refusal to accept the subordinate, docile, passive role assigned to women by Occidentalist domestic ideology and, indeed, because of the war she wages on those characters who do accept and play out their appropriate gender roles (most obviously Henriquez and Lilla, whose relationship Victoria physically destroys). Thus most critics point out that Victoria comes to seem physically more powerful—more masculine in a reductively literal sense—through the novel, and not only in contrast with the hyperfeminized Lilla. Of course, because of the way in which Victoria is ultimately destroyed at the end of the novel, while *Zofloya* does in one sense elaborate a critique of early nineteenth-century British domestic ideology, it also symbolically marks the triumph of that ideology by containing and destroying this upstart of a threat to it, while signaling all along (by narratorial interjections) the need for men and women to regulate themselves and behave in accordance with the Occidental social norms gradually being institutionalized at the time of the novel's composition in early nineteenth-century Britain.

What is missing from the accounts of Zofloya's gender and sexual dynamics in the existing scholarship, and what I would like to add here, is a sense of the relationship between the sexual and the racial or civilizational components of the novel, which have so far been taken far too much for granted. Thus, most of the scholarship tends to read the Moorish character Zofloya—whose profound attractiveness is depicted as inseparable from his powerful masculinity—as a kind of "black" foil for the sexually inadequate, even quasi-impotent, "white" male characters, especially Berenza and Henriquez.

Although much of the literary scholarship on Moorish characters in English literature from, say, *Othello* on tend to misread Moors as African rather than Arab, Moors were, culturally and linguistically speaking, affiliated with the Arab world, and specifically al-Andalus and Arab Spain, where Zofloya himself comes from (thus depictions of Moorish "blackness" need to be seen in comparison with depictions of Indian "blackness" in the eighteenth and nineteenth centuries). I'm not just splitting hairs here: the difference is significant because, especially in a novel like *Zofloya*, Arab characters need to be read as representatives of the Orient, rather than of Africa. And indeed so it is with Zofloya himself.

But what about the "white" characters who occupy the other pole of the black/white dichotomy with which most of the extant scholarship has framed Dacre's novel? Precisely because of the powerful presence of Zofloya the Moor, all the scholarship so far reads Berenza, Henriquez, Lilla, Victoria, and the other Italian characters as "white." That may be a tempting move, partly, perhaps, because it would allow us to underscore Diane Hoeveler's characterization of the novel as "racist, xenophobic and misogynistic," but I don't think it is historically, culturally, or politically accurate, any more than it would be to lump all the Italian characters together as "Western," in opposition to Zofloya's Easternness.

Zofloya's setting in fifteenth-century Venice is the key here, precisely because, even less than England, Italy in general (and Venice in particular) would hardly have been considered a "civilized," Westernized space in the early nineteenth century (never mind the fifteenth century). This explains perhaps why Dacre set the novel in Venice rather than back in England (and this sort of thinking goes for the gothic genre in general, at least that major strand of it preoccupied with southern European spaces, above all Italy). It also makes sense of the peculiarity that most critics register with little more than bemusement, namely, the transposition of a story ultimately concerned with nineteenth-century British domestic ideology to fifteenth-century Venice. Perhaps it would have been easier for an early nineteenth-century British audience to recognize Italy as an undeveloped space and the Venetians as not quite—or at least not automatically—Occidental.

Consider how Venice is depicted in *Zofloya*. The Venetians, we read, are a proud people. "In no country was the pride of nobility carried to a greater extent; their manners, also, received a deep and gloomy tincture from the nature of their government, which in its nature was jealous and suspicious, dooming sometimes to a public, sometimes to a private death, on mere surmise or apprehension of design against the state, and always by secret trial, its most distinguished members." The Venetians, the narrator adds, united "the Spanish and Italian character in its most sublimated state of passion. . . . Sanguinary and violent by nature, climate, habit, and education, the hatred

of the Venetians once excited became implacable, and endured through life."
Held in thrall by fear of the dreadful Inquisition and Il Consiglio de Dieci,
the novel's Venetians are, in short, essentially Orientalized; for are these not
essentially Oriental features—jealousy, fear, paranoia, violence, political and
judicial arbitrariness, religious extremism?

If we accept this point, however, it is no longer possible to impose—
as most of the scholarship on *Zofloya* does—a relatively straightforward
West/East, white/black, civilized/barbarian interpretive grid on the novel.
If we accept that Venice itself is Orientalized, in other words, it would be
difficult to argue that Zofloya is *more* Oriental than the Italian characters:
Orientalist discourse does not admit of degrees of Orientalism. So the binary breaks down.

After all, Zofloya himself is hardly the only hyper-Orientalized character in the novel. It is only later on that one appreciates the significance of
what seems to be a passing reference to Victoria's skin tone rather early in
the novel, where the narrator refers to the "Orient tint" on her cheek. In her
violent confrontation with Lilla toward the end of the novel, most critics
have pointed out the opposition the novel plays with between the "masculine features" of Victoria on the one hand and the "fairy delicacy" of Lilla.
Fewer have noted also that a racial discourse is consistently deployed in the
descriptions of Victoria. In sharp contrast with the "snowy" and "alabaster"
(and of course blonde) features of Lilla, our attention is repeatedly drawn
to Victoria's "black-fringed eyelids, reposing upon a cheek of dark and animated hue," and her "raven tresses hanging unconfined," an opposition that
helps mark the fall of Lilla to her "barbarous enemy." Lilla herself echoes
the narrator in recognizing the opposition, denouncing her tormentor less
than a page after this first reference to barbarism as "barbarous Victoria."

Nor is the Orientalization and barbarization of Victoria a matter of skin
and hair color; rather, those features signify in recognizably racial terms the
interior barbarism (i.e., literally the uncivilized state) of Victoria's mind.
"From her infancy untaught, therefore unaccustomed to subdue herself,
she had no conception of that *refined* species of virtue which consists in
self-denial," we are told; "the proud triumph of mind over the weakness
of the heart, she had ever been unconscious of; education had never corrected the evil propensities that were by nature hers; hence pride, stubborn-
ness, the gratification of self, contempt and ignorance of the nobler proper-
ties of the mind, with a strong tincture of the darker passions, revenge, hate,
and cruelty, made up the sum of her early character. Example, a *mother's*
example, had more than corroborated every tendency to evil, and the un-

happy Victoria was destitute of a single actuating principle, that might, in consideration of its guilt, deter her from the pursuit of a favorite object. *Her mind, alas, was an eternal night, which the broad beam of virtue never illumined.*" Thus the novel deploys a frankly civilizational discourse to describe Victoria's state of mind. And in stark contrast with Lilla's pleasure, we learn that Victoria's was not "that innocent vivacity which springs at once from the purity and sanity of the heart; *it was the wild and frightful mirth of a tyrant, who condemns his subjects to the torture, that he may laugh at their agonies;* it was the brilliant glare of the terrible volcano, pregnant even in its beauty with destruction!" And of course she expresses "the wildest phrenzy of passion, *the most ungovernable hate,* and thirst, even for the blood of all who might oppose her." Again, all of these terms draw on what were by the time of the novel's publication in 1807 well-established components of the Orientalist repertoire.[46]

And on this point too it's difficult to argue that Zofloya himself is *more* Oriental than Victoria. It's on this very issue, in fact, that it becomes essential, as I hinted earlier, to consider that the character Zofloya is mistakenly read by most critics as "black" or at any rate simply non-European. The *real* Zofloya plays only a passing role in the novel; he is spotted by Victoria briefly and then he suddenly disappears—as I mentioned earlier, it turns out that he has been murdered by a fellow servant, who confesses to his crime. The "Zofloya" that dominates the action of the second half of the novel is then not an Arab; he is the devil who has embodied the form of the departed Arab servant, about whom neither we nor Victoria know anything. And there's significance in the distinction. The devil takes the form of Zofloya when he appears to Victoria (first in a dream, then in "real life") because that cluster of tendencies she associates in her own mind with Zofloya (violence, raw sexuality, desire, and so on—the essences of the East) are projected into an image that takes the shape of those desires. The devil in this sense is a projection emanating from Victoria. He is no more Arab than she is. On the other hand, he is also no more Occidental—or white— than she is either. Let's put it this way: the false "Zofloya" is literally the embodiment of the desires and motivations that drive Victoria but that the emergent Occidentalist ideology of early nineteenth-century England would mark as improper, wrong, off-limits. Zofloya is the undiluted, unambiguous, unambivalent embodiment of the uncivilized inner nature of Victoria; he is more her twin than her other; or he is her perfection, her distillation into a pure position.

With this in mind, we are now in a position to return to the critical consensus regarding the novel's gender and sexual dynamics. If the emergent ideology of Occidentalist domesticity (as embodied so paradigmatically in the character of little sweet innocent blonde Lilla) can be thought of in racial or civilizational terms as "Westernness," then the threat to that ideology (as embodied in Victoria just as much as in her projected inner devil, "Zofloya") is Orientalized. What this suggests more than ever, though, is that it is insufficient to read the novel as narrating a Western woman's desire for the non-Western other: for the desiring woman herself is *already* non-Western precisely because her desires are as unregulated as her "raven tresses hanging unconfined." Indeed, female desire itself is shown to be not civilized precisely to the extent that it is not Western. And though the novel's preoccupation is with specifically female desire, I would argue that the same thing could be said of male desire as well. Moreover, I'd add—and I think Blake and Spinoza help us see this—that desire need not be restricted to the field of sexuality. Civilization is the regulation of desire, precisely as Norbert Elias argues (see the Introduction). Think of the "priests in black gowns / walking their rounds / and binding with briars / my joys and desires" that we see in Blake's "Garden of Love" in *Songs of Experience*, where desire is not merely sexual—it is the very essence of man, as Spinoza puts it in a not dissimilar context.

Westernness as it is elaborated in Charlotte Dacre's novel, then, can only comprehend a certain mode of feminine desire, the one embodied in Lilla—which is a mode of desire so severely curtailed that it can hardly be considered desire at all; it's the palest shadow of desire. And again I would say that what goes for sexuality goes for the whole range of desires, thoughts, affects, and emotions: only one norm is shown to be acceptable; the others must be civilized, Occidentalized. What that suggests of course is that the boundary between the civilized and the uncivilized is not simply a boundary that lies between Europe and its others at the distant, dusty and bloody frontiers of empire—it is a boundary that lies, even more specifically within Europe, within and among Europeans themselves. In becoming Western, Occidental, Europe had to purge itself of its own Easternness, and Europeans of their inner Orients.

This then is the real accomplishment of Dacre's novel: that it shifts the struggle between East and West away from the colonial frontier and to the Occidentalizing process taking place in Europe itself. And this takes us back to Byron, who also saw the Orient not simply as an external space but also as an imaginary space onto which questions of desire and ontology could be projected. There are, however, some major differences between Byron's engagement with Orientalism and Dacre's. What Byron was interested in is the preservation of a kind of no-man's-land between East and West as a site from which (in both imaginative and material terms) to resist Occidentalism and its civilizing process. But what *Zofloya* maps out is what happens when the civilizing process encounters its other and goes, as it were, off-script: instead of seeking to transform and civilize otherness, it annihilates it.

CHAPTER FIVE

The Occidental Imperative

The gap between the kind of Orientalism expressed by Byron and that expressed by Dacre, which the previous chapter explored, would not stay open indefinitely. As the nineteenth century progressed, one kind of Orientalism began to consolidate itself as the dominant form, and it was, as I suggested in the Introduction and in other chapters, increasingly fused with Occidentalism. The threat posed by the other kind of Orientalism—the one less invested in, or even quite critical of, the Occidentalist project to make England Western—would begin to recede, though it would never quite disappear and would in fact recur in various post-Romantic formulations later in the nineteenth century and on into the twentieth (Richard Burton and T. E. Lawrence come to mind as examples).

In this chapter I want to argue that it was in the 1830s that the critical—if not quite finally the terminal—blow was struck by the now-dominant form of Orientalism against its residual opponent and that the blow took the form of the devastating attack launched by Thomas Macaulay on the poet laureate Robert Southey. In the clash between Macaulay and Southey we can see the resolution of the tension between two different forms of Orientalism that had first come to the surface back in the 1790s. Macaulay's attack on Southey can be seen, point by point, as an all-but-verbatim replication of the attack launched by 1790s radicals on Burke, with the difference that in the 1790s radical ideas and the logic of Occidentalism with which they were infused were still genuinely oppositional, whereas by the 1830s they had become institutionalized in the corridors of power. In the span of just four decades, in other words, we can see the transition by which Occidentalism went from an emergent cultural mode to a dominant one.

For Macaulay, as we will see, to be modern is to be Western. But his critique of Southey makes it clear that England itself was not always either modern or Western; indeed, its status as modern and Occidental has to be asserted against forces that would, according to Macaulay, drag it back into the past. It is as the very embodiment of those forces that the unfortunate Southey enters Macaulay's narrative. The most striking thing for the purposes of my argument here, however, is that Macaulay's critique of Southey runs in parallel with his critique of those forces who would also resist the British empire's modernization and improvement of India. In both cases, in effect, to resist the inexorable progress of modernization is to cling to an Oriental logic. Thus Macaulay translates what he sees as Southey's stubborn resistance to the process of the modernization of England into an Oriental idiom. Just as it is necessary to break down any form of resistance to the inevitable modernization of India, so is it necessary to break down any last resistance to the modernization of England itself. Nowhere more clearly than in Macaulay, then, do we see the extent to which the process of modernizing England, making it Western, had to involve purging the last traces of Oriental detritus from the land—including the poet laureate himself, if need be.

"It would be scarcely possible for a man of Mr Southey's talents and acquirements to write two volumes so large as those before us," writes Thomas Macaulay in the opening lines of his devastating critique of Southey's *Colloquies on the Progress and Prospects of Society*, "which should be wholly destitute of information and amusement." He had previously registered his disapproval of some of the poet laureate's earlier works, Macaulay continues, but now, he says, Southey has "done his worst." To a task demanding the highest intellectual and moral qualities of the philosophical statesman, Southey brings "two faculties which were never, we believe, vouchsafed in measure so copious to any human being, the faculty of believing without reason, and the faculty of hating without a provocation." It is, Macaulay adds, "most extraordinary, that a mind like Mr Southey's, a mind richly endowed in many respects by nature, and highly cultivated by study, a mind which has exercised considerable influence on the most enlightened generation of the most enlightened people that ever existed, should be utterly destitute of the power of discerning truth from falsehood."[1]

Macaulay's Southey is not only incapable of distinguishing truth from falsehood while hating without provocation and believing without reason; he exceeds even Burke's "fierce and ungovernable sensibility," with which, according to Macaulay, Southey shares strong affinities. For while Burke "chose his side like a fanatic, and defended it like a philosopher," and while he could "defend the wildest course by arguments more plausible than those by which common men support opinions which they have adopted after the fullest deliberation," in the mind of Southey "reason has no place at all, as either leader or follower, as either sovereign or slave. He does not seem to know what an argument is. He never uses arguments himself. He never troubles himself to answer the arguments of his opponents. It has never occurred to him, that a man ought to be able to give some better account of the way in which he has arrived at his opinions than merely that it is his will and pleasure to hold them. It has never occurred to him that there is a difference between assertion and demonstration, that a rumour does not always prove a fact, that a single fact when proved, is hardly foundation enough for a theory, that two contradictory propositions cannot be undeniable truths, that to beg the question is not the way to settle it, or that when an objection is raised, it ought to be met with something more convincing than 'scoundrel' and 'blockhead.'"

In case all this has not already helped us to identify Southey as essentially a bilious old nabob—which, not coincidentally, is how Macaulay mocks the apparition of Thomas More in the *Colloquies*—there remains one more moment in this thoroughgoing Orientalization of the poet laureate (for Orientalization is precisely what this is) by the end of which Southey seems of a piece with the Orient, "its vast cities, its gorgeous pagodas, its infinite swarms of dusky population, its long-descended dynasties [and] its stately etiquette." For, Macaulay concludes, drawing on what was by the 1830s the full spectrum of Orientalist thought, "it would be absurd to read the works of such a writer for political instruction. The utmost that can be expected from any political system promulgated by him is that it may be splendid and affecting, that it may suggest sublime and pleasing images. His scheme of philosophy is a mere day-dream, a poetical creation, like the Domdaniel cavern, the Swerga, or Padalon [references to Southey's Oriental epics], and indeed it bears no inconsiderable resemblance to those gorgeous visions. Like them, it has something of invention, grandeur, and brilliancy. But, like them, it is grotesque and extravagant, and perpetually violates even that conventional probability which is essential to the effect of works of art."[2]

It should come as no surprise, then, that—having Orientalized it—Macaulay should find Southey's work intellectually and aesthetically barren ("wholly destitute of information and amusement"), since that was also his assessment of Oriental culture in the *Minute on Indian Education*, which he wrote only shortly after his review of Southey. He argues in this document that India's vernacular languages "contain neither literary nor scientific information" and that the sum total of historical information contained in even the learned languages of India (Arabic, Persian, Sanskrit) "is less valuable than what may be found in the most paltry abridgments used at preparatory schools in England." This too should hardly come as a surprise, since, according to the *Minute*, those learned languages express "medical doctrines, which would disgrace an English farrier,—Astronomy, which would move laughter in girls at an English boarding school,—History, abounding with kings thirty feet high, and reigns thirty thousand years long,—and Geography, made up of seas of treacle and seas of butter."[3]

Perhaps in part because Macaulay launched his attack on Southey at exactly the same time as he was deepening his interest in Oriental and imperial affairs, Southey thus emerges from this critique a thoroughly Orientalized figure, privileging belief over reason, mixing truth and falsehood, expressing hatred without provocation, and conveying a philosophical system which, precisely like those of the Orient, might perhaps offer glimpses of pleasure, grandeur, affect, sublimity—though at the expense of being finally negated or overcome by a dreamlike extravagance, excessive irrationality, and of course intellectual barrenness. Southey's Orientalization is not merely inseparable from what Macaulay claims are his intellectual and philosophical faults: it expresses those faults exactly. Southey is Orientalized to the extent that he is wrong, misguided, deluded, irrational, inaccurate, and extravagant, and he is wrong, misguided, deluded, irrational, inaccurate, and extravagant precisely to the extent that he is Orientalized.

In thus Orientalizing Southey, Macaulay is, of course, reiterating some of the key components of what had been stabilized long before his time as a standard radical critique of the ancien régime (best exemplified perhaps by the attack launched by Tom Paine and Mary Wollstonecraft on Edmund Burke in the 1790s), with whose established traditions and customs he identifies Southey. As I pointed out in the Introduction, Orientalism played a crucial role in that critique, fusing the criticisms of the supposed corruption, degradation, irrationality, extravagance, and unnaturalness of the ancien régime to its Orientalization.

Macaulay is in part demonstrating his affinities with that earlier form of radical thought (and thereby illustrating its reemergence with far more profound political affiliations in both domestic and imperial politics—for many of the discourses that had been oppositional in the 1790s would become institutionalized by the 1830s). And in so doing, he is also sharply differentiating his own view of the East from Southey's and hence is signaling the abrupt end of one version of Orientalism—the one that had helped to set the stage for Romanticism—and the emergence of another, one much more clearly articulated with Occidentalism and first expressed in the work of 1790s radicals such as Paine and Wollstonecraft.

For we can also locate in Macaulay a fully consolidated version of Occidentalism, according to which the putative West itself must be purged of the last traces of the Orient, even if they are embodied in the person of the poet laureate himself. In Macaulay's schema, that is, the Occident can be seen to have become recognizably itself by having been Occidentalized, having already largely experienced the same kinds of transformation which Macaulay now advocates exporting to India. Occidentalism offers in this sense the cultural paradigm of an ultimately global culture.

The differences between Macaulay and Southey actually express in part the differences between those two momentous cultural and political periods to which they belonged, which are nowhere more clearly articulated than in Macaulay's absolute condemnation of Oriental culture, in his now infamous assertion in the *Minute on Indian Education* that "a single shelf of a good European library [is] worth the whole native literature of India and Arabia." Not only did Macaulay's argument register a whole new attitude toward the cultural politics of empire: it did so in a way that necessarily condemned the infatuation with otherness that was so essential to Romanticism.

Southey's intervention in the busy field of Orientalist adventures and Macaulay's response to it need to be read as part of a dispute over the difference between putatively Occidental and Oriental forms of style and hence subjectivity. Southey, for his part, claimed that his Oriental epics—*Thalaba the Destroyer* and *The Curse of Kehama*—differed from the actual Oriental texts and traditions in which they were, however, rooted. Derived from the East (or at any rate from the extensive knowledge of Eastern cultures and languages pouring into Europe during what has been referred to as the Oriental Renaissance of the late eighteenth century),[4] but differing from it at the same time, the Orient elaborated by Southey thus existed in a kind of adversarial relationship with the Orient "out there." It drew its inspiration from what we might guardedly refer to as the "real" Orient (it being understood, of course, that the Orient does not exist as such);[5] but at the same time it sought to create a substitute version of the "real thing": a spectacle for European consumption, or in other words, a second-order spectacle, the image of an image—given that the Orient "itself" was already a spectacle to begin with. This simulacral relationship explains much of the ambivalence and anxiety reflected in Southey's Orientalism, which has been seen as an attempt to neutralize the threat posed by Eastern culture precisely by imitating it—and thereby transforming it into a second-order image.[6]

In certain passages of the notes and prefaces to *Thalaba* and *Kehama*, Southey goes out of his way to denigrate Eastern culture—the monstrous "deformities" of Hinduism, for example, or the austere "despotism" of

Islam.[7] "A waste of ornament and labor characterizes all the works of the Oriental[s]," he writes in one of the notes to *Thalaba*. "I have seen illuminated Persian manuscripts, that must each have been the toil of many years, every page painted, not with representations of life and manners, but usually like the curves and lines of a Turkey carpet, conveying no idea whatever, as absurd to the eye as nonsense-verses to the ear. The little of their literature that has reached us is equally worthless," he adds, claiming that "The Arabian Tales . . . have lost their metaphorical rubbish in passing through the filter of a French translation."[8] In generating his spectacular Orient, Southey thus sought to draw on the East while also claiming to filter out what he considered its wasteful, undesirable, or downright dangerous elements. "The spirit of the poem was Indian," he writes in the 1838 preface to *The Curse of Kehama*, "but there was nothing Oriental in the style. I had learnt the language of poetry from our own great masters and the great poets of antiquity."[9]

But of course a great deal of the distancing that Southey attempted to build into the later prefaces of his Oriental works was retrospective, and it has a distinctly disingenuous ring to it—often flatly at odds with claims he made in the original prefaces to the same works (*Thalaba*, 1801; *Kehama*, 1810). "The story is original, but, in all its parts, consistent with the superstition upon which it is built," he claims, "for example, in the original preface to *Kehama*."[10] And whereas he retrospectively sought to claim—in the 1838 preface to *Kehama*—that there was nothing authentically Oriental about its style, in one of the early prefaces to *Thalaba* Southey was happy to announce that the poem's style offers "the Arabesque ornament of an Arabian tale."[11] Such prevarication suggests that Southey was a great deal more ambivalent about his relationship to the Orient than he was willing to admit in later life.

For although works like *Thalaba* devote considerable energy to the construction and elaboration of their complex Oriental settings—especially in visual terms—the Orient here is not merely a spectacle for easy visual consumption. It serves, rather, as one setting for what Southey conceived of as a universal history—one that he would, through his career, trace not only in the myths (genuine or otherwise) of India and Arabia but also in those of Wales, Portugal, Spain, Germany, Brazil, and England itself, without feeling it necessary to resort to the device of grouping all of these myths into an obvious hierarchy or ranking them according to a scale of development. If Javed Majeed is right to suggest that Southey seems to have been hard at work in a kind of "laboratory of cultures, experimenting with and constructing different cultural identities,"[12] what was at stake in this experimentation was not merely each culture's identity unto itself, but rather the complex relationship of all of these cultures to each other and to some larger (universal) unity. The Oriental spectacle here comes to serve as one setting of a universal story—revealing Southey for the cosmopolitan intellectual that he really was.

"Several years ago," writes Southey in the 1838 preface to *Kehama*, "I had formed an intention of exhibiting the most remarkable forms of mythology which have at any time been obtained among mankind, by making each the groundwork of a narrative poem." He continues, "I began with the Mahommedan religion, as being that with which I was then best acquainted myself, and of which every one, who had read the 'Arabian Nights Entertainments,' possessed all the knowledge necessary for readily understanding and entering into the intent and spirit of the poem. Mr Wilberforce thought that I had conveyed in it a very false impression of that religion, and that the moral sublimity which he admired in it was owing to this flattering misrepresentation. But 'Thalaba the Destroyer' was professedly an Arabian tale. The design required that I should bring into view the best features of that system of belief and worship which had been developed under the Covenant with Ishmael, placing in the most favorable light the morality of the 'Koran,' and what the least corrupted of the Mahommedans retain of the patriarchal faith."[13]

Not only was Southey engaged in producing a universal history in which different cultures might be read alongside one another, rather than according to a rigid hierarchy with European cultures lording it over supposedly inferior non-European cultures: he was also willing to weave elements of these cultures into one another. Thus he would often cut from one culture to another as a way of asserting not merely their interrelationship but their interdependence—and in so doing, he would substantially head off any European claims to superiority based on cultural difference. In a note to the lines in *Thalaba*, "Praise to the Lord our God, / He gave, he takes away," for example, Southey acknowledges what might be considered by some to be the strangeness of placing "a Scripture phrase in the mouth of a Mahommedan, but," he explains, "it is a saying of Job, and there can be no impropriety in making a modern Arab speak like an ancient one." Moreover, he adds that, rather than using a line from the Koran, "I thought it better to express a feeling of religion in that language with which our religious ideas are connected."[14] Here, quite explicitly, Southey is articulating a view of cultures surprisingly similar to Blake's: for it is only if the same concepts (like Blake's Poetic Genius) are manifested and articulated differently in different cultures that it could make sense to suggest that a line from the Bible could stand in for one from the Koran—that we could, paradoxically, best approximate the spirit of Islam by invoking the Bible. In another passage of *Thalaba*, Southey borrows a line from what he says is a traditional English ballad— which he cites in full in the notes—and transposes it to an Arab context. Again, this suggests a certain degree of commonality among cultures.

This repeated cultural cross-fertilization undoubtedly boosted the cosmopolitan energies of Southey's works; it also helped him to deploy the Orient as a spectacular setting for moral instruction. Using the Orient this way was of course, in itself, nothing new by the early nineteenth century (Addison and Steele had deployed the tactic a hundred years earlier), but in the context of expanded knowledge and greater imperial commitments such a gesture had altogether different significance in the early nineteenth century, as the more charitable views of people like William Jones started to fade away, to be gradually replaced by the outright cultural hostility of people like James Mill, Charles Grant, and, ultimately, Macaulay himself. Many of the concerns that Southey elaborates in the spectacular setting of *Thalaba* are identical to the concerns he would elaborate in his explicitly English works, notably the *Colloquies* and such essays as "On the Rise and Progress of Popular Disaffection" or "On the Means of Improving the People."

Not only, for example, does *Thalaba* evoke the same concern for the instruction of "the multitude" that would prove one of the dominant concerns of Southey's essays on England; it also offers a warning of what happens to societies that allow material concerns to eclipse their moral and religious commitments. The warning issued by Aswad in one of the early passages of *Thalaba* is precisely the kind of lesson that one finds reiterated throughout Southey's work, especially the work devoted to England:

> Boy, who hast reached my solitude,
> Fear the Lord in the days of thy youth!
> My knee was never taught
> To bend before my God;
> My voice was never taught
> To shape one holy prayer.
> We worshipped Idols, wood and stone;
> The work of our own foolish hands
> We worshipped in our foolishness.
> Vainly the Prophet's voice
> In frequent warning raised,—

'REPENT, AND BE FORGIVEN!'
We mocked the messenger of God;
We mocked the Lord, long-suffering, slow to wrath.[15]

Here once again a distinctly Christian line—"repent, and be forgiven,"—is spoken by a Muslim, and the well-known Muslim hostility to idolatry and the worship of material things is seen to bear an uncanny resemblance to the warning echoing through England in the late eighteenth and early nineteenth centuries that, to quote Oliver Goldsmith, "where wealth accumulates . . . men decay."[16]

Certainly, this is one of the recurring themes of Southey's *Colloquies*, whose main concerns are the moral consequences of "the uncontrolled dominion of that worldly spirit which it is the tendency of the commercial system to produce and foster," and hence the "undisputed and acknowledged supremacy" which Mammon—a false god like the false idols of *Thalaba*—"seems to have obtained in commercial countries, and in no country more decidedly than in this [England]. The spirit which built and endowed monasteries is gone," points out the ghost of Thomas More; "are you," he asks Montesinos, "one of those persons who think it has been superseded for the better by that which erects steam-engines and cotton-mills?"[17] Clearly, for Southey, not only do steam and steel represent the modern-day equivalent of the primitive wood and stone idols denounced by Aswad, but the need to assert the moral rehabilitation of societies in which the spirit of materialism has gone out of control applies no more to the Orient than it does to England itself, where Southey advocates a system of national education (including moral and religious instruction) that might extend the benefits of civilization to "those classes who are brutalized by the institutions of society."[18]

Clearly, too, the brutalized workers of England—victims of a system that, according to the ghost of More, is founded on "slavery direct or indirect, abroad or at home" and that "employs men unremittingly in pursuits unwholesome for the body, and unprofitable for the mind"—are no better off, no more intellectually and culturally developed, than the Arab workers in *Thalaba*, where we see that only "the labor and pain of multitudes" made possible the creation of the short-lived material wealth of Ad, whose people discover far too late that the Lord does not hear the prayers abroad of those "who made no prayers at home."[19] The threat of moral decay brought about by the unchecked pursuit and accumulation of material wealth links the fate of the English to that of Indians and Arabs, cultures tied together in the face of a common enemy. Southey's cosmopolitan surveys of cultures threatened by the worldly spirit of vulgar materialism refuses to privilege one society over another, much less one over all the others.

Southey's cosmopolitan commitments rested, however, on an extremely unstable set of assumptions, which were themselves built on the shifting terrain of arguments concerning imperial policy running through his entire career, from the 1780s to the 1830s. It should hardly come as a surprise, then, that his position should be shot through with contradictions. Ironically, for example, it was Southey's universalist and cosmopolitan interests (which were derived from one stage of imperial policy, in the 1780s and 1790s) that led to his advocacy of the evangelical attitude toward Britain's imperial possessions in Asia (which would take hold in a radically—indeed self-consciously—contradictory set of imperial policies in the early nineteenth century). The kind of Orientalism elaborated by Southey, as well as by other writers, from Walter Savage Landor to Tom Moore and Byron, was not the only form of Orientalism in the Romantic period; it existed in sharp contrast with, for example, the distinctly more hostile Orientalism of writers such as Volney, Paine, Wollstonecraft, Shelley, and De Quincey— but both forms emerged in the gap arising between these different stages of imperial rule.[20] When that gap closed, with the consolidation of a new set of attitudes, embodied in new policies (of which Macaulay would—and this is the point of this stage of my argument—be one of the prime advocates), these contradictions would themselves be resolved. It would then become more difficult, if not impossible, to engage in the kinds of spectacular Orientalist projects that so interested Southey (or Byron, or Moore).

We can locate this gap in the transition from the approach to imperial policy advocated by Warren Hastings in the 1780s to the new policies that would be first announced in the Cornwallis reforms of 1793 but would really come to be put into practice only after 1813 (when missionaries were first officially allowed to work in India) and would not actually be consolidated until after the debates in the 1830s in which Macaulay's *Minute on Indian Education* would prove such a significant intervention. The new approach to imperial policy was first advocated in a systematic fashion by Charles Grant, who, arguing explicitly against the openness to Oriental cultures that animated scholars like William Jones, insisted that the Orient— far from being "the nurse of sciences, the inventress of delightful and useful arts, the scene of glorious actions, fertile in the productions of human genius"—was essentially a scene of intellectual, aesthetic and moral degradation. "We cannot avoid recognizing in the people of Hindostan," Grant wrote as early as 1792, "a race of men lamentably degenerate and base; retaining but a feeble sense of moral obligation; yet obstinate in their disregard of what they know to be right, governed by malevolent and licentious passions, strongly exemplifying the effects produced on society by a great and general corruption of manners, and sunk in misery by their vices."[21] Echoed by William Wilberforce and others, Grant's view of what he called the "moral improvement" of the natives, beginning with their conversion to Christianity, was one of the main driving forces behind the move toward the 1813 reforms in the East India Company charter.

We can recognize in Grant's work the early stirrings of what would merge into full-blown Occidentalism, in the sense that it conveys the need to "improve" and "civilize" both at home and abroad; to align all societies along the track of unilinear, progressive time; and to pull lesser or undeveloped or stalled peoples forward into the time of the West. As we have seen in previous chapters, precisely the same sort of perspective was emerging in England at the same time in the drive to civilize and improve what the Reverend George Greatbatch saw as the "unenlightened and uncivilized" barbarism of provincial backwaters (in which the advocates of such improvement found a "heathenism as dense as any in Polynesia or Central Africa")[22] or the savagery of London, where, in the face of which alarmed observers argued that "a veritable heathen mission is as much wanted in the interior of London as in the interior of Africa,"[23] there emerged a whole range of projects to settle and bring order to the darkness of the metropolis, as we saw in chapter 1. In Grant we can recognize the extent to which, as I suggested in the Introduction, Occidentalism and Orientalism are not opposites, as they are sometimes taken to be, but rather operate on a continuum. It was the same civilizing process that was being played out both in England and in colonial possessions, including India: in England, in order to purge the last traces of Oriental contamination from what was supposed to be an Occidental space; and in the colonial world, in order to begin the challenging process of converting Oriental "vice and misery" into the universal culture of Occidental modernity.

In the case of Southey, there are many ironies in this regard. For one thing, although he was profoundly interested in and influenced by the work emerging from the Oriental Renaissance of the 1780s and 1790s, he was also a champion of the very same evangelical approach to India called for by men like Grant and Wilberforce, whose hostility to Eastern cultures was unflinching. "When," Southey asked as early as 1803, "will the East India Company be convinced that it is in their ultimate interest, as well as their immediate duty, to convert their subjects?"[24] Southey denounced the Church of England for neglecting what he regarded as its moral duty in the East, especially in comparison with dissenting and Roman Catholic mis-

sionaries. If "we had served our God with half the zeal" of Catholic missionaries, he argues in an 1814 article in the *Quarterly Review*, "the tree of
life would long ere this have stuck deep roots in Hindostan."[25] Thus fraught
with contradictions, Southey was, in other words, interested in eradicating
the very same cultural traditions that he also drew on for inspiration for his
own work; indeed, that's precisely what makes his position Romantic, in
that it emerged from the ideological gap I already mentioned.

The more significant irony attending Southey's engagement with Orientalist discourses, however, is that he in turn would come to be Orientalized,
by Macaulay among others. And if Southey's work was torn with contradictions, Macaulay, on the other hand, did not suffer from such contradictions
or their attendant anxieties, which is why he could be so sweeping in his
condemnation both of Southey and of the Oriental literatures in which the
poet laureate was actually (for all his retrospective attempts at denial and
distancing) very interested. Macaulay saw nothing of value in Oriental civilization, let alone any possible source of inspiration for anyone writing for
what he claimed was the most enlightened generation of the most enlightened people that ever existed. "To have found a great people sunk in the lowest depths of slavery and superstition, to have so ruled them as to have made
them desirous and capable of all the privileges of citizens, would indeed be
a title to glory all our own," Macaulay argues in his Speech in the Charter
Debate of 1833. "The scepter may pass away from us. Unforeseen accidents
may derange our most profound schemes of policy. Victory may be incon-
stant to our arms. But there are triumphs which are followed by no reverse.
There is an empire exempt from all natural causes of decay. Those triumphs
are the pacific triumphs of reason over barbarism; that empire is the imperishable empire of our morals, our literature and our arts."[26] Such an attitude
clearly requires a relatively stable sense of who "we" are and hence what
"our morals" and so forth stand for: a sense of stability that would have been
unavailable to writers from the Romantic period, including Southey.

What we see in Macaulay, then, is a sense of confirmation that the questions that once haunted Romantic-era writers, especially around the question of Occidentalism and where the limits of the Occident are—and how
Occidental "we" and "our" space are—are now being settled. This emergent
sense of a settlement or normalization of Occidentalism may itself help us
to draw a line between the Romantic and the Victorian periods, even where
they overlap chronologically, as in the case of Southey and Macaulay. The
point is not that there was no haunting or questioning of Occidentalism in
the Victorian period, of course (Dickens, as we will see in the next chapter,
had many doubts and questions), but that the questions and their attendant

anxieties gradually seem to ease as "we" gradually settle into a more nor-
malized sense of identity, a sense of who "we" are and what it means to be
one of "us" as opposed to one of "them." As we saw in previous chapters,
writers like Wordsworth, Austen, and Byron were seized with doubts as to
the stability of "our" identity in cultural terms, certainly its stability as
opposed to a whole range of others; is the Old Man Travelling one of "us"?
Is Simon Lee? Is Conrad? Is the Giaour? Is young Tom Bertram? Is Sir Walter Eliot? In Macaulay there are no longer any such doubts. "We" know
who "we" are; "we" know what it means to invoke in an uncomplicated
way "the imperishable empire of our morals, our literature and our arts."
It is difficult to imagine the Wordsworth of 1798 making such a sweeping
statement.

In his book on the English utilitarians and India, Eric Stokes argues that
little of the cultural hostility revealed by Macaulay in such texts as the
speech on the Charter Debate was new, that "everywhere his speech rings
with ideas which the elder Charles Grant and Wilberforce had uttered nearly
forty years before."[27] But it is important to note that despite the similarities,
there were also some profound differences between Macaulay's position and
the older evangelical position on which he would draw. For one thing, Macaulay sought to secularize what had been a frankly religious discourse (distinguishing "our morals" from "our religion"), while advocating religious
tolerance in India and the refusal to encourage the missionary project. On
this point of course he differed not only from evangelicals like Grant but
also from Southey, for, against Southey's claim that "it is from religion that
power derives its authority, and laws their efficacy," Macaulay fires back
the question "from what religion does our power over the Hindoos derive
its authority, or the law in virtue of which we hang Brahmins its efficacy?"[28]

More significantly, however, even when he echoed older voices (like
Grant or Wilberforce), Macaulay's position suffered from none of the contradictions that hobbled theirs: for while their approach might be considered conservative in an English context (i.e., upholding what it conceived
of as the traditional culture, or at least one version of a traditional culture),
it was radically destabilizing in the imperial context—seeking to uproot
and destroy local institutions and traditions and to replace them with new
imports. Macaulay, on the other hand, was all for radical transformation in
England (and Britain generally of course, bearing in mind his own Scottish
roots) as well as in India, even if he thought that government, in the form of
the East India Company, was ideal for the task in India and hopeless at it in
England. He was an eager advocate of what Marx would later identify as the
mission to "put an end to all feudal, patriarchal, idyllic relations," to "tear

asunder the motley feudal ties that bound man to his 'natural superiors,'" to batter down Chinese walls and "force the barbarians' intensely obstinate hatred of foreigners to capitulate," and to compel them to "introduce what it calls civilization into their midst."[29] And he was as quick to demand and endorse such a defeat of barbarism at home in England as he was to demand and endorse it in places like India. What differentiates Macaulay from Grant is that he anticipates the defeat of barbarism and the progress of civilization as processes to which "we" too have been subject, in our own prior Occidentalization—which included the destruction of the outmoded cultures, political systems, beliefs, and languages to which we would attempt to cling at our peril and their replacement by new and appropriately modern forms of culture, politics, belief, and language.

As much as the various imperial and Oriental questions, in fact, this Occidentalism is what manifestly distinguishes Macaulay's position from Southey's; or, to be more precise, this is what fuses Macaulay's attack on Southey's Oriental tendencies to his critique of Southey's domestic politics. (It also, by the way, distinguishes Macaulay's position from that of utilitarians like James Mill, who believed that institutional and legal—rather than cultural and intellectual—reforms held the key to progress in India.)[30] The point here is that, for Macaulay, the process and discourse of progress unfolds across all cultures and all times; what Norbert Elias would later identify as the "civilizing process" had brought Occidental civilization to England and would now bring it to India.[31] England is not inherently superior to India, in other words; it is merely further along in the process of Occidentalization—a process to which the people of England and their own indigenous languages, dialects, traditions, and cultures had already been subject. Thus, according to Macaulay, if it falls to England to bring enlightenment to India in the nineteenth century, and if the English are now the most enlightened people that ever existed, that is only because England and the English received enlightenment from others in their turn at an earlier moment in the same civilizing process. "What the Greek and Latin were to the [English] contemporaries of More and Ascham, our tongue is to the people of India," Macaulay argues in the *Minute on Indian Education.* "Had our ancestors . . . neglected the language of Cicero and Tacitus; had they confined their attention to the old dialects of our own island; had they printed nothing and taught nothing at the universities but Chronicles in Anglo-Saxon, and Romances in Norman-French, would England have been what she now is?"[32]

Macaulay's argument thus anticipates Marlow's assertion in *Heart of Darkness* that England too "has been one of the dark places of the earth."

If the civilizing process unfolds universally, what had happened in England to make it Occidental would also have to happen to India to make it in turn—how else can one express this?—Occidental; which is to say, modern. The point here is not just that Macaulay fuses modernity with Occidentalism, so that to be modern is necessarily to be Western, but that he makes it clear that Occidentalism is subservient to modernity; what gives the Occident value is that it is modern, not the other way around. At the same time, Macaulay reveals more clearly than anyone else at the time the extent to which Orientalism and Occidentalism operate on the same continuum: as a society moves from irrational, primitive savagery, it loses the taint of the Oriental and gains the value of the Occidental. Occidentalization is an index of modernization; resistance to it hence involves falling back on Oriental values.

This explains both Macaulay's unremitting hostility toward Eastern cultures and his profound disagreement with Southey. For on Macaulay's reading of Southey's *Colloquies*, the poet laureate is as much an advocate of obstinate English traditions and stubborn but worn-out English customs—if not quite Chinese walls—stubbornly trying to keep the spirit of innovation and progress at bay in England as the sages and *ulema* of the East are said to be doing in the Orient itself. Southey, according to Macaulay, "abhors the spirit of the present generation, the severity of its studies, the boldness of its inquiries, and the disdain with which it regards some old prejudices by which his own mind is held in bondage. He dislikes an utterly unenlightened age; he dislikes an investigating and reforming age. The first twenty years of the sixteenth century would have suited him perfectly."[33] What is most interesting for our purposes, however, is the way in which Macaulay stages this final moment of his critique of Southey in his review of the *Colloquies*.

He quotes a long passage from one of the colloquies, in which Montesinos (i.e., Southey) contrasts English weather-stained cottages of former times, "such as the poet and the painter equally delight in beholding. . . . the rose-bushes beside the door, the little patch of flower-ground, with its tall hollyhocks in front; the garden beside, the bee-hives, and the orchard with its bank of daffodils and snow-drops" with the ugly and uniform housing of modern industrial workers. How is it, asks Montesinos, "that every thing which is connected with manufactures presents such features of unqualified deformity? From the largest of Mammon's temples down to the poorest hovel in which his helotry are stalled, these edifices have all one character. Time will not mellow them; nature will neither clothe nor conceal them; and they will remain always as offensive to the eye as to the mind."[34]

Macaulay responds fiercely to such an assessment of progress. "Here is wisdom," he fumes; "here are the principles on which nations are to be governed. Rose-bushes and poor-rates, rather than steam-engines and independence. Mortality and cottages with weather-stains, rather than health and long life with edifices which time cannot mellow. We are told," Macaulay goes on, "that our age has invented atrocities beyond the imagination of our fathers; that society has been brought into a state, compared with which extermination would be a blessing; and all because the dwellings of cotton-spinners are naked and rectangular. Mr Southey has found out a way, he tells us, in which the effects of manufactures and agriculture may be compared. And what is this way? To stand on a hill, to look at a cottage and a factory, and to see which is the prettier. Does Mr Southey think that the body of the English peasantry live, or ever lived, in substantial or ornamented cottages, with box-hedges, flower-gardens, bee-hives and orchards? If not, what is his parallel worth?"[35]

Macaulay's point here is twofold. He obviously wishes to contest Southey's assessment of the reality of England's material progress and to argue that the common people are far better off in the nineteenth century than they were in some idyllic and mythical pre-industrial age of the Romantic imagination. Just as importantly, though, he wants to reassert the convergence of the Oriental with the resistance to modernity and hence the flip side of that, which is the convergence of the modern with the Occidental. Here he is anticipating John Stuart Mill's argument that "strong prejudices of any kind" and "obstinate adherence to old habits"—which is exactly what Macaulay accuses Southey of—are among the worst "obstacles to progress in civilization."[36] According to Mill, after all, "one of the strongest hindrances to improvement, up to a rather advanced stage, is a inveterate spirit of locality,"[37] or in other words a stubborn clinging to local ways and customs. "The despotism of custom is everywhere the standing hindrance to human advancement, being in unceasing antagonism to that disposition to aim at something better than customary, which is called, according to circumstances, the spirit of liberty, or that of progress or improvement," Mill would go on to argue. "The greater part of the world has, properly speaking, no history, because the despotism of custom is complete. This is the case over the whole East."[38] It was also, clearly, at some point, the case over the whole of what-would-become-the-West.

For Mill, progress is good partly because it breaks down custom and locality and allows for a greater integration of people within a more progressive and larger—ultimately universal—community of what must ultimately be thought of as the West (the opposite of the stalled and degenerate

East, where "the despotism of custom is complete"). What Mill argues for the "inferior and more backward portion of the human race"[39]—he names Bretons, Basques, the Welsh, and Scottish Highlanders as examples—within Europe also goes, according to Macaulay, for the English as well. And one can recognize in Macaulay's depiction of Southey just the kind of stubborn refusal of progress that Mill would condemn in his work, where he says it would be better for the "backward" person to embrace progress than to "sulk on his own rocks, the half-savage relic of past times, revolving in his own little mental orbit, without participation or interest in the general movement of the world."[40] For this is exactly what Macaulay accuses Southey of because of his stubborn clinging to outmoded practices, values, forms of science, technology, and language itself.

As I argued in the Introduction (and I will return to this same point in the next chapter as well), the emergence of the Eurocentric claim that historical time defines the distance between the West and the non-West also applies to spaces and populations within what would become the West itself.[41] The discourses of modernity and of Occidentalism are in this sense coextensive with one another: to be modern, for Macaulay, is in effect to be Western also. What Macaulay sees in Southey, then, is a stubborn defense not simply of vestigial premodern structures ("rose-bushes and poor-rates, rather than steam-engines and independence"), but also, in effect, of the pre-Western. That is exactly why Macaulay's condemnation of Southey's Romanticism is expressed in terms of Orientalism: if Occidentalism and modernization are two sides of the same coin, then to defend the archaic and the premodern is to be Oriental.

It is not merely coincidental that in Macaulay's account this stubborn refusal to accept the imperative to modernize and Occidentalize assumes an aesthetic component as well. In saying that Southey wants "to stand on a hill, to look at a cottage and a factory, and to see which is the prettier," and thereby judge the difference between modern industrial society on the one hand and an outmoded agricultural society on the other, he is arguing against the use of images (the pretty cottage, the ugly factory) as political devices, which is what he accuses Southey of doing—and (and this is the point) not only with regard to the Orient but with regard to England as well. Southey's investment in Orientalism is here revealed to be inextricable from his investment in a more general economy of false and misleading images; for, just as Orientals are said to prefer false images to actual realities, so too does the poet laureate. For Macaulay, however, in exactly the same way that it is essential to show that the splendid and affecting—"sublime and pleasing"—images of the Orient amount to little more than daydreams and fantasies, it is also essential to show that it is folly of precisely the same kind to elaborate would-be political or philosophical arguments (in England as much as in India) on the basis of images alone. Hence the absurdity of trying to assess the comparative value of manufactures and agriculture according to the prettiness of the landscapes associated with them is exactly indicative, he says, of the absurdity of substituting prettified aesthetics for serious political economy, or in other words abandoning hard-nosed reason in the name of image and spectacle.

This is precisely what Macaulay accuses Southey of doing. Not only is the poet laureate utterly destitute of the power of discerning truth from falsehood and guilty of those peculiarly Oriental sins of believing without reason and hating without provocation; he is also guilty of substituting images for realities—yet another Oriental trait. "Government is to Mr Southey one of the fine arts," Macaulay writes. "He judges of a theory, of a public measure, of a religion or a political party, of a peace or a war, as men judge of a picture or a statue, by the effect produced on his imagination. A chain of associations is to him what a chain of reasoning is to other men; and what he calls his opinions are in fact merely his tastes." Thus, he concludes, "Mr Southey's political system is just what we might expect from a man who regards politics, not as a matter of science, but as a matter of taste and feeling."[42] For Macaulay, of course, progress is made possible precisely by allowing science and discipline to override not only taste and feeling but also long-established customs, stubborn prejudices, and outmoded practices—in England as much as in India.

The Orient—and Orientalist investments such as Southey's—represent for Macaulay the embodiment of the pursuit of the spectacular rather than the substantive and the material, and of the foolhardy substitution of an image economy for genuine political economy. As far as Macaulay is concerned, they are both to be brought under control and disciplined: a process that would involve the eradication of forms of thought incompatible with the disciplinary logic of a new age—an age of improvement and civilization, in England as in India, which Romanticism itself would not survive. Just as the inauguration of the era of British Romanticism had been announced by Sir William Jones's 1772 "Essay on the Poetry of the Eastern Nations," its demise was signaled by Macaulay's *Minute on Indian Education.* Jones's essay had helped make available to British writers a whole new cultural and literary world, on which—their appetites having already been whetted earlier in the century by translations (genuine and otherwise) of the *Arabian Nights*—they would steadily feast for the following five decades, transforming themselves and British literary culture in the process. Macaulay's 1835 essay, however, scorned Jones and anyone who took seriously his advice to seek inspiration and gather raw material for poetry from what Macaulay regarded as the backward and thoroughly degenerate East, and hence it marked the termination of the cultural and literary project that had been inaugurated by Jones. In between Jones and Macaulay, British Romanticism emerged, grew, flourished—and died.

In the new imperial policies advocated by Macaulay, image and spectacle would henceforth be entirely secondary in their importance when compared to supposedly genuine material realities—the "facts" espoused by Gradgrind in Dickens's *Hard Times*—and the rigor of improvement, civilization, or what we would now call Westernization. Since it is impossible to educate the mass of the population of India, Macaulay would famously argue in the *Minute*, "we must at present do our best to form a class who may be interpreters between us and the millions whom we govern; a class of persons, Indian in blood and colour, but English in taste, in opinions, in morals, and in intellect."[43] This we can readily recognize as an imperialist project being projected on to India. But when we re-read Macaulay's encounter with Southey's *Colloquies*, we are reminded that Englishmen too had to be made "English in taste, in opinions, in morals, and in intellect," and that involved the overcoming or sweeping away of any gesture of resistance to the relentless process of Occidentalism, as England was made Western.

PART 3

Occidentalism in Crisis

"Irregular Modernization": Charles Dickens and the Crisis of Occidentalism

An ancient English Cathedral town? How can the ancient English Cathedral town be here! The well-known massive grey square tower of its old Cathedral? How can that be here! There is no spike of rusty iron in the air, between the eye and it, from any point of the real prospect. What IS the spike that intervenes, and who has set it up? Maybe, it is set up by the Sultan's orders for the impaling of a horde of Turkish robbers, one by one. It is so, for cymbals clash, and the Sultan goes by to his palace in long procession. Ten thousand scimitars flash in the sunlight, and thrice ten thousand dancing-girls strew flowers. Then, follow white elephants caparisoned in countless gorgeous colors, and infinite in number and attendants. Still, the Cathedral tower rises in the background, where it cannot be, and still no writhing figure is on the grim spike. Stay! Is the spike so low a thing as the rusty spike on the top of a post of an old bedstead that has tumbled all awry? Some vague period of drowsy laughter must be devoted to the consideration of this possibility.

Shaking from head to foot, the man whose scattered consciousness has thus fantastically pieced itself together, at length rises, supports his trembling frame upon his arms, and looks around. He is in the meanest and closest of all rooms. Through the ragged window-curtain, the light of early day steals in from a miserable court. He lies, dressed, across a large unseemly bed, upon a bedstead that has indeed given way under the weight upon it. Lying, also dressed and also across the bed, not longwise, are a Chinaman, a Lascar, and a haggard woman. The two first are in a sleep or stupor; the last is blowing at a kind of pipe, to kindle it. And as she blows, and shading it with her lean hand, concentrates its red spark of light, it serves in the dim morning as a lamp to show him what he sees of her.

"Another?" says this woman, in a querulous, rattling whisper. "Have another?"[1]

T he extraordinary opening lines of Charles Dickens's last (and unfinished) novel, *The Mystery of Edwin Drood*, plunge us into—and slowly
extract us from—the disoriented and volatile consciousness of John Jasper
as he emerges from an opium-induced stupor in a squalid den somewhere
in east London. Although many other novels by Dickens reveal the author's
interest in imperial affairs and in the whole relationship between England
as a center of empire and various colonial peripheries under British control,
none has quite the level of imperial intensity as *Edwin Drood*. In *Bleak
House*, for instance, the imperial realm is comfortably distant: so distant,
in fact, that characters like Mrs. Jellyby can be satirized for their obsession
with the improvement of such faraway places as Borrioboola-Gha while literally overlooking disorder much closer to (or at) home.[2] In *Great Expectations*, similarly, empire functions by virtue of its distance, serving both as
a site to which certain marginalized characters (notably Magwitch) can be
temporarily displaced, and as a place toward which aspiring middle-class
characters, like Pip and Herbert Pocket, can look to fulfill their commercial
aspirations. And although throughout Dickens's work (as is also the case
with that of his Victorian contemporaries) there are countless references to
colonial commodities, from Chinese tea and Caribbean sugar to Turkey car-
pets and Morocco leather, they end up serving as reminders of the distance
of exoticism rather than its proximity.

While Pip's and Herbert's interest in Egypt as a commercial venue in
Great Expectations is echoed in Edwin Drood's long-standing engineering ambition to go "to wake Egypt up a little,"[3] the later novel's engagement with questions of empire is far more profound than that earlier effort.
As Grace Moore points out, *Edwin Drood* is the first novel by Dickens in
which imperial questions are not merely a matter of distanced or deferred
side interest, but rather among the plot's central preoccupations.[4] Not only
is the empire a site to which characters can be sent; it is also—much more
unusually for Dickens—an origin from which characters arrive, whether
from imperial service (in the case of Lt. Tartar) or from a place of childhood
and upbringing (in the case of the Ceylonese Landless orphans, Neville and
Helena).

Moreover, in *Edwin Drood* "the colonial commodity is no longer the
awkward obstacle that clutters the homes of *Bleak House* or the various
junk shops Dickens depicts in his [other] novels," Moore notes. "Rather it
is something all-consuming and potentially all-engulfing," and the novel's

primary setting, the cathedral city of Cloisterham, is, as she puts it, "awash with delicacies from the East."[5] Exotic goods are such a constant, quotidian presence in *Edwin Drood* that they end up losing much of their exoticism and slide into that banal familiarity generated by the domestication of the formerly foreign (in the way that chicken tikka masala is today said to be Britain's national dish). Most of the major characters, and many of the minor ones too, have a repeatedly expressed, often daily interest in products brought to England by the global networks of empire. Rosa, for example, for all her seeming innocence, is addicted to Turkish Delight. Crisparkle and his mother regularly consume Souchong tea sourced from China, tamarind and ginger from south and southeast Asia, and Constantia wine from South Africa. Sapsea, for all his xenophobia, makes up for what he lacks in travel by the consumption of colonial goods at home: "I see some cups and saucers of Chinese make, equally strangers to me personally: I put my finger on them, then and there, and I say 'Pekin, Nankin, and Canton,'" he boasts to Jasper. "'It is the same with Japan, with Egypt, and with bamboo and sandalwood from the East Indies; I put my finger on them all.'"[6] And of course there is Jasper himself and his opium habit.

"The attention to foreign and especially Oriental and exotic commodities demonstrates a subtle indictment of the domestic consumption that fueled the colonial presence of England in the colonies and the colonies in England," Miriam O'Kane Mara argues. The real mystery of *Edwin Drood*, she adds, is "the insidious seeping of consumption and, thus, empire into a quiet English town."[7] Even Crisparkle, surely the most "white" and "English" of the characters—he seems to be, as David Faulkner has observed, "a pure specimen of the genus 'muscular Christian,' a cultural ideal of Anglo-Saxon vigor and virtue"[8]—is implicated in colonial consumption.[9]

So far, so good. Yet far more is at stake in *Edwin Drood's* treatment of empire than plot devices, characters, or the forms of contamination that are brought about through colonial trade. "The colonial presence here is neither a subordinated theme nor exotic grace-note," Faulkner argues, "but a transformative historical and psychological *pressure*, a paradigm-shift legible in the deep structure of the novel."[10] The novel is in one sense a meditation on imperial culture: on what it means to inhabit empire as an open and continuous space of flows in which a rigid distinction between the familiar and the exotic, the domesticated and the foreign, the metropolis and the periphery, "here" and "there," and ultimately "us" and "them" is unsustainable, insofar as the two spaces, their goods—and, more importantly, their populations—are seen to be interpenetrating and overlapping. Thus, for all its spectacular theatricality, the novel's opening opium dream sequence nevertheless also offers a glimpse at a material reality: that it is no longer possible (leaving aside whether or not it ever was or will be) to cleanly demarcate the space of the self from that of the other; the space of "whiteness" from that of "blackness"; the space of Occident from that of Orient; or for that matter an Occidental "us" from an Oriental "them."

Certainly, one way of understanding this collapse of distinctions is to think of it in terms of contamination or corruption. That is where much of the scholarship on *Edwin Drood* takes us, urging us to see Dickens recoiling against the colonial infiltration of, as Mara puts it, "a quiet English town." For all its undoubted appeal, however, such an approach presupposes and takes for granted the normative stability and homogeneity of the English-ness which is seen to have been thus infiltrated and contaminated. What I want to argue in this chapter is that, in addition to offering a meditation on imperial culture, the profound revelation of Dickens's last novel is that that Englishness—and hence that sense of modernity, that sense of white or Oc-cidental superiority—was never quite as stable, secure, and homogeneous as it was (and still is) often assumed to be, including by Dickens himself in much of his earlier work.

What *Edwin Drood* reveals, in other words, is not that an idealized En-gland has been infiltrated and corrupted by colonial contamination, but rather that that idealized England never existed in the first place. So to go back to the opening dream sequence: its revelation is not that the Orient has contaminated the Occident or that an Oriental dream is invading or undermining an Occidental reality, but that both Occident and Orient are imaginary geographies.[11] What we are left with is the sense that there was never a "real" Occident to begin with, at least not as a pure homogeneous form—as the embodiment and expression of all those virtues of progressive development, modernization, and enlightenment celebrated, for example, by Macaulay in his attack on Southey or in his *Minute on Indian Educa-tion*—that might, from a position of prior purity, be subjected to contamina-tion or corruption from the East.

Students of *Edwin Drood* are surely right to note, then, a difference in tone in this novel compared to earlier works by Dickens. The author's often starkly expressed attitudes have long informed scholarship on his atti-tudes to empire—what John DeWind sees as his ardent imperialism and un-bounded faith in the superiority of Western civilization.[12] For example, Dick-ens's well-known claim, in an 1848 piece he wrote for *The Examiner* on the Niger Expedition, that "between the civilized European and the barbarous African there is a great gulf set" is often cited as evidence of such attitudes,[13] as are such frankly racist essays as "The Noble Savage," the ironically titled and quasi-genocidal piece he published in *Household Worlds* in 1853.[14] Indeed, Dickens's widely cited letter to Angela Burdett-Coutts in the wake of the Indian uprising of 1857—in which he expresses a vengeful desire "to exterminate the Race upon whom the stain of the late cruelties rested . . . to blot it out of mankind and raze it off the face of the Earth"[15]—suggests, as many scholars have noted, more than merely an attitude of disparagement toward cultural others.[16]

Dickens's novels do not generally betray the same level of violent xenophobia as comes across in his journalism or letters, however (if only, perhaps, because they tend to keep imperial settings out of view and referred to from a safe distance). And in some of them there is a quite explicit working through of the relationship—both the similarities and the differences—between overseas barbarism and domestic wretchedness and savagery (a question in which Dickens was long engaged, not least in his writing on London, as I discussed in chap. 1). This theme is most prominent in *Bleak House*, especially in the treatment of the impoverished street-sweeping orphan, Jo. He is "not one of Mrs. Pardiggle's Tockahoopo Indians; he is not one of Mrs. Jellyby's lambs, being wholly unconnected with Borrioboola-Gha; he is not softened by distance and unfamiliarity; he is not a genuine foreign-grown savage; he is the ordinary home-made article," the narrator tells us. "Homely filth begrimes him, homely parasites devour him, homely sores are in him, homely rags are on him: native ignorance, the growth of English soil and climate, sinks his immortal nature lower than the beasts that perish."[17]

However, such a comparison of the English to the foreign savage raises an important problem of emphasis. Are we are meant to see Jo as just as other as the "savage" Africans reviled by Dickens in his Niger Expedition piece (which would have the effect of collapsing the distinction between the civilized metropolis and the savage periphery)?[18] Or, on the contrary, are we to identify all the more closely with Jo because he is, after all, English and hence one of "us" (which would have the effect of reinforcing the difference between a putatively civilized, or at least civilizable, "us" as opposed to a resolutely uncivilizable "them")?[19]

I am inclined toward the latter reading of *Bleak House*. The scene of Jo's death appeals to the language of sentiment in order to generalize from him as an individual character to that wider population of English people awaiting the civilizing mission at home: "our" home, around "us." At that point, the character becomes merely a placeholder for the novel's larger sentimental claims on its Victorian readers. After Jo dies in the middle (well, actually at the beginning) of repeating the Lord's Prayer after Allan Woodcourt, the narrator proclaims: "Dead, your Majesty. Dead, my lords and gentlemen. Dead, Right Reverends and Wrong Reverends of every order. Dead, men and women, born with Heavenly compassion in your hearts. And dying thus around us, every day."[20] What makes Jo exceptional is not that he can be compared to an African; it is that he is a provisional or temporary savage, one who can make a justifiable claim on "our" space; the impetus then is to incorporate him rather than expunge him: to make him more appropriate for "our" space, or, in short, to make him into one of "us." And the first step toward that comes with recognizing that he is indeed one of "us" in the first place. Ironically, in other words, rather than collapsing London into Africa, what enables the narrator of *Bleak House* to compare Jo with an African savage is exactly that there is—or ought to be—a sense of difference between the two spaces, the domestic and the foreign.

In *Edwin Drood* such self/other, here/there, us/them, foreign/domestic oppositions don't function in the same binary way because of the destabilization of the opposition, the mixture, hybridization, or (if you prefer) contamination of one set of terms by the other. There is no longer an external "there" against which an internal "here" can be cleanly opposed because the outside has come in. "The sentimental contrast between a starving, neglected, uneducated poor and John Chinaman or Mrs. Jellyby's distant Borrioboolans—the stridently asserted division between a socialized self and a racialized other in *Bleak House*—no longer makes sense" in *Edwin Drood*, Tim Dolin points out, because "the Orient has found its way to England."[21] In other words, it is not the case in *Edwin Drood* that there are pockets of primitive darkness in, as Allan Woodcourt puts it in *Bleak House*, the "heart of a civilized world."[22] The civilized world is overrun with primitive darkness.

John Jasper is the perfect embodiment of this collapse of distinctions. Not only is jasper, the gemstone after which he is named, an impure variety of chalcedony that owes its characteristic reddish-brown color to the iron oxide impurities it contains, but the English word "jasper" itself is of Oriental origin (from Arabic and Persian).[23] The combination of constitutive impurity and foreign derivation define Jasper, who is set up—and I want to emphasize that it is a set-up—to be read in dualistic terms, as though in anticipation of Dr. Jekyll and Mr. Hyde: cathedral choirmaster in gowns on the "outside," Orientalized opium fiend on the "inside." Taken for granted, this external/internal or surface/depth mode of reading Jasper—essential to most of the scholarship on the novel—threatens to re-impose the very grid of binaries otherwise undermined by the novel, which is why we need to be wary of it; it also misses much of what is interesting about Jasper, since much of his cultural otherness is actually manifest, not latent.

Jasper is described, for one thing, as a "dark man" who "looks older than he is, as dark men often do."[24] It is true that he indulges his opium habit more or less in secret (though he does confess it to Edwin at one point),[25] either on his visits to the Princess Puffer's London opium den or when he retires to his own rooms, fills his pipe—"but not with tobacco"[26]—then lights it "and delivers himself to the Spectres it invokes at midnight."[27] But the effects of the drug are also made visible on the outside, alarming Edwin, for instance, when he notices "a strange film" over his uncle's eyes, which is explained away by Jasper's confession of his habit and his insistence that "the effects of the medicine steal over me like a blight or a cloud, and pass. You see them in the act of passing; they will be gone directly."[28] And when, following the novel's opening sequence, Jasper returns to Cloisterham a "jaded traveller," Crisparkle and Tope, noticing his unhealthy look and manner, ask each other whether he is "quite himself."[29]

That is a good question, though the temptation is for us to think that there are two John Jaspers, two "himselfs" rather than one. When at one point Crisparkle startles the sleeping Jasper into wakefulness, we learn that "long afterwards he had cause to remember how Jasper sprang from the couch in a delirious state between sleeping and waking, crying out, 'What is the matter? Who did it?'"[30] Such passages do indeed suggest that Jasper exists in two different and mutually exclusive states or modes of being, split by sleep and wakefulness or intoxication and sobriety. In his life of Dickens, John Forster says that the author wrote to him, concerning the plot of what would turn out to be his last novel, that the story "was to be that of the murder of a nephew by his uncle; the originality of which was to consist in the review of the murderer's career by himself at the close, when its temptations were to be dwelt upon as if, not he the culprit, but some other man, were the tempted."[31] This reinforces the sense of a kind of double personality for Jasper, the one part of his self not knowing what the other has been up to, or, as Rosemarie Bodenheimer argues this point, "allowing him to discuss himself as if he were somebody else."[32]

The circumstantial evidence from Forster and others aside, however, the novel also contains evidence to suggest that Jasper can also at times establish, even provisionally, a kind of coherence. For instance, on several occasions he can be seen pretty clearly setting up false or misleading evidence or circumstances to frame Neville for Edwin's apparent murder or to convict him in other people's minds before he is convicted in a court of law.[33]

Similarly, when Jasper learns from Grewgious that Rosa and Edwin are no longer engaged and hence that at least one of the possible motivations for his murdering his nephew as a rival claimant to Rosa's hand renders that violent act superfluous, he dissolves into a state of shock suggestive of his consciousness of his guilt—and the needlessness of his crime.[34] Moreover, a long strand of scholarship on the novel reads Jasper as a fully conscious practitioner of the Indian cult of Thuggee, with which Victorian Britain was obsessed.[35] This approach has been questioned by other critics, but, in addition to necessitating Jasper's provisional coherence in plotting and carrying out the ritual murder of Edwin in accordance with the right set of signs and circumstances (augured, perhaps, from celestial observations made on his midnight visits to the cathedral in the company of Durdles), it would also underscore the hybridization of Orient and Occident in the figure of a putatively white man gone "native" while at home in England.

Much of the most interesting scholarship on the novel, however, has been structured in terms of dualism. This runs from Hillis Miller's influential reading of *Edwin Drood* as irreconcilably split between a daytime surface and dark and hidden depths, to Charles Mitchell's argument that sees the text documenting a war between inner and outer selves, to Eve Sedgwick's reading of the Gothic structure of the text in terms of doubles and oppositions (dark and contaminated Jasper's murderously homoerotic desire for Edwin against the more conventional and heteronormative structures underlying the novel's "wholesome and blond characters"),[36] and so on, to more recent scholarship, much of which still falls back on the binary framework with which *Edwin Drood* itself unquestionably tempts us.[37]

Although most of the more recent scholarly approaches to the novel are less metaphysical and more cultural and political in orientation than the readings proposed in the 1950s and 1960s, many, taking their cues from *Edwin Drood's* saturation with Oriental references, are predicated on a structuring opposition between Orient and Occident and in particular to an alignment of Jasper's apparent self-divisions in relation to his opium habit and hence the Orient. Joachim Stanley, for example, notes the "increasingly pathological self-divisions" that the drug produces in Jasper, while Miriam Mara sees in his split consciousness the very embodiment of the destructiveness of colonial addiction.[38] For similar reasons, others see Jasper's opium addiction rupturing a complacent Western surface by bringing up Eastern impulses from below; or documenting "the increasing savagery of English domestic life," as Suvendrini Perera puts it, "the narrative of a civilization contaminated to its very core" as "a product of the imperial connection"; or, as Grace Moore argues, offering a fearful meditation on the loss of cultural identity, even the possibility of an "atavistic backsliding" brought about through imperial expansion and contact with other cultures.[39] Similarly, in arguing that "the difficulty of regulating appetite in its various forms so as to safeguard the health of the national body constitutes the text's main source of anxiety," Angelia Poon re-imposes a grid opposing the supposedly healthy national body to foreign contamination.[40]

Such readings of the novel make perfect sense for all kinds of reasons, partly because they position Dickens as building on and elaborating British fears of Oriental contamination brought about by imperial expansion, and the expansion of Eastern trade in particular: a tradition that has a long and culturally persuasive heritage, going back through Wilkie Collins (although *The Moonstone* also offers a critique of empire) and Thomas De Quincey (whose *Confessions of an English Opium Eater* was likely one of the sources Dickens drew on for *Edwin Drood*)[41] at least as far back as Goldsmith and *The Deserted Village*, if not earlier in the eighteenth century.[42] I have no argument against this approach to *Edwin Drood* as far as it goes, but I don't think it goes far enough.

As paradoxical as it might seem, what I want to argue at this stage of the chapter is that the novel's Orientalism—which forms not merely the point of departure but also the ultimate interpretive horizon for almost all the scholarship on *Edwin Drood*—amounts to something of a red herring in terms of understanding the forms of contradiction, discontinuity, and cultural breakdown it sets out to explore. This is so for two main reasons: first, because, besides Jasper, there are plenty of other characters in the novel who also have split personalities, if not altogether misfiring forms of subjectivity and individuality, and none of those other cases comes about as a by-product of Oriental contamination, or at least not one as fully—and hence perhaps misleadingly—developed as that of Jasper the opium fiend. Hence, they prompt us to ask, first, if the Orient or Oriental contamination is not (or not solely) responsible for such dissolutions, malformations, or breakdowns of subjectivity, what is? And second, it is not clear that selfhood as such—the mode of individual self-regulating subjectivity in the sense in which we have become familiar with it from, say, the 1790s on as one of the ideological bases of Occidentalism, as discussed in previous chapters of this book—is even fully operative or functional in *Edwin Drood* on a consistent basis.

In the case of Jasper, when Crisparkle and Tope ask each other whether Jasper is "quite himself" after his return from London, we are undoubtedly immediately tempted to think of that question in Oriental or Orientalized terms. After all, the scene of his return to Cloisterham, where they notice their colleague's poor appearance, follows on the scene in the east London bedsit, with its meditation on the instability of cultural forms and identities and the "unclean spirit of imitation" with which one culture borrows from, parasitizes on, or simply merges into another.[43] Right before the question of whether or not Jasper is "quite himself," we have seen, through his eyes, that the haggard opium dealer, Princess Puffer, "has opium-smoked herself into a strange likeness of the Chinaman. His form of cheek, eye, and temple, and his color, are repeated in her."[44] Most critics of the novel see this line as reinforcing a sense that the problematic being worked through in *Edwin Drood* is the erosion of cultural (and specifically English) purity. But that line also invites us to take a different approach: what if there is no cultural purity in the first place? After all, what evidence does the novel offer of such purity in an uncomplicated—let alone altogether uncompromised—way? (In other words, and I will shortly come back to this point: where is there a culturally pure space or character in this entire novel? And what does it do to our reading of the novel as a meditation on corruption of purity if there is none?) Under circumstances in which there is no cultural purity, we have to consider what it might mean to be "quite oneself" at all. Is the hybrid form of the haggard woman—its "unclean spirit of imitation" of the Chinaman—any less real than her original form? Might one's form, one's mode of subjectivity, inherently unstable in the first place, change according to changing circumstances?

The novel seems inclined toward such a position. When Crisparkle and Tope ask about Jasper, he has also just been identified by the narrator as "a jaded traveller," which it is, again, impossible for us not to think of in Oriental terms, since Jasper has just returned from his Oriental opium dream and his commingling with the Chinaman and the Lascar, as though that experience could have turned one stone—jasper—into another, even more Orientalized stone—jade—through (I can't help this) the act of having been stoned. But actually the question we should be asking ourselves here is not whether Jasper the choirmaster is the same person as Jasper the opium addict, but whether it is even possible to think not just of Jasper as "quite himself," but really of *any* character as "quite" him- or herself in a meaningfully sustained way, here or elsewhere in a novel so interested in the possibilities and consequences of what Durdles at one point refers to as a "mixing of things,"[45] that is, a mixing of modes and states of being, including the sleep and wakefulness, life and death (Durdles's main obsession), and also *this* culture and *that* one, the domestic and the foreign.

Not only do we see Jasper's "scattered consciousness" being deconstituted and reconstituted (which implies of course that consciousness and subjectivity are far from being given in a fixed and stable form once and for all), but there are also elements to Jasper's character that suggest more than a touch of the supernatural at work in him. The reference in the passage I quoted earlier to Jasper delivering himself to midnight specters may be rather less figurative than we might otherwise think, and he is at different times described as ghastly or diabolical.[46] In general, as Eve Sedgwick has pointed out, Jasper takes us quite deeply into the Gothic mode with which Dickens had experimented in other works (*Barnaby Rudge* among others) and here elaborates more fully in a thinking through of empire and sexuality.[47] In few other texts, in fact, are the affiliations between the colonial and the Gothic which Laura Doyle has explored more fully thought through than they are in this novel.[48]

It is not without reason that several characters feel a distinct discomfort in Jasper's presence, a sense of being watched by him. Even Durdles (who hardly seems the most aware character) is repeatedly "conscious of his [Jasper's] watchful eyes."[49] This sensation is especially disturbing to Rosa. "He terrifies me. He haunts my thoughts, like a dreadful ghost," she explains to Helena. "I feel that I am never safe from him. I feel as if he could pass in through the wall when he is spoken of."[50] In such moments, Jasper's being seems not simply split between two forms (inside/outside, Oriental/Occidental), but rather to exceed the constraints of individual selfhood and even material containment in the body, and in ways that have nothing immediately to do with opium and the Orient. This excess seems to enable him to project his being beyond the scale of the ordinary five senses that normally define our sensorium and hence, according to Locke and his descendants, the outer, structural, limits of our subjectivity. "He has made a slave of me with his looks. He has forced me to understand him, without his saying a word; and he has forced me to keep silence, without his uttering a phrase," Rosa complains. "When I play, he never moves his eyes from my hands. When I sing, he never moves his eyes from my lips. When he corrects me, and strikes a note, or a chord, or plays a passage, *he himself is in the sounds*, whispering that he pursues me as a lover, and commanding me to keep his secret. I avoid his eyes," she adds, "but he forces me to see them without looking at them. Even when a glaze comes over them (which is sometimes the case), and he seems to wander away into a frightful sort of dream in which he threatens most, he obliges me to know it, and to know that he is sitting close at my side, more terrible to me then than ever."[51]

Such episodes might be dismissed as projections of Rosa's own discomfort with her tutor (and who can blame her?), but the sense that Jasper's being exceeds—and can be projected beyond—the limits of his ordinary self (into sound, for example) is consistently corroborated by other characters, as well as by the omniscient narrator. So disconnected is Jasper's subjectivity from his senses that they can essentially split from him as well as the other way around. When, for example, Edwin first arrives at Jasper's flat, we see the uncle gazing intently at his nephew, but a subtle shift takes place: "Once for all, a look of intentness and intensity—a look of hungry, exacting, watchful, and yet devoted affection—is always, now and ever afterwards, on *the Jasper face* whenever *the Jasper face* is addressed in this direction. And whenever *it* is so addressed, *it* is never, on this occasion or any other, dividedly addressed; *it* is always concentrated."[52] Rather than Jasper's projecting his subjectivity beyond the limits of the five senses, what we see here is the reverse: the five senses, or one of them at least, expresses a form of agency quite autonomous from its supposed possessor. For it is not that Jasper has become reduced to his face, but rather that his face is acting as though it had, so to speak, a mind of its own. In such circumstances, it becomes impossible to say what it means to ask whether Jasper is "quite himself," not just because we are tempted to think of the Oriental Jasper and the Occidental Jasper, or the homosexual Jasper and the heterosexual Jasper, but because "Jasper," it turns out, is merely a temporarily or provisionally coherent assemblage of different elements or forces that may disarticulate at any moment, either *into* or *beyond* its various subcomponents. Bizarrely, we are here much closer to Blake and Spinoza than we are to the author of the far more bourgeois *Oliver Twist* or *Great Expectations*.[53]

This is surely what explains the most expressly supernatural scene in the novel, when, as Grewgious explains to him that Edwin (by then disappeared, presumably killed) and Rosa have broken their engagement, Jasper quite literally melts away, in a passage well worth quoting in full:

> Mr. Grewgious, alternately opening and shutting the palms of his hands as he warmed them at the fire, and looking fixedly at him [Jasper] sideways, and never changing either his action or his look in all that followed, went on to reply.
>
> "This young couple, the lost youth and Miss Rosa, my ward, though so long betrothed, and so long recognizing their betrothal, and so near being married—"
>
> Mr. Grewgious saw a staring white face, and two quivering white lips, in the easy chair, and saw two muddy white hands gripping its sides. But for the hands, he might have thought he had never seen the face.
>
> "This young couple came gradually to the discovery, (made on both sides pretty equally, I think), that they would be happier and better, both

in their present and their future lives, as affectionate friends, or say rather as brother and sister, than as husband and wife."

Mr. Grewgious saw a lead-coloured face in the easy chair, and on its surface dreadful starting drops or bubbles, as if of steel.

"This young couple formed at length the healthy resolution of interchanging their discoveries, openly, sensibly, and tenderly. They met for that purpose. After some innocent and generous talk, they agreed to dissolve their existing, and their intended, relations, for ever and ever."

Mr. Grewgious saw a ghastly figure rise, open-mouthed, from the easy chair, and lift its outspread hands towards its head.

"One of this young couple, and that one your nephew, fearful, however, that in the tenderness of your affection for him you would be bitterly disappointed by so wide a departure from his projected life, forbore to tell you the secret, for a few days, and left it to be disclosed by me, when I should come down to speak to you, and he would be gone. I speak to you, and he is gone."

Mr. Grewgious saw the ghastly figure throw back its head, clutch its hair with its hands, and turn with a writhing action from him.

"I have now said all that I have to say: except that this young couple parted, firmly, though not without tears and sorrow, on the evening when you last saw them together."

Mr. Grewgious heard a terrible shriek, and saw no ghastly figure, sitting or standing; saw nothing but a heap of torn and miry clothes upon the floor.

Not changing his action even then, he opened and shut the palms of his hands as he warmed them, and looked down at it.[54]

As Grewgious unfolds his narrative, Jasper begins disarticulating. First, Jasper as unified or articulated subject is replaced by the sum of his individual parts—face, hands, lips, and so on. Each of these parts seems in turn disarticulated from the others (but for the hands Grewgious might not have seen the face, for example). Then these parts begin to assume their own autonomy, to act independently of their supposed possessor: it is not Jasper *as Jasper* who reacts to Grewgious's unfolding story, but rather the lips, the hands, the face. Under such circumstances it is meaningless to speak of Jasper as a unified subject; he is not even recognizably human, alternating between the mechanical ("sweating" drops of steel as he melts) and the supernatural (the ghastly, the spectral). At the end of the scene, the disarticulated components of the character formerly known as Jasper disappear altogether, leaving behind only his empty clothes. And what makes the

scene more powerful still is that the entire narrative takes place through the
validation of Grewgious: by far the driest and most unimaginative character
in the novel, the one least likely to imagine or project a supernatural scene;
and yet the one who corroborates it through that series of statements, "Mr
Grewgious saw."

Now, it could well be (as various scholars have suggested) that this dissolution of self is the inevitable outcome of Jasper's Orientalization and, as
Sedgwick puts it, the homosexual panic to which it is tied.[55] But the draw-
back with readings of the novel that focus too narrowly on Jasper—as most
do—is that they miss much of what is stake in other characters as well and
tend to take for granted that if Jasper is the embodiment of corruption or
deviance, of which this dissolution of self is a sure indicator, there must be
some "normal," pure, clean, uncompromised character serving as his foil.
That is not so straightforward a proposition as it might seem.

For example, both Poon and Sedgwick (with whose readings of Jasper, as
far as they go, I am otherwise sympathetic) assume that since what marks
Jasper as problematic is his "darkness" and his proximity to or internalization of the Orient (literally, in the case of opium consumption), then we
must look to his apparent opposites, Crisparkle and Tartar, as the representatives of wholesome, patriotic whiteness. On Sedgwick's reading, since
"the novel in many ways connives in a view of Englishness, of culture and
race, or simply of 'psychology,' that insulates Jasper's existence from that
of the novel's wholesome and blond characters," it makes perfect sense to
see Crisparkle as representing "the English racial ideal" who occupies "the
moral center of the novel," and Tartar as "Crisparkle's other, more vital,
more virile, simply more national protégé."[56] Poon takes a similar position.
"The text solicits approval for Rosa's attraction to the sailor, Tartar, on the
basis of his role as a 'healthier' alternative to Jasper," she argues. "Tartar is
'brown,' tanned and sunburned from his sea voyages abroad in the nation's
service. That he, again unlike Jasper, is inured against the potentially con-
taminating influence of empire despite his exposure to foreign places is suggested by his extremely clean and ordered room—'the neatest, the cleanest,
and the best-ordered chambers ever seen under the sun, moon, and stars.'"[57]

Neither of these accounts, however, takes sufficient note of the considerable ironies attending the characterization of Crisparkle and Tartar. And
yet it is impossible not to laugh at Crisparkle, who comes off as a caricature,
a parody, rather than a serious model, of the muscular Christian, with his
absurd sparring and mock boxing in front of the mirror, his habit of plung-
ing his head into frozen rivers, and his hardly model-like family life (in his
forties, he is still living with his mother and under her thumb, never hav-

ing matured beyond that, remaining more of a boy than a man; moreover, their home is, as I mentioned earlier, bursting with Oriental and colonial commodities). David Faulkner is right to point out that although the novel seems to pit a degenerate, Orientalized Jasper against the virtuous, English Crisparkle, in fact "Crisparkle's 'purity' as a muscular Christian is never unadulterated."[58]

Sedgwick does admit that "the novel, especially toward the beginning, takes a certain pleasure in exploring the fatuity of the Crisparkle type," but she still wants to insist that his homosocial " 'manliness,' his Englishness," is "clean, clean, clean."[59] Yet at no point does the novel really leave off its parody of Crisparkle, and indeed it ties its mockery to his cleanliness: for example, to his propensity for ice-plunging. More than that, it incorporates his racial whiteness directly into the parody as well: "Mr. Crisparkle, Minor Canon, fair and rosy, and perpetually pitching himself head-foremost into all the deep running water in the surrounding country; Mr. Crisparkle, Minor Canon, early riser, musical, classical, cheerful, kind, good-natured, social, contented, and boy-like."[60] The point here is that the "spark" or light that seems to be given off by Crisparkle, his "whiteness," is misleading, even false—just another will-o'-the-wisp like his six brothers who died in infancy, to whom he owes his name (Septimus), who "went out, one by one, as they were born, like six weak little rushlights, as they were lighted."[61] He hardly serves as a genuine alternative to Jasper.

As for Tartar, although both Sedgwick and Poon read him as the embodiment of patriotic values, neither points out the irony that this apparently most manly and in that sense English character in the novel has such a clearly foreign—indeed, Oriental—name. In the case of Crisparkle, the novel deploys the language of parody in his characterization, but it turns to a childish language, and specifically the language of children's stories, to frame Tartar. "Mr Tartar's chambers were the neatest, the cleanest, and the best-ordered chambers ever seen under the sun, moon, and the stars," we read. "The floors were scrubbed to that extent, that you might have supposed the London blacks emancipated for ever, and gone out of the land for good. Every inch of brass-work in Mr Tartar's possession was polished and burnished, till it shone like a brazen mirror. No speck, nor spot, nor spatter soiled the purity of any of Mr Tartar's household gods, large, small, or middle sized."[62] As with the treatment of Crisparkle, the characterization here rests on exaggeration to the point of absurdity, but more than in the other case, there is, apart from his name, more than a racial tinge to Tartar as well.[63]

As Ina Rae Hark points out, Dickens has overwhelmed Tartar with both

Oriental and fairy-tale associations.[64] For example, the hyperbolic language used to describe Tartar's quarters is not coincidentally reminiscent of the language of the *Arabian Nights*, or, more precisely, a children's version of the same. And when Rosa accompanies him down the street in London, her girlish fancy is fired up with her own imagination of herself seeming, as though she had fallen into the pages of a fairy tale, "very little and very helpless, contrasted with the strong figure that could have caught her up and carried her out of any danger, miles and miles without resting."[65] She then falls into a dreamy swoon, which, the narrator tells us, "may account for her never afterwards quite knowing how she ascended (with his help) to his garden in the air, and seemed to get into a marvelous country that came into sudden bloom like the country on the summit of the magic beanstalk. May it flourish for ever!"[66] Once in his quarters, we switch back again from *Jack in the Beanstalk* to *Arabian Nights*, as Tartar presents "a dazzling enchanted repast. Wonderful macaroons, glittering liqueurs, magically preserved tropical spices, and jellies of celestial tropical fruits, displayed themselves profusely at an instant's notice."[67] Hark is quite right to suggest that what we have here is a mix of the fairy tale and the exotic, neither a suitable alternative nor a foil to Jasper's Orientalism. "While there can be no doubt that Rosa becomes infatuated with Tartar almost instantly, the images that surround him suggest that her attachment is not altogether healthy," Hark argues. "Tartar is not a person at all, in the sense that Rosa or Jasper or Edwin is a person, but a fantasy come to life, appearing magically when the need arises like a friendly wizard or Cinderella's fairy godmother. . . . He is a living symbol of both the virtues and the perils of the imagination."[68] There is more to what Hark is saying than she seems to realize: what I find significant here is not just that Tartar is a fairy-tale character but also that that very status takes us back to the question of what constitutes the reality of a person or a subject in the first place.

It may seem straightforward enough, then, to read the character of Jasper as corrupted or degenerate, but if we look through the novel for supposedly more wholesome or healthy alternatives—the Occidental characters to balance Jasper's insidious Orientalism, necessary to any binary reading of the novel—we exhaust the list of possibilities pretty quickly. Neither Crisparkle nor Tartar, as we have seen, offer much of a stable, reassuring alternative. To whom, then, might we look? We might turn to Miss Twinkleton, the headmistress of Rosa's school, who ought surely to offer some kind of model of Victorian propriety. But she, too, is compromised, another composite subject, split even more radically than, say, Wemmick of *Great Expectations*, with his two distinct personalities, one for home, the other for work: "As, in some cases of drunkenness, and in others of animal magnetism, there are two states of consciousness which never clash, but each of which pursues its separate course as though it were continuous instead of broken (thus, if I hide my watch when I am drunk, I must be drunk again before I can remember where), so Miss Twinkleton has her two distinct and separate phases of being."[69] She is not only split, but chronologically cut off from herself. Moreover, her name is oddly, and not coincidentally, reminiscent of Crisparkle's: in a novel obsessed with the misfiring symbols of light and darkness, here too we have a misleading light—twinkling—to match the Minor Canon's sparkling, rather than shining strongly. For there is no strong shining light in *Edwin Drood*, and that is part of the point.

Grewgious might suggest himself as a stabilizing, normalizing, Westernizing alternative. Since he is the least exciting character in the novel, he ought to represent, if we may borrow from Walter Scott, "the humble English post-chaise, drawn upon four wheels, and keeping his Majesty's highway," in contrast to "the conveyance of Prince Hussein's tapestry, or Malek the Weaver's flying sentry-box,"[70] represented by Jasper; that is, predictable, dull, law-abiding: the very embodiment of the stultifying lack of excitement, indeed the lethargy, that John Stuart Mill identifies as one of the indispensable requirements of a civilized life.[71]

And yet in Grewgious too we find a bundle of unstable contradictions. Even his person is consistently described in the novel as incomplete. "He was an arid, sandy man, who, if he had been put into a grinding-mill, looked as if he would have ground immediately into high-dried snuff," we learn. "The little play of feature that his face presented, was cut deep into it, in a few hard curves that made it more like work; and he had certain notches in his forehead, which looked as though Nature had been about to touch them into sensibility or refinement, when she had impatiently thrown away the chisel, and said: 'I really cannot be worried to finish off this man; let him go as he is.'"[72] Grewgious, then, more like Jasper than unlike him in this respect, represents yet another form of temporal distortion, a subject out of synch with time. He is acutely aware of this himself. "Young ways were never my ways," he tells Rosa; "I was the only offspring of parents far advanced in life, and I half believe I was born advanced in life myself."[73] Rosa is in some sense the perfect match for him: the rosebud that has never opened and probably never will; the child who will never grow up, who will cling to the "forever" world of fairy tales.

From the moment of its conception as such, the Occident, as the self-proclaimed center of modernity, was supposed to represent an antidote to the Orient's suspension of time and progress or to the vertiginous loss of

stable temporality said to be characteristic of Orientalized opium dreams
from Coleridge's "Kubla Khan" onward. But if the Occident is meant to offer stable, chronometric predictability and ultimately the sense of a "present unified in historical contemporaneity," which, as Jonathan Grossman
shows,[74] was intimately woven into many of Dickens's earlier novels, the
supposedly Occidental characters of *Edwin Drood*—the ones to whom we
should be able to turn in escape from the Oriental contamination of Jasper—fail that test one by one. Crisparkle is stuck in time as a permanent
boy; Tartar, a man "with a young face, but with an older figure,"[75] offers
only an escape into the childish world of fairy tales and Oriental dreams;
Rosa is a bud that will never bloom; Edwin, weighed down by the promises
of the past and full of ambitious dreams about the future, ends up cut off
from both; Miss Twinkleton exists in two distinct and temporally discontinuous phases of being; Grewgious is out of synch with time itself; and
Durdles—ah, Durdles—is more interested in tapping and ferreting out the
"old 'uns" in the cathedral crypts than in actually mixing with the living in
the open air outside.

   "Stony" Durdles is in some sense the real hero of this story, the perfect
match for Jasper. "Yours is a curious existence," Jasper tells him at one
point. "Yours is another," comes the perfectly balanced reply.[76] Durdles the
stone mason is the leading authority on the cathedral crypt, which with his
tapping and probing he methodically maps out in a perpetually incomplete
project to try to synchronize the living and the dead, to align them in a
common space. He talks of the dead—the "old 'uns," as he calls them—on
a perfectly familiar basis, as though they were in fact living. And, in "that
hazy state of his," "always an uncertain state," his own subjectivity is, like
that of the other characters, un- or mal-formed, or simply misfiring.[77] "He
often speaks of himself in the third person; perhaps being a little misty as
to his own identity when he narrates," the narrator tells us. "Thus he will
say, touching his strange sights: 'Durdles come upon the old chap,' in reference to a buried magnate of ancient time and high degree, 'by striking right
into the coffin with his pick.'"[78] Not merely burrowing through the stone,
he is himself stoned in his own way, "covered from head to foot with old
mortar, lime, and stone grit,"[79] as though he has been absorbed into the very
material with which he is supposed to be working: the subject defined and
framed by his object, rather than the other way around. His permanently
incomplete residence, we are told, is "a little antiquated hole of a house
that was never finished: supposed to be built, so far, of stones stolen from
the city wall. To this abode there is an approach, ankle-deep in stone chips,
resembling a petrified grove of tombstones, urns, draperies, and broken col-

umns, in all stages of sculpture. Herein," the narrator adds, "two journeymen incessantly chip, while other two journeymen, who face each other,
incessantly saw stone; dipping as regularly in and out of their sheltering
sentry-boxes, as if they were mechanical figures emblematical of Time and
Death."[80]

Time and Death: perhaps they, rather than Durdles, can claim to be the
real heroes of *Edwin Drood*, the truest representatives of the Occidentalism
against which Jasper's Orientalism is supposed to be defined. For this is a
novel saturated with references to what time means in and for modernity:
it offers a meditation on time and its death. Time in *Edwin Drood* is stalled,
broken, splintered: not what it is supposed to be in the culture of modernity. There is no unified present in *Edwin Drood*, and contemporaneity itself
seems to have broken down beyond repair.

I don't intend to rehearse here the vast body of scholarly arguments on
time and modernity, which I have discussed in great detail in other books
and throughout the preceding chapters.[81] Suffice it to say that a certain conception of progressive and synchronized time is foundational to most conventional understandings of what we now think of as Occidental culture,[82]
and, moreover, that (as I argued in the chapter on London in the present
volume) the normative conception of self-regulating subjectivity that was
consolidated in England from the late eighteenth through the nineteenth
centuries was also expressly conceived of in relation to progressive, linear
time and its history.

Tied immediately to these notions of time and subjectivity was a very
clear understanding of racial and cultural specificity: this way of inhabiting of being and time, and hence history, does not apply to other races and
cultures, which explains "their" inferiority and "our" superiority; thus we
have James Mill's dismissal of Indian history or Macaulay's claims for the
superiority of English over Arabic or Persian as the appropriate vehicle of
modernity (as was discussed in chap. 5).[83] The only question the advocates
of colonialism asked themselves is whether or not it falls to "us" to bestow
the privileges of linear time and history, and self-regulating subjectivity, on
"our" subject peoples; and (though this would really become more of a question a bit later in the nineteenth century, the moment of Wells, Kipling, and
Conrad) whether these others are even up to the task of such improvement.
Macaulay, for his part, clearly thought they were (some of them anyway),
hence his urge to form "a class of persons, Indian in blood and color, but English in taste, in opinions, in morals and in intellect."[84]

By the late 1860s, when Dickens was thinking through and starting to
write his last novel, there was a quite solidly established sense—not with-

out its critics and its anxieties, to be sure—that certain societies were moving through the stream of progressive time while others had stalled by the wayside of history and were patiently waiting for repairs, spare parts, and a friendly tow into the future. Nowhere is this sense more fully articulated than in the work of John Stuart Mill, for whom the distinction between "stationary" and "progressive" societies is inseparable from either his doctrine of liberalism or his attitude toward empire.

Since, as Mill argues in *On Representative Government*, "the best government is that which is most conducive to Progress,"[85] the question is what to do about societies that have stalled in their development. "The Egyptian hierarchy, the paternal despotism of China, were very fit instruments for carrying those nations up to the point of civilization which they attained. But having reached that point, they were brought to a permanent halt for want of mental liberty and individuality," he argues.[86] Halted in time, such a society needs outside intervention, the benign and civilizing influence of empire, or in other words—and stated somewhat more frankly—the externally induced destruction of the "despotism" of local cultural, social, and political custom, which "is everywhere the standing hindrance to human advancement, being in unceasing antagonism to that disposition to aim at something better than customary, which is called, according to circumstances, the spirit of liberty, or that of progress or improvement."[87] And yet, if according to Mill "the indispensable virtue . . . in a government which establishes itself over a people of this sort is that it make itself obeyed," and hence even if such a government "must be nearly, or quite despotic," its ultimate task is the series of lessons "which the pupils, in this stage of their progress, require."[88] To grant such a debased people Liberty and Representative Government—that is, sovereign independence—would lead to utter disorder and retrogression, Mill argues. "Their improvement can not come from themselves, but must be superinduced from without," he argues. "They have to be taught self-government."[89]

These are all by now familiar arguments.[90] The point is that Mill's assessment of empire rested on the fundamental assumption that, as he argued in an 1836 essay, "Civilization," which he published in the *Westminster Review*—of which, incidentally, Francis Place produced a very long and detailed, albeit unpublished, critique[91]—the progressive elements of civilization "exist in modern Europe, and especially in Great Britain, in a more eminent degree, and in a state of more rapid progression, than at any other place or time."[92] Hence, of course, Britain's responsibilities toward its as yet uncivilized colonial "pupils."

Dickens, for his part, would disagree with Mill about the civilizing

mission overseas, which he considered, if not altogether "useless and fu-
tile," given the "great gulf set" between the civilized European and barbarous "savages," then at least a lower priority than the need for a civilizing mission at home in England.[93] Nevertheless, he expresses in much of
his journalism and other writings a boundless faith in the superiority of
Western and specifically British civilization over others (albeit a faith that
is sometimes tempered in his fiction with the skepticism of novels such
as *Hard Times* and *Bleak House*). And his celebration of the superiority of
Western culture runs essentially in parallel with that of Mill, since it is also
structured in terms of time. Nowhere is this clearer than in a piece he co-
authored for *Household Worlds* with Richard Horne on the Great Exhibition of 1851 (about which Dickens actually had various reservations), com-
paring the accomplishments of Britain with those of the Chinese, "a people
who came to a dead stop, Heaven knows how many hundred years ago."[94]
For in such pieces the contrast between "our" civilization and "their" barbarism does not depend simply on the sheer material superiority of British over Chinese technology (as suggested in the contrast drawn between a
bamboo palanquin and a railway car, or a British ship and the "ridiculous
abortion" presented by a Chinese junk).[95] Rather, it depends on the contrast between what the article refers to as "Stoppage" and "Progress," or the
sense that "we" are moving and progressing while "they" are stuck in time.

"There may be an odd, barbarous, or eccentric nation, here and there,
upon the face of the globe, who may see fit to exercise its free will, in the
negative form of will-not, and who may seclude itself from the rest of the
world, resolved not to move on with it," Dickens and Horne argue. "For
the rest of the earth's inhabitants, the shades, and steps, and gradations of
the ascending scale will be various, and no doubt numerous; but that we are
moving in a right direction towards some superior condition of society,"
they add, "we humbly yet proudly, and with heartfelt joy that partakes of
solemnity, do fully recognize as a great fact."[96] Thus, the Africans whose
savagery Dickens condemns in his "Niger Expedition" piece may eventually, in theory anyway, be improved and civilized, even though to change
the customs of "ignorant and savage races is a work which, like the progressive changes of the globe itself, requires a stretch of years that dazzles
in the looking at."[97] But for Orientals stuck in time, and especially for the
Chinese, with their "glory of yellow jaundice," past, present and future are
jumbled indiscriminately together in stalled time.[98]

Part of the argument in this view of Oriental despotism, which emerges
from the same tradition articulated by Mill, is one that we have seen at
work in the discussion in the London chapter of this book of the changing

Victorian conceptualizations of the metropolis: namely, the sense that progress or movement in time depends on a connection to global movements
and circulations, a notion to which Dickens himself was undoubtedly committed earlier in his career. This is one of the lessons of Jonathan Grossman's recent book *Charles Dickens's Networks*, the fullest account yet of
time and circulation in Dickens. Grossman tracks the unfolding elaboration
of the engagement in Dickens's novels with Britain's developing passenger
transport network, especially in terms of time. He traces the movement
from the first awareness of this kind of networking and its contraction of
time in early novels like *Pickwick* to the later and much more elaborate
sense of spatiotemporal entanglement we get in *Little Dorrit*, in which the
standardization of time at home is tied into the growing awareness—what
Fredric Jameson identifies as a cognitive map—of an international network
spanning the globe.[99]

As Grossman shows, the development—or rather, the imposition—of
standard time on local time in England as it took place from the 1850s on,
mostly at the behest of railroad companies to allow for the greater coordina-
tion of their schedules (Greenwich Mean Time was not officially adopted
until 1880), led to a profound transformation at a personal phenomenologi-
cal and epistemological level. "The older mode of keeping time helped hold
an epistemology, a structure of meaning, in place for human activity," he
argues. "It meant that anything done at a distance from home matters only
when it comes across distance, which is in fact time, to affect home and in
doing so necessarily occupies a position in the past, however tremendously
important its effects might be. By contrast," he notes, "standard time is pre-
mised upon the semi-omniscient awareness that what is going on is going
on simultaneously at different places, such that the relation—the shrunken
distance, two trains speeding toward each other—between these places now
amounts to a zone of human contact, a space shared in time."[100] As a result,
Grossman argues, the difficulty encountered by the characters of *Little Dorrit*, who confront the limitation of their perspectives, "is not—as some later
modernist writers will have it—that their modern world is fragmented and
disconnected. It is just the opposite. The density and extensivity of people's
interconnections exceeds their capacity to grasp them, producing a bewil-
dering incompleteness in the understanding people have of what's going on
around them."[101] What that 1857 novel leaves us with, then, is a sense of a
world ever more densely integrated, both spatially and epistemologically,
through the synchronization of time, the alignment of various formerly currents into one coordinated and necessarily progressive flow.

Dickens would not have been far from Mill in such an assessment of linear, synchronized time in the 1850s. But by the time of *Edwin Drood*, something has clearly changed, in the atmosphere of the novel, if not in the mind of Dickens himself. And here too there is something to be learned from Mill. For, whether consciously, deliberately, or otherwise, the novel articulates one of the great fears that also attends Mill's celebration of progress and civilization, a fear that haunts Mill's writing from that quite early *Westminster Review* piece all the way through *On Representative Government* and *On Liberty*, which is not merely that, even in Britain, there are threats to liberty and individuality (increasing dissipation and intellectual laziness, the tyranny of mediocrity and conformity, the development of a mass culture in which, as he puts it, "power passes from individuals to masses, and the weight and importance of an individual, as compared with the mass, sink into greater and greater insignificance"),[102] but above all that, with enough counterpressures, progress might simply grind to a halt.

"The very same social causes—the same beliefs, feelings, institutions, and practices—are as much required to prevent society from retrograding as to produce a farther advance," Mill cautions. "Were there no improvement to be hoped for, life would not the less be an unceasing struggle against causes of deterioration, as it even now is."[103] And deterioration, he warns, "once begun, would proceed with increasing rapidity, and become more and more difficult to check, until it reached a state often seen in history, and in which many large portions of mankind even now grovel; when hardly any thing short of superhuman power seems sufficient to turn the tide, and give a fresh commencement to the upward movement."[104] Under certain circumstances, he adds, it is possible to imagine Europe and even Britain itself becoming "another China."[105] The forward, progressive movement of time is therefore for Mill not something to be counted on or taken for granted as either inevitable or inexorable.[106] We might go Oriental ourselves; we too might fall back into—might become—one of the dark places of the earth.

For all Dickens's famous reformist optimism, there are signs that, like Mill, he did not take the progressive movement of time completely for granted—and again the Orient, and specifically China, figures as the other haunting the self, a warning of what we too might slide back into if we stall. "The true Tory spirit," that Great Exhibition piece warns, "would have made a China of England, if it could."[107] Toryism in this sense represents the very same clinging to the despotism of custom which Macaulay identifies in Southey and which Mill sees as "the standing hindrance to human advancement."[108] But the sense we get from that jingoistic and optimistic Great Exhibition piece is that Toryism is a *former* threat: something that perhaps *could have* held England back—had the Southeys of an earlier era prevailed, for example—but that has now lapsed as a danger. In *Edwin Drood*, however, the danger of retrogression and backsliding is everywhere, and it is no longer identified in party terms but rather as an omnipresent condition: if not a state "we" have entered into by sliding back into it then, worse, a state from which we had never actually propelled ourselves as we liked to proclaim in such an endlessly self-congratulatory way. It is as though, like the narrator of Blake's "The Garden of Love," we can now see what we "never had seen"—not because it wasn't there, but because we had persistently misrecognized it, not seen it for what it was all along; mistaking tombstones for flowers, as in the Blake poem, and not noticing the priests in black gowns walking their rounds and binding with briars our joys and desires.[109]

Cloisterham cathedral, which ought to be the last bastion and inner keep of Occidental culture—a fortress of what the novel refers to as "oppressive respectability"—turns out to be the very heart of the darkness that haunts *The Mystery of Edwin Drood*, a darkness that spills over into the rest of the town as well. This too is not seen by those critics who insist on reading the novel as a narrative of Oriental contamination of the healthy Occidental body, which almost inevitably takes for granted the normative stability of Cloisterham as "a quiet English town."[110] Nothing could be further from the truth. It is worth quoting the initial description of the town—usually read as a stand-in for Dickens's native Rochester—at length, since much of what I want to say about it is contained in this passage:

> For sufficient reasons which this narrative will itself unfold as it advances, a fictitious name must be bestowed upon the old Cathedral town. Let it stand in these pages as Cloisterham. It was once possibly known to the Druids by another name, and certainly to the Romans by another, and to the Saxons by another, and to the Normans by another; and a name more or less in the course of many centuries can be of little moment to its dusty chronicles.
>
> An ancient city, Cloisterham, and no meet dwelling-place for any one with hankerings after the noisy world. A monotonous, silent city, deriving an earthy flavor throughout, from its cathedral crypt, and so abounding in vestiges of monastic graves, that the Cloisterham children grow small salad in the dust of abbots and abbesses, and make dirt-pies of nuns and friars; while every ploughman in its outlying fields renders to once puissant Lord Treasurers, Archbishops, Bishops, and such-like, the attention which the Ogre in the story-book desired to render to his unbidden visitor, and grinds their bones to make his bread.
>
> A drowsy city, Cloisterham, whose inhabitants seem to suppose,

with an inconsistency more strange than rare, that all its changes lie behind it, and that there are no more to come. A queer moral to derive from antiquity, yet older than any traceable antiquity. So silent are the streets of Cloisterham (though prone to echo on the smallest provocation), that of a summer-day the sunblinds of its shops scarce dare to flap in the south wind; while the sun-browned tramps who pass along and stare, quicken their limp a little, that they may the sooner get beyond the confines of its oppressive respectability. This is a feat not difficult of achievement, seeing that the streets of Cloisterham city are little more than one narrow street by which you get into it and get out of it: the rest being mostly disappointing yards with pumps in them and no thoroughfare—exception made of the Cathedral-close, and a paved Quaker settlement, in color and general conformation very like a Quakeress's bonnet, up in a shady corner.

In a word, a city of another and a bygone time is Cloisterham, with its hoarse cathedral bell, its hoarse rooks hovering about the Cathedral tower, its hoarser and less distinct rooks in the stalls far beneath. Fragments of old wall, saint's chapel, chapter-house, convent, and monastery, have got incongruously or obstructively built into many of its houses and gardens, much as kindred jumbled notions have become incorporated into many of its citizen's [*sic*] minds.

All things in it are of the past. Even its single pawnbroker takes in no pledges, nor has he for a long time, but offers vainly an unredeemed stock for sale, of which the costlier articles are dim and pale old watches apparently in a slow perspiration, tarnished sugar-tongs with ineffectual legs, and odd volumes of dismal books.[111]

Cloisterham is a place where time goes to die; the "slow perspiration" of the pawnbroker's stock of pale old watches the perfect echo of Jasper's steel-like sweat, and a sign that this Occident is not any more stable than that Orient. The first temptation when reading this remarkable passage is to suspect that what we have here is a description that may apply to a dull provincial backwater, but not to a thriving modern metropolis, so let me begin by preempting that temptation and by pointing out that the novel's descriptions of London (to which I will shortly return) convey exactly the same sense of stalled time and of a present supersaturated with a past from which it cannot escape, so the condition being described here has nothing to do with mere provinciality. The second thing to point out is that nowhere here is there a reference to Jasper, opium, or Oriental contamination and corruption. On the contrary, if Cloisterham has stalled in time, that stall has nothing to do with the East or opium: it has been stalled for a long time, from long before the age of empire; in a sense, it has always been stalled.

Cloisterham is a city which has accumulated pasts and histories, which, instead of being overcome and transcended each in its turn, instead overlap in palimpsestic layers or are endlessly reformulated in its spaces. Its history is discontinuous and fragmented, apprehended—to the extent that it is apprehended at all—in the form of an indefinite and disorganized recycling by which the present is not only indelibly tainted by the past but structured and defined by it. The present is in fact nothing but the haphazard accumulation of the fragments of the past. And the future is more of the same, since all transformation seems to be in the past: a notion identified with antiquity and thereby suggesting all the more strongly that the modern is already the antique and always has been, or in other words that the future itself is already behind us in some sense, that we are living in the past.

Moreover, the endless recycling of the past that takes place here—literally *giving* place to the city by *taking* it, as the old is taken apart and rebuilt into the new—occurs both in an architectural sense and in an organic one. Just as the modern urban fabric of the town is constituted by the recycling of material from past fabrics, its modern population sustains itself by recycling and consuming its ancient population, the brutal truth of this ghoulish cannibalism disguised only by the fact that the recycling takes place through the mediation of agriculture as the dead fertilize the nourishment of the living.

The specific reference to the Ogre of "Jack in the Beanstalk" ("Fee, fie, fo, fum, / I smell the blood of an Englishman. / Be he alive or be he dead, / I'll grind his bones to make my bread")[112] is especially intriguing, however, because of the connection to the whimsical fairy-tale world that Rosa inhabits. Here "real life" involves the material enactment of what the darkest moment of the fairy tale only threatened as mere narrative. These scenes of the quotidian banality of life's imitation of art—the children growing "small salad" in the dust of abbots—underscore the extent to which the opposition of the real and the imaginary is little more than facile. What we have here in other words is not the opposition of colorful Oriental fantasies to hard, empirical Occidental realities, never mind the colonization of the latter by the former, but rather the sense that the Occident's own fairy tales are in some sense also its realities, and are all the more banal— "monotonous" is the term used here—for that. In such a context, nationalist and culturalist bravado rings all the more hollow. "We are, sir," Sapsea tells Datchery, "an ancient city, and an ecclesiastical city. We are a constitutional city, as it becomes such a city to be, and we uphold our glorious privileges." Such jingoism does little to disguise the rather more brute fact of Englishmen grinding each other's bones to dust; such has England become—such it has always been.

It is not just that the process of modernization is here revealed to be uneven: it is that modernity itself is revealed to be a state of recycled incompletion. This state is reflected over and over again in the various architectural spaces in the novel, from Durdles's "antiquated hole" of an unfinished house, in which those workers so emblematic of time and death perpetually labor in a "petrified grove of tombstones, urns, draperies and broken columns, in all stages of sculpture"; to Tope's residence, with its "ancient walls" containing rooms that "rather seemed to have been dug out of them, than to have been designed beforehand"; to the "warped and distorted" Travellers' Twopenny; to Sapsea's premises, which are "of about the period of the Nuns' House, irregularly modernized here and there, as steadily deteriorating generations found, more and more, that they preferred air and light to Fever and the Plague."[113]

As we saw in the previous chapter, the process of modernization as charted by Macaulay in his scathing critique of Southey—the one to which Dickens seems so committed in so much of his work—follows an uncomplicated linear path forward. Thus, "steam-engines and independence," "health and long life with edifices which time cannot mellow," matter more to him than "rose-bushes and poor-rates" or "mortality and cottages with weatherstains."[114] To be fair, Macaulay is redeploying Southey's own language, but in both cases modernity is identified with the absence of temporal markings, as though the modern could transcend the ancient and rid itself of the marks of antiquity. What we have in *Edwin Drood*, however, is a sense of modernity as saturated and bound up with antiquity and of modernization as necessarily "irregular," simultaneously one step forward and one step back—the "deteriorating generations" succeeding each other not in uniform progress (as Macaulay would have it), but rather, paradoxically, in a steady progressive decline, moving forward and backward at the same time.

Given Dickens's intense and long-standing engagement in the question of transport and time, it makes sense that Cloisterham's "irregular modernization" is also described in relation—or rather in opposition—to the transportation system tying the town to the rest of the country and the world. The density and extensiveness of interconnections whose traces Jonathan Grossman detects in *Little Dorrit* do not function in at all the same way in *Edwin Drood*. For all that Cloisterham is shown to be saturated with exotic goods, the town has a very awkward and unsynchronized relationship to the transport network, especially the railroad system. "In those days, there was

no railway to Cloisterham, and Mr Sapsea said there never would be. Mr
Sapsea said more; he said there never should be," we read. "And yet, marvelous to consider, it has come to pass, in these days, that Express Trains
don't think Cloisterham worth stopping at, but yell and whirl through it on
their larger errands, casting the dust off their wheels as a testimony against
its insignificance."[115]

The town goes, in short, from being disconnected to the network to being irrelevant to the network. In the meantime, the characters' travels to
and from London involve several different modes of transport, including
walking, coach, and train. Traffic into the town comes via "some remote
fragment of Main Line to somewhere else," we note, "sneaking in from an
unprecedented part of the country by a back stable-way, for many years la-
beled at the corner: 'Beware of the Dog.'"[116] The novel's sense of irregular
modernization is captured perfectly in the very irony of that conjuncture:
the abstract, synchronized, mechanized, impersonal logic of the network in-
terfacing awkwardly and unevenly with the intensely local, personal, individual, and (in every sense of the term) the pedestrian.

Here, again, however we need—as I mentioned earlier—to be careful, for
it is tempting to think that this sense of irregular modernization may perhaps be appropriate to a backwater cut off from the network in a way that
it could never be to the heart of the network. But what we see of London in
the novel is not very different at all from what we see of Cloisterham: its
own modernity is just as irregular and broken down. This is so not simply
because of the tainting of London by virtue of its contact with Oriental
commerce—hinted at for example when we see the London fog make Edwin's eyes smart "like Cayenne pepper"[117]—or because of our awareness
that London has its own internal Orients, its own Easts, such as the one
Jasper goes to in order to feed his opium habit ("Eastward and still eastward
through the stale streets he takes his way").[118]

For in London, too, time has stalled. As Rosa crosses the metropolis in
a cab, she absorbs the sense of stasis—lethargy, even atrophy—she sees all
around her as she makes her way "through deserts of gritty streets, where
many people crowded at the corners of courts and byways to get some air,
and where many other people walked with a miserably monotonous noise
of shuffling feet on hot paving-stones, and where all the people and all their
surroundings were so gritty and so shabby."[119] In the chapter on London
earlier in this book, I discussed Dickens's very early depiction of the Seven
Dials in *Sketches by Boz*. In that account, we see streets and courts "lost in
the unwholesome vapour which hangs over the house-tops, and renders the
dirty perspective uncertain and confined," and, "lounging at every corner,

as if they came there to take a few gasps of such fresh air as has found its way so far, but is much too exhausted already, to be enabled to force itself into the narrow alleys around," we see "groups of people, whose appearance and dwellings would fill any mind but a regular Londoner's with astonishment."[120] The very same sense of listlessness and lethargy that characterized Seven Dials in that early account as an *exceptional* space (contained within a wider metropolitan atmosphere of dizzying and energizing movement, circulation, and speed) now, in *Edwin Drood*, seems to have become generalizable to all of London: the more it moves, the more it seems to stand still.

For the grit, the dirt, and the sense of stifling, airless suffocation and the attendant lethargy that pervades London are also associated with a feeling of suspension in time. London's lack of air underscores, in other words, the feeling that "everything had a strange and an uncomfortable appearance on it of seeming to wait for something that wouldn't come."[121] This feeling of London "waiting for something that never came"[122] (a phrase the novel repeats) is partly felt through Rosa's perspective by the use of free indirect style, but it is seen also through the perspective of the omniscient narrator and consistently reinforced in the novel's representations of the great metropolis.

The description of Holborn and areas around it is key here. "Behind the most ancient part of Holborn, London, where certain gabled houses some centuries of age still stand looking on the public way, as if disconsolately looking for the Old Bourne that has long run dry, is a little nook composed of two irregular quadrangles, called Staple Inn," the narrator tells us. "It is one of those nooks, the turning into which out of the clashing street, imparts to the relieved pedestrian the sensation of having put cotton in his ears, and velvet soles on his boots."[123] This account of Holborn is significant partly because of the juxtaposition of the sense of listless nostalgia on the one hand with what ought to be the energy of the "clashing street" on the other.

However, Holborn amounts to far more than merely a particularly busy part of the metropolis. It also offers a palimpsest of modes of transport from modernity back into antiquity: in some sense the most obvious place, in Dickens's lifetime, to witness London slowly—and painfully—becoming modern. The Bourne toward which Staple Inn nostalgically looks, and after which Holborn itself is named, is a stream (a tributary to the Fleet, which is in turn a tributary to the Thames) along which the Romans built a road following the stream's curving track (an arc that remains intact in the modern incarnation of Holborn) through the once marshy ground to the west, toward what would become Oxford Street. Staple Inn (already in Dickens's time the last remaining Inn of Chancery) occupies a site adjacent to where the Holborn bars had been: tollgates erected in medieval times (and removed only in the eighteenth century, though still commemorated today by the granite posts which stand on either side of the street) at the edge of the City of London.[124] This was once an area of coaching inns: one of the staging points for journeys in and out of London, frequently depicted in Dickens's novels (inspired in part, no doubt, by his own residence in Furnival's Inn on the north side of the street here).

But just as the Roman period had yielded to the medieval, so the medieval had yielded to the modern, and the inns were mostly demolished during the growth of the railroads in the nineteenth century. Much of the rest of the urban fabric of this part of the metropolis was also transformed during the years leading up to the publication of *Edwin Drood* by the construction of the Holborn viaduct (which opened in 1869) just to the east, across what had been the valley of the Fleet, and the nearby massive works, home demolitions, population removals, and construction projects associated with the development of the Farringdon Road and Farringdon station (which opened in 1863), which is presumably the "yet unfinished and undeveloped railway station," near Grewgious's quarters in Staple Inn to which Crisparkle and Neville repair.[125]

Even here, in other words—at the very hub of the revolution and modernization of both the local and the national transport systems—modernity seems somehow out of synch with itself, and modernization seems to involve a process of an indefinitely deferred arrival, so that we fall back into a mode hovering between nostalgia for what had been and that paralyzing feeling of "waiting for something that never came" with which the novel's depictions of London are suffused. This is a novel that is truly third world in spirit: we are closer to Naguib Mahfouz's Cairo or Rashid Daif's Beirut than to the London of, say, Shaftesbury or Chadwick, for modernity turns out to be much messier when we actually inhabit it than when we project it into a utopian future.

The feeling of nostalgia articulated by the novel combines both spatial and temporal elements: it is a longing for a lost past, but also a yearning for a state of (apparent) rural innocence. Both are conveyed in the account of Staple Inn, with its "deluded sparrows" who "twitter in smoky trees, as though they called to one another, 'Let us play at country,'" and "rheumatically hopped, like little feathered cripples who had left their crutches in their nests," making "an imperfect sort of music . . . that would have been melody in the country."[126] Those birds in turn are recalled in the listless music that Rosa hears in the streets of London, the dull barrel organ and distant chapel bells and "flat wind-instruments" that "seemed to have cracked their hearts and souls in pining for the country."[127] The country here stands for a certain form of nostalgia, similar to what we see in Keats, for a state of innocence never actually experienced in the metropolitan imagination but longed for nonetheless, that very longing translating the feeling of temporal displacement attendant on the sense of stalled modernization into a imaginary geographical one.

The novel's depiction of London, then, offers no alternative to the sense of temporal breakdown and confusion characterizing Cloisterham: the sense of layerings and accretions of different and contradictory moments of time, fragments of memories and histories both—and indistinguishably—real and imagined. The London scenes remind us all the more profoundly that this is a novel primarily about a breakdown in, and of, time. *Edwin Drood* is not about the infiltration and corruption of a pure Occident by Oriental degeneration, in other words, but rather about what it means to live the present of Occidental modernity not with an eye to the future that the civilizing and modernizing process is supposed to hold forth and yet keeps perpetually being deferred, but rather as haunted by the sense of a past that hangs over and lives on into the present; a past that was never truly transcended in the leap into modernity.

Nowhere is this more apparent than in the treatment of the romance—or rather lack of romance—between Edwin and Rosa. Their betrothal is, after all, not the result of their own agency but rather, quite literally, an inheritance from the past which they both find suffocating. "My dead and gone father and Pussy's dead and gone father must needs marry us together by anticipation," Edwin complains to Jasper. "Why the—Devil, I was going to say, if it had been respectful to their memory—couldn't they leave us alone?"[128] He adds, "*You* can take it easily. *Your* life is not laid down to scale, and lined and dotted out for you, like a surveyor's plan. *You* have no uncomfortable suspicion that you are forced on somebody, nor has anybody an uncomfortable suspicion that she is forced upon you, or that you are forced upon her. *You* can choose for yourself. Life, for *you*, is a plum with the natural bloom on; it hasn't been over-carefully wiped off for *you*."[129] What is at issue here, however, is not merely a dead romance, one which is characterized, as Edwin puts it disconsolately, by "a certain unavoidable flatness that attends our love-making, owing to its end being all settled beforehand."[130] It is, as well, a feeling of loss of agency; of immobilization by—and in effect in—a past that cannot be escaped.

And the whole question of the past determining and dictating to the

present, holding it hostage, is loaded with symbolic baggage in both the
political and the colonial contexts of the nineteenth century. The revolution
of modern political and social formations against those of the ancien régime
was, after all, consistently depicted as an *intifada*, a dusting-off, of the grip
of the dead over the living. "I am contending for the rights of the *living*, and
against their being willed away, and controuled and contracted for, by the
manuscript assumed authority of the dead," Tom Paine famously declared
in *Rights of Man*, "and Mr. Burke is contending for the authority of the dead
over the rights and freedom of the living."[131] In finding themselves subject
to the manuscript assumed authority of the dead, Edwin and Rosa discover
all over again the need to stage the rebellion of the modern against the ancient, as though that revolution—which was supposed to have launched
England into a state of Occidental modernity—had not already taken place.
In other words, it is as though the characters were not already inhabiting a
modern state, but rather a state that may want or claim to be modern but is
in fact still entirely held in the clutches of the past, and in the grip of custom which is everywhere, according to J. S. Mill, "the standing hindrance
to human advancement." The real discovery here, though, is that that state
is precisely that of modernity.

Moreover, the language of surveying and planning which Edwin uses to
explain his predicament to Jasper also carries with it a set of immediately
colonial implications. Edwin's ambition is, after all, to go "engineering into
the East," a project which he sees as indispensable to changing "the whole
condition of an undeveloped country."[132] His role in his father's firm—that
is, his expectation that he will go "engineering into the East"—is, along
with his engagement to Rosa, one of the dispensations of his father's will.
Thus the engagement and Edwin's colonial ambitions must be read alongside and in relation to one another.

On this score, however, we cannot fail to notice that Rosa dreads the
prospect of moving to Egypt, given her distaste not only for "boilers and
things" but also for "Arabs, and Turks, and Fellahs, and people,"[133] and the
whole scene of Oriental ruination with which Egypt and all its antiquarian
paraphernalia are associated.[134] For Edwin, in other words, explorers like
Belzoni and engineers like Ferdinand de Lesseps (whose Suez Canal, like
the Holborn Viaduct, was opened the same year Dickens started work on
Edwin Drood) are an inspiration; for Rosa, they are a nightmare.[135] She has
been bored by Miss Twinkleton's going on about the pyramids of Egypt, and
the "tiresome old burying-grounds! Isises, and Ibises, and Cheopses, and
Pharaohses; who cares about them?" she asks. She adds, "And then there

was Belzoni or somebody, dragged out by the legs, half choked with bats and dust."[136]

Yet in Rosa's disdain for Egypt something suddenly becomes quite clear, in this novel so heavily invested in the past, in the dead, in excavations, and in "tiresome old burying-grounds." For what else is Cloisterham other than a giant burying ground in which, as we saw already, the living excavate and continuously re-use the material of the dead? We might recall from the discussion of London in chapter 1 of the present volume that Belzoni also figures in Dickens's depiction of the Seven Dials in *Sketches by Boz*, representing the intrepid traveler who dares to enter the maze of squalid, festering streets in close proximity to St. Giles's.[137] Here too, as with the meditation on paralyzing atrophy, what had once seemed to make the Seven Dials an exceptional space earlier in Dickens's career (exceptional in contrast to a surrounding space of speed and movement, and hence development) comes to stand in for much more. England itself turns out to be stuck in the "condition of an undeveloped country," and Edwin's Belzoni-like ambition to awaken the past is at least as appropriate for an England trapped in time as it is for Egypt.

This brings us back again, one last time, to the cathedral, and also to the character of Grewgious, the one most out of synch with the dictates of progressive time. At one point during a visit to Cloisterham, Grewgious stops at the door of the cathedral. "'Dear me,'" he says, peeping in; "'it's like looking down the throat of Old Time.'"

Old Time heaved a mouldy sigh from tomb and arch and vault; and gloomy shadows began to deepen in corners; and damps began to rise from green patches of stone; and jewels, cast upon the pavement of the nave from stained glass by the declining sun, began to perish. Within the grill-gate of the chancel, up the steps surmounted loomingly by the fast darkening organ, white robes could be dimly seen, and one feeble voice, rising and falling in a cracked monotonous manner, could at intervals be faintly heard. In the free outer air, the river, the green pastures, and the brown arable lands, the teeming hills and dales, were reddened by the sunset: while the distant little windows in windmills and farm homesteads, shone, patches of bright beaten gold. In the Cathedral, all became gray, murky, and sepulchral, and the cracked monotonous mutter went on like a dying voice, until the organ and the choir burst forth, and drowned in a sea of music. Then the sea fell, and the dying voice made another feeble effort, and then the sea rose high, and beat its life out, and

lashed the roof, and surged among the arches, and pierced the heights of
the great tower; and then the sea was dry, and all was still.[138]

This beautifully melancholic passage offers the novel's fullest treatment
of the two major themes running through it: time and light. The jewels
scattered on the floor of the nave are projections of the fading sunlight
streaming through the cathedral's stained-glass windows; with the music,
they help sustain a sense of life, however fleeting, in the sepulchral gloom
within. Death is symbolized by the enfolding silence and darkness. But
the point about these jewels is that their glittering—which inevitably recalls the names of Crisparkle and Twinkleton—is not merely misleading,
but necessarily transitory, evanescent: a vain attempt to forestall the very
movement of time of which it is in fact the product.

The question that remains is whether that movement of time is actually
going—taking us—anywhere; or in other words whether time flows in the
unilinear stream that was so important to the ideologues of modernization
or in some other pattern. The novel's other profound meditation on jewels
and time offers us a way to resolve this question. When Grewgious—who is
so acutely aware of the presence of Old Time in peeping in at the cathedral
entrance—contemplates the ring which Rosa's father had used to signify
his marriage to her mother, and which, passed on through the lawyer as
intermediary, Edwin was in turn to use to mark his own betrothal to Rosa,
he says, "If I had any imagination (which it is needless to say I have not), I
might imagine that the lasting beauty of these stones was almost cruel."[139]
Unlike the evanescent twinkling jewels of light cast in the cathedral nave,
these jewels are permanent; their very permanence seems not exactly to
defy the passage of time but, rather, to *contain* the flow of time, to try to re-
capture it within a structure insistently defined by the past; in other words,
to trap both the present and the future within the claims of the past.

After all, the ring was given to Grewgious to give to Edwin to put on
Rosa's finger to mark the "maturity" of their betrothal in accordance with
their fathers' wills. "Your placing it on her finger," he warns Edwin, "will
be the solemn seal upon your strict fidelity to the living and the dead. You
are going to her, to make the last irrevocable preparations for your marriage. Take it with you."[140] Later, having broken the engagement, Edwin
reflects on the ring, which he still holds in his hand, and considers that its
jewels "were but a sign of broken joys and baseless projects; in their very
beauty they were (as the unlikeliest of men had said) almost a cruel satire
on the loves, hopes, plans, of humanity, which are able to forecast nothing,
and are so much brittle dust." Upon further consideration, he decides that

"he would restore them to her guardian when he came down; he in his turn would restore them to the cabinet from which he had unwillingly taken them; and there, like old letters or old vows, or other records of old aspirations come to nothing, they would be disregarded, until, being valuable, they were sold into circulation again, to repeat their former round."[141] Thus, breaking their engagement does not offer solace to Edwin and Rosa, but rather, all the more intensely, a reminder that they are the objects of hopes and plans expressed in the past that have now come to naught. Whether in fulfillment or disappointment, the present and the future offer no hope of truly transcending or escaping the claims of the past. We are much closer here to Burke than to Paine after all. For as we see time recycling and re-peating itself with a different cast of characters we become all the more aware that we are witnessing "the mode of existence decreed to a perma-nent body composed of transitory parts," in which, according to Burke, "the whole, at one time, is never old, or middle-aged, or young, but in a condi-tion of unchangeable constancy," moving on "through the varied tenor of perpetual decay, fall, renovation and progression."[142]

The novel's meditations on time convey the sense that time both stands still and repeats itself (the permanence of the jewels capturing perfectly the way in which time is periodically reset), really capturing Burke's no-tion of the social organism as inhabiting a time of both perpetual motion and unchangeable constancy. The one thing time certainly does not do in this novel is to progress in a straightforward linear fashion.[143] In this con-text the novel's repeated, even insistent, references to the breakdown of time attain an even greater clarity. It is not just, for example, that Edwin finds himself in Cloisterham feeling "surrounded by vestiges of old time and decay,"[144] but that that feeling is continually corroborated by external markers and references suggesting that something is broken in "the vast iron-works of time and circumstance."[145] On the eve of his murder, Edwin's watch runs down and he is ominously warned by the jeweler not to let it happen again.[146] If we follow the inevitable temptation to read this as a sign indicating Edwin's own looming fate, we ought surely to follow the same logic when confronted by the scene of the hands of the cathedral clock being blown away in a storm, leaving the town bereft of time.[147] Critics are surely right to point to the significance of Jasper's shadow falling on the sundial in his final confrontation with Rosa, "setting, as it were, his black mark upon the very face of the day,"[148] but it becomes clearer than ever that the tempo-ral breakdown is anything but a simple or direct product or outcome of his Oriental contamination; it has become a general condition. For Jasper is not the only one at odds with time.

Hence the significance of another of the novel's most melancholically beautiful passages, one describing Cloisterham at Christmas, also in terms of time. To those who have returned to their native town from other places, the sound of the cathedral bells reminds them of earlier times, "like the voices of their nursery time," we are told. "To such as these, it has happened in their dying hours afar off, that they have imagined their chamber floor to be strewn with the autumnal leaves fallen from the elm trees in the Close: so have the rustling sounds and fresh scents of their earliest impressions revived when the circle of their lives was very nearly traced, and the beginning and the end were drawing close together."[149] What ought to be the diachronic sequence of an individual life is here once again captured into the cyclical pattern of breakdown and repetition, accretion and layering, that mark the entire urban fabric of Cloisterham. The time of the beginning and the time of the end come round to touch each other, "to repeat their former round," as Edwin had put it with reference to Rosa's ring. The movement of time amounts to repetition and recycling, the dust of the dead giving the transient gift of life to the living, who are at one point described "looking as if they were just made of the dust of the earth, so very dusty are they,"[150] and hence already anticipating their own recycling in turn, as if future and past (dust to dust) could be mingled with the present (yet more dust) in Occidentalizing England just as much as in the Oriental China scornfully condemned by Dickens earlier in his career.

It has to be noted that Dickens left the novel incomplete when he died, so it is impossible to say with certainty that this same sense of cyclicality and return, rather than an escape into the new, would have characterized the ultimate version of the novel had he been able to complete it. But most of the endings that have been projected either by people who knew Dickens (including Forster) or by more recent scholars don't assume a sudden reversal of the trends developed toward the point where what we have now ends.[151] Even if Forster is right that the novel was meant to end with Jasper's confession, that still would not suffice to undo the gloom gathered around Cloisterham or London; if anything, it might have confirmed it. John DeWind argues that the most hopeful version of the ending, the marriage plots pairing Rosa with Tartar and Helena with Crisparkle, would hinge on a domestic containment of the exotic threat, bringing together England and the Orient "in a harmonious whole in which the former balances, controls and channels the latter, and together they symbolize a full and happy life," thereby confirming Dickens's imperialist vision of "just, beneficial rule of the East by the West."[152] As we have already seen, however, both Crisparkle and Tartar are profoundly compromised as representatives of the West, so such a set of pairings doesn't quite seem as optimistic, let alone triumpha-list, as DeWind suggests.

It is tempting to think of the novel's meditation on time and cyclicality as marking what Edward Said identifies as late style, a phase in which an author—not necessarily toward the end of his or her career or indeed life, although that would be the case here—suddenly turns against the pattern developed earlier, in the way that Beethoven, for example, used some of his late work (Op. 111, the last piano sonata, and Op. 133, the *Grosse Fuge* for strings, are the most impressive examples) to challenge or even undo all of the compositional patterns he had spent decades developing in his other work.[153] And it could well be that this accounts for part of what we see in *Edwin Drood*, which similarly ruptures and overturns the sense of a commitment to optimistic, progressive reformism, not to say Occidental self-congratulation, characteristic of much of Dickens's earlier novels and other works. In some strange way, the Dickens of *Edwin Drood* really does have the feeling of having nearly traced the circle of his life, of witness-ing, like those simultaneously celebrating and mournful children-turned-adults-turned-children who return to Cloisterham at Christmas, the "be-ginning and the end drawing close together." It is unlikely to be merely a coincidence that the London scenes of Dickens's last novel are set not only exactly across Holborn from where Dickens temporarily lived at the begin-ning of his career (Furnival's Inn), but also within a two-minute walk from where the Artful Dodger brings Oliver Twist into London at the other end of Dickens's career as a novelist: Saffron Hill the Great, which had by 1869–70 been swallowed up in the giant works surrounding the improvement of Farringdon, just down the road from Holborn.

But there is surely more at stake in the novel than merely the novel-ist's own sense of approaching biographical closure. What *Edwin Drood* of-fers us is something more than merely a meditation on what it means to inhabit imperial culture as an open space in which the distinction between "us" and "them," Occident and Orient, here and there has broken down. For, in the hands of writers from Wollstonecraft through Shelley and on to Macaulay and Mill, those distinctions were all predicated on a form of tem-poral opposition in which the Occident was moving and progressing while the Orient had broken down and stalled: an image of stasis so profoundly woven into texts such as Shelley's "Alastor."[154] In *Edwin Drood*, the Occi-dent, seen structured as an alternating progressive and degenerative cycle of return and repetition, cannot possibly be opposed to the Orient, and not just because, as David Faulkner points out (also in disagreeing with readings of the novel that take for granted a binary Occidental/Oriental opposition), the gulf between home and abroad is always already bridged, so that "the metropolitan self and culture may be inhabited, indeed constituted, by heterogeneous otherness," leading us to recognize that "cultural difference lies not between but within."[155] Certainly, as I have already argued, the novel portrays identities across the scale from personal to national and civilizational to be always provisional, and anything but homogeneous, secure, and permanently stable in the way that Occidental culture was—and still is—so often assumed to be. Durdles turns out to be by far the most self-aware character in the novel, precisely because he is "a little misty as to his own identity."[156] He has grasped that identity is always a little misty. For the same reason, Jasper is actually far more normative than the scandalized characters surrounding him, for one is never quite oneself at all. It is the pretense at stability that turns out to be deviant in some way.

What is at stake here, however, involves not merely an awareness of the temporary and provisional nature of identity, but also a recognition that that temporariness is also structured in terms of time. Cloisterham, London, England, the Occident have not actually degenerated or suffered a backslide into stalled time: their condition is expressive of the true nature of modernity as an uneven and incomplete accumulation of recycled pasts. Far from proposing a narrative of the Oriental infiltration and corruption of a pure Occidental space, *Edwin Drood* offers us a profound understanding of modernity as permanently incomplete. And far from proposing a vision of the world divided between, on the one hand, a progressive Occident basking in the glow of modernity and, on the other hand, a degenerate Orient mired in which "the despotism of custom is complete" (which Mill assures us is the case "over the whole East"),[157] Dickens's final novel reveals to us that modernity itself involves the linking together of different kinds of identities and spaces in a structurally articulated process of uneven development. It turns out to be Durdles, after all, who most embodies the spirit of the modern in recognizing that modernity involves, as he puts it, the "mixing of things."

CONCLUSION

To try to draw together the various strands of argument running through this book, I want to return to where we began in the first chapter: to the project, inaugurated at the turn of the nineteenth century, to make London Western. I hope the intervening chapters will have made clearer that when we encounter a character such as Hannah More's Betty Brown we are witnessing the unfolding of the individual subject extracted from a massified, savage, Oriental existence—an existence supposedly incompatible with individual selfhood, according to people like John Stuart Mill—and launched into the unilinear stream of developmental time and narrative which was essential to the cultural logic of Occidentalism.

Hannah More's work, or at least that short story, is significant because it helps us recognize the point of convergence (important differences notwithstanding) between the conservative project of someone like More and the radical project of Francis Place or many others like him: Richard Carlile, James Griffin, John Wade, and so on.[1] In both cases, according to this new convergence that began to span the ideological spectrum, the individual subject is the contested site of moral improvement. The workingman who drinks and, in drinking, is stuck in time has to be rescued and given hope in Place's account, for instance, by being connected to the flow of linear, progressive time—to which Betty Brown must also be connected in Hannah More's account.

Hence the explosion of projects of moral reform in the early nineteenth century, documented by M. J. D. Roberts in *Making English Morals*.[2] This was after all the common ground invested in by both, for example, Wilberforce's Proclamation Society and its successor the Society for the Suppression of Vice (founded in 1802) and, on the other side, radicals like Place or Richard Carlile. The drive for moral reform at the individual level is a recurring topic of interest in most London-based radical periodicals from this period. Carlile's *Moralist*, for instance, which ran from 1823 to 1824, features extensive discussions of drunkenness,[3] theft,[4] lying,[5] filthiness,[6] idleness,[7] swearing and "coarse and offensive speech,"[8] and so on: all topics frequently mapped out by Place in his various notebooks as well. The same range of concerns comes up repeatedly in Carlile's *Newgate Monthly Magazine*, which, claiming that "the progress of knowledge tends to civilize and cultivate the understanding," repeatedly published calls for a moral education on a mass scale and for redirecting missionary energies from overseas missions to educating the poor at home in England.[9]

To be sure, as Kevin Gilmartin has so assiduously demonstrated, Hannah More, like other conservative writers, placed extremely circumscribed limits on the scope of development allowed to individual plebeian subjects; for her, moral improvement was expressly tied to an authoritarian political regime of surveillance and disempowerment.[10] For Place and similar radicals, however, the whole point of moral improvement or education in the widest sense was self-determination and self-representation. "'Knowledge is power,' in whose hands soever it may be placed, whether in the hands of the rulers, or in the hands of the people," notes a clipping from the radical magazine *The Gorgon* approvingly pasted into Place's notebooks. "In the hands of the former, it may be used to keep the people in slavery, by keeping them immersed in ignorance and superstition; but, in the hands of the latter, it must always be an invincible instrument, to preserve or recover their freedom, or promote their happiness."[11] For his part, and throughout his work, Place consistently insists, as he does in his unpublished manuscript essay on civilization (a critique of J. S. Mill's early essay on that topic), on "the real and beneficial advance of every thing whose tendency is the improvement of the happiness of mankind."[12]

Clearly, the radical project and the conservative one were in the long run directly opposed and mutually incompatible; radicals like Place were more generous; they secularized the indefinite future held out by evangelicals like More, and in so doing they made it available for actual attainment by working people. But the two projects, liberal and conservative, did nevertheless share this point of convergence in the terrain of the individual, self-regulating subject, which is why we can see, in the convergence itself, the first steps toward the consolidation of Occidentalism as a cultural and political project, even if it would take decades to be secured, and if even then—and all along—it would face criticism, opposition, and resistance also spanning the ideological spectrum.

When we see in Francis Place's massive archive of papers, clippings, and notes his painstaking documentation of improvement in morals, manners, drinking, learning, reading, building, sexuality, fighting, art, diet, medicine, transportation, writing, literature, and so forth—much of it projected onto that spatiotemporal imaginative map of London which I discussed in chapter 1—what we are seeing is the evidence he was gathering that the people of London (and hence of England more generally) were no longer all of them merely indeterminate parts of an indistinct mass: from the mass we can begin to detect the emergence of discrete self-regulating individuals entering the stream of Occidental time.

"It was, at one time, but too common, in certain quarters, to ridicule the idea of diffusing useful knowledge among the people, and the phrases, 'march of mind,' 'march of intellect,' &c. were regularly laid hold of by those who wished to deride the endeavours of all those who looked forward to the improvement of their countrymen," notes an 1827 article in the *Morning Chronicle* that I think we can safely attribute to Place, among whose manuscript notes on morals and manners it is pasted in.[13] "It has been reserved to our times to make the discovery, that the prevalence of ignorance among the lower orders is incompatible with the peace of society and the establishment of good order. Wherever a mass of prejudices exist, the lash governs the slave. But where the lower orders are not slaves, but *free agents*, it becomes of the utmost consequence that the mainspring of their actions should be properly regulated." Thus, the article concludes, "the savage and the ignorant seek relief from the tedium of life in violent emotions. Hence, in proportion as men are ignorant, they are cruel and fond of inebriation. The great pleasure of the savage and the boor is rapid and beastly intoxication. The man who has entered the threshold of knowledge finds himself exempted from this necessity through the perpetual gratification afforded to him by the treasures successively presented to him. If of an active disposition, he avails himself of his information to better his situation, and to employ his energies not in purposes hostile to society; and if he be of a quiet contemplative disposition, he devises means for rendering his situation less irksome." As we saw in Place's piece on the improvement of the people, which I discussed at the opening of chapter 1, the workingman who drinks and is thereby trapped in time is equated to the savage, not on moral grounds, but because, like a savage, he is trapped in a time prior to his own individualization, development, and civilization, prior to his assimilation into a recognizably Occidental culture.[14]

Place's exhaustive notes on the civilization of London reveal how much improvement has taken place in the decades since his own childhood. But there was yet more to be done. "If we compare our present state with that in which Caesar found its inhabitants, it may be called a high state of civilization, but every observing reasoning man must conclude that we are far indeed from being a really civilized people, and that we have many very serious and perhaps painful changes to go through before we shall deserve the title of highly civilized," he writes. "Considerable advance has been made, it will be continually accelerated, and it may be safely concluded that no ordinary circumstance can greatly impede our progress nor any but uncommon and unlooked for events cause any considerable delay in that progress. These are exhilarating prospects and the more they are entertained the more rapid and less painful will be the progress."[15]

That mingling of pain with pleasure in anticipation of future civilization was all too appropriate. For what we see the proponents of the emergent Occidentalism struggling with in the early years of its formation was precisely the need to resolve the contradictions and tensions inherent in the fact that "we" are not all really "we" in this period, that there are those among us—and not just out in India—who need to be civilized like "us." As we have seen in different ways in each of the chapters of this book, the recurring problem that this Occidentalism had to confront, in other words, was that there was a gap between, on the one hand, the assertion of cultural and civilizational homogeneity among "us" as opposed to "them" and, on the other hand, the very messy reality of a total lack of homogeneity even in the heart of the metropolis itself. The discourse of Occidentalism did not coincide, in other words, with a truly Occidental space, and this contradiction needed to be resolved somehow—and at someone's expense.

This exposes a pressing contradiction in the liberal thought into which the radical imperatives of the 1790s would gradually evolve. Uday Mehta argues that, for John Stuart Mill, individual identities are trumped by the civilizational categories within which they are enclosed, so that "the limitations that Mill places on the reach of the principle [of liberty] are not narrowly tailored to exclude human beings below a certain threshold that is defined in individual terms," but instead depend explicitly upon "a civilizational, and therefore communal, index," so that "we now have a principle of liberty whose applicability is limited to those adults who are members of advanced civilizations."[16] One can't, on this reading, think of individual Arabs or Indians being civilized, and worthy of liberty, insofar as they belong to backward societies, because thinking of civilizations as homogeneous blocs allows no room for the extraction of individual exceptions to the rule within each bloc. But the same logic that dictates that one can't isolate an individual worthy of liberty in an otherwise backward society also dictates that there shouldn't be backward individuals—or a savage, Oriental mass—

in a society that wants to think of itself as having advanced into civilization. Those that don't fit in have to be made to fit in, like Betty Brown or the individuals whose rescue from a mass existence Place so exhaustively chronicles. Or they have to go—in one way or another.

It is all too tempting to downplay or ignore the work of people like Place and to forget just how much work it took to bring a recognizably Occidental civilization to England, or in other words just how much of a monumental struggle it was to make England Western, for good or for ill. The temptation here is to take the Occidentalist narrative of progress completely for granted or, even worse, to assume that England or other Western spaces have always been Western in the sense preached by Occidentalism. After all, the idea of the so-called clash of civilizations between West and East that has provided one of the ideological justifications for a belligerent foreign policy in our own time necessarily takes for granted that "we" in the West share, and have somehow always shared, certain values that homogeneously distinguish "us" from an Eastern other. It ought to be clear that this is an absurd proposition and that many of the transhistorical characterizations of Western culture that we see in the work of the proponents of the clash of civilizations thesis are as reductive and nonsensical—sustaining caricatures just as crude—as their characterizations of Islam and the East.

What I hope to have made clear in the preceding chapters is that the West, in the way in which that concept is generally deployed today—as the locus of supposedly liberal, moderate, regulated, tolerant, secular, progressive, democratic cultures, ways of life and political systems—had to be made Western and that we can date the onset of the project to make (in the particular case in which this book has been interested) England Western to a very specific cultural and political moment at the turn of the nineteenth century. Moreover, we can map out the many forms of opposition or resistance with which this project had to contend, which in a sense tie together such otherwise quite distinct and disparate figures as Blake, Byron, Southey, and some of the others I have discussed in the preceding chapters. This helps explain their common refusal (which recurs in different forms throughout Romanticism) of the progressivist notion of linear time, their refusal to uncritically accept the imposition of a universal history across different cultural locations and populations, and their interest instead in notions of time and space as uneven, fractured, dissonant.

Resistance or opposition to the smooth unfolding logic of Occidentalism did not end in the Romantic period, of course; as we saw in chapter 6, Dickens's novel *Edwin Drood* offers an exploration of the kinks and distortions in time, space, and the self persisting into the state of modernity that completely undermine many of the self-congratulatory claims of the Occidentalist imperative. And the critique of smooth developmental time that we see in *Edwin Drood* would recur again and again through the close of the nineteenth century and on into the twentieth. We can see evidence of it in forms as disparate as the later novels of Hardy, the poetry of T. S. Eliot, the novels of Virginia Woolf, and the body of work—by Wilfred Owen, Siegfried Sassoon, and David Jones, among others—that emerged from the trenches of the Western Front in World War I, which seemed to so many to be the very graveyard of smooth time, smooth space, and the calmly self-regulating Western subject: goodbye to all that, as the memorable title of Robert Graves's 1929 war memoir captures it so perfectly.[17]

In my earlier book *William Blake and the Impossible History of the 1790s*, I discuss Blake's critique of the self-regulating subject and the modes of space and of time with which it was bound up at the other end of the period which would come to an end at Passchendaele and the Somme. In concluding this book, which emerged directly out of that one, I want to revise and extend the account I offered there in certain ways. One of the points I argued in *Impossible History* was that the best-known radicals of the period, among them Paine and Wollstonecraft, elaborated a mode of subjectivity—a mode of being—that was dependent on, and inseparable from, not merely a modern, progressive sense of time but also, with it, an underlying contrast with the Orient.[18] Their celebration of the "natural," vigorous, masculine, rational, honest, forthright, disciplined, manly, self-regulating, and therefore rights-endowed individual subject developing in time depended, in other words, on their attack on "unnatural" Oriental decadence, idleness, effeminacy, dishonesty, femininity and dissipation out of time, or before time, or in stalled time. The sheer scale of Oriental references in radical works from the 1790s helps establish this point: Wollstonecraft's disparagements of Islam, for instance, begin on the first page of her *Vindication of the Rights of Woman*—a text that at face value ought to have nothing whatsoever to do with the Muslim Orient—and carry on from there. There is no other way to explain the extraordinary saturation of radical works with Oriental references and tropes than to see that they were developing, as I argued this point in *Impossible History*, a specifically Western or Occidental mode of identity, subjectivity, citizenship: one that depended both on linear time and on a recurring contrast with Oriental otherness of the kind with which they sought to taint their aristocratic European enemies. *They*—indolent and luxuriating and supine and immobilized—are Oriental; *we*—active and manly and vigorous and on the move—are Occidental. Though it was a relatively contained point in *Impossible*

History, this argument formed the kernel of what I have come to develop in this book into the idea of Occidentalism.

What I also argued in *Impossible History* is that this set of attitudes toward the Orient that emerges in so much—but not all—1790s radicalism can be seen to anticipate later developments in imperial ideology. In its condemnation of Oriental dissipation, idleness, luxuriousness, weakness, inarticulateness, deceitfulness, wiliness, seductiveness, femininity, lack of self-control, and so on, I wrote, this strand of radicalism can be recognized as the antecedent of James Mill's assessment of Orientals as born liars; of Cromer's sense that "want of accuracy . . . is, in fact, the main characteristic of the Oriental mind"; of T. E. Lawrence's claim that Arabs are entirely lacking in "organization of mind or body"; of Balfour's insistence that self-government is a notion of which Orientals have not even a passing familiarity; and so on and on in the tedious archive of Western imperial self-congratulation.[19] Orientals, this drearily familiar set of arguments goes, can't tell fact from fiction; they are unable to acquire knowledge of themselves, let alone to actually manage their own affairs; like children, they fundamentally *need* us to hold their hands and show them the path to development and prosperity. On this point, my argument dovetails with that of Uday Mehta's account of liberal imperialism.[20]

What I am adding here, both to my own account in *Impossible History*— which actually makes this point but doesn't take it as far as I would now— and to Mehta's account in *Liberalism and Empire*, is that the sense of Oriental otherness that was developed in order to enable the mobilization of a properly Occidental mode of being, subjectivity, and citizenship, in time, could and did locate that otherness not just out "there" in the space of the empire, but right "here" in the very heart of the metropolis. It could be found among the aristocracy, to be sure (this is a point I make in *Impossible History*), but also in the chaos and disorder and temporal suspension or immobility of certain quarters of London. It could be seen in the animalized, swarmlike mode of life in those overcrowded quarters; in the sense that those spaces and their populations had stopped developing and fundamentally required intervention to extract them from the anonymous mass and salvage them as individual units inserted into the smooth flow of the time of modernity and development. And it can be seen even in the disavowal and jettisoning of a certain earlier tradition of radical thought, one that (as in Blake) utterly refused the Occidentalist imperative, or, much more straightforwardly, could not be accommodated with the new radical march of mind and clung tenaciously to a certain kind of roughness, or a refusal to engage in the respectable mode, or a commitment to satire rather than

moral earnestness, or a language of religiously inspired communism connected directly to antinomians, to the Ranters and to Winstanley in the seventeenth century (a tradition that I discuss at length in *Impossible History*).

By the end of the 1820s, as Iain McCalman points out, veteran radicals of an older generation still tied to those seventeenth-century notions of
collective struggle, collective ownership, collective being—as in the work
of Robert Wedderburn or the Spencean Thomas Evans, William and John
Dugdale, "Old" Palmer, and so on—"were regarded as embarrassingly un-
respectable in artisan and middling radical circles."[21] The proponents of that
now outmoded kind of radicalism lingered on, eking out a kind of existence as they "begged, borrowed, stole, blackmailed, pimped, informed and
peddled smut," while remaining true to the cause to transform a society
which they found to be quite intolerable. They were not only disavowed by
radicals more invested in respectability and individual subjectivity but also
remorselessly hunted down by the state. "Few English men and women experienced so directly the repressive force that England's ruling classes could
muster when threatened," McCalman argues, and yet the most committed
"persisted with their plots, agitations and propaganda, apparently indifferent to their vulnerability, powerlessness and obscurity."[22] These rough-and-
ready ultraradicals, as they emerge from McCalman's account, are completely uninterested in the reform of the individual subject, self-regulation,
self-composure, and the rest of the civilizing mission, whether applied at
home via Occidentalism or in some imperial contact zone.[23]

As these ultraradicals faded away (though, as McCalman notes, they did
keep alive in the nineteenth century "a tradition of plebeian unrespectabil-
ity and irreverence in the face of powerful countervailing forces"),[24] at a time
when a modern, secularized form of communism had not yet emerged—
though it is anticipated in Robert Owen—their places were taken all the
more comprehensively by a reinvigorated mainstream form of radicalism,
one that came out of that other, more dominant, strand of radicalism that
emerged in the 1790s, which I want here to distinguish as a specifically Occidentalist radicalism: one firmly committed to the development of the self
and hence to moral improvement.

Clearly, not all radicals fell under the spell of Occidentalism. There
were exceptions to the rule, including William Hone, whose commitment
to an older tradition of radical satire in defiance of moral earnestness persisted well into the nineteenth century, as Ben Wilson reminds us.[25] There
were certain strands of the London Corresponding Society that were ada-
mant that their struggle for liberty was partly inspired by and predicated
on the struggles of slaves and other non-Europeans with whom they made

common cause, expressing a sense of solidarity in a global struggle of "the unrepresented" rather than "the people" more narrowly defined in national, racial, or civilizational terms—a kind of radical proto-International.[26] There was Hazlitt, "an intellectual to his fingertips, and a militant, an extreme democrat who suffered martyrdom for his opinions," as C. L. R. James put it, seeing in him the last expression of a kind of outmoded political and intellectual creativity, freedom, and commitment that the new age would not readily allow. "The possibility of such completeness of expression," James argues, "ended with him and has not yet returned."[27] There was Robert Owen, one of the forerunners of modern socialism, who, in his searing critique of individualization, refused the idea that the self-regulating individual ought to be the point of departure for social thought and insisted on understanding and altering the social formation itself in order to produce changes in the individuals produced by and inhabiting it.[28] There was the cabal of radical insurrectionists whom McCalman describes slowly fading away into the background of moral improvement.

And there was Blake, who could see that a world of individual self-regulating subjects priding themselves on their moral virtue would necessarily lead to efforts to coerce or control Others who were not seen as equally moral or capable of self-regulation ("The Moral Virtues are continual Accusers of Sin & promote Eternal Wars & Domineering over others").[29] His point was that the insistence on the moral development of the individual self-regulating subject necessarily implies an Other who is not so developed, or who is incapable of development, or who is supposedly seen to be in need of help—our help—in order to develop. Blake refused to go along with the dictates of the new cultural dominant ("certainly a happy state of agreement to which I for one do not agree")[30] and the civilizational and temporal dictates of a reforming Occidentalism. For he never gave up on other ways of imagining time and history and the acceptably knowable itself, or the range of alternative possibilities in his insistence that "the history of all times & places is nothing else but improbabilities and impossibilities; what we should say, was impossible if we did not see it always before our eyes."[31]

In few places, indeed, is the spirit of resistance to Occidentalist triumphalism as comprehensively—and as presciently—thought through as in the work of Blake. It informs his refusal of that mode of self-justifying moral virtue that led, as he recognized, to domineering over others, whether overseas or at home. It is there in his developing aesthetic alternatives to the flow of smooth, progressive, mechanical time: the form of time that, as we have seen repeatedly in these pages, was built right into the cultural logic of Occidental modernity. And it is there is his interest in different modes of thought, different forms of imagination, of being, even—or perhaps especially—when they take us away from the straight line, the path of least resistance. "Improvement makes strait roads," he writes in those lines in *The Marriage of Heaven and Hell* from which I derived the epigraph at the beginning of this book; "but the crooked roads without Improvement, are roads of Genius."[32] Blake was not alone in refusing to take the straight road of improvement, progress, modernization, and empire, the path of least resistance charted out by an emergent conventional wisdom. But few were as keen to convey at least a glimpse of those crooked roads—the ones that take us to places where what we were so often told was impossible turns out to be possible after all.

NOTES

PREFACE

1. On the modern state's claim to racial and cultural homogeneity, see David Theo Goldberg, *The Racial State* (Oxford: Blackwell, 2002), p. 16. On the relationship between national identity and race in the case of Britain, see Paul Gilroy, *There Ain't No Black in the Union Jack: The Cultural Politics of Race and Nation* (Chicago: University of Chicago Press, 1991), p. 45. Such claims of homogeneity would always remain subject to revision and qualification. After all, Matthew Arnold saw, even among "we English," philistines and barbarians. And yet, for all that, he would also insist on "the impulse of the English race towards moral development and self-conquest." Thus, despite his sense that the mass of the English people were "raw and uncultivated," he always maintained not only the hope that they might yet be reached by sweetness and light but also his belief that there remain profound differences between the Englishman, of whatever rank, and other, lesser peoples. "We can have no scruple at all about abridging, if necessary, a non-Englishman's assertion of personal liberty," Arnold argues. "The British Constitution, its checks, and its prime virtues, are for Englishmen. We may extend them to others out of love and kindness; but we find no real divine law written on our hearts constraining us so to extend them. And then the difference between an Irish Fenian and an English rough is so immense, and the case, in dealing with the Fenian, so much more clear! He is so evidently desperate and dangerous, a man of a conquered race, a Papist, with centuries of ill-usage to inflame him against us, with an alien religion established in his country by us at his expense, with no admiration of our institutions, no love of our virtues, no talents for our business, no turn for our comfort!" The rioter in London's Hyde Park is an altogether different being for Arnold: "He is our own flesh and blood; he is a Protestant; he is framed by nature to do as we do, hate what we hate, love what we love." See Matthew Arnold, "Culture and Anarchy," in Stefan Collini, ed., *Arnold: Culture and Anarchy and Other Writings* (Cambridge: Cambridge University Press, 1993), pp. 67, 68, 87.

2. Thus, as Paul Gilroy points out, by the time of Enoch Powell's infamous 1968 "Rivers of Blood" speech, the black presence in Britain could be "constructed as a problem or a threat against which a homogeneous, white, national 'we' could be unified."

See Gilroy, *There Ain't No Black in the Union Jack*, p. 48. On nationalism and imagined community, see Benedict Anderson, *Imagined Communities* (London: Verso, 2006).

3. See Suvir Kaul, *Poems of Nation, Anthems of Empire: English Verse in the Long Eighteenth Century* (Charlottesville: University Press of Virginia, 2000).

4. "If the complaint continues throughout the [eighteenth] century that the poor were indisciplined, criminal, prone to tumult and riot, one never feels, before the French Revolution, that the rulers of England conceived that their whole social order might be endangered," as E. P. Thompson points out; "the insubordination of the poor was an inconvenience; it was not a menace." All that changed from the 1790s on. See E. P. Thompson, *Customs in Common* (New York: New Press, 1993), p. 42.

5. See Gretchen Gerzina, *Black London: Life before Emancipation* (New Brunswick, NJ: Rutgers University Press, 1997), pp. 17–19.

6. Lauren Benton, *A Search for Sovereignty: Law and Geography in European Empires, 1400–1900* (Cambridge: Cambridge University Press, 2010), p. 2.

7. Ian Baucom, *Out of Place: Englishness, Empire, and the Locations of Identity* (Princeton, NJ: Princeton University Press, 1999), p. 8. Hence the significance of the 1981 Nationality Act, according to Baucom.

8. See Stuart Hall, "Race, Articulation, and Societies Structured in Dominance," in *Sociological Theories: Race and Colonialism* (Paris: UNESCO, 1985), pp. 305–45.

9. See Edward Said, *Orientalism* (New York: Vintage, 1977), p. 120.

10. I discuss radical Orientalism quite extensively in *William Blake and the Impossible History of the 1790s* (Chicago: University of Chicago Press, 2003).

11. Frantz Fanon, *The Wretched of the Earth* (Harmondsworth: Penguin, 1961), p. 37.

12. See Upamanyu Pablo Mukherjee, *Crime and Empire: The Colony in Nineteenth-Century Fictions of Crime* (Oxford: Oxford University Press, 2003).

13. See David Lloyd, *Irish Culture and Colonial Modernity, 1800–2000* (Cambridge: Cambridge University Press, 2011), pp. 2–3.

14. On the freeborn Englishman, see, of course, E. P. Thompson, *The Making of the English Working Class* (New York: Vintage, 1966), esp. pp. 77–101. Also see Laura Doyle, *Freedom's Empire: Race and the Rise of the Novel in Atlantic Modernity, 1640–1940* (Durham, NC: Duke University Press, 2008), esp. pp. 1–23.

15. James Pycroft, *Twenty Years in the Church: An Autobiography* (London, 1859), pp. 43–44.

16. Walter Thornbury, *Old and New London*, vol. 3 (London, 1878), p. 202.

17. For example, the "two nations" problem or the North/South contrast, or in the Condition of England debate, etc. As James Buzard points out, debates around the condition-of-England question saw essayists and moralists asking "whether England was in fact one nation or two (rich and poor, capitalist and worker)." See *Disorienting Fiction: The Authoethnographic Work of Nineteenth-Century British Novels* (Princeton, NJ: Princeton University Press, 2005), p. 8.

18. See Goldberg, *The Racial State*, p. 23.

19. See Craig Calhoun, *The Question of Class Struggle: Social Foundations of Popular Radicalism during the Industrial Revolution* (Chicago: University of Chicago Press, 1982).

20. "The personality is strangely composite," Gramsci argues; it contains "Stone Age elements and principles of a more advanced science, prejudices from all past phases of

history . . . and intuitions of a future philosophy." Antonio Gramsci, *Prison Notebooks,*
p. 324, quoted in Stuart Hall, "Gramsci's Relevance to the Analysis of Racism and Ethnicity," in the proceedings of the International Seminar on Theoretical Issues of Race and
Ethnicity, Milan, Italy, 1985 (published by UNESCO), p. 34.

21. See Douglas Lorimer, *Colour, Class and the Victorians: English Attitudes to the
Negro in the Mid-Nineteenth Century* (Leicester: Leicester University Press, 1978), esp.
pp. 21–44; and Gerzina, *Black London,* esp. pp. 1–28. "In spite of incidents of discrimina-
tion, the black poor did not suffer from universal or even widespread objections to their
colour, and, as isolated individuals rather than as an identifiable group, blacks mixed
reasonably freely with the commonality of Englishmen," Lorimer argues. "Outbursts of
anti-Negro feeling only occurred after the First World War, when an increase in the number of African and West Indian sailors in London, Liverpool, Manchester and particularly
Cardiff, together with a shortage of jobs in the merchant service led to violence. During
the nineteenth century, blacks in England never constituted a threat to any interest or
group, nor did they present a convenient scapegoat for the failures and frustrations of
society." See Lorimer, *Colour, Class and the Victorians,* p. 43. Also see Gilroy, *There
Ain't No Black in the Union Jack,* as quoted in note 2 above.

22. Thomas Carlyle, "Occasional Discourse on the Nigger Question," in *Collected
Works of Thomas Carlyle,* vol. 13 (London: Chapman & Hall, 1864), pp. 1–28, esp. pp. 3,
4, 24.

23. See Carlyle, "Occasional Discourse on Nigger Question," p. 20. For instance, in
the "Distressed Needle-Women" he complains about those who refuse honest work just
like "the blacks of Demerara." It's worth noting too that when Carlyle wants to find the
measure "in quantity of intellect, faculty, docility, energy, and available human valour
and value" for the black population of the British West Indies, he points to St. Giles's as a
kind of index. See p. 2.

24. See Linda Colley, *Britons* (New Haven, CT: Yale University Press, 1992); Anderson, *Imagined Communities;* see also the critique of Anderson in Gilroy, *"There Ain't No
Black in the Union Jack,"* pp. 44–45.

25. See Gilroy, *There Ain't No Black in the Union Jack,* p. 38. He talks about multiple forms of racism; I don't exactly disagree, but I think that defers the question of how
the kind of racism I am talking about in the nineteenth-century context, directed against
what would come to be regarded as a "white" population in the twentieth century, is
related to anti-black racism in the contemporary United Kingdom, which is Gilroy's primary emphasis.

26. See, for example, David Cannadine, *Ornamentalism: How the British Saw Their
Empire* (Oxford: Oxford University Press, 2002). Cannadine argues pretty much the
inverse of what I am arguing here. He makes the case that the British empire was more
interested in the replication of sameness overseas and in particular in discovering the
mirror images of the traditional, class-riven, unequal society of the metropolis. Admit-
ting that the British saw in their own inner cities "analogies" to Africa, he argues that
other notions of superiority and inferiority—articulated along class lines—were brought
into play in the empire, on an individual rather than a collective basis. "For the British
in India, and for their friends, allies, and collaborators, hierarchy was indeed 'the axis
around which everything turned,'" he argues on p. 56, adding, "the same could, of course,

be said of Britain, and this was scarcely a coincidence." There are several problems with his account. First, he has far too static a sense of "Britons" and "the British," and far too static a sense of the empire itself, as though a single set of terms of reference, a single set of imperial ideologies, prevailed intact from the eighteenth century through the nineteenth, which is far from the case. (I argue exactly the opposite in *Romantic Imperialism*: that there was a profound transformation in the cultural logic of the empire in this period, a shift from the cultivation to the elimination of difference, gauged, for instance, in the yawning abyss between colonial administrators like Hastings and Jones on the one hand and Macaulay and J. S. Mill on the other.) More pressingly, he at times seems to take for granted that class structures at home were also static all through this period, as though the aristocracy dominated late nineteenth-century Britain in the way they had done a hundred years previously—and when he does acknowledge that shifts have taken place (as on p. 57), he says that those who were dissatisfied with those transformations at home were all the more keen to seek out the "traditional hierarchies" that "still flourished east of Suez." He thus refuses to distinguish between the narrow vision of a particular group of people who saw the romantic possibilities of empire and on the other hand a much larger, more inclusive sense of national and imperial identity, and he allows no sense of a gap between a clutch of people, including disaffected aristocrats hanging on to a particular view of the empire (for there is no doubt such types existed), and the generality of "Britons." This leads him not only to misread the dynamics and articulations of race and class at home but also to offer profound misreadings of British policy overseas. His account of British policy in Palestine, for example, substitutes certain colorful self-representations ("a large new imperial dominion based on a romantic, admiring, escapist view of Arab social structure, which closely resembled Rudolph Valentino's celebration of the Bedouin characteristics of 'nobility, dignity, manliness, gracefulness and virility' in his film *The Sheikh*") for a reading of the much more brutal reality of British connivance with the ambitions of Zionist settler-colonialism and French imperialism (as in the Sykes-Picot agreement, according to which the British and the French amicably divided the heart of the Arab world between themselves: an event that merits no mention in Cannadine's account).

27. "The struggle between Islam and the West is now . . . no longer one between competing religions, between peoples each of whom look upon the other as deluded and aberrant, yet all of whom belong to worlds that are mutually intelligible," according to Anthony Pagden, for example. Thus, he concludes, "the struggle is between two mutually unintelligible worlds. In one world are the Muslim militants who still cling to beliefs that correspond very closely to those Saladin's soldiers might have shared," and "in the other world is the modernized West (which now includes most of Southeast Asia), overwhelmingly secular as regards all matters of policy and almost all of its social and domestic life as well. Between the two [worlds] any dialogue on almost anything of real significance is virtually impossible. They may be able to tolerate each other when they do not conflict, but they can never assimilate with each other. All the other great religions of the world—Hinduism, Buddhism, Taoism, Confucianism—have succeeded in accommodating themselves to modernity, and in some cases have hasted its progress. Islam, by contrast, at least in its dominant form, remains resolutely opposed." Anthony Pagden, *Peoples and Empires* (New York: Modern Library, 2003), pp. 172–73. Also see Niall Ferguson, *Empire:*

The Rise and Decline of the British World Order and the Lessons for Global Power (New York: Basic Books, 2004).

INTRODUCTION

1. See Edward Said, *Culture and Imperialism* (New York: Vintage, 1993), pp. 80–97.

2. Said, *Culture and Imperialism*, p. 32.

3. Johannes Fabian, *Time and the Other* (New York: Columbia University Press, 1986).

4. Dipesh Chakrabarty, *Provincializing Europe: Postcolonial Thought and Historical Difference* (Princeton, NJ: Princeton University Press, 2000), p. 7.

5. Edward Said, *Orientalism* (New York: Pantheon, 1978), p. 54.

6. Krishnan argues that De Quincey produces a "double and contradictory image [of] London [in which it] is visualized as transit and terminus, at once wild and domesticated: it is both the heterogeneous, undeveloped empty spaces from which raw materials are extracted *and* the unseen boardrooms for a homogenous reckoning of profit and power." Sanjay Krishnan, *Reading the Global: Troubling Perspectives on Britain's Empire in Asia* (New York: Columbia University Press, 2007), pp. 70–71. I make a very similar argument with respect to Wordsworth in *Romantic Imperialism*. See Saree Makdisi, *Romantic Imperialism: Universal Empire and the Culture of Modernity* (Cambridge: Cambridge University Press, 1998), pp. 23–44, and in the opposite way for Blake, pp. 154–72.

7. I intend something quite different by the term "Occidentalism" than what seems to be suggested by most of the recent books that have assumed that title. Most of those are explicitly concerned with representations of the "West" by the "non-West," taking too much for granted that there is a West/East divide that occurs more or less along geographical lines, something that I am obviously arguing against here. See, e.g., Ian Buruma and Avishai Margalit, *Occidentalism: The West in the Eyes of Its Enemies* (London: Penguin, 2005); James Carrier, ed., *Occidentalism: Images of the West* (Oxford: Oxford University Press, 1995). Couze Venn comes closer to the spirit of what I am arguing here, but his book proposes a largely theoretical argument in which the kind of historical processes and cultural ambiguities that I am exploring play no role; he is more interested in the convergence of modernity and the rubric of "the West," so his is a very different project in the end, though we overlap to a certain extent in our mutual interest in the question of the centrality of individual subjectivity to the culture of modernity, something that both of my other books on this question have explored extensively. See Couze Venn, *Occidentalism: Modernity and Subjectivity* (London: Sage, 2000). Meanwhile, Walter Mignolo uses the term "Occidentalism" with reference to the New World; I am using it to refer to "the West" as a geocultural formation. See Walter Mignolo, *Local Histories/Global Designs: Colonialty, Subaltern Knowledges, and Border Thinking* (Princeton, NJ: Princeton University Press, 2000).

8. The earliest reference to the West in a cultural-political rather than merely a geographical sense recorded in the *Oxford English Dictionary* (*OED*) is actually by Wordsworth, in *Extinction of the Venetian Republic* (1802): "Once did She hold the gorgeous east in fee; / And was the safeguard of the west." But the term does not recur in this sense until the 1860s and later. Kipling's famous "East is East and West is West" is from 1895.

9. Said, *Culture and Imperialism*, p. 51.

10. Said, *Culture and Imperialism*, p. 52.

11. See Ian Baucom, *Out of Place: Englishness, Empire and the Locations of Identity* (Princeton, NJ: Princeton University Press, 1999).

12. "Ironically, the approach to fiction that flows from Said's and other postcolonialist analyses actually outdoes the defensive nation-making efforts of the nineteenth-century English novel itself, by blotting out so completely all those fine differentiations (of class, of region, of religion, and so forth) observable *within* the imperial nation and regarding 'England' or 'Britain' (or even 'the West') as one unanimous whole, poised against the whole it coercively constructs of its 'Other.'" James Buzard, *Disorienting Fiction: The Autoethnographic Work of Nineteenth-Century British Novels* (Princeton, NJ: Princeton University Press, 2005), p. 43.

13. Bernard Porter, *The Absent-Minded Imperialists: Empire, Society, and Culture in Britain* (Oxford: Oxford University Press, 2006), p. 19.

14. Porter, *The Absent-Minded Imperialists*, p. 20. Also see p. 311.

15. Porter, *The Absent-Minded Imperialists*, p. xii.

16. Porter, *The Absent-Minded Imperialists*, p. 308.

17. Porter, *The Absent-Minded Imperialists*, p. 309.

18. It is worth recalling here Craig Calhoun's critique of E. P. Thompson on the question of class and class-consciousness. See Craig Calhoun, *The Question of Class Struggle: Social Foundations of Popular Radicalism during the Industrial Revolution* (Chicago: University of Chicago Press, 1982).

19. See Gilroy, *There Ain't No Black in the Union Jack*; also see Ann Laura Stoler, *Race and the Education of Desire* (Durham, NC: Duke University Press, 1995).

20. See Stuart Hall, "Race, Articulation, and Societies Structured in Dominance," in *Sociological Theories: Race and Colonialism* (Paris: UNESCO, 1985), pp. 305–45.

21. Porter, *The Absent-Minded Imperialists*, p. 308.

22. Porter, *The Absent-Minded Imperialists*, p. 21.

23. Porter, *The Absent-Minded Imperialists*, p. 25.

24. Porter, *The Absent-Minded Imperialists*, p. 22.

25. Porter, *The Absent-Minded Imperialists*, pp. 314–15.

26. See David Theo Goldberg, *The Racial State* (Oxford: Blackwell, 2001).

27. Gilroy, *There Ain't No Black in the Union Jack*, p. 11.

28. Henry Mayhew, *London Labour and the London Poor*, vol. 1 (London, 1861), pp. 1–2.

29. See Gilroy, *There Ain't No Black in the Union Jack*, p. 45.

30. The Earl of Cromer, *Modern Egypt* (New York: Macmillan, 1908), p. 144.

31. Cromer, quoted in Said, *Orientalism*, p. 39.

32. Porter, *The Absent-Minded Imperialists*, p. xv.

33. Simon Gikandi, *Maps of Englishness: Writing Identity in the Culture of Colonialism* (New York: Columbia University Press, 1996), p. x.

34. Warren Hastings, "Introductory Letter," in *The Bhagavad-Geeta, or Dialogues of Kreeshna and Arjoon*, trans. Charles Wilkins (London, 1785).

35. The early eighteenth-century split between entertainment and instrumental knowledge (or even knowledge as such) is illustrated by the fact that the publication of Antoine Galland's *Les mille et une nuits* in 1704 was swiftly followed by the first of

many English translations of the *Arabian Nights Entertainments* and inspired a wave of other "translations," amendments, variations, "discoveries" of new tales or fragments, and even something of a cottage industry in quasi-Oriental storytelling and essay writing; whereas Barthélemy d'Herbelot's 1697 *Bibliothèque orientale*, a compendium of Oriental knowledge, was never translated into English, presumably because there was no market for it, even though Galland himself had edited d'Herbelot's manuscript and had had it posthumously published for him in French.

36. Warren Hastings, Letter to East India Company Court of Directors, 3 November 1772, quoted in Bernard Cohn, *Colonialism and Its Forms of Knowledge: The British in India*. (Princeton, NJ: Princeton University Press, 1996), p. 26.

37. Javed Majeed, *Ungoverned Imaginings* (Oxford: Clarendon Press, 1992), p. 52.

38. Cohn, *Colonialism*, p. 21.

39. Asia, according to Jones, is "the nurse of sciences, the inventress of delightful and useful arts, the scene of glorious actions, fertile in the productions of human genius, abounding in natural wonders, and infinitely diversified in the forms of religion and government, in the laws, manners, customs, and languages, as well as in the features and complexions of men;" it also offers a source of literary inspiration to Europeans. "I must request," Jones writes, in the conclusion to one of his essays on the poetry of the Eastern nations, that "in bestowing these praises on the writings of Asia, I may not be thought to derogate from the merit of the Greek and Latin poems, which have been justly admired in every age; yet I cannot but think that our European poetry has subsisted too long on the perpetual repetition of the same images, and incessant allusions to the same fables: and it has been my endeavour for several years to inculcate this truth, that, if the principal writings of the Asiaticks, which are reposited in our public libraries, were printed with the usual advantage of notes and illustrations, and if the languages of the Eastern nations were studied in our great seminaries of learning, where every other branch of useful knowledge is taught to perfection, a new and ample field would be opened for specu-lation; we should have a more extensive insight into the history of the human mind; and we should be furnished with a new set of images and similitudes; and a number of excellent compositions would be brought to light, which future scholars might explain and future poets might imitate." Jones, "A Discourse on the Institution of a Society," pp. 359–60.

40. William Wordsworth, "Essay, Supplementary to the Preface [of *Lyrical Ballads*, 1815]," in William Knight, ed., *The Prose Works of William Wordsworth* (London: Mac-millan, 1896), vol. 2., p. 252.

41. John Thelwall, "Rights of Britons," in *The Politics of English Jacobinism: Writ-ings of John Thelwall*, ed. Gregory Claeys (University Park: Pennsylvania State Univer-sity Press, 1995), p. 473.

42. See John Barrell, *The Infection of Thomas De Quincey: A Psychopathology of Imperialism* (New Haven, CT: Yale University Press, 1991).

43. See *William Blake and the Impossible History*, pp. 204–59, among other places.

44. See Olivia Smith, *The Politics of Language 1791–1819* (Oxford: Clarendon Press, 1984).

45. See Tom Paine, *Rights of Man* [1792], in *The Political Writings of Thomas Paine* (New York, 1830), vol. 2, p. 57.

46. Stoler, *Race and the Education of Desire*, p. 12. She goes on to argue that "the 'civilizing mission' of the nineteenth century was a bourgeois impulse directed not only at the colonized as often assumed, but at recalcitrant and ambiguous participants in imperial culture at home and abroad." See her pages 108–9.

47. See Benedict Anderson, *Imagined Communities* (London: Verso, 2006); Linda Colley, *Britons: Forging the Nation, 1707–1837* (New Haven, CT: Yale University Press, 1992).

48. See Norbert Elias, *The Civilizing Process* (Oxford: Blackwell, 2000), pp. 367, 370, 411.

49. Karl Polanyi, *The Great Transformation: The Political and Economic Origins of Our Time* (1944; reprint, Boston: Beacon, 2001), p. 87.

50. See Polanyi, *Great Transformation*, pp. 81–89; also see E. P. Thompson, *The Making of the English Working Class* (New York: Vintage, 1966), pp. 220–25; Eric Hobsbawm, *Industry and Empire* (New York: New Press, 1999), pp. 82–83.

51. See Polanyi, *Great Transformation*, esp. pp. 59–115, and p. 60 in particular. "To allow the market mechanism to be the sole director of the fate of human beings and their natural environment indeed, even of the amount and use of purchasing power, would result in the demolition of society," he notes on p. 76. "For the alleged commodity 'labor power' cannot be shoved about, used indiscriminately, or even left unused, without affecting also the human individual who happens to be the bearer of this peculiar commodity. In disposing of a man's labor power the system would, incidentally, dispose of the physical, psychological, and moral entity 'man' attached to that tag." The Romantic period marked, in short, a kind of hiatus, a blurred, transitional, gray zone between two totally different if not mutually exclusive social formations and the class systems associated with them—and it was characterized above all by the social cataclysm resulting from the discordant combination and overlap of those two social systems. It was truly the worst of both worlds: this attempt to combine the logic of paternalism with that of a modern wage system was disastrous—wages plunged, and workers were trapped in their local parishes, disabled from taking their labor power elsewhere (which is why, as Polanyi notes, there was no national labor market in this period). The result was catastrophic, as the human flotsam and jetsam flowing through the pages of *Lyrical Ballads* always remind us. "If the Reform Bill of 1832 and the Poor Law Amendment of 1834 were commonly regarded as the starting point of modern capitalism, it was because they put an end to the rule of the benevolent landlord and his allowance system," Polanyi argues. "The attempt to create a capitalistic order without a labor market had failed disastrously. The laws governing such an order had asserted themselves and manifested their radical antagonism to the principle of paternalism." In the Speenhamland period from 1795 to 1834, then, society was torn by two opposing forces, Polanyi concludes, "the one emanating from paternalism and protecting labor from the dangers of the market system; the other organizing the elements of production, including land, under a market system, and thus divesting the common people of their former status, compelling them to gain a living by offering their labor for sale, while at the same time depriving their labor of its market value." Polanyi, *Great Transformation*, p. 84. In order to establish a labor market, labor power had to be separated from other areas of life and social organization and—once stripped naked and cut off from those restraints—subjected to the laws of the market. To

do so, as Polanyi says, required smashing previous social formations in order to release individuals, as the bearers of labor power, from their grip. See Polanyi, *Great Transformation*, pp. 171–73.

52. See, for example, Felicity Nussbaum, ed., *The Global Eighteenth Century* (Baltimore: Johns Hopkins University Press, 2003); Felicity Nussbaum, *The Limits of the Human: Fictions of Anomaly, Race and Gender in the Long Eighteenth Century* (Cambridge: Cambridge University Press, 2003); Kathleen Wilson, *The Island Race: Englishness, Empire and Gender in the Eighteenth Century* (London: Routledge, 2003).

53. Marx, quoted in Philip Corrigan and Derek Sayer, *The Great Arch: English State Formation as Cultural Revolution* (Oxford: Blackwell, 1985), p. 186.

54. Corrigan and Sayer, *Great Arch*, pp. 117, 186.

55. Corrigan and Sayer, *Great Arch*, pp. 114–15.

56. "The moderation of spontaneous emotions, the tempering of affects, the extension of mental space beyond the moment into the past and the future, the habit of connecting events in terms of chains of cause and effect—all these are different aspects of the same transformation of conduct which necessarily takes place with the monopolization of physical violence, and the lengthening of the chains of social action and interdependence," Elias argues. "The denser the web of interdependence becomes in which the individual is enmeshed with the advancing division of functions, the larger the social spaces over which this network extends and which become integrated into functional or institutional units—the more threatened is the social existence of the individual who gives way to spontaneous impulses and emotions, the greater is the social advantage of those able to moderate their affects, and the more strongly is each individual constrained from an early age to take account of the effects of his or her own or other people's actions on a whole series of links in the social chain." See Elias, *Civilizing Process*, pp. 370, 382–87, 411. Also see Kevin Gilmartin, *Writing against the Revolution: Literary Conservatism in Britain, 1790–1832* (Cambridge: Cambridge University Press, 2008), esp. pp. 55–95.

57. *The Life and Correspondence of Major Cartwright*, ed. F. D. Cartwright, vol. 1 (London, 1826), p. 91. Also quoted in Gerald Newman, *The Rise of English Nationalism: A Cultural History, 1740–1830* (London: Macmillan, 1997), p. 199.

58. See Michael Hechter, *Internal Colonialism: The Celtic Fringe in British National Development* (Berkeley: University of California Press, 1975).

59. See Makdisi, *William Blake and the Impossible History*, pp. 204–59.

60. See Katie Trumpener, *Bardic Nationalism: The Romantic Novel and the British Empire* (Princeton, NJ: Princeton University Press, 2007).

61. See Susan Thorne, *Congregational Missions and the Making of an Imperial Culture in Nineteenth-Century England* (Berkeley: University of California Press, 1999); and "'The Conversion of Englishmen and the Conversion of the World Inseparable': Missionary Imperialism and the Language of Class in Early Industrial Britain," in Frederick Cooper and Ann Laura Stoler, eds., *Tensions of Empire: Colonial Cultures in a Bourgeois World* (Berkeley: University of California Press, 1997), pp. 238–55.

62. Quoted in Thorne, "Missionary Imperialism," p. 238.

63. Both quoted in Thorne, "Missionary Imperialism," p. 247.

64. Quoted in David Solkin, *Painting Out of the Ordinary: Everyday Life in Early Nineteenth-Century Britain* (New Haven, CT: Yale University Press, 2008), p. 58.

65. G. Alston, quoted in Friedrich Engels, *The Condition of the Working Class in England* (Harmondsworth: Penguin, 1987), p. 73.

66. Some of the political and indeed imperial ramifications of language were explicit in the period's own writing. In explaining the plan for his *Dictionary*, for example, Dr. Johnson famously compares the attempt to bring order to the English language to a difficult, if not impossible, attempt to civilize the country itself, and he expresses his hope "that, though I should not complete the conquest, I should at least discover the coast, civilize part of the inhabitants, and make it easy for some other adventurer to proceed farther, to reduce them wholly to subjection, and settle them under laws." In hoping to settle and subdue the language, as Barrell points out, Johnson aimed in some measure to help settle and subdue the inhabitants of England themselves. See Samuel Johnson, *The Plan of a Dictionary of the English Language* (London, 1747), p. 33. This, as Barrell notes, raises the inevitable question of whose usage it was Johnson intended to secure. "The immediate and most obvious answer [to that question] can be found by leafing through the dictionary itself," Barrell writes. "Like the OED, it is to be regarded as a dictionary of the written, not the spoken language, and of the written language as it is to be found in the pages of polite authors, though as far as possible purged of the barbarisms that from time to time even the politest have admitted." John Barrell, *English Literature in History, 1730–1780: An Equal, Wide Survey* (London: Hutchinson, 1983), pp. 110–75, esp. p. 155.

67. Janet Sorenson, *The Grammar of Empire in Eighteenth-Century British Writing* (Cambridge: Cambridge University Press, 2000), pp. 63, 88.

68. See Thomas Spence, Grand Repository of the English Language (Newcastle, 1775); Barrell, *English Literature*, pp. 170–71. Also see Joan Beal, *English Pronunciation in the Eighteenth Century* (Oxford: Oxford University Press, 2002), pp. 69–180.

69. See Pierce Egan, ed., *Grose's Classical Dictionary of the Vulgar Tongue* (London, 1823); Noel McLachlan, ed., *The Memoirs of James Hardy Vaux, Including his Vocabulary of the Flash Language* (London: Heinemann, 1964).

70. Robert Miles, *Racism after "Race Relations"* (London: Routledge, 1993), p. 88. As I explained in the Preface, however, I don't find the formulation of "racialization" very productive.

71. Miles, *Racism*, p. 91.

72. See Eugen Weber, *Peasants into Frenchmen: The Modernization of Rural France, 1870–1914* (Palo Alto, CA: Stanford University Press, 1976).

73. Gustav Le Bon, quoted in Tzvetan Todorov, *On Human Diversity*, trans. Catherine Porter (Cambridge, MA: Harvard University Press, 1993), p. 113.

74. See Thomas Holt, *The Problem of Freedom: Race, Labor and Politics in Jamaica and Britain, 1832–1938* (Baltimore: Johns Hopkins University Press, 1992), pp. 307–9.

75. Antonio Gramsci, *Selections from the Prison Notebooks*, edited and translated by Quintin Hoare and Geoffrey Nowell Smith (New York: International Publishers, 1983), p. 71.

76. Lombard women, one League politician claims, "have always transmitted to their children the culture and traditions of Lombardy, based on our values of: mutual respect, honesty, hard work, altruism, etc. Presently our centralist state under southern hegemony has forced on Lombardy southern culture in which unfortunately predominate: cleverness, the dominance of the strongest, arrogance, corruption and often even

violence." Quoted in Jeffrey Cole, *The New Racism in Europe* (Cambridge: Cambridge University Press, 1997), p. 98.

77. Stoler, *Race and the Education of Desire*, p. 123.

78. See *William Blake and the Impossible History*, pp. 204–59.

79. See the discussion in the Preface of Gramsci and Hall on the articulation of race and class.

80. Quoted in Barrell, *English Literature*, p. 138.

81. Robert Malcolmson, "'A Set of Ungovernable People': The Kingswood Colliers in the Eighteenth Century," in John Brewer and John Styles, eds., *An Ungovernable People: The English and Their Law in the Seventeenth and Eighteenth Centuries* (London: Hutchinson, 1980), pp. 85–127. I quote from p. 85.

82. William Godwin, *Caleb Williams* (Peterborough: Broadview, 2000), pp. 109, 110.

83. Godwin, *Caleb Williams*, pp. 109–10.

84. Godwin, *Caleb Williams*, p. 305.

85. See John Thelwall, *The Peripatetic*, ed. Judith Thompson (Detroit: Wayne State University Press, 2000), pp. 90–91.

86. See Ghassan Hage, *Against Paranoid Nationalism: Searching for Hope in a Shrinking Society* (London: Pluto Press, 2003), pp. 7–9.

87. Godwin, *Caleb Williams*. p. 393. The village is in Wales, but I don't think that matters here; there is nothing specifically Welsh about the villagers, in the way that the Scottish characters of Scott's novels are marked as specifically Scottish.

88. "You may look through the whole history of the Orientals in what is called, broadly speaking, the East, and you never find traces of self government," claimed Lord Balfour, author of the notorious eponymous Declaration of 1917; "conqueror has succeeded conqueror; one domination has followed another; but never in all the revolutions of fate and fortune have you seen one of those nations of its own motion establish what we, from a Western point of view, call self-government." Quoted in Said, *Orientalism*, pp. 32–33.

89. See David Theo Goldberg, *The Racial State* (Oxford: Blackwell, 2002), esp. pp. 13–16.

90. This is what is missing from the recent wave of studies in the eighteenth century, which has otherwise done so much to radically transform our sense of the relationship between England and the colonial and global scenes. The work of Felicity Nussbaum, Ros Ballaster, Kathleen Wilson, Srinivas Aravamudan, and others has thrown wide open the previously limited, even myopic, spectrum through which eighteenth-century British culture had been viewed. But for all that it offers in terms of opening up a hitherto insular sense of culture to imperial and global influences—which is salutary—some of this work also has the tendency to unintentionally reinscribe the very sense of normative sameness and identity that it sets out to decenter. While expanding the frontiers of literary and cultural discussion to include the Orient, Africa, Caribbean, and the Pacific, and the range of tropicopolitan selves that Aravamudan has so brilliantly described, the underlying theme in some of this work is a recurring set of oppositions to a norm—let's call it a norm of English whiteness—whose status is necessarily taken for granted as the center against which various Others can be counterposed. What I have been arguing here is that that there was no dominant, secured, normative form of racial and cultural identity in

England in the years around 1800: there was a struggle to locate and secure the space in which such an identity might be consolidated. "One of the most important contributions of the renewed attention to the imperial frame of eighteenth-century British history has been the revelation of that 'middle ground' that empire produced, a space disrupting comfortable binary oppositions about insiders and outsiders posted by eighteenth-century European intellectuals to make sense of the wider world," Kathleen Wilson argues, for example. "West/Orient, white/black, free/slave, masculine/effeminate, parents/children, social/natural, home/abroad, are some of the oppositions that are visibly undone by the products of empire itself: the mulatto, the free black and the Eurasian, the indentured servant and the imported or extirpated 'native,' the Creole and the métis, as much as sugar and tobacco give embodied form to the permeability and instability of national and hemispheric boundaries and to the fact of cultural miscegenation." Englishness, she adds, "became a performance of non-English and even non-British peoples, a trope of white civilization, maintained through social and theatricalized practices and displays at all levels that attempted to set off its performers from 'indigenous' savagery." There are two problems with this account: for one thing, it seems to have put the cart before the horse, for the empire itself created the binaries themselves, not just the in-between spaces. To whom, after all, are these binaries "comfortable?" They were essential for the work of the empire. The other problem is that Englishness was not just something for natives to perform; it was something for the English themselves to perform as well. Here as in other passages Wilson ends up reinscribing a normative center even while it looks like she is deconstructing it. The problem, in other words, is that the idea of a non-white as specifically other to those whom we would presume to be white (that is, middle-class white men) seems to imply a kind of stability to the normative whiteness which the all-too-predictable range of others on view in her book ends up reinscribing all over again. If the only "others" are those whom we think of as "other" in the first place, the normative self is restabilized, rather than undermined, for it is against that self that the other can be measured. In other words, the others are other to a normative white male self whose whiteness and Englishness again goes unchallenged. There remains a stable center, a dominant metropole, after all. What I have been arguing is that that center was not there at all, or at least not in a way that can be taken for granted in this way. It was other to itself, fractured internally, riven with difference; one does not have to look to African and Irish immigrants to find the traces of difference in England. See Wilson, *The Island Race*, pp. 16–18. Also see Nussbaum, *The Global Eighteenth Century*, and *The Limits of the Human*; Wilson, *The Island Race*; Kathleen Wilson, ed., *A New Imperial History: Culture, Identity and Modernity in Britain and the Empire, 1660–1840* (Cambridge: Cambridge University Press, 2004); Srinavas Aravamudan, *Tropicopolitans: Colonialism and Agency, 1688–1804* (Durham, NC: Duke University Press, 1999); Ros Ballaster, *Fabulous Orients: Fictions of the East in England, 1662–1785* (Oxford: Oxford University Press, 2005); Roxann Wheeler, *The Complexion of Race: Categories of Difference in Eighteenth-Century British Culture* (Philadelphia: University of Pennsylvania Press, 2000).

    91. Colley, *Britons*, p. 6.

    92. See Gerald Newman, *The Rise of English Nationalism: A Cultural History, 1740–1830* (London: Macmillan, 1997), esp. pp. 128–33. Krishnan Kumar has developed a strong critique of Newman's account, but I find the critique problematic because it depends on

the deployment of a sense of Englishness which flattens out the very kinds of internal cultural and class differences attended to by Newman into a homogeneous identity. "The English," he argues, for example, "were conscious that Britain and the empire were their creations. But rather than assertive, this made them cautious about insisting on their national identity. When you are in charge, or think you are in charge, you do not go about beating the drum." This takes too much for granted: as I have been arguing, not all "the English" were the same. See Krishnan Kumar, *The Making of English National Identity* (Cambridge: Cambridge University Press, 2003), esp. pp. 178–87.

93. See Baucom, *Out of Place*, p. 5.

94. Victor Kiernan, *The Lords of Human Kind* (New York: Columbia University Press, 1986), p. 316.

95. Kiernan, *Lords of Human Kind*, p. 316.

96. Etienne Balibar and Immanuel Wallerstein, *Race, Nation, Class: Ambiguous Identities* (London: Verso, 1991), esp. pp. 204–15.

97. Miles, Racism, p. 89.

98. Holt, *Problem of Freedom*, p. 309.

99. Calhoun, *Question of Class Struggle*, p. 55.

100. See Calhoun, *Question of Class Struggle*, p. 7.

101. John Brewer and John Styles, "Introduction," in *An Ungovernable People*, p. 19.

102. Henry Fielding, *Joseph Andrews* (Oxford: Oxford University Press, 1999), pp. 136–37. Part of the passage is quoted in V. A. C. Gatrell, *The Hanging Tree: Execution and the English People* (Oxford: Oxford University Press, 1996).

103. See Gattrell, *Hanging Tree*, pp. 280–97.

104. Michel Foucault, *Society Must Be Defended: Lectures at the College de France, 1975–1976*, trans. David Macey (New York: Picador, 2003), p. 256.

105. John Brewer, *The Common People and Politics, 1750–1790s* (Cambridge: Chadwyck-Healey, 1986), p. 21.

106. Brewer, *Common People*, p. 39.

107. See Ranajit Guha, "The Prose of Counter-Insurgency," in Ranajit Guha and Gayatri Spivak, *Selected Subaltern Studies* (Oxford: Oxford University Press, 1988), pp. 45–86.

108. Solkin, *Painting out of the Ordinary*, pp. 4, 22.

109. Upamanyu Pablo Mukherjee, *Crime and Empire: The Colony in Nineteenth-Century Fictions of Crime* (Oxford: Oxford University Press, 2003), pp. 47–49, 123.

110. See John Barrell, *The Dark Side of the Landscape: The Rural Poor in English Painting, 1730–1840* (Cambridge: Cambridge University Press, 2006), esp. pp. 35–88.

111. Ranajit Guha, "The Prose of Counter-Insurgency," p. 82.

112. Gayatri Spivak paraphrases this dilemma: "How can we touch the consciousness of the people, even as we investigate their politics? With what voice-consciousness can the subaltern speak?" Spivak's contention is that these questions are fraught with difficulty, for to try to represent and speak for the subaltern as such runs the risk of perpetuating and reproducing the conditions of that very subalternity. At the very least, as Dipesh Chakrabarty warns, translating subaltern life-worlds into a modern idiom comes with a price: it necessarily excludes as much as it seeks to include. See Gayatri Spivak, "Can the Subaltern Speak?" in Cary Nelson and Lawrence Grossberg, eds., *Marxism and the Inter-*

pretation of Culture (Champaign-Urbana: University of Illinois Press, 1988), pp. 271–313. I quote from p. 285. Also see Chakrabarty, *Provincializing Europe*, esp. pp. 72–96.

113. Pier Paolo Pasolini, *Heretical Empiricism*, trans. Ben Lawton and Louise Barnett (Washington, DC: New Academia Publishing), pp. 84–85, 87.

114. See Barrell, *Dark Side of the Landscape*, pp. 72–73.

115. Solkin, *Painting Out of the Ordinary*, p. 29.

116. See Hage, *Against Paranoid Nationalism*, pp. 12–21.

CHAPTER I

1. Mary Thale, ed., *The Autobiography of Francis Place* (Cambridge: Cambridge University Press, 1972), p. 14.

2. Francis Place, notes on songs and specimens of songs sung about the streets of London, British Library Add. Mss. 27825, pp. 144–45.

3. See Place, British Library Add. Mss. 27828, p. 53.

4. See Place, British Library Add. Mss. 27828, p. 53.

5. See Place, British Library Add. Mss. 27826, p. 43.

6. Place, British Library Add. Mss. 27826, p. 97.

7. Place, British Library Add. Mss. 27826, p. 172.

8. See Vic Gatrell, *City of Laughter: Sex and Satire in Eighteenth-Century London* (New York: Walker, 2006), p. 582.

9. Gatrell, *City of Laughter*, p. 581.

10. In a published piece on the improvement of the working people, Place insists, for example, that the common people's "acquisition of knowledge, and the reformation of manners, are almost wholly attributable to their own unaided exertions." Francis Place, *Improvement of the Working People* (written 1829; published London, 1834), p. 6.

11. Gatrell, *City of Laughter*, p. 583.

12. See Pierce Egan, *Boxiana; or, Sketches of Ancient and Modern Pugilism, from the Days of the Renowned Broughton and Slack, to the Championship of Cribb* (London, 1830).

13. Thale, *Autobiography of Francis Place*, p. 20. Emphasis added.

14. Place, *Improvement*, p. 6.

15. Place, *Improvement*, p. 8. Emphasis added.

16. Place, *Improvement*, p. 9.

17. Place, *Improvement*, p. 11.

18. Place, *Improvement*, p. 9.

19. "I have frequently and very lately conversed with elderly people, now most respectably circumstanced, and having genteel families, whose improvement has been so gradual and so long that they themselves were scarcely conscious of it," Place notes in his autobiography; "and when I have led them back to the state of morals and the common conduct of those of their own rank in their boyish days, they have invariably ejaculated their surprise at the very great changes which have taken place without their having particularly noticed them as they went on and as they had not before been recalled to their recollection." Thale, *Autobiography of Francis Place*, p. 51.

20. W. Weir, "Some Features of London Life of Last Century," in Charles Knight, ed.,

London, vol. 2 (London, 1841), pp. 345–68. Weir does not name Place or engage his argument, but he does provide a similar account of London.

21. See Charles Dickens, *Oliver Twist* (1837; Harmondsworth: Penguin, 2003), pp. 204–5.

22. Weir, "Some Features of London Life," pp. 351–52.

23. Here and elsewhere, I will be using the term "London" to refer to the metropolitan area, rather than specifically the City as such.

24. Weir, "Some Features of London Life," p. 352.

25. Donald Low, *Thieves' Kitchen: The Regency Underworld* (London: J. M. Dent, 1982), p. 19.

26. Low, *Thieves' Kitchen*, p. 20.

27. Low, *Thieves' Kitchen*, p. 20.

28. See *The Memoirs of James Hardy Vaux*, ed. Noel McLachlan (London: Heinemann, 1964), pp. 152, 168, 172.

29. Friedrich Engels, *The Condition of the Working Class in England*, trans. Florence Wischnewetzky, ed., V. G. Kiernan (1844; Harmondsworth: Penguin, 1987), p. 71.

30. Charles Dickens, "On Duty with Inspector Field," in *Charles Dickens: Selected Journalism 1850–1870*, ed. David Pascoe (London: Penguin, 1997), p. 307.

31. Edmund Burke, letter to Robert Dodge, 29 February 1792; quoted in Roy Porter, *London: A Social History* (Harmondsworth: Penguin, 2000), p. 150.

32. Porter, *London*, p. 118.

33. See John Barrell, *The Spirit of Despotism: Invasions of Privacy in the 1790s* (Oxford: Oxford University Press, 2004), p. 20.

34. See Mary Thale, ed., *Selections from the Papers of the London Corresponding Society* (Cambridge: Cambridge University Press, 1983), p. 148; Henry Burd, *Joseph Ritson: A Critical Biography* (Urbana: University of Illinois, 1916), p. 32; Bertrand Bronson, *Joseph Ritson: Scholar-at-Arms* (Berkeley: University of California Press, 1938), vol. 1, p. 163.

35. See Pierce Egan, *Life in London* (London, 1821), e.g., p. 269. Also see Porter, *London*, pp. 185, 301; David Taylor, *The New Police in Nineteenth-Century England* (Manchester: Manchester University Press, 1997), esp. pp. 12–43.

36. See Patrick Colquhoun, *Treatise of the Police of the Metropolis* (London, 1797).

37. Low, *Thieves' Kitchen*, p. 19.

38. Simon Joyce, *Capital Offenses: Geographies of Class and Crime in Victorian London* (Charlottesville: University of Virginia Press, 2003).

39. John Nash, quoted in Barrell, *Spirit of Despotism*, p. 25.

40. See Jerry White, *London in the Nineteenth Century: A Human Awful Wonder of God* (London: Vintage, 2008), pp. 23–25.

41. White, *London in the Nineteenth Century*, p. 24.

42. Barrell, *Spirit of Despotism*, p. 27.

43. Robert Southey, Letter VII in *Letters from England* (1808; London: Crescent Press, 1951), p. 49.

44. See Gareth Stedman Jones, *Outcast London: A Study in the Relationship between Classes in Victorian Society* (New York: Pantheon, 1984), esp. pp. 159–214. Also see White, *London in the Nineteenth Century*, pp. 28–35; Porter, *London*, pp. 312–38.

45. See Francis Sheppard, *London, 1808–1870: The Infernal Wen* (Berkeley: University of California Press, 1971), pp. 90–91.

46. Weir, "Some Features of London Life," p. 352.

47. See Barrell, *Spirit of Despotism*, p. 26.

48. "Cadge: to beg. The *cadge* is the *game* or profession of begging." From James Hardy Vaux's *Vocabulary of the Flash Language*, in Vaux, *Memoirs*, p. 231.

49. See *Sinks of London Laid Open; a Pocket Companion for the Uninitiated* (London, 1848), which is a repackaged version of the original *Dens of London Exposed* reviewed by Hunt's journal. Also see Anonymous, *The Dens of London Exposed* (London, 1835); *Leigh Hunt's London Journal*, no. 59 (13 May 1835), p. 145.

50. In fact, Monmouth Street was, as Thomas Beames points out, a rookery in its own right. See Thomas Beames, *Rookeries of London: Past, Present and Prospective* (London, 1851), p. 30.

51. See Leigh Hunt, *A Saunter through the West End* (London, 1861), and *The Town* (London, 1848).

52. Anon., *The Compete Modern London Spy* (London, 1781), p. 85.

53. Anon., *The New London Spy* (London, 1771), pp. 138, 143, 144.

54. *Sinks of London*, p. 6.

55. Engels, *Condition of the Working Class*, p. 71.

56. Sheppard, *London, 1808–1870*, p. 363.

57. William Baer, "The Seven Dials: 'Freak of Town-Planning,' or Simply Ahead of Its Time?" in *Journal of Urbanism*, vol. 3, no. 1 (2010), pp. 1–18. Also see W. Edward Riley and Laurence Gomme, eds., *Survey of London*, vol. 5 (London: London City Council, 1914), pp. 112–14; W. Weir, "St, Giles's, Past and Present," in Charles Knight, ed., *London*, vol. 3 (London, 1851), pp. 257–72. Also see the Web site of the Seven Dials Monument Charity, www.sevendials.com.

58. See Baer, "Seven Dials," p. 10.

59. John Gay, *Trivia; Or, the Art of Walking the Streets of London* (London, 1716), p. 26.

60. This is according to the Seven Dials Charity, which commissioned a replica pillar based on the original design and had it installed in 1989; it is still there. http://www.sevendials.com/the_seven_dials_monument_charity.htm.

61. Dickens, "Seven Dials," in *Sketches by Boz* (1837; reprint, London: Penguin, 1996), pp. 91–92.

62. Weir, "St, Giles's, Past and Present," p. 267.

63. Walter Thornbury, *Old and New London*, vol. 3 (London, 1878), p. 205.

64. It was Belzoni who brought the great bust of Rameses II to the British Museum, helping to inspire Shelley's "Ozymandias."

65. Dickens, "Meditations in Monmouth-street," in *Sketches by Boz*, p. 96.

66. Dickens, "Monmouth-street," p. 98.

67. Weir, "St. Giles's, Past and Present," p. 258.

68. Peter Ackroyd, *London: The Biography* (New York: Anchor Books, 2003), p. 127.

69. Beames, *Rookeries of London*, pp. 27, 34, 37.

70. Beames, *Rookeries of London*, p. 20.

71. Southey, *Letters from England*, p. 147.

72. Beames, *Rookeries of London*, p. 8.

73. Beames, *Rookeries of London*, p. 41.

74. Beames, *Rookeries of London*, p. 17.

75. Dickens, "Inspector Field," pp. 306–11.

76. *Sinks of London*, p. 19.

77. Dickens, "Seven Dials," p. 92.

78. See Steven Johnson, *The Ghost Map: A Street, a City, an Epidemic and the Hidden Power of Urban Networks* (London: Penguin, 2006), esp. pp. 25–79.

79. Dickens, "Seven Dials," p. 93.

80. Weir, "St. Giles's, Past and Present," p. 267.

81. Weir, "St. Giles's, Past and Present," p. 270.

82. Weir, "St. Giles's, Past and Present," p. 270.

83. Weir, "St. Giles's, Past and Present," p. 270.

84. See Gatrell, *City of Laughter*, e.g., 29–50. In developing this argument, he ends up reading Blake as an example of high-minded canonical moral earnestness, which is surely a mistaken approach.

85. See Joyce, *Capital Offenses*, pp. 13–58, esp. pp. 18–19, 28.

86. Mary Robinson, "January, 1795," in *The Norton Anthology of English Literature*, ed. Jack Nicholson and Deidre Lynch, vol. D (New York: Norton, 2005), pp. 68–69.

87. Mary Robinson, "London's Summer Morning," in *Norton Anthology*, p. 69.

88. Charles Lamb, letter to Thomas Manning, 28 November 1800, in J. E. Morpurgo, ed., *Charles Lamb: Selected Writings* (New York: Routledge, 2003), p. 158.

89. Southey, *Letters from England*, pp. 49–50.

90. Southey, *Letters from England*, p. 53.

91. Wordsworth, *The Prelude* (1805–6), lines 133, 156–58, 165–67, in William Wordsworth, *The Prelude: A Parallel Text*, ed. J. C. Maxwell (London: Penguin, 1986), pp. 257–58.

92. Wordsworth, *The Prelude*, lines 185–88.

93. Wordsworth, *The Prelude*, lines 206–8.

94. Wordsworth, *The Prelude*, lines 198–99.

95. Wordsworth, *The Prelude*, line 196.

96. Wordsworth, *The Prelude*, line 209.

97. Wordsworth, *The Prelude*, lines 176–77.

98. See Saree Makdisi, *Romantic Imperialism* (Cambridge: Cambridge University Press, 1998), pp. 23–44.

99. Wordsworth, "Composed upon Westminster Bridge, September 3, 1802," in the Norton *Anthology*, p. 317.

100. William Blake, "Holy Thursday," in *Songs of Innocence*, lines 2–3, in William Blake, *Songs of Innocence and of Experience* (London, 1794).

101. Blake, "London," in *Songs of Experience*, lines 1–2, in Blake, *Songs of Innocence and of Experience*.

102. Hannah More, "Betty Brown, the St. Giles's Orange Girl," in More, *Tales for the Common People*, ed. Clare Shaw (Nottingham: Trent, 2002), p. 55.

103. See More, "Betty Brown," p. 62.

104. P. 63 and note 16 on pp. 162–63 of More's "Betty Brown."

105. More, quoted in Anne Stott, *Hannah More: The First Victorian* (Oxford: Oxford University Press, 2003), p. 186.

106. See "Rookery" in *Oxford English Dictionary*.

107. Beames, *Rookeries of London*, p. 6.

108. Weir, "St. Giles's, Past and Present," p. 267.

109. Dickens, *Sketches by Boz*, p. 94.

110. *Dens of London*, p. 19.

111. Dickens, "Inspector Field," p. 309.

112. Beames, *Rookeries of London*, p. 48.

113. *Dens of London*, pp. 13–14.

114. George Reynolds, *Mysteries of London*, vol. 1 (London, 1845), pp. 406–7.

115. Mary Wollstonecraft, *Maria; or, the Wrongs of Woman* (1798; New York: Norton, 1998), p. 102.

116. Henry Mayhew, *London Labour and the London Poor*, vol. 1 (London, 1861), p. 1.

117. Mayhew, *London Labour*, p. 2.

118. Mayhew, *London Labour*, p. 3.

119. See Ian Baucom, *Out of Place: Englishness, Empire and the Locations of Identity* (Princeton, NJ: Princeton University Press, 1999), esp. pp. 3–14. I quote from p. 5.

120. See Ghassan Hage, *Against Paranoid Nationalism: Searching for Hope in a Shrinking Society* (Annandale NSW: Pluto Press Australia, 2003), esp. pp. 12–18.

121. George Godwin, *London Shadows: A Glance at the "Homes" of the Thousands* (London, 1854), pp. 1–2.

122. Thornbury, *Old and New London*, p. 202.

123. Thomas Guthrie, quoted in Lydia Murdoch, *Imagined Orphans: Poor Families, Child Welfare and Contested Citizenship in London* (New Brunswick, NJ: Rutgers University Press, 2006), p. 25.

124. Lord Shaftesbury, also quoted in Murdoch, *Imagined Orphans*, p. 25.

125. James Greenwood, *Seven Curses of London* (Boston, 1869), pp. 4–5; Charles Dickens, "Underground London," in *All the Year Round*, 30 July 1861, p. 390.

126. See Murdoch, *Imagined Orphans*, p. 25; for street Arabs in theater, also see Heidi Holder, "The East End Theatre," in *Cambridge Companion to Victorian and Edwardian Theatre*, ed. Kerry Powell (Cambridge: Cambridge University Press, 2004), pp. 257–76.

127. Murdoch, *Imagined Orphans*, p. 25.

128. James Pycroft, *Twenty Years in the Church: An Autobiography* (London, 1859), pp. 43–44.

129. Pycroft, *Twenty Years*, p. 36.

130. See Susan Thorne, *Congregational Missions and the Making of an Imperial Culture in Nineteenth-Century England* (Berkeley: University of California Press, 1999).

131. Weir, "Some Features of London Life," p. 851.

132. Weir, "St, Giles's, Past and Present," p. 264.

133. Weir, "St. Giles's, Past and Present," p. 258.

134. Beames, *Rookeries of London*, p. 8; Thornbury, *Old and New London*, 202.

135. See Beames, *Rookeries of London*, p. 136.

136. Beames, *Rookeries of London*, p. 214.

137. Beames, *Rookeries of London*, p. 219.

138. Johannes Fabian, *Time and the Other: How Anthropology Makes Its Object* (New York: Columbia University Press, 1983), p. 17.

139. "A Looking-Glass for London," *The Penny Magazine of the Society for the Diffusion of Useful Knowledge*, 30 December 1837.

140. Thornbury, *Old and New London*, p. 206.

141. Thornbury, *Old and New London*, p. 209.

142. Weir, "St. Giles's, Past and Present," p. 271.

143. See the discussion of James Mill and others in my *Romantic Imperialism*, pp. 100–121.

144. James Mill, quoted in my *Romantic Imperialism*, p. 114.

145. See Upamanyu Pablo Mukherjee, *Crime and Empire: The Colony in Nineteenth-Century Fictions of Crime* (Oxford: Oxford University Press, 2003).

146. Uday Mehta, *Liberalism and Empire: A Study in Nineteenth-Century British Liberal Thought* (Chicago: University of Chicago Press, 1999), p. 78.

147. See Mehta, *Liberalism and Empire*, pp. 81–82.

148. See Andrew Bell, *An Experiment in Education Made at the Male Asylum in Madras* (London, 1797).

149. Graham Wallas, *The Life of Francis Place, 1771–1854* (London, 1898), p. 93.

150. See Place, British Library Add. Mss. 27,825.

151. Patrick Colquhoun, *New and Appropriate System for the Education of the Labouring People* (London, 1806), p. 11.

152. See Francis Place, *A New Proposal for Establishing in the Metropolis a Day School, in which An Example may be Set of the Application of the Methods of Dr Bell, Mr. Lancaster and Others* (London, 1817), which is included in British Library Add. Mss. 27,825.

153. Wallas, *Life of Francis Place*, p. 95.

154. *Manual of the System of the British and Foreign School Society of London* (London, 1816), p. viii.

155. See Stedman Jones, *Outcast London*, pp. 159–78. I quote from p. 169.

156. See Boyd Hilton, *A Mad, Bad and Dangerous People? England, 1783–1846* (Oxford: Oxford University Press, 2006), p. 574.

157. See Michelle Allen, *Cleansing the City: Sanitary Geographies in Victorian London* (Athens: Ohio University Press, 2008), p. 2.

158. Allen, *Cleansing the City*, p. 6.

159. See, for example, E. P. Thompson, *The Making of the English Working Class* (New York: Vintage, 1966), pp. 77–101..

160. Godwin, *London Shadows*, p. 2, emphases added.

161. Godwin, *London Shadows*, p. 10. He does add, however, that "it is at the same time necessary that other accommodation should first be provided for those who are driven out."

162. Godwin, *London Shadows*, p. 3.

163. Quoted in Stedman Jones, *Outcast London*, pp. 166–67.

164. Beames, *Rookeries of London*, p. 138.

CHAPTER 2

1. See the discussion of Wordsworth and Romantic Orientalism in chap. 5 of Saree Makdisi, *William Blake and the Impossible History of the 1790s* (Chicago: University of Chicago Press, 2003).

2. Henry Mayhew, *London Labour and the London Poor*, vol. 1 (London, 1862), p. 275. Mayhew is quoting another (unnamed) authority here.

3. See Philip Connell and Nigel Leask, "What Is the People?" in Philip Connell and Nigel Leask, eds., *Romanticism and Popular Culture in Britain and Ireland* (Cambridge: Cambridge University Press, 2009), pp. 3–48, p. 6.

4. See Ian Newman, "Tavern Talk: Literature, Politics and Conviviality, 1780–1840" (PhD dissertation, UCLA Department of English). Also see Nigel Leask, "'A Degrading Species of Alchymy': Ballad Poetics and the Meanings of Popular Culture," in Connell and Leask, *Romanticism and Popular Culture*, pp. 51–71.

5. See Newman, "Tavern Talk," esp. chap. 3.

6. *Monthly Review* on 1798 *Lyrical Ballads*, in Michael Gamer and Dahlia Porter, eds., *Lyrical Ballads, 1798 and 1800* (Peterborough: Broadview, 2008), p. 156.

7. *New London Review* on 1798 *Lyrical Ballads*, in Gamer and Porter, *Lyrical Ballads, 1798 and 1800*, p. 152. Emphases in original.

8. See Philip Connell, "How to Popularize Wordsworth," in Connell and Leask, *Romanticism and Popular Culture*, pp. 262–82, p. 279.

9. See Newman, "Tavern Talk."

10. See Nick Groom, *The Making of Percy's* Reliques (Oxford: Clarendon Press, 1999), esp. pp. 145–92.

11. Dianne Dugaw, "The Popular Marketing of 'Old Ballads': The Ballad Revival and Eighteenth-Century Antiquarianism Reconsidered," in *Eighteenth-Century Studies*, vol. 21, no. 1 (Autumn 1987), pp. 71–90.

12. Robert Mayo, "The Contemporaneity of the Lyrical Ballads," in *PMLA*, vol. 69, no. 3 (June 1954), pp. 486–522, esp. p. 495.

13. Mayo, "The Contemporaneity of the Lyrical Ballads," p. 491.

14. Quoted in Anne Stott, *Hannah More: The First Victorian* (Oxford: Oxford University Press, 2004), p. 172.

15. Letter from Bishop Porteus to Hannah More, 1794, in William Roberts, *Memoirs of the Life and Correspondence of Mrs. Hannah More*, vol. 1 (New York: Harper & Brothers, 1837), p. 457.

16. Connell and Leask, "What Is the People?" p. 19.

17. See Charles Hindley, *The History of the Catnach Press* (London, 1887); Leslie Shepard, *John Pitts: Ballad Printer of Seven Dials* (London: Private Libraries Association, 1969).

18. Charles Dickens, *Sketches by Boz* (1837; reprint, London: Penguin, 1996), p. 96.

19. See Anonymous, *The Dens of London Exposed* (London, 1835), pp. 13–14.

20. Patrick Colquhoun, *Treatise on the Police of the Metropolis* (London, 1797), p. xi.

21. Wordsworth, *The Prelude*, line 209.

22. Colquhoun, *Treatise on the Police*, p. 625.

23. See Mayhew, *London Labour*, vol. 1, p. 220. The "seven bards" reference is to Hindley, *History of the Catnach Press*, pp. 40–41.

24. Mayhew, *London Labour*, p. 213.

25. Mayhew, *London Labour*, p. 214.

26. Mayhew, *London Labour*, p. 214.

27. See Kathryn Sutherland, "The Native Poet: The Influence of Percy's Minstrel from Beattie to Wordsworth," in *Review of English Studies*, vol. 33, no. 132 (November 1982), pp. 414–33.

28. See Marilyn Butler, "Antiquarianism (Popular)," in Iain McCalman, ed., *An Oxford Companion to the Romantic Age* (Oxford: Oxford University Press, 2001), pp. 328–38.

29. Jon Mee, *Dangerous Enthusiasm* (Oxford: Oxford University Press, 1994), p. 114.

30. Joseph Ritson, "A Historical Essay on National Song," in *A Select Collection of English Songs* (London, 1813), p. lxvii.

31. *Monthly Review*, new series, vol. XI, pp. 72–77 (May, 1793), quoted in Bertrand Bronson, *Joseph Ritson: Scholar-at-Arms* (Berkeley: University of California Press, 1938), vol. 1, p. 172.

32. *Critical Review*, new series, vol. IV, pp. 55–58 (January, 1792), quoted in Bronson, *Joseph Ritson*, vol. 1, pp. 172–73.

33. Bronson, *Joseph Ritson*, p. 163.

34. "To Daniel Isaac Eaton," in *Politics for the People: or, a Salmagundy for Swine*, vol. 2 (London: Daniel Isaac Eaton, 1794), p. 400.

35. "A New Song," in *Politics for the People*, vol. 2, p. 319.

36. "A Song," in *Pigs' Meat; or, Lessons for the Swinish Multitude*, vol. 2 (London: Thomas Spence, 1795), p. 67.

37. "The Americans Happy," in *Pigs' Meat*, vol. 2, p. 283.

38. For more on that elite tradition and its gradual erasure, see Newman, "Tavern Talk," chaps. 3 and 4.

39. See Makdisi, *William Blake and the Impossible History of the 1790s*, especially chap. 2.

40. Roberts, *Memoirs of the Life and Correspondence of Mrs. Hannah More*, p. 457.

41. *Publications Printed by Special Order of the Society for Preserving Liberty and Property from Republicans and Levellers, at the Crown and Anchor, in the Strand* (London, 1793), p. 16.

42. *A New Loyal Song*, for the 1st of January 1793 (London, 1792).

43. *The Contrast* (London, 1793).

44. Kevin Gilmartin, *Writing against the Revolution: Literary Conservatism in Britain, 1790–1832* (Cambridge: Cambridge University Press, 2008), pp. 55–95.

45. Roberts, *Memoirs of the Life and Correspondence of Mrs. Hannah More*, pp. 456–57.

46. *The Life, Death, and Wonderful Atchievements* [sic] *of Edmund Burke: A New Ballad* (Edinburgh: 1792?).

47. John Thelwall, *John Gilpin's Ghost; or, the Warning Voice of King Chanticleer: An Historical Ballad* (London, 1795), p. 2.

48. Anon., *Ballad of the French Revolution* (London, 1791), p. 7.

49. See the book catalog of the Wordsworth Trust. I am grateful to Jon Mee for bringing this to my attention.

50. *New London Review* on 1798 *Lyrical Ballads*, in Gamer and Porter, *Lyrical Ballads, 1798 and 1800* , p. 154.

51. Linda Venis suggests that the volume bridges class boundaries. See "The Problem of Broadside Balladry's Influence on the *Lyrical Ballads*," in *SEL* vol. 24, no. 4 (Autumn 1984), 617–32. My claim here involves more than merely class; see the Preface and Introduction.

52. See Francis Place, "The Specimens of Songs Sung about the Streets of London," British Library Add. Mss. 27,825, pp. 141–67.

53. Place, British Library Add. Mss. 27,825, p. 165.

54. Mayhew, *London Labour*.

55. See Place, British Library Add. Mss. 27,825, pp. 141–67.

56. Place, British Library Add. Mss. 27,825, pp. 141–67.

57. Manoah Sibly, *The Genuine Trial of Thomas Hardy for High Treason* (London: JS Jordan, 1794), vol. 2, p. 222.

58. Mary Moorman, *William Wordsworth: A Biography: The Early Years, 1770–1803* (Oxford: Clarendon Press, 1957), p. 470.

59. See David Simpson, *Wordsworth, Commodification and Social Concern: The Poetics of Modernity* (Cambridge: Cambridge University Press, 2009).

60. Letter to Mathews, 23 May 1794, in Ernest De Selincourt, ed., *The Letters of William and Dorothy Wordsworth: The Early Years, 1770–1803* (Oxford: Clarendon Press, 1967), p. 119.

61. Letter to Mathews, 8 June 1794, in De Selincourt, *Letters*, p. 125.

62. See Wordsworth's letter to John Taylor, 9 April 1801, De Selincourt, *Letters*, p. 325.

63. Connell and Leask, *Romanticism and Popular Culture*, p. 5, quoting Jon Klancher, *The Making of English Reading Audiences, 1790–1832* (Madison: University of Wisconsin Press, 1987), p. 139.

64. Or so I argue in my *Romantic Imperialism*.

65. Letter to Thomas Poole, 9 April 1801, in De Selincourt, *Letters*, p. 322. Emphasis in original.

66. See letter to Poole, De Selincourt, *Letters*, pp. 322–23.

67. Letter to Mathews, 24 October 1795, in De Selincourt, *Letters*, p. 154.

68. Dorothy Wordsworth, letter to Mrs John Marshall, 30 November 1795, in De Selincourt, *Letters*, p. 162.

69. David Bromwich, *Disowned by Memory* (Chicago: University of Chicago Press, 1998), p. 40.

70. See Louis Althusser, *Essays on Ideology* (London: Verso, 1984), esp. p. 48.

71. See Kenneth Johnston, *Wordsworth and the Recluse* (New Haven, CT: Yale University Press, 1984); David Simpson, *Wordsworth's Historical Imagination* (New York: Methuen, 1987), pp. 162, 165.

72. See Johannes Fabian, *Time and the Other* (New York: Columbia University Press, 1983).

73. Simpson, *Wordsworth's Historical Imagination*, p. 163. Emphasis in original.

74. Dipesh Chakrabarty, *Provincializing Europe: Postcolonial Thought and Historical Difference* (Princeton, NJ: Princeton University Press, 2000), pp. 103–4.

75. Chakrabarty, *Provincializing Europe*, p. 105.

76. I am, of course, paraphrasing Fredric Jameson's well-known argument. See Fredric Jameson, *The Political Unconscious* (New York: Routledge, 2006), p. 20.

77. Pier Paolo Pasolini, *Heretical Empiricism*, trans. Ben Lawton and Louise Barnett (Washington, DC: New Academia Publishing), pp. 84–85,

78. All are collected in the excellent Cornell edition. See Stephen Gill, ed., *The Salisbury Plain Poems of William Wordsworth* (Ithaca, NY: Cornell University Press, 1975).

79. Dorothy Wordsworth to Jane Pollard, 30 August 1793, in De Selincourt, *Letters*, p. 109; also see Moorman, *William Wordsworth*, p. 232.

80. See Frederick Garber, *Wordsworth and the Poetry of Encounter* (Champaign-Urbana: University of Illinois Press, 1971).

81. *Preface* to Lyrical Ballads, in Gamer and Porter, *Lyrical Ballads, 1798 and 1800*, p. 177.

82. Karl Polanyi, *The Great Transformation: The Political and Economic Origins of Our Time* (1944; reprint, Boston: Beacon, 2001), pp. 171, 173.

83. See Norbert Elias, *The Civilizing Process* (Oxford: Blackwell, 2000), p. 411.

84. Alan Bewell, *Wordsworth and the Enlightenment: Nature, Man and Society in the Experimental Poetry* (New Haven, CT: Yale University Press, 1989), p. 31.

85. E. P. Thompson, *The Romantics: England in a Revolutionary Age* (New York: New Press, 1997), p. 33.

86. Even as discerning a reader as David Bromwich, who seeks to complicate and challenge the critical orthodoxy established by the political and new historical readings of Wordsworth the apostate in the 1980s—partly by insisting on Wordsworth's enduring fidelity to a certain democratic idealism—begins his 1998 book *Disowned by Memory* by declaring that "Wordsworth turned to poetry after the revolution to remind himself that he was still a human being," which suggests that Wordsworth's poetry is something that happened after his revolutionary commitments had been put to rest. Bromwich, *Disowned by Memory*, p. 1.

87. Simpson, *Wordsworth, Commodification and Social Concern*, p. 75.

88. Anne Janowitz, *Lyric and Labour in the Romantic Tradition* (Cambridge: Cambridge University Press, 1988), pp. 33–61. I quote from p. 34.

89. See Marilyn Butler, "Antiquarianism (Popular)," pp. 328–38.

90. See Alan Boehm, "The 1798 *Lyrical Ballads* and the Poetics of Late Eighteenth-Century Book Production," *ELH*, vol. 63, no. 2 (Summer 1996), pp. 453–87, p. 457.

91. Mary Jacobus, *Tradition and Experiment in Wordsworth's "Lyrical Ballads"* (Oxford: Oxford University Press, 1976), p. 196.

92. Wordsworth, letter to William Mathews, 23 May 1794, in De Selincourt, *Letters*, p. 118.

93. Quoted in Thompson, *The Romantics*, p. 38. Also see Kenneth Johnston, *The Hidden Wordsworth* (New York: Norton, 1998), pp. 598–608.

94. Venis, The Problem of Broadside Balladry's Influence, p. 621.

95. Quoted in G. H. Spinney, "Cheap Repository Tracts, Hazard and Marshall Edition," in *The Library*, fourth series, vol. xx (1940), p. 296.

96. Spinney, "Cheap Repository Tracts," pp. 298–99, 309.

97. Spinney, "Cheap Repository Tracts," p. 296.

98. Thompson, *The Romantics*, p. 34.

99. Francis Jeffrey, review of Southey's *Thalaba the Destroyer* (which also discusses *Lyrical Ballads*), *Edinburgh Review*, October 1802; reproduced in Michael Gamer and Dahlia Porter, *Lyrical Ballads, 1798 and 1800* , pp. 409–17.

100. Scott McEathron, "Wordsworth, *Lyrical* Ballads and the Problem of Peasant Poetry," *Nineteenth-Century Literature*, vol. 54, no. 1 (June 1999), pp. 1–26, p. 4.

101. McEathron, "Wordsworth," p. 24. My emphasis.

102. McEathron, "Wordsworth," p. 5.

103. M. H. Abrams, "On Political Readings of *Lyrical Ballads*," in *Romantic Revolutions*, ed. Kenneth Johnston et al. (Bloomington: Indiana University Press, 1990), pp. 320–49.

104. On the notion of worldliness, see Edward Said, *The World, the Text and the Critic* (Cambridge, MA: Harvard University Press, 1983).

105. Mayo, "The Contemporaneity of the Lyrical Ballads," p. 511. Also see pp. 507–8.

106. See Janowitz, *Lyric and Labour*.

107. See, for example, Jacqueline Labbe, *Writing Romanticism: Charlotte Smith and William Wordsworth, 1784–1807* (London: Palgrave, 2011).

108. Simon Gikandi, *Maps of Englishness: Writing Identity in the Culture of Colonialism* (New York: Columbia University Press, 1996), p. 19.

CHAPTER 3

1. Edward Said, *Culture and Imperialism* (New York: Knopf, 1993), pp. 80–97.

2. See, in particular, Susan Fraiman, "Jane Austen and Edward Said: Gender, Culture and Imperialism," in Deidre Lynch, ed., *Janeites: Austen's Disciples and Devotees* (Princeton, NJ: Princeton University Press, 2000), pp. 206–24; and Katie Trumpener, *Bardic Nationalism: The Romantic Novel and the British Empire* (Princeton, NJ: Princeton University Press, 1997), esp. pp. 161–92.

3. One of the classic works on this subject remains C. L. R. James, *The Black Jacobins* (New York: Vintage, 1989); I quote from p. 51. Also see Robin Blackburn, *The Overthrow of Colonial Slavery, 1776–1848* (London: Verso, 1989); and Eric Williams, *Capitalism and Slavery* (Chapel Hill: University of North Carolina Press, 1994).

4. See Claudia Johnson, *Jane Austen: Women, Politics and the Novel* (Chicago: University of Chicago Press, 1988), pp. 94–120; I quote from p. 97.

5. Blake, annotations to Berkeley, in David Erdman, ed., *The Complete Poetry and Prose of William Blake* (New York: Anchor Books, 1988), p. 664.

6. Johnson, *Jane Austen*, p. 99.

7. Johnson, *Jane Austen*, p. 103.

8. See Johnson, *Jane Austen*, p. 112.

9. See Johnson, *Jane Austen*, pp. 99–100.

10. See Jill Heydt-Stevenson, *Austen's Unbecoming Conjunctions: Subversive Laughter, Embodied History* (New York: Palgrave Macmillan, 2005).

11. John Stuart Mill, *Considerations on Representative Government* (London, 1861), p. 39. Emphasis in original.

12. Mill, *Considerations*, p. 39.

13. See Trumpener, *Bardic Nationalism*.

14. Jane Austen, *Mansfield Park* (Harmondsworth: Penguin, 1985), p. 206.

15. Austen, *Mansfield Park*, p. 206.

16. Austen, *Mansfield Park*, p. 448.

17. Marilyn Butler, *Jane Austen and the War of Ideas* (Oxford: Oxford University Press, 2002), pp. 247–49.

18. Clara Tuite, "Domestic Retrenchment and Imperial Expansion: The Property Plots of *Mansfield Park*," in *The Postcolonial Jane Austen*, ed. You-me Park and Rajeswari Sunder Rajan (London: Routledge, 2000), p. 99.

19. Tuite, "Domestic Retrenchment," p. 99.

20. See Linda Colley, *Britons: Forging the Nation, 1707–1837* (New Haven, CT: Yale University Press, 1994).

21. Austen, *Mansfield Park*, p. 451.

22. Tuite, "Domestic Retrenchment," p. 95.

23. Maaja Stewart, *Domestic Realities and Imperial Fictions: Jane Austen's Novels in Eighteenth Century Contexts* (Athens: University of Georgia Press, 1993), p. 131.

24. See Marilyn Butler, *Jane Austen and the War of Ideas*.

25. See Heydt-Stevenson, *Austen's Unbecoming Conjunctions*, pp. 137–58.

26. Stewart, *Domestic Realities*, pp. 110, 131.

27. Gary Kelley, *Women, Writing and Revolution* (Oxford: Clarendon Press, 1993), p. 5.

28. Said, *Culture and Imperialism*, p. 85.

29. See Johnson, *Jane Austen*, p. 100.

30. This is a question I discuss at length in *William Blake and the Impossible History of the 1790s* (Chicago: University of Chicago Press, 2003).

31. Samuel Taylor Coleridge, "Lectures on Revealed Religion: Lecture 6," in *Collected Works*, ed. Kathleen Coburn and Bart Winer (Princeton, NJ: Princeton University Press, 1969), vol. 2, p. 229.

32. Paula Byrne, "A Simple Story: From Inchbald to Austen," in *Romanticism*, vol. 5, no. 2 (Fall 1999).

33. See Elizabeth Inchbald, *A Simple Story*, ed. Anna Lott (Peterborough: Broadview Press, 2007).

34. See Mary Wollstonecraft, *Original Stories from Real Life* (London: Joseph Johnson, 1791).

35. Eleanor Ty, *Unsex'd Revolutionaries: Five Women Novelists of the 1790s* (Toronto: University of Toronto Press, 1993), p. 100.

36. See Mary Wollstonecraft, review of *A Simple Story* for the *Analytical Review*, in Elizabeth Inchbald, *A Simple Story*, p. 381.

37. Jane Austen, *Persuasion* (London: Penguin, 2003), p. 10.

38. Austen, *Persuasion*, p. 20.

39. Austen, *Persuasion*, pp. 7, 24.

40. Austen, *Persuasion*, p. 12.

41. Austen, *Persuasion*, p. 169.

42. This is, again, an issue I discuss at much greater length in my *William Blake and the Impossible History of the 1790s*.

43. See Said, *Orientalism*, p. 81.

44. Balfour, quoted in Said, *Orientalism*, pp. 32–33.

45. See Thomas Macaulay, "Minute on Indian Education," in Barbara Harlow and Mia Carter, eds., *Archives of Empire, vol. 1: From the East India Company to the Suez Canal* (Durham, NC: Duke University Press, 2003), pp. 227–39.

46. See Frantz Fanon, *Black Skin, White Masks*, trans. Constance Farrington (New York: Grove Press, 1994).

47. Hannah More, quoted in Colley, *Britons*, p. 275.

48. Colley, *Britons*, p. 275.

49. Moira Ferguson, *Subject to Others: British Women Writers and Colonial Slavery, 1670–1834* (London: Routledge, 1992), p. 6.

50. See Deirdre Coleman, "Conspicuous Consumption: White Abolitionism and English Women's Protest Writing in the 1790s," in *ELH* 61, pp. 341–62.

CHAPTER 4

1. George Gordon, Lord Byron, "Lara," in *The Works of Lord Byron* (London: Murray, 1823), vol. 4, p. 16.

2. Byron, "Lara," p. 16.

3. See Immanuel Kant, "Toward Perpetual Peace," in Kant, *Toward Perpetual Peace and Other Writings on Policy, Peace and History*, ed. Pauline Kliengeld (New Haven, CT: Yale University Press, 2006), pp. 67–109.

4. Byron, *The Corsair* (London: Murray, 1814), p. 14.

5. Byron, "The Siege of Corinth," in *The Works of Lord Byron* (London: Murray, 1823), vol. 4, p. 72.

6. George Gordon, Lord Byron, *The Giaour: A Fragment of a Turkish Tale* (London: Murray, 1813), pp. 39–40, lines 798–813.

7. See Andrew Elfenbein, *Byron and the Victorians* (Cambridge: Cambridge University Press, 1996), pp. 14–15. "My overall concern," he writes, "is not with how Byron revealed himself in his heroes but with what in his writing made his first readers certain that he did."

8. Abigail Keenan, *Byron's Othered Self and Voice: Contextualizing the Homographic Signature* (New York: Peter Lang, 2003), p. 146.

9. See Louis Crompton, *Byron and Greek Love: Homophobia and 19ᵗʰ-Century England* (Berkeley: University of California Press, 1985).

10. Leask, *British Romantic Writers and the East: Anxieties of Empire* (Cambridge: Cambridge University Press, 1992), p. 2.

11. See Peter Cochran, *Byron and Orientalism* (Newcastle: Cambridge Scholars Press, 2006).

12. Byron letter to Moore, in Leslie Marchand, ed., *Byron's Letters and Journals* (Cambridge, MA: Harvard University Press, 1974), vol. 3, p. 101.

13. Leask, *British Romantic Writers*, p. 12. Also see Peter Kitson, "Byron and Post-Colonial Criticism: The Eastern Tales," in Jane Stabler, ed., *Palgrave Advances in Byron* (London: Palgrave, 2007), pp. 106–29, 114.

14. Marilyn Butler, "Byron and the Empire in the East," in Andrew Rutherford, ed., *Byron: Augustan and Romantic* (New York: St. Martin's Press, 1990), pp. 75, 80.

15. So, at least, I argue in *Romantic Imperialism* (Cambridge: Cambridge University Press, 1998), esp. chaps. 4 and 5.

16. See Marchand, *Byron's Letters*, p. 36.

17. See Marchand, *Byron's Letters*, p. 142.

18. Caroline Franklin, *Byron's Heroines* (Oxford: Oxford University Press, 1993), p. 119.

19. Elfenbein, *Byron and the Victorians*, pp. 209–10.

20. Nigel Leask, "Byron and the Eastern Mediterranean," in Drummond Bone, ed., *The Cambridge Companion to Byron* (Cambridge: Cambridge University Press, 2004), pp. 99–117, p. 114.

21. Alan Richardson, "Escape from the Seraglio: Cultural Transvestism in Don Juan," in *Rereading Byron*, ed. Robert N. Keane and Alice Levine (New York: Garland, 1993), pp. 175–85, p. 184.

22. Andrew Elfenbein, "Byron: Gender and Sexuality," in Drummond Bone, ed., *The Cambridge Companion to Byron* (Cambridge: Cambridge University Press, 2004), pp. 56–76, p. 59.

23. Elfenbein, "Byron," 60.

24. See Ian Baucom, *Out of Place: Englishness, Empire and the Locations of Identity* (Princeton, NJ: Princeton University Press, 1999).

25. See Saree Makdisi, *William Blake and the Impossible History of the 1790s* (Chicago: University of Chicago Press, 2003), p. 7.

26. Byron, *The Giaour*, line 810.

27. Byron, *The Giaour*, lines 787–97.

28. Byron, *The Giaour*, line 180.

29. Byron, *The Giaour*, lines 230–31.

30. Byron, *The Giaour*, lines 1040–41.

31. Byron, *The Giaour*, lines 1131–34.

32. William Marshall, "The Accretive Structure of Byron's 'The Giaour,'" *Modern Language Notes*, vol. 76, no. 6 (June 1961), pp. 502–9, p. 502.

33. Robert Gleckner, *Byron and the Ruins of Paradise* (Baltimore: Johns Hopkins University Press, 1967), p. 97.

34. Here I am drawing on the work of Ghassan Hage, in "Eavesdropping on Bourdieu's Philosophers," *Thesis 11* (February 2013), and in "Critical Anthropological Thought and the Radical Political Imaginary Today." Via his readings of Pierre Bourdieu, Hage urges us to think not about reality as a single site of contestation but rather, instead, about the conflict among multiple realities, in which the winners impose both their reality and their practical mastery over it on others. "There are dominant and dominated people within a reality," Hage argues, "but just as, if not more, importantly, there are dominant and dominated realities." Hage, "Eavesdropping." In a related vein, drawing on the elaboration of multinaturalism in the work of Viveiros de Castro, Hage argues that

the notion of multinaturalism, with its multiplicity of realities or natures, "stands in opposition to the discourses of multiculturalism which presuppose one nature/'objective reality' and a multiplicity of cultures/subjectivities." Hage, "Critical Anthropological Thought and the Radical Political Imaginary Today," in *Critique of Anthropology*, vol. 32, no. 3 (September 2012).

35. Eve Sedgwick, *Between Men: English Literature and Male Homosocial Desire* (New York: Columbia University Press, 1985), p. 21.

36. Byron, *The Giaour*, lines 447–54.

37. Byron, *The Giaour*, line 718.

38. See Marshall, "Accretive Structure of Byron's 'The Giaour,'" pp. 502–3.

39. See Byron, *The Giaour*, lines 257–64.

40. Byron, *The Giaour*, line 273.

41. Byron, *The Giaour*, lines 316–19.

42. See my *William Blake and the Impossible History*, esp. pp. 78–203.

43. James Dunn, "Charlotte Dacre and the Feminization of Violence," *Nineteenth-Century Literature*, vol. 53, no. 3 (December 1988).

44. Diane Hoeveler, "Charlotte Dacre's *Zofloya*: A Case Study of Miscegenation as Sexual and Racial Nausea," *European Romantic Review*, vol. 8, no. 2 (Spring 1997).

45. See Anne Mellor, "Interracial Sexual Desire in Charlotte Dacre's *Zofloya*," *European Romantic Review*, vol. 13, no. 2 (Spring 2002).

46. Charlotte Dacre, *Zofloya* (London, 1806), vol. 2, pp. 102, 253.

CHAPTER 5

1. Thomas Macaulay, "Southey's *Colloquies*," *Edinburgh Review*, 1830; reprinted in *The Complete Works of Thomas Babington Macaulay* (New York: Houghton & Mifflin, 1910), vol. 1, pp. 496–545, p. 496.

2. Macaulay, "Southey's *Colloquies*," pp. 497–99.

3. Macaulay, *Minute on Indian Education*, in Barbara Harlow and Mia Carter, eds., *Archives of Empire* (Durham, NC: Duke University Press, 2003), vol. 1, pp. 227–38, p. 232.

4. See Raymond Schwab, *The Oriental Renaissance: Europe's Rediscovery of India and the East, 1680–1880*, trans. Gene Patterson-Black and Victor Reinking (New York: Columbia University Press, 1986).

5. This is of course the key argument of Said's *Orientalism*. See Edward Said, *Orientalism* (New York: Pantheon, 1978).

6. Majeed makes a similar argument, though he is less interested in the question of second-order images. See Javed Majeed, *Ungoverned Imaginings* (Oxford: Clarendon Press, 1992), p. 84.

7. Hinduism, he writes, for example, is "of all false religions the most monstrous in its fables and the most fatal in its effects." Robert Southey, 1838 Preface to *The Curse of Kehama*, in *The Complete Works of Robert Southey, Collected by Himself* (London, 1838), vol. 8, p. 23. Also see Robert Southey, *Thalaba the Destroyer* (Boston, 1812).

8. Robert Southey, note to *Thalaba the Destroyer*, vol. 1, p. 39.

9. Southey, 1838 Preface to *Curse of Kehama*, p. xvii.

10. Southey, 1810 Preface to *Curse of Kehama*, p. xxiii.

11. Southey, Preface to the fourth edition of *Thalaba*, p. 2.

12. Majeed, *Ungoverned Imaginings*, p. 53.

13. Southey, 1838 Preface to *Curse of Kehama*, p. xiii.

14. Southey, notes to *Thalaba*, p. 37.

15. Southey, *Thalaba*, p. 16.

16. Oliver Goldsmith, "The Deserted Village."

17. Robert Southey, *Sir Thomas More; or, Colloquies on the Progress and Prospects of Society* (London, 1831), pp. 154, 158.

18. Southey, *Colloquies*, p. 132.

19. Southey, *Colloquies*, pp. 168–70; *Thalaba*, pp. 18, 20.

20. I discuss this tension extensively in *Romantic Imperialism*, pp. 100–153.

21. Charles Grant, *Observations on the State of Society among the Asiatic Subjects of Great Britain, particularly with respect to Morals and on the Means of Improving it, Written chiefly in the Year 1792* (London, 1797), p. 71.

22. Quoted in Susan Thorne, "'The Conversion of Englishmen and the Conversion of the World Inseparable': Missionary Imperialism and the Language of Class in Early Industrial Britain," in Frederick Cooper and Ann Laura Stoler, eds., *Tensions of Empire: Colonial Cultures in a Bourgeois World* (Berkeley: University of California Press, 1997), pp. 238–55, pp. 238, 247. See the Introduction, above.

23. James Pycroft, *Twenty Years in the Church: An Autobiography* (London, 1859), pp. 43–44. See chap. 1, above.

24. Robert Southey, *"Asiatick Researches" Annual Review for 1803*, quoted in Majeed, *Ungoverned Imaginings*, p. 82.

25. Robert Southey, "Forbes' *Oriental Memoirs*," *Quarterly Review* (October 1814), quoted in Majeed, *Ungoverned Imaginings*, p. 82.

26. Thomas Macaulay, Speech in the Charter Debate, 10 July 1833 (quoted in Eric Stokes, *The English Utilitarians and India* [Oxford: Oxford University Press, 1989], pp. 43–45).

27. Stokes, *The English Utilitarians*, p. 45.

28. Macaulay, "Southey's *Colloquies*," p. 522.

29. Karl Marx and Friedrich Engels, *The Communist Manifesto*.

30. See Stokes, *The English Utilitarians*, pp. 55–58.

31. See Norbert Elias, *The Civilizing Process*, trans. Edmund Jephcott (Oxford: Blackwell, 2000); also see chap. 1, above.

32. Macaulay, *Minute on Indian Education*, p. 232.

33. Macaulay, "Southey's *Colloquies*," p. 533.

34. Southey, *Colloquies*, quoted in Macaulay, "Southey's *Colloquies*," p. 511.

35. Macaulay, "Southey's *Colloquies*," p. 511.

36. John Stuart Mill, *Considerations on Representative Government* (London, 1861), pp. 77, 79.

37. Mill, *Considerations on Representative Government*, pp. 76–77.

38. Mill, *On Liberty*, chap. 3.

39. Mill, *Considerations on Representative Government*, p. 300.

40. Mill, *Considerations on Representative Government*, p. 300.

41. See Introduction, above. Also see Dipesh Chakrabarty, *Provincializing Europe: Postcolonial Thought and Historical Difference* (Princeton, NJ: Princeton University Press, 2000), p. 7.

42. Macaulay, "Southey's *Colloquies*," p. 497.

43. Macaulay, "Minute on Indian Education," p. 237.

CHAPTER 6

1. Charles Dickens, *The Mystery of Edwin Drood* (1870; reprint, Harmondsworth: Penguin, 1974), p. 37.

2. See, among other works on Dickens's attitudes to empire, Edward Said, *Culture and Imperialism* (New York: Random House, 1994), esp. pp. 62–110; Grace Moore, *Dickens and Empire: Discourses of Class, Race and Colonialism in the Works of Charles Dickens* (Aldershot: Ashgate, 2004); Wendy Jacobson, ed., *Dickens and the Children of Empire* (London: Palgrave Macmillan, 2001); Suvendrini Perera, *Reaches of Empire: The English Novel from Edgeworth to Dickens* (New York: Columbia University Press, 1991); and, on *Bleak House* in particular, Timothy Carens, "The Civilizing Mission at Home: Empire, Gender, and National Reform in *Bleak House*," *Dickens Studies Annual* vol. 26 (1998), 121–45.

3. Dickens, *Edwin Drood*, p. 96.

4. Moore, *Dickens and Empire*, p. 181.

5. Grace Moore, "Turkish Robbers, Lumps of Delight, and the Detritus of Empire: The East Revisited in Dickens's Late Novels," in *Critical Survey*, vol. 21, no. 1 (2009), 74–87, p. 86, and *Dickens and Empire*, p. 183.

6. Dickens, *Edwin Drood*, p. 64.

7. Miriam O'Kane Mara, "Sucking the Empire Dry: Colonial Critique in *The Mystery of Edwin Drood*," in *Dickens Studies Annual*, vol. 32 (2002), pp. 233–45, p. 236.

8. David Faulkner, "The Confidence Man: Empire and the Deconstruction of Muscular Christianity in *The Mystery of Edwin Drood*," in Donald Hall, ed., *Muscular Christianity: Embodying the Victorian Age* (Cambridge: Cambridge University Press, 1994), pp. 175–93, p. 175. He cautions, however, that "Crisparkle's 'purity' as a muscular Christian is never unadulterated" (p. 183).

9. See Mara, "Sucking the Empire Dry," p. 236.

10. Faulkner, "The Confidence Man," p. 186. Emphasis in original.

11. See Edward Said, *Orientalism* (New York: Pantheon, 1978), for the notion of imaginative geography.

12. John DeWind, "The Empire as Metaphor: England and the East in *The Mystery of Edwin Drood*," in *Victorian Literature and Culture*, vol. 21 (1993), pp. 169–89, esp. pp. 169, 186.

13. Charles Dickens, "The Niger Expedition," in *Miscellaneous Papers by Charles Dickens* (London: Chapman & Hall, 1911), pp. 117–35, p. 133.

14. See, for example, John Drew, *Dickens the Journalist* (London: Palgrave Macmillan, 2003), pp. 98–100; Deirdre David, *Women, Empire and Victorian Writing* (Ithaca, NY: Cornell University Press, 1995), pp. 61–62; Patrick Brantlinger, "Victorians and Africans: The Genealogy of the Myth of the Dark Continent," in Henry Gates, ed., *Race,*

Writing and Difference (Chicago: University of Chicago Press, 1985), pp. 185–222, esp. p. 193; Carens, "The Civilizing Mission at Home," pp. 121–45, p. 134. Also see Charles Dickens, "The Noble Savage," in David Pascoe, ed., *Charles Dickens: Selected Journalism, 1850–1870* (London: Penguin, 1997), pp. 560–65, which concludes with the following grim lines: "My position is, that if we have anything to learn from the Noble Savage, it is what to avoid. His virtues are a fable; his happiness is a delusion; his nobility, nonsense. We have no greater justification for being cruel to the miserable object, than for being cruel to a WILLIAM SHAKESPEARE or an ISAAC NEWTON; but he passes away before an immeasurably better and higher power than ever ran wild in any earthly woods, and the world will be all the better when his place knows him no more."

15. Charles Dickens, letter to Angela Burdett-Coutts (4 October 1857), in Charles Osborne, ed., *Letters of Charles Dickens to the Baroness Burdett-Coutts* (London: Murray, 1931), pp. 188–89.

16. See, for example, Lillian Nayder, "Class Consciousness and the Indian Mutiny in Dickens's 'The Perils of Certain English Prisoners,'" in *Studies in English Literature*, vol. 32, no. 4 (Autumn 1992), pp. 689–705, esp. pp. 695–98; Garrett Ziegler, "The Perils of Empire: Dickens, Collins and the Indian Mutiny," in Grace Moore, ed., *Pirates and Mutineers of the Nineteenth Century: Swashbucklers and Swindlers* (Farnham: Ashgate, 2011), pp. 149–64, esp. pp. 149–50; and Patrick Brantlinger, *Rule of Darkness: British Literature and Imperialism, 1830–1914* (Ithaca, NY: Cornell University Press, 1988), pp. 199–226, esp. pp. 206–10.

17. Charles Dickens, *Bleak House* (London: Bradbury & Evans, 1853), p. 452.

18. This is the argument proposed by Timothy Carens, who argues, in view of the treatment of Jo, that in *Bleak House* Dickens creates a world "in which the 'condition of England' belies the presumed distinction between the 'civilized' imperial metropole and the 'savage' periphery," so that "Jo's ignorance collapses the privileged distinction between the 'native' Briton and the African 'native.'" See Carens, "The Civilizing Mission at Home," pp. 121–45, pp. 121, 134.

19. Thus argues Grace Moore, who maintains that Dickens challenges the racialization of the poor in the case of Jo, whose "homeliness" undermines his seeming otherness. Unlike other, more explicitly racist depictions of working-class or plebeian savages at home, she says, "Dickens attempts to assert a common nationality and humanity between the revolting Jo and his readers." See Moore, *Dickens and Empire*, pp. 30–34.

20. Dickens, *Bleak House*, p. 459.

21. Tim Dolin, "Race and the Social Plot in *The Mystery of Edwin Drood*," in Shearer West, ed., *The Victorians and Race* (Aldershot: Scolar Press, 1996), pp. 84–100, p. 94.

22. See Carens, "The Civilizing Mission at Home," p. 121.

23. See entries for "Jasper" in John Daintith, ed., *A Dictionary of Chemistry* (Oxford: Oxford University Press, 2008) and, for its etymology, in the *Oxford English Dictionary*.

24. Dickens, *Edwin Drood*, p. 43.

25. "I have been taking opium for a pain," Jasper tells Edwin. Dickens, *Edwin Drood*, p. 47.

26. Dickens, *Edwin Drood*, p. 77.

27. Dickens, *Edwin Drood*, p. 77.

28. Dickens, *Edwin Drood*, p. 47.

29. Dickens, *Edwin Drood*, pp. 39, 41.

30. Dickens, *Edwin Drood*, p. 130.

31. See John Forster, *The Life of Charles Dickens* (London: Chapman & Hall), vol. 3, p. 366.

32. Rosemarie Bodenheimer, *Knowing Dickens* (Ithaca, NY: Cornell University Press, 2007), p. 124.

33. For example, he seemingly deliberately draws Sapsea's attention to his (Jasper's) diary entries expressing a worry about the danger that Neville's savagery seems to pose to Edwin (Dickens, *Edwin Drood*, p. 132), and he encourages Sapsea's estimation of Neville's tigerish "un-Englishness" (*Edwin Drood*, p. 180), which will clearly prove useful in framing Neville in Sapsea's mind.

34. See Dickens, *Edwin Drood*, pp. 191–92.

35. See the classic, though often discredited, Howard Duffield, "John Jasper—Strangler," in *The Bookman*, vol. 70, no. 6 (February 1930), pp. 581–89; Edmund Wilson, *The Wound and the Bow: Seven Studies in Literature* (New York: Oxford University Press, 1965), pp. 69–78; Wendy Jacobson, "John Jasper and Thuggee, in *Modern Language Review*, vol. 72, no. 3 (July 1977), pp. 526–37; Perera, *Reaches of Empire*, p. 120.

36. Eve Sedgwick, *Between Men: Literature and Male Homosocial Desire* (New York: Columbia University Press, 1985), p. 198. I will return to Sedgwick's reading shortly.

37. See J. Hillis Miller, *Charles Dickens: The World of His Novels* (Cambridge, MA: Harvard University Press, 1958); Charles Mitchell, "*The Mystery of Edwin Drood*: The Interior and Exterior of Self," in *ELH*, vol. 33, no. 2 (June 1966), pp. 228–46. See, by way of comparison, the more recent Angelia Poon, *Enacting Englishness in the Victorian Period: Colonialism and the Politics of Performance* (Aldershot: Ashgate, 2008), pp. 114–24, to which I will return shortly.

38. See Joachim Stanley, "Opium and *Edwin Drood*: Fantasy, Reality and What the Doctor Ordered," in *Dickens Quarterly*, March 2004, pp. 12–27, p. 13; Mara, "Sucking the Empire Dry," p. 242. Stephanie Peña-Sy goes so far as to argue that "the discontinuity of Jasper's selfhood and the disconnection of that discontinuous selfhood from personal identity" could well have been taken seriously as arguments for his innocence in a Victorian court of law; see her "Intoxication, Provocation, and Derangement: Interrogating the Nature of Criminal Responsibility in *The Mystery of Edwin Drood*," in *Dickens Studies Annual*, vol. 40 (2009), pp. 215–30, p. 228.

39. See Joachim Stanley, "Opium and *Edwin Drood*," esp. p. 12; Perera, *Reaches of Empire*, p. 108; Moore, *Dickens and Empire*, p. 184.

40. Poon, *Enacting Englishness*, p. 121.

41. See Robert Tracy, "'Opium is the True Hero of the Tale': De Quincey, Dickens, and *The Mystery of Edwin Drood*," *Dickens Studies Annual*, vol. 40 (2009), pp. 199–213.

42. See Saree Makdisi, "Literature, Nation and Empire," in Tom Keymer and Jon Mee, eds., *The Cambridge Companion to English Literature, 1740–1830* (Cambridge: Cambridge University Press, 2004), pp. 61–79.

43. Dickens, *Edwin Drood*, p. 39.

44. Dickens, *Edwin Drood*, p. 38.

45. Dickens, *Edwin Drood*, p. 154.

46. See, e.g., Dickens, *Edwin Drood*, pp. 159, 192.

47. See Sedgwick, *Between Men*, pp. 180–200.

48. See Laura Doyle, "At World's Edge: Post/Coloniality, Charles Maturin, and the Gothic Wanderer," in *Nineteenth-Century Literature*, vol. 65, no. 4, pp. 513–47.

49. Dickens, *Edwin Drood*, p. 156; see also pp. 157–58 for more of the same.

50. Dickens, *Edwin Drood*, p. 95.

51. Dickens, *Edwin Drood*, p. 95. Emphasis added.

52. Dickens, *Edwin Drood*, p. 44. Emphases added.

53. For my take on Blake's critique of unitary subjectivity, see my *William Blake and the Impossible History of the 1790s* (Chicago: University of Chicago Press, 2003).

54. Charles Dickens, *Edwin Drood* (London: Chapman & Hall, 1870), pp. 120–21. Unless otherwise noted, other references to the novel are to the 1974 Penguin edition.

55. See, e.g., Poon, *Enacting Englishness*, p. 119; Sedgwick, *Between Men*, p. 191.

56. Sedgwick, *Between Men*, pp. 185, 186.

57. Poon, *Enacting Englishness*, p. 122.

58. Faulkner, "The Confidence Man," pp. 183.

59. Sedgwick, *Between Men*, pp. 185–86.

60. Dickens, *Edwin Drood*, p. 42.

61. Dickens, *Edwin Drood*, p. 78.

62. Dickens, *Edwin Drood*, p. 247.

63. The reference to the emancipation of the "London blacks" seems especially intriguing here. The editors of the two editions of the novel I am consulting point out that the phrase was commonly used to refer to soot and dust; and yet the term "emancipation" necessarily reiterates the racial dimension of the ordinary domestic language, representing another collapse of the exotic and the familiar.

64. Ina Rae Hark, "Marriage in the Symbolic Framework of *The Mystery of Edwin Drood*, in *Studies in the Novel*, vol. 9 no. 2 (Summer 1977), pp. 154–68, p. 162.

65. Dickens, *Edwin Drood*, p. 246.

66. Dickens, *Edwin Drood*, p. 247.

67. Dickens, *Edwin Drood*, p. 252.

68. Hark, "Marriage," pp. 162–63.

69. Dickens, *Edwin Drood*, p. 53.

70. See Walter Scott, *Waverley* (London: Black, 1895), p. 30. The narrator's point here is that he will be devoted to possibly boring realities rather than misleading flights of fancy.

71. See John Stuart Mill, *Considerations on Representative Government* (New York: Henry Holt, 1882), p. 47. I will return to this point a little later.

72. Dickens, *Edwin Drood*, pp. 109–10.

73. Dickens, *Edwin Drood*, p. 114.

74. See Jonathan Grossman, *Charles Dickens's Networks: Public Transport and the Novel* (Oxford: Oxford University Press, 2012); I quote from p. 24.

75. Dickens, *Edwin Drood*, p. 214.

76. Dickens, *Edwin Drood*, p. 74.

77. Dickens, *Edwin Drood*, pp. 70–71.

78. Dickens, *Edwin Drood*, p. 68.

79. Dickens, *Edwin Drood*, p. 74.

80. Dickens, *Edwin Drood*, pp. 68–69.

81. See esp. the Introduction and chap. 1 above; also see Saree Makdisi, *Romantic Imperialism* (Cambridge: Cambridge University Press, 1998), esp. pp. 23–44, and *William Blake and the Impossible History*, esp. pp. 155–203.

82. Bernard Lewis, who may be usefully thought of as the leading ideologue of Occidentalism in our contemporary world, says exactly this, albeit in a totally unself-conscious and, of course, celebratory rather than critical, way, in his post-September 11 justification of the absurd "clash of civilizations" thesis, which he originated (Huntington only picked up on it afterward). See, for example, his *What Went Wrong? Western Impact and Middle Eastern Response* (Oxford: Oxford University Press, 2001).

83. Uday Mehta's *Liberalism and Empire* (Chicago: University of Chicago Press, 1999) remains a key book on this question.

84. Thomas Macaulay, "Minute on Indian Education," in G. M. Young, ed., *Speeches by Lord Macaulay* (1935; reprint, New York: AMS Press, 1979), p. 359.

85. John Stuart Mill, *Considerations on Representative Government*, p. 34.

86. Mill, *Considerations on Representative Government*, p. 51.

87. John Stuart Mill, *On Liberty* (Boston: Ticknor & Fields), p. 135.

88. Mill, *Considerations on Representative Government*, p. 47. Mehta, *Liberalism and Empire*, discusses all of these questions at great length as well.

89. Mill, *Considerations on Representative Government*, p. 49. Hence, he says, on p. 46, "Institutions need to be radically different, according to the stage of advancement already reached. The recognition of this truth, though for the most part empirically rather than philosophically, may be regarded as the main point of superiority in the political theories of the present above those of the last age, in which it was customary to claim representative democracy for England or France by arguments which would equally have proved it the only fit form of government for Bedouins or Malays."

90. Mehta's *Liberalism and Empire* still presents the most thorough analysis of these arguments.

91. "Mr Mill like many others has been led astray by treating of this country as one in a high state of civilization," Place argues. "If we compare our present state with that in which Caesar found its inhabitants, it may be called a high state of civilization, but every observing reasoning man must conclude that we are far indeed from being a really civilized people, and that we have many very serious and perhaps painful changes to go through before we shall deserve the title of highly civilized. Considerable advance has been made, it will be continually accelerated, and it may be safely concluded that no ordinary circumstance can greatly impede our progress nor any but uncommon and unlooked for events cause any considerable delay in that progress. These are exhilarating prospects and the more they are entertained the more rapid and less painful will be the progress." Francis Place, "Civilization," unpublished manuscript in British Library, Add. Mss. 27,827, pp. 202–41.

92. John Stuart Mill, "Civilization," in *London and Westminster Review*, April 1836, pp. 1–28, p. 3.

93. Dickens, "Niger Expedition," p. 133. He adds, "No amount of philanthropy has a right to waste such valuable life as was squandered here. Between the civilized European and the barbarous African there is a great gulf set." See Carens. "The Civilizing Mission

at Home," on Dickens's critique of "telescopic philanthropists" such as Mrs. Jellyby in *Bleak House.*

94. Charles Dickens and Richard Horne, "The Great Exhibition and the Little One," in *Household Worlds* vol. 8 (Leipzig, 1851), pp. 281–88, p. 283; also see Sabine Clemm, *Dickens, Journalism, and Nationhood* (New York: Routledge, 2009), esp. pp. 30–37; Paul Young, *Globalization and the Great Exhibition: The Victorian New World Order* (London: Palgrave Macmillan, 2009), esp. pp. 118–42; Anthony Chennells, "Savages and Settlers in Dickens: Reading Multiple Centers," in Jacobson, *Dickens and the Children of Empire,* pp. 153–72; also see Elizabeth Hope Chang, *Britain's Chinese Eye: Literature, Empire, and Aesthetics in Nineteenth-Century Britain* (Stanford: Stanford University Press, 2010).

95. See Dickens and Horne, "The Great Exhibition," p. 285.

96. Dickens and Horne, "The Great Exhibition," p. 285. "In brief," they write on p. 281, "we consider that our present period recognizes the progress of humanity, step by step, towards a social condition in which nobler feelings, thoughts, and actions, in concert for the good of all, instead of in general antagonism, producing a more refined and fixed condition of happiness, may be the common inheritance of great and small communities, and of all those nations of the earth who recognize and aspire to fulfill this law of human progression."

97. Dickens, "Niger Expedition," p. 133. What he is really saying here, it should be noted, is that the improvement of African savages will take so much time that it is a waste of resources to even attempt it in the present, pending the full civilization of areas much closer to (or at) home.

98. "Well may the three Chinese divinities of the Past, the Present, and the Future be represented with the same heavy face. Well may the dull, immoveable, respectable triad sit so amicably, side by side, in a glory of yellow jaundice, with a strong family likeness among them! As the Past was, so the Present is, and so the Future shall be, saith the Emperor. And all the Mandarins prostrate themselves, and cry Amen." Dickens and Horne, "The Great Exhibition," p. 284.

99. On cognitive maps, see Fredric Jameson, "Cognitive Mapping," in Cary Nelson and Lawrence Grossberg, eds., *Marxism and the Interpretation of Culture* (Carbondale: University of Illinois Press, 1990), pp. 347–60.

100. Grossman, *Charles Dickens's Networks,* pp. 185–86.

101. Grossman, *Charles Dickens's Networks,* p. 195.

102. Mill, "Civilization," p. 8.

103. Mill, *Considerations on Representative Government,* p. 35.

104. Mill, *Considerations on Representative Government,* p. 36. "A people, it appears, may be progressive for a certain length of time, and then stop: when does it stop?" he asks in *On Liberty;* "when it ceases to possess individuality." Mill, *On Liberty,* p. 137.

105. Mill, *On Liberty,* p. 139.

106. For more on Mill and the character of the liberal individual as he imagined it, see Elaine Hadley's excellent *Living Liberalism: Practical Citizenship in Mid-Victorian Britain* (Chicago: University of Chicago Press, 2010), pp. 63–124, esp. pp. 70–74.

107. Dickens and Horne, "The Great Exhibition," p. 283.

108. Mill, *On Liberty,* p. 135.

109. See William Blake, "The Garden of Love," in *Songs of Innocence and of Experience* (London, 1794).

110. This is how Mara puts it on p. 236 of "Sucking the Empire Dry." Also see Stanley, pp. 12–13; Moore, *Dickens and Empire*, pp. 183–84.

111. Dickens, *Edwin Drood* (Chapman & Hall edition, 1870), pp. 12–13.

112. Entry for "Jack and the Beanstalk," in Graham Seal, *Encyclopedia of Folk Heroes* (Santa Barbara: ABC-CLIO, 2001), pp. 119–20.

113. Dickens, *Edwin Drood*, pp. 69, 219, 76, 63.

114. Thomas Macaulay, "Southey's Colloquies," originally published in the *Edinburgh Review* (January 1830), in Macaulay, *Critical, Historical, and Miscellaneous Essays and Poems*, vol. 1 (Boston: Estes & Lauriat, 1882), p. 487.

115. Dickens, *Edwin Drood*, p. 83.

116. Dickens, *Edwin Drood*, p. 83.

117. Dickens, *Edwin Drood*, p. 136.

118. Dickens, *Edwin Drood*, p. 266.

119. Dickens, *Edwin Drood*, p. 235.

120. Dickens, "Seven Dials," p. 92. Also see the discussion of London in chap. 1, above.

121. Dickens, *Edwin Drood*, p. 258.

122. Dickens, *Edwin Drood*, p. 263.

123. Dickens, *Edwin Drood*, p. 134.

124. See Ed Glinert, *The London Compendium* (London: Penguin, 2004), p. 4.

125. Dickens, *Edwin Drood*, p. 213.

126. Dickens, *Edwin Drood*, pp. 114, 208.

127. Dickens, *Edwin Drood*, p. 235.

128. Dickens, *Edwin Drood*, p. 47.

129. Dickens, *Edwin Drood*, p. 47. Emphases in original.

130. Dickens, *Edwin Drood*, p. 50.

131. Tom Paine, *Rights of Man* (London: JS Jordan, 1791), p. 12.

132. Dickens, *Edwin Drood*, pp. 50, 59.

133. "Fellah" means "farmer" in Arabic, though in the hands of English writers it often seems to signify an ethnic designation.

134. Dickens, *Edwin Drood*, p. 59.

135. Hyungji Park notes that Belzoni and De Lesseps serve as examples for Edwin's "going engineering into the East." See Hyungji Park, "'Going to Wake up Egypt': Exhibiting Empire in *Edwin Drood*," *Victorian Literature and Culture* (2002), pp. 529–50, p. 538.

136. Dickens, *Edwin Drood*, p. 59.

137. "The stranger who finds himself in 'The Dials' for the first time, and stands Belzoni-like, at the entrance of seven obscure passages, uncertain which to take, will see enough around him to keep his curiosity and attention awake for no inconsiderable time," writes Dickens in *Boz*. See chap. 1, above.

138. Dickens, *Edwin Drood*, pp. 117–18.

139. Dickens, *Edwin Drood*, p. 144.

140. Dickens, *Edwin Drood*, p. 145.

141. Dickens, *Edwin Drood*, pp. 168–69.

142. Edmund Burke, *Reflections on the Revolution in France*, in *The Works of Edmund Burke*, vol. 3 (Boston: Little & Brown, 1839), p. 53.

143. This sense of temporal repetition and recycling is reinforced all the more strongly by our growing awareness that Grewgious had originally been enamored of Rosa's mother. Dry as he is, his growing fondness for Rosa is motivated in part by his feeling that she resembles her mother ("Good God," he says to himself on p. 146, "how like her mother she has become!"). If he picks up where Edwin leaves off by making love (in the Victorian sense of that phrase) to Rosa, he would in effect be returning to his own youth and resituating Rosa as her mother.

144. Dickens, *Edwin Drood*, p. 179.

145. Dickens, *Edwin Drood*, p. 169.

146. See Dickens, *Edwin Drood*, pp. 176–77.

147. See Dickens, *Edwin Drood*, p. 183.

148. Dickens, *Edwin Drood*, p. 228. Stephen Franklin says that this situates Jasper as the "enemy of time." See Stephen Franklin, "Dickens and Time: The Clock without Hands," in *Dickens Studies Annual*, vol. 4 (1975), pp. 1–35, p. 33.

149. Dickens, *Edwin Drood*, p. 171.

150. Dickens, *Edwin Drood*, p. 225.

151. For example, the marriage plots imagined in most of the projected endings, in pairing Helena and Crisparkle on the one hand and Rosa and Tartar on the other do not offer satisfactory resolutions, given what has already been said about Crisparkle and Tartar.

152. DeWind, "Empire as Metaphor," pp. 170, 187.

153. See Edward Said, *On Late Style: Music and Literature against the Grain* (New York: Pantheon, 2006).

154. See my discussion of "Alastor" in Makdisi, *Romantic Imperialism*, pp. 122–54.

155. Faulkner, "The Confidence Man," pp. 181–82, 186.

156. Dickens, *Edwin Drood*, p. 68.

157. Mill, *On Liberty*, p. 136.

CONCLUSION

1. For useful overviews of radical culture in the 1820s and 1830s, see Iain McCalman, *Radical Underworld* (Cambridge: Cambridge University Press, 1988), pp. 181–237; E. P. Thompson, *The Making of the English Working Class* (New York: Vintage, 1963), pp. 711–832.

2. See M. J. D. Roberts, *Making English Morals: Voluntary Association and Moral Reform in England, 1787–1886* (Cambridge: Cambridge University Press, 2004).

3. *The Moralist*, no. 2, vol. 1.

4. *The Moralist*, no. 4, vol. 1.

5. *The Moralist*, no. 5, vol. 1.

6. *The Moralist*, no. 6, vol. 1.

7. *The Moralist*, no. 7, vol. 1.

8. *The Moralist*, no. 9, vol. 1.

9. See "To Our Fellow Republicans," *Newgate Monthly Magazine*, vol. 1, no. 5 (Janu-

ary 1825), p. 200; "Thoughts on the Present System of Education," *Newgate Monthly Magazine*, vol. 1, no. 1 (September 1824), pp. 28–33, and other *Newgate* articles on education at that time; "Missionary Labours," *Newgate Monthly Magazine*, vol. 1, no. 1, pp. 44–45, and related *Newgate* articles.

10. See Kevin Gilmartin, *Writing against the Revolution: Literary Conservatism in Britain, 1790–1832* (Cambridge: Cambridge University Press, 2008), esp. pp. 55–95.

11. *The Gorgon*, no. 48 (17 April 1819), in British Library Add. Mss. 27,825.

12. See Francis Place, "On Civilization," unpublished ms. critique of John Stuart Mill's essay "Civilization," which was published in the *London and Westminster Review* (April 1836), British Library Add. Mss. 25,827, p. 206.

13. Clipping from *The Morning Chronicle*, 27 May 1827, in British Library Add. Mss. 27,827. Emphasis added. I attribute this to Place because it recapitulates the arguments that consistently appear throughout his work.

14. "The laws criminal and civil were much more barbarous and cruel than they are now, punishments were approved of, which if they now existed would cause even the commonest of the people to hold them in abhorrence," Place writes of that former age, which he saw fading away. "The state of the Goals [*sic*] and Debtors Prisons were such as could not, would not now be endured, the treatment of the actually poor was barbarous in the extreme, little or no care was taken of them, disease abounded, ignorance prevailed, and the popular population scarcely increased at all, disease and death were prevalent in excess and epidemic disorders destroyed the people in almost incredible numbers. Drinking and whoring were scarcely unusual offenses and the almost incredible debauchery, drunkenness and filthiness of the common people is attested by the several acts of parliament and the numerous enactments intended by force to correct their grovelling vices. The mass of the people were enormously ignorant and brutish and were treated accordingly by their *betters* who when compared with men of the same classes in the present day were as barbarous as the common people. Evidence of the depraved state of society from the top to the bottom abounds, and shews with conclusive certainty that our almost immediate ancestors, even, were an ignorant, narrow minded, gross, selfish, cruel, community." See Place, "On Civilization," p. 204.

15. Place, "On Civilization," p. 219.

16. See Uday Mehta, *Liberalism and Empire* (Chicago: University of Chicago Press, 1999), pp. 101–2.

17. See Robert Graves, *Goodbye to All That* (1929; reprint London: Penguin, 2000).

18. See Makdisi, *William Blake and the Impossible History*, pp. 204–59, esp. pp. 204–32.

19. See Makdisi, *William Blake and the Impossible History*, pp. 230–31.

20. See Mehta, *Liberalism and Empire*.

21. McCalman, *Radical Underworld*, p. 192.

22. McCalman, *Radical Underworld*, p. 234.

23. See, for instance, McCalman's discussion of Wedderburn's speech on the question of the American project to "civilize" the Indians, in which, according to a spy's report, he argued that "ignorance was better than knowledge." McCalman, *Radical Underworld*, p. 117.

24. McCalman, *Radical Underworld*, p. 237.

25. See Ben Wilson, *The Laughter of Triumph: William Hone and the Fight for the Free Press* (London: Faber & Faber, 2005).

26. Jon Mee has drawn my attention to the extent to which the founder of the LCS, Thomas Hardy, thought of his own project in international solidarity with that of others, a feature of the radical struggle of those Hardy himself refers to as "the unrepresented," which was accentuated by the roles played in it by ex-slaves like Equiano or Robert Wedderburn. See Mee's forthcoming work *The Laurel of Liberty: Print and Sociability in London Radicalism, 1792–1795* (still in manuscript as this book was going to press).

27. C. L. R. James, *Beyond a Boundary* (Durham, NC: Duke University Press, 1993), p. 160.

28. See Robert Owen, *A New View of Society* (London, 1817); also see the discussion of Owen in Karl Polanyi, *The Great Transformation: The Political and Economic Origins of Our Time* (1944; Boston: Beacon, 2001), esp. pp. 133–35.

29. Blake, annotations to Berkeley, in David Erdman, ed., *The Complete Poetry and Prose of William Blake* (New York: Anchor, 1997), p. 660.

30. Blake, letter to Cumberland, 12 April 1827, in Erdman, *Complete Poetry and Prose of William Blake*, p. 783.

31. Blake, *Descriptive Catalogue*, in Erdman, *Complete Poetry and Prose of William Blake*, p. 543.

32. William Blake, *The Marriage of Heaven and Hell*, plate 10, in Erdman, *Complete Poetry and Prose of William Blake*, p. 37.

Page numbers in italics refer to illustrations.

abolitionism, 149
Abrams, M. H., 127
Allen, Michelle, 84
Anderson, Benedict, 8, 17
antinomians, 240
Arab, as designation of racial and civilizational otherness. *See* City Arabs of London
Arabian Nights, 11, 191, 210, 248n35
Aravamudan, Srinivas, 253n90
Arnold, Matthew, 243n1
Ascham, Roger, 187
Association for Preserving Liberty and Property from Republicans and Levellers, 100–101, 105, 127
Austen, Jane: interest in education of women, 144; *Persuasion,* 17, 20, 145–47, 167
Austen, Jane, *Mansfield Park,* 1–2, 17, 20; class formation at expense of kinship relations, 142; critique of slave trade tied to critique of outmoded forms of power among landed gentry, 135; and emergent ideology of Occidental domesticity, 141, 143; relationship to Inchbald, 144–45; role of women in self-regulation, 133; Said's reading of, 142–43; and self-regulating subject, 133, 135, 137, 138–39, 140–41, 143, 148; situated between radical discourse of 1790s and Occidental discourse of 1830s, 149; subversive critique of patriarchal repression, 137

Baer, William, 54
Balfour, Lord, 147, 148, 239
Balfour Declaration, 148, 253n88
Balibar, Etienne, 28
ballad(s): association with radical politics, 99, 102, 104; attack of Bishop of London on, 101–2, 105; countersubversive, 100–102, 105, 125–26; dangerous associations by 1790s, 128–29; in Eaton's *Politics for the People,* 99; flash ballads, 39; hawkers of, 96; increasingly associated with plebeian culture, 87–88; lyrical, 128, 129; mapping of, 89–97; political, in elite Whig circles as well as plebeian culture, 90; political pressure against, 93, 96, 105; production of in Seven Dials, 93; revival of in late eighteenth century, 90
Ballad of the French Revolution, 102
ballad singers, 39
ballad warehouses, 93
Ballaster, Ros, 253n90
Balzac, Honoré de, 22
Barrell, John, 22, 23–24, 53, 252n66; on attempts by writers and artists to deny plebeian consciousness, 34; *The Dark Side of the Landscape,* 32; on language as a marker of class, 21; on London in eighteenth and nineteenth centuries, 47–51; on pseudo-Oriental style, 14; on St. Giles's Rookery, 51
Baucom, Ian, xi, 4, 27, 75, 159–60

Beames, Thomas: *Rookeries of London: Past, Present and Prospective*, 59, 65, 68–69, 70, 79–80, 86, 258n50

Beckford, William, 14, 130

Beethoven, Ludwig van, 231

Bell, Andrew, 82

Belzoni, Giovanni Battista, 58, 226–27, 278n135

Bentham, Jeremy, 82, 83

Benton, Lauren, xi

Bewell, Alan, 121

blackness and whiteness, as racial markers of location from savage to civilized, 25

black population, London, 243n2; increase in late eighteenth and early nineteenth centuries, x; mixed freely with other communities in nineteenth century, xviii, 245n21; referred to as "St. Giles's blackbirds," 71

Blake, William, 63, 99, 206; alternatives to progressive, mechanical time, 241–42; "Garden of Love" in *Songs of Experience*, 172, 218; "Holy Thursday" of *Songs of Innocence*, 66; illustrations for Ritson volumes, 97, 103; "London," 66; *The Marriage of Heaven and Hell*, 242; on moral virtues as justification for imperialism, 136; and Poetic Genius, 180; rejection of linear narrative, 66; rejection of notion of linear time and self-regulating subjectivity, 19, 66, 100, 144, 147, 166, 239, 241; rejection of Occidentalism, 13, 16, 241

Bodenheimer, Rosemarie, 201

Boehm, Alan, 123

Bonaparte, Napoleon, 147

Bond, Thomas, 47

Boswell, James, 40–41

Bourdieu, Pierre, 269n34

Bow Street Runners, 48

Brand, John, 97

Brewer, John, 29, 30, 31

British and Foreign Bible Society, 35

British and Foreign School Society, 83

British imperialism. *See* imperialism, British

British Tree of Liberty, 85

broadsides, 91

Bromwich, David, 110, 122, 265n86

Brontë, Charlotte: *Jane Eyre*, 2

Burdett-Coutts, Angela, 199

Burke, Edmund, 47, 150, 159, 226; attack on by Paine and Wollstonecraft, 177; notion

of social organism occupying time of motion and constancy, 229; *Reflections on the Revolution in France*, 14, 15

Burney, Charles, 90

Burton, Richard, 174

Butler, Marilyn, 123, 142; reading of *The Giaour*, 156–57

Buzard, James, 4, 244n17, 248n12

Byrne, Paula, 144

Byron, Lord (George Gordon), 13, 116, 183; anti-bourgeois self-Orientalization, 14, 16, 17; critique of chivalry, 158; desire to leave England, 158; refusal of Occidentalist imperative, 157, 159, 165; reinforcement of Orientalism, 157–58; and relationship between personal and cultural identity and place, 159; Romantic spirit of resistance to modernization, 166

Byron, Lord (George Gordon), Eastern tales, 152–66; alternative forms of desire and temporality, 152–53, 160; binary opposition between East and West, 160; characters who belong nowhere, 153–55; characters within multidimensional spatiotemporal force field, 161; *The Corsair*, 153–54; culturally ambiguous spaces, 160; eroticism as force to open up limits of Occidentalism, 152; irony of claim that Byron sought to subvert Orientalism, 155–56; *Lara*, 153; Orient as imaginary locus of alternative forms of desire, 172–73; refusal of Occidentalist imperative, 159, 160; *The Siege of Corinth*, 154. *See also* Byron, Lord (George Gordon), *The Giaour*

Byron, Lord (George Gordon), *The Giaour*, 152, 160–66; charged force field of multiple realities, 163–65; description of a man out of place and of unknown origin, 162–63; differing narrative voices, 162; discordant and contradictory frames, 161–62, 165; eroticism as part of relations generated by multiple realities, 164–65; flashbacks and forward leaps, 162–63, 165; identity as lack of identity, 162; publishing history and editions, 163

cadgers, 51, 52, 258n48

Calhoun, Craig, 28, 29

Cannadine, David, 245n26

canting language, 22

Carens, Timothy, 273n18

Carlile, Richard, 107, 233; *Moralist*, 234; *Newgate Monthly Magazine*, 234

Carlyle, Thomas: *Discourse on the Nigger Question*, xviii; "Distressed Needle-Women, 245n23

Castro, Viveiros de, 269n34

Catnach, James, 93, 96

Césaire, Aimé, 2

Chadwick, Edwin, 84

Chakrabarty, Dipesh, 2, 114–15, 255n112

chapbook, 91

Chartist period, x, 28

Cheap Repository Tracts, 101, 102, 125–26

Choir Clubs, 39

cholera, 61

Church of England, 82

City Arabs of London, xiv, xv–xvi, 2, 6, 17, 21, 77, 78

civilizing mission, 20; of all societies along track of progressive time, 184; and annihilation of other, 172–73; in both England and colonial possessions, 184, 186–87; carried out by evangelicals or radicals, 35; against individual decadence and idleness, 135; and internal others not capable of assimilation, 75–76; and literary works, 35; and national development, 75–76; and Occidentalism, 184; and politicization of individual morality, 135; and project to make England Western, 151; and transformation of individual personality structures, 120–21. *See also* London, civilizing of

clash of civilizations thesis, 237, 276n82

class: instability of concept in England at turn of nineteenth century, 6; language as a marker of, 21; unstable relationship with race, xvii–xviii, 23

Clausewitz, Carl von, 126

Cochran, Peter, 155

Cock and Hen Clubs, 39

Cohn, Bernard, 11–12

Cole, Charles, 47

Coleman, Deirdre, 150

Coleridge, Samuel Taylor, 103, 123, 126, 144, 145, 149

Colley, Linda, 17, 141, 149; *Britons*, 26–27

Collins, Wilkie: *The Moonstone*, 203

colonial consumption, 197

Colquhoun, Patrick, 48; educational scheme,

82, 83; *Treatise on the Police of the Metropolis*, 32, 93, 96

Committee for the Relief of the Black Poor, 71

Complete Modern London Spy, The, 51

Connell, Philip, 88, 90, 93, 107

Conrad, Joseph: *Heart of Darkness*, 136, 187

consciousness, and question of language, 33–34

Cornwallis reforms of 1793, 183

Corrigan, Philip, 19, 20

costermongers, 96

Cottle, Joseph, 123

countersubversive ballads and songs, 100–102, 105, 125–26

Cromer, Lord, 8, 147

Crompton, Louis, 155

Dacre, Charlotte, *Zofloya; or, The Moor*, 152, 166–73; civilizing process annihilates the other, 172–73; embraces both colonization and homogenization of cultural spaces, 166; hyper-Orientalized and barbarized characters, 170–71; Orientalization of Venice, 169–70; Oriental threat to Occidentalist domesticity, 172–73; relationship between sexual and racial or civilizational components, 168; scholarship on, 168, 169

Dens of London, 52, 53, 61, 69–70, 70, 93

De Quincey, Thomas, 7, 63, 183, 247n6; *Confessions of an English Opium Eater*, 203

desire: civilization as regulator of, 172; Orient as locus of alternative forms of, 151, 172–73

DeWind, John, 198, 230–31

Dicey, William and Cluer, 91

Dickens, Charles: *Barnaby Rudge*, 205; *Bleak House*, 196, 199, 200, 215, 273n18, 273n19; considered overseas reform mission less important than mission in England, 214–15; faith in superiority of Western civilization, 215; fear of deterioration of culture, 217; "The Great Exhibition and the Little One," 277n94, 277n96; *Great Expectations*, 196, 206, 210; *Hard Times*, 192, 215; *Household Words*, 46–47; *Little Dorrit*, 216, 221; "Niger Expedition," 198, 199, 215, 276n93, 277n97; "The Noble Savage," 198–99, 273n14; *Oliver Twist*, 45, 206; *Pickwick Papers*, 216; piece on Great

Dickens, Charles (*continued*)
   Exhibition of 1851, 277n98; piece on
      Seven Dials, 227, 278n137; reference to
      "City Arabs," 77; *Sketches by Boz*, 51,
      93, 96; sketch of Seven Dials, 51, 57, 58,
      68, 69, 70, 93, 222–23; and St. Giles's,
      61; xenophobia in journalism and letters,
      198–99
Dickens, Charles, *The Mystery of Edwin
   Drood*, xix, 63; absence of any culturally pure space or character, 203–4;
   awkward and uneven transportation
   network, 221–22; civilized world and
   the primitive, 200; collapse of binary
   distinctions, 200–201; critique of smooth
   developmental time, 237–38; danger of
   retrogression and backsliding, 218; and
   dissolution of self, 206–8; emphasis on
   colonial commodities, 196–97; England
   as stuck in condition of undeveloped
   country, 227; excavation and recycling of
   material of the dead by the living, 227;
   feeling of nostalgia for spatial and temporal elements, 224–25; hybridization of
   Orient and Occident in one character,
   202; impossibility of opposing Occident
   to Orient, 231–32; instability of Occidental superiority, 198, 208–13; intertwining
   of domestic and foreign spaces, 197–98;
   as meditation on imperial culture, 196,
   197; meditation on jewels and time, 227–
   29; mixing of modes and states of being,
   204–5; modernity as state of recycled incompletion, 220, 221, 232; both Occident
   and Orient as imaginary geographies,
   198; scholarship on, 198, 202–3; sense of
   stalled time and present saturated with
   past, 218–21, 222–26; temporal breakdown and irregular modernization in
   both village and metropolis, 220–25, 232;
   temporal repetition and recycling, 213,
   229–30, 279n143; treatment of romance,
   225–29
Douce, Francis, 97
Doyle, Laura, xiv, 205
drinking songs, in elite Whig circles as well
   as plebeian culture, 90
Drury, Henry, 157
Dugaw, Dianne, 91
Dunn, James, 167

East India Company, 11, 12, 184, 186
Eaton, Daniel Isaac, 98–99, 102, 127; *Politics
   for the People*, 99
Edgeworth, Maria, 158
education: adapted from imperial India to
   England, 82; Colquhoun's scheme, 82, 83;
   Southey's system of, 182
Egan, Pierce, 22, 41; *Life in London*, 50, 51
Elfenbein, Andrew, 155, 158, 159
Elias, Norbert, 18, 19–20, 120–21, 172, 187,
   251n56; *The Civilizing Process*, 28
Eliot, T. S., 238
Engels, Friedrich, 46; visits to St. Giles's
   rookery, 52–53
England, in decades around 1800: began
   formation as metropolitan center,
   ix–x; breakup of parish-based society
   dominated by rural landlords, 19; differentiation of spaces and peoples, x–xi;
   emergence of Occidental identity, xvi;
   emergent "us"/"them" distinction, x–xi,
   xix; increasing literary and political
   participation, x; lack of dominant
   normative form of racial and cultural
   identity, xvi, 18; middle-class view of
   plebeian population as "savages," 20;
   new concepts of race and nation, x; new
   cultural notion of "West" in opposition
   to Orient, xii–xiii; overlapping relation
   between emergent metropolitan and
   colonial spaces, xi, xix; state formation,
   and cultural regulation, 19; struggle
   to become Western, 13, 20, 237; "two
   nations" problem, 244n17; unstable
   relationship of race and class, xvii–xviii.
   See also imperialism, British; London,
   civilizing of
England, later nineteenth century: depiction
   of ordinary life in nineteenth-century
   painting, 30–31; formation of market
   society, 18; growth of competitive labor
   market after 1834, 18; imposition of
   standard time on local time, 216
English feminism. *See* women's rights
English slang, dictionaries of, 22
English terror, 19
Equiano, Olaudah, 281n26
Eurocentrism, 190
evangelicals, civilizing mission of in England,
   28, 35

Fabian, Johannes, 2; *Time and the Other*, 80
Fanon, Frantz, xiii–xiv, 2; *Black Skin, White Masks*, 148
Faulkner, David, 197, 209, 231
Ferguson, Moira, 149
Fielding, Henry, 45, 48; *Joseph Andrews*, 29
flash ballads, 39
flash houses, 46
flash language, 22, 72
Forster, John, 201, 230
Foucault, Michel, 29–30
France, racial discourse, 22
Franklin, Carolyn, 158
Free and Easys, 39
"Free-Born Englishmen," 84
Friendly Societies, 35
Frith, Richard, 47

Gainsborough, Thomas, 34
Galland, Antoine: *Les mille et une nuits*, 248n35
Gandhi, Mohandas, 20
Gatrell, Vic, 29, 62; *City of Laughter*, 41; on Place's project, 40–41, 42, 43
Gay, John: *Trivia; Or, the Art of Walking the Streets of London*, 57
Gikandi, Simon, 10, 130
Gillray, James, 30, 245n25; "London Corresponding Society, Alarm'd," 30, 31, 71
Gilmartin, Kevin, 19, 101
Gilroy, Paul, xviii, xix, 6, 7, 8, 243n2
Girard, René, 164
Gleckner, Robert: *Byron and the Ruins of Paradise*, 163
Goddard, Lorriman, 105
Godwin, William, 35, 76, 85, 98; *Caleb Williams*, 24–25, 28, 30, 49–50, 108
Goldberg, David Theo, 26
Goldsmith, Oliver, 182; *The Deserted Village*, 203
Gorgon, The, 234
Gramsci, Antonio, xvii, 23, 32, 244n20
Grant, Charles, 157, 183–84, 186
Graves, Robert, 238
Greatbatch, George, 20, 184
Greenwich Mean Time, 216
Greenwood, James, 77
Griffin, James, 233
Grose, Francis, 97; *Classical Dictionary of the Vulgar Tongue*, 22

Grossman, Jonathan: *Charles Dickens's Networks*, 212, 216, 221
Guha, Ranajit, 30, 33
Guthrie, Thomas, 77; Ragged Schools, 78

Hage, Ghassan, 25, 75, 269n34
Halhed, Nathaniel Brassey: *A Code of Gentoo Laws*, 11
Hall Stuart, xi, xvii, 6
Hardy, Thomas (founder of London Corresponding Society), 281n26; trial for high treason, 105
Hardy, Thomas (novelist and poet), 238
Hark, Ina Rae, 209–10
Hastings, Warren, 10, 11, 19, 136, 157, 183
Hazlitt, William, 63, 241
Hechter, Michael: *Internal Colonialism*, 20
Heydt-Stevenson, Jill, 137, 142, 150
Hilton, Boyd, 84
historicism, 2
Hoeveler, Diane, 167, 169
Holcroft, Thomas, 98
Holt, Thomas, 22–23, 28
Hone, William, 107, 240
hope, discourse of, and remaking of savages into Englishmen, 25, 35
Horne, Richard, 215, 277n94, 277n96, 277n97
Hunt, Leigh, 51, 63; *Saunter through the West End*, 51; *The Town*, 51

imperialism, British, 10; centrality of subjectivity to new mission, 12, 148–49; changes in imperial policy in period around 1800, 135–36, 157, 183; in Dickens's *The Mystery of Edwin Drood*, 196, 197; expansion of, 149; and expansion of Eastern trade, 203; and free trade, 134; justification for in Romantic period radicalism, 147–48; mission to teach non-Europeans to regulate themselves, 148; moral virtues as justification for, 136; new brand of colonial administrators, 149; new form of depicted in Austen's *Mansfield Park*, 133, 135, 137, 138–39, 143, 148; new ideology and women's rights, 150; shift in empire from Western hemisphere to colonial holdings in Asia, 134; and slavery, 134; transformation from exploitation of difference to

imperialism, British (*continued*)
  eradication of difference, 19; and virtuous
  despotism, 148
Inchbald, Elizabeth: *A Simple Story*, 144–45
India: attitudes toward imported back to
  England, 32; counterinsurgent writing
  of colonials, 33; viewed as in need of
  same kind of development as spaces in
  England, 81–82, 186–87
Indian uprising of 1857, 199
industrial revolution, 18
internal racism, 7
Irish fever, 59
Irish in London, 20, 71
Italy, attitudes of some Northern Italians
  toward people of the Mezzogiorno, 23

Jacobins, 143
Jacobus, Mary, 123, 124
James, C. L. R., 134, 241; *The Black Jacobins*,
  134
Jameson, Fredric, 216
Janowitz, Anne: *Lyric and Labour in the
  Romantic Tradition*, 122, 129
Jeffrey, Francis, 126, 159
Jermyn, Henry, 47
Johnson, Ben: *Dictionary*, 21
Johnson, Claudia, 135, 137, 143–44, 150
Johnson, Joseph, 97, 103
Johnston, Kenneth, 124
Jones, David, 238, 249n39
Jones, Gale, 30
Jones, Gareth Stedman: *Outcast London*, 83
Jones, Sir William, 10, 12, 19; *Grammar of
  the Persian Language*, 11
Jones, William, 157, 1833; "Essay on the
  Poetry of the Eastern Nations,"
  191–92
Joyce, Simon, 48, 53, 66; *Capital Offenses*,
  62–63

Kant, Immanuel, 153
Kaul, Suvir, x
Keats, John, 116
Keenan, Abigail, 155
Kelley, Gary, 142
Kiernan, Victor, 27
Kinnaird, Douglas, 158
Kipling, Rudyard, 213
Klancher, Jon, 107, 127
Knight, Charles: *London*, 45, 52

Krishnan, Sanjay, 3, 247n6
Kumar, Krishnan, 254n92

Lakeland poets, 63
Lamb, Charles, 63, 64
Lancaster, Joseph, 82
Lancasterian day schools, 35, 82
Lancasterian method, 83
Landor, Walter Savage, 183; *Gebir*, 130
language: biological and racial language, to
  describe marginalized populations in
  England, 23, 25, 68–69, 70–71, 72, 75;
  canting language, 22; distinction between
  provincial and vulgar usage and "proper"
  language, 21–22; as marker of class and
  national identity in eighteenth century,
  21; political and imperial ramifications
  of, 252n66; used to map interior spaces
  of London, 76
"Lascars," 71
Lawrence, T. E., 147, 174, 239
Leask, Nigel, 88, 90, 93, 107, 155, 156, 158
Le Bon, Gustave, 22
Lee, Richard "Citizen," 85
Leroux, Jacob, 47
Lesseps, Ferdinand de, 226, 278n135
Lewis, Bernard, xiii, 276n82
liberty, of self-regulating subject, 144
Liberty of the Savoy on the Strand, 47, 48
*Life, Death, and Wonderful Atchievements
  of Edmund Burke, The*, 102
literature, Romantic through mid-Victorian
  period: account of common people in,
  35; alternation of flickers and flashes and
  sustained narrative, 63–68; approaches
  to relation of narrative to time, 62–68;
  London as spatiotemporal problematic
  in, 62–68; question of genre, 63. *See also*
  popular literature
Little London Arabs, The, 77
Little Scrigget, the Street Arab, 77
Lloyd, David, xiv
Locke, John, 205
Lombard League, 23
London, civilizing of, 78–86; ambivalent
  duality of project, 84; city viewed as in
  need of same kind of development as
  India, 81–82; "civilizing" of rookeries,
  78–86; movement of traffic and air linked
  to movement of time, 79–82; number of
  people displaced by street development

projects, 49, 50, 83–84; reform of those who could be reformed and removal of those who could not, 83; rookeries, 78–86; view that spatiotemporal layout produces a certain kind of population, 85–86. *See also* City Arabs of London

London, Romantic to mid-Victorian periods: administrative and legal heterogeneity, 48; advent of Metropolitan Police in 1830s, 48; density, 53, 68–79; islands of prosperity surrounded by criminal areas, 46, 52; lack of central planning, 47; making Western, 39–45, 233; neighborhoods that precluded individual distinction or movement, 68–69; Oriental spaces and populations, xv–xvi, 3; rookeries of, 45, 68–86; spatial unevenness, 45–54; temporal unevenness, 54–62; unnavigable space between West End and City, 49–51

"London blacks," emancipation of, 275n63

London City Mission, 78

London Corresponding Society (LCS), 105, 240–41; Gillray's print of, 30, *31*, 71; suppression of in 1798-99, 104; voice of politically marginalized population, 33

London Journal, 51

London locations: Bermondsey, 53; Berwick Street, Soho, 85; Bethnal Green, 53; Carlton House, 49; Charing Cross, 49, 78; Church Lane, xv; City of London, 47, 48, 49; Clerkenwell, 47; Cock and Pye fields, 54; Covent Garden, 45; Drury Lane, 45; Ely Place, 47–48; Farringdon Road, 50, 83, 224, 231; Farringdon station, 224; Field Lane, 45, 50, 81; Fleet Market, 45; Fleet Street, 45, 50; Fleet valley, 53, 224; Furnival's Inn, 224, 231; Holborn Street, 49, 50, 62, 223, 231; Holborn Viaduct, 50, 224, 226; Houndsditch, 53; Hundreds of Drury, 45; Jennings Buildings, 53; Kensington High Street, 53; Lambeth, 47; Liberty of the Savoy, 48; Lincoln's-Inn-Fields, 45; Lisson Grove, 53; Marylebone Square, 50; Mayfair, 49; Middle and Inner Temples, 48; Monmouth Street, 51, 58, 78, 80, 258n50; New Oxford Street, 49, 50, 80, 81, 83; Oxford Street, 49, 62; Piccadilly, 47, 50; Piccadilly Circus, 49; pillory at Charing Cross, 40; Regent's Park, 49; Regent Street project, 48–49, 58, 78; Rotherhithe, 53; Saffron Hill, 50, 53,

231; Shaftesbury Avenue, 49, 50, 51, 58, 78, 80; Shoe Lane, 50, 81; Soho, 47, 49, 81; Somers Town, 47; Southwark Street, 53, 83; Spitalfields, 53, 78; Staple Inn, 223, 224; St. George's Square, 50, 53; St. James's Square, 3, 47, 50; St. Martin's Lane, 80; St. Marylebone, 53; Strand, 49, 50; Swallow Street, 58, 78; Trafalgar Square, 78; Tyburn hangings, 40, 50, 58; West End, 49, 50; Westminster, 47, 49, 53; Whitechapel, 53; Whitecross Street, 53. *See also* Seven Dials; St. Giles's parish

London Spy books, 51–52, 71

Lorimer, Douglas, xviii

Low, Donald, 45, 48, 53

lyrical ballad, 128, 129

Macaulay, Thomas, 12, 18, 149; advocated radical transformation in England and India, 186–87; associated modernity with West, 190; attacked India's languages and literature, 176–77, 178, 213; attacked Robert Southey, 15, 17, 157, 174–78, 185–92, 198, 221; on Burke, 175–76; and centrality of subjectivity to new imperial mission, 148–49; condemned use of images as political tools, 190–91; as cultural paradigm of global culture, 178; equated Oriental with resistance to modernity, 189; *Minute on Indian Education*, 148, 176–77, 178, 183, 187, 198; normalization of Occidentalism, 185–86; related Orientalism to Occidentalism, 177; saw nothing of value in Oriental civilization, 185; Speech on the Charter Debate of 1833, 185, 186; urged creation of class of Indians to resemble English, 160, 213; viewed modernization following linear path forward, 221; viewed Occidentalism as index of modernization, 188

Macaulay, Zacharay, 125

"Madras System" of education, 82

Mahomet, A. J.: From Street Arab to Evangelist, 77

Majeed, Javed, 11, 179

Makdisi, Saree: *Romantic Imperialism*, 65–66, 157, 246n26, 247n6; *William Blake and the Impossible History of the 1790s*, 6, 99–100, 166, 238–40

Malcolmson, Robert, 24

Malthus, Thomas, 149
Mara, Miriam O'Kane, 197, 202
Marshall, William, 163
Marx, Karl, 19, 186
match boys, 48
Mathews, William, 106
Mayhew, Henry: biological and racial language to describe poor, 72, 75; "The Coster-Girl," 74; division between nomadic and settled, 71–72; "The Intensity of Ignorance," 9; "The London Costermonger," 73; London Labour and the London Poor, 7–8, 127; "Long-Song Seller," 94; on nomadic habits of "patterers," 96–97; "The Street-Stationer," 95; view of ballads and ballad singers, 87, 96–97, 104–5; view of slang in racial terms, 22
Mayo, Robert, reading of Lyrical Ballads, 91–92, 128, 129
McCalman, Iain, 240, 241
McEathron, Scott, 127
Mechanics' Institutes, 35
Mee, Jon, 97, 281n26
Mehta, Uday, 81–82, 83, 234, 276n90; Liberalism and Empire, 239
Mellor, Anne, 168
middle class: and "racial" differentiation of various English populations, 6; writers' view of lower classes as savages, 108
Miles, Robert, 22, 28
Mill, James, 81, 83, 149, 157, 187, 239
Mill, John Stuart, 81, 100, 211, 226, 232, 236; "Civilization," 214, 234; Considerations on Representative Government, 276n89; distinction between stationary and progressive societies, 214; fear of deterioration of culture, 217; on "inferior" groups of mankind, 190; On Liberty, 217; On Representative Government, 138, 214, 217; on value of progress to integrate people into West, 189–90; view of adherence to local customs as hindrance to improvement, 189
Miller, Hillis, 202
missionaries, and "uncivilized" population of England, 20–21, 78
Mitchell, Charles, 202
modernism, 63; association with West, 190; in Dickens's work, 213, 220–26, 232, 237–38; efforts to bring Oriental differ-ence into universal culture of, 16; linear space-time of, 63, 64, 79, 80; and lyrical ballad, 129; and Occidentalism, 188, 190, 211, 241; Orientalized populations and spaces as out of sync with or resistant to, 2, 84, 147, 175, 189; Romantic spirit of resistance to, 166; rookeries of London as disruption in flow of, 80, 81; threatened by plebeian oral culture, xiv; Wordsworth and, 122, 129

monitorial system of education, 82
Moore, Grace, 196–97, 202–3, 273n19
Moore, Thomas, 156, 183; Lalla Rookh, 130
Moorish characters, in English literature, 168–69
Moorman, Mary, 106
moral reform, 233–34
More, Hannah, 19, 92, 127, 129, 149, 158, 187; battle against moral and political corruption, 96; battle against popular political ballads, 100; Betty Brown, the St. Giles's Orange Girl, 51, 66–68, 75, 78, 233; "The Hackney Coachman," 67; limits on development allowed to plebeian subjects, 234; publishing of countersubversive ballads and songs in Cheap Repository Tracts, 101, 125; Shepherd of Salisbury Plain, 34; Village Politics, 34
Mukherjee, Pablo, 31, 81
Murdoch, Lydia, 77

Nares, Robert, 22
Nash, John, 48, 49
nationalism, xix, 26, 27
Neale, Thomas, 47, 54, 55
Newgate Monthly Magazine, 234
New London Review, critique of Lyrical Ballads, 90
New London Spy, 51–52
Newman, Gerald, 27, 90
Newman, Ian, 88, 90
New Oxford Street project, 80, 81, 83
New Right, Britain, 75
Nussbaum, Felicity, 253n90

Occidentalism: based on feeling of superiority over Eastern other, 13, 15; and clearing of space for white Western self, 26; on continuum with Orientalism, 10, 12–13, 16–17, 157, 174, 184, 188; difficulty of locating Western self, 17–18; distinguished from hierarchies of aristocracy, 100; emergence of in decades around 1800, xvi; and erotics of self, 151–52; importance of progressive, linear time in, 184, 213, 231; as index of modernism, 188, 190, 211, 241; internal, as necessary correlate of external, 3, 10; and modern sense of imperial and national subjectivity, 12; and need for internal other to be assimilated or purged, 5, 8, 17, 236–37; and need to contain threat of politics of the multitude, 100; normalization of, 174, 185–86; recent scholarship on, 247n7; reinforced by describing internal others using language of foreignness, 77; and self-regulating subject, 88, 135, 136. *See also* civilizing mission

Orient, as locus of alternative forms of desire and subjectivity from 1790s on, 151

Orientalism: applied to spaces and populations in London, xv–xvi, 3; British use of knowledge of to conquer from within, 10–12; on continuum with Occidentalism, 10, 12–13, 16–17, 157, 174, 184, 188; developed to enable Occidental mode, 239; eighteenth-century split between entertainment and knowledge goals, 248n35; as essential part of British cultural and political self-definition, 12, 16; European use of knowledge of for aesthetic purposes, 12; and gender and sexuality discourse, 152; as imaginative geographical construct, 2–3; internal, as necessary correlate of external, xii, 3; new cultural notion of "West" contrasted with, xii–xiii; Occidental subjectivity contrasted with, 143, 238–39; projection of Oriental traits onto aristocracy by radicals of 1790s, 14, 147, 177, 239; pseudo-style, 14, 15; view of relation to modernism, 2, 84, 147, 175, 189

Orientalist press, 130

Oriental Renaissance, 178, 184

the Other: need for assimilation or purging of by civilizing mission, 5, 8, 17, 75–76, 172–73, 236–37; relationship of self to, 88; "us"/"them" opposition between English and Orientalized other, 2–3, 6, 72, 199, 200, 237. *See also* Orientalism

Owen, Robert, 82, 240, 241

Owen, Wilfred, 238

Pagden, Anthony, 246n27

Paine, Thomas, 149, 183, 238; *Rights of Man*, 14–15, 226

Pasolini, Pier Paolo, 33, 116, 129

patois of criminal subculture, 22

Peel, Robert, 32

Peña-Sy, Stephanie, 274n38

Percy, Thomas, 103; differences with and from Joseph Ritson, 97–98; *Reliques of Ancient English Poetry*, 91; sanitized ballads, 97–98

Perera, Suvendrini, 202

Pieces of Ancient Popular Poetry, 97

Piozzi, Hester, 92

Pitts, John, 93

Place, Francis, 28, 50, 100, 107, 149, 233, 256n19; account of his father, 41–43, 45, 72, 75; advocacy of moral improvement for self-determination and self-representation, 234; archive of plebeian London life in years around 1800, 39–45, 234–36; contrast between "then" and "now" of London, 40–41; critique of Mill's "Civilization," 214; description of political pressure on popular ballads, 105; explanation for why a working man drinks, 43–44; hope as basis for politics, 44; *Improvement of the Working People*, 43; on improvement of working people, 256n10; involvement with Lancasterian method of education, 82–83; and morality as marker of movement of time and history, 43; movement in time as basis of hope, 44; on obscene and politically subversive songs and prints, 39–40, 104; "On Civilization," 234, 276n91, 280n14; on popular ballad form, 129; on space and hope, 53

plebeian consciousness: caricatured or negated by elite writers and artists, 33, 34; defused by translation into bourgeois terms, 35; in visual and verbal culture in Romantic period, 33; Wordsworth and, 109–21

plebeian subcultures: attitudes toward reflected attitudes toward external others, 22; biological and racial language used to describe, 23, 25, 68–69, 71, 72, 75; discourse of barbarism and savagery with respect to, 20–21, 108; representations of, 30

Polanyi, Karl, 18, 19, 120, 135, 240n51
Politics for the People, 99
Poole, Thomas, 107
Poon, Angelia, 203
Poor Law Amendment of 1834, 18, 240n51
popular literature: flourishing of into nineteenth century, 92–93; reclamation for new purposes, 90–91. *See also* ballad(s)
Porter, Bernard, 5–7, 8, 10, 28, 53; *The Absent-Minded Imperialists*, 1–2
Porter, Roy, 47
Powell, Enoch, 243n2
power, key component of relationship between domestic and imperial or elites and plebeians, 29, 32
Proclamation Society, 35, 233
pseudo-Oriental style, 14
Pycroft, James, xiv, xv, 78

racial discourse: blackness and whiteness as racial markers of location from savage to civilized, 25; on civilization of Europe, 22; and modern state, 7; in regard to "others" within the domestic space and in colonial world, xvi–xvii, 23–24, 26, 28, 29–30; in regard to plebeian subcultures in England, 23, 25, 68–69, 70, 71, 72, 75; role in formation of class identity, 23; and twentieth-century racism, 75
radicals of earlier seventeenth century, 240
radicals of 1790s, 19; association with popular culture, 97; civilizing project of people of England, 28; Occidentalist radicalism, 240; projection of Oriental traits onto aristocracy, 14, 177, 239; and regulation of subjectivity, 143–44, 147, 148, 149; subjectivity as differentiating feature of Occidental and Oriental, 238–39; surveillance of and crackdown on in 1790s, 105; transgression of literary and aesthetic formulas, 102–3; and treason trials of mid-1790s, 105
Ragged Schools, 77, 78
Ranters, 240
realist novel, 4
Reeves, Charles, 48
Reform Bill of 1832, 18, 240n51
Religious Tract Society, 35
Renan, Joseph Ernest, 22
Reynolds, George: *Mysteries of London*, 70–71
Ricardo, David, 82

Richardson, Alan, 155, 158–59
Ritson, Joseph, 48, 103, 125, 127, 129; *Ancient Songs, From the Time of King Henry the Third to the Revolution*, 103; challenge to Thomas Percy, 97–98, 104; and leading radicals of 1790s, 98; *Pieces of Ancient Popular Poetry*, 98, 103; *A Select Collection of English Songs*, 103
Roberts, M. J. D.: *Making English Morals*, 233
Robin Hood, 97
Robinson, Henry Crabb, 159
Robinson, Mary: "January, 1795," 63; "London's Summer Morning," 64
Romanticism: demise of signaled by Macaulay's *Minute on Indian Education*, 191–92; spirit of resistance, 166
Romantic period: attempt to combine paternalism with modern wage system, 250n51; discourse of race and civilization prevalent among those in power, 27–28; discourses permeated by contrasts between Occidental self and Oriental other, 13, 16; efforts to resist pressure of Occidentalism, 13; equivalence of representations of English plebeian subcultures and cultures of Africa or India, 30; framed by decades of 1790s and 1830s, 18; and location of England as Occidental space, 4–5; plebeian consciousness in visual and verbal culture, 33
rookeries of London, 68–79; association with imposture, 70; "civilizing" of, 78–86; represented disruption in flow of modernity, 80, 81; use of biological and racial language to describe inhabitants and spaces of, 68–69, 70, 71. *See also* St. Giles's Rookery

Said, Edward, 127, 138; assumption of separation between domestic national space and empire, 1–2, 8; *Culture and Imperialism*, 1–2, 4, 133–34; discussion of imaginative geography, 2–3, 152; and late style, 231; *Orientalism*, 2–3, 12, 155, 156; reading of Austen's *Mansfield Park*, 1–2, 142–43; use of term "counterpoint," 4
Sassoon, Siegfried, 238
satirical prints, 62
Sayer, Derek, 19, 20
Scott, Walter, 211
Scottish, 26

Scottish Highlanders, 20

Sedgwick, Eve, 202, 205, 209; *Between Men*, 164

Select Collection of English Songs, 97

self-regulation: in Austen's *Mansfield Park*, 133, 135, 137, 138–39, 140–41, 143, 148; Blake's rejection of, 19, 66, 100, 144, 147, 166, 239, 241; importance to radicals of 1790s, 143–44, 147, 148, 149; and Occidentalism, 88, 135, 136; as virtuous despotism, 144, 145, 148; women as exerters of, 133, 149

separate-spheres ideology, 149

Seven Dials, 47, 54–55; accounts of stale air, 61; area around, 1799, 55, 56; Dickens's sketch of, 51; discourse of spatiotemporal dissonance in regard to, 55, 57–58, 80; part of St. Giles parish, 51; "Seven Dials," from Walter Thornbury, *Old and New London*, 58

Seven Dials Charity, 258n60

Shaftesbury, Lord, 77

Sheikh, The, 246n26

Shelley, Percy Bysshe, 116, 166, 183, 231

Sheppard, Francis, 53

Simpson, David, 106, 114; *Wordsworth, Commodification and Social Concern*, 122

slavery: abolished in British empire in mid-1830s, 134, 148; British critique of tied to domestic English cultural and political alignment, 134–35; Mill on, 138

Smith, Charlotte, 129–30

Smollett, Tobias, 45, 78

Snow, John, 83

Society for the Diffusion of Useful Knowledge, 35, 80

Society for the Suppression of Vice, 35, 233

Solkin, David, 30–31, 34–35

Sorenson, Janet, 21

Southern Question, in Italy, 23

Southey, Robert, 12, 103; association of identity and place in Orientalist epics, 159–60; *Colloquies on the Progress and Prospects of Society*, 175–78, 181, 182; contention that societal improvements never reach the poor, 59; *The Curse of Kehama*, 156–57, 178, 179; denigration of Eastern culture in some works, 178–79, 185; evangelical approach to India, 183, 184–85; interruption of narrative flow, 64–65; later prefaces of Oriental works,

179; *Letters from England*, 50; Macaulay's attack on, 174–92; "On the Means of Improving the People," 181; "On the Rise and Progress of Popular Disaffection," 181; Orientalism as spectacle for European consumption, 178; Orientalized by Macaulay and others, 175, 176, 177, 185; Orient as setting for moral instruction, 181; rejection of progressivist notion of linear time, 166; shifting arguments on imperial policy, 183; *Thalaba the Destroyer*, 130, 178, 179–80, 181–82; use of Eastern culture while filtering out dangerous elements, 179; use of Orient as setting for universal history, 179–82; views on national education, 182; warning to societies that allow material concerns to overcome moral commitments, 181–83

Speenhamland system, 18, 250n51

Spence, Thomas, 98, 103, 127; phonetic spelling system for English, 22; *Pig Meat*, 99, 103

Spenser, Edmund: *The Faerie Queen*, 116

Spenserian stanza, 116, 117

Spinney, G. H., 125

Spinoza, Baruch, 172, 206

Spivak, Gayatri, 255n112

Stanley, Joachim, 202

Stewart, Maaja, 141–42, 142

"St. Giles's Greek," 22

St. Giles's parish, 45, 47, 49, 50, 57; Church Lane, 76–77; displacement of people by "civilizing" development, 83; disruption in flow of modernity, 59–62, 80; opening up of spaces to flow of civilization, 81; Orientalization, 3; otherness, xv; place of transients, 58; St. Giles's church, 55

St. Giles's Rookery, 46–47, 51–52, 76; accounts of stale air, 61; descriptions of animal existence, 70–71; Engels's visit to, 52–53; in mid-1840s, 52–53; referred to as Holy Land because of Irish population, 71; transformation of inhabitants into Arabs, 76–77; "Views in the Rookery, St. Giles's," from Walter Thornbury, *Old and New London*, 60; Weir's description of, 51, 57, 61–62, 65, 69. *See also* Beames, Thomas

Stokes, Eric, 186

Stoler, Ann, 6, 16, 23, 250n46

Street Arab, The, 77
street children, transformation into Arabs, 76, 77
Styles, John, 29
subaltern groups, parallels in surveillance and control of in England and India, 32
Subaltern Studies group, 33
Suez Canal, 226

Taylor, Jane, 158
Thale, Mary, 42
Thelwall, John, 14, 35, 103, 105, 107, 127, 129; *John Gilpin's Ghost; or, the Warning Voice of King Chanticleer*, 102; lectures at the Beaufort Buildings, 48, 98; member of London Corresponding Society, 98; *The Peripatetic*, 25, 103
Thompson, E. P., 84, 122, 124, 126, 244n4
Thornbury, Walter, xv, xvi, 57, 76–77, 80
Thorne, Susan, 20, 23, 78
Thornton, Thomas, 158
Thuggee, Indian cult of, 202
time, linear and progressive: as basis of hope, 44; and civilizing mission of all societies, 79–82, 184; and civilizing of London, 54–68, 85–86; and modernism, 63, 64, 79, 80; morality as marker of, 43; and Occidentalism, 184, 213, 231
Todorov, Tzvetan, 22
trades-union movement, 150
Trumpener, Katie, 20, 138
Tuite, Clara, 141
Ty, Eleanor, 145
typhus, 59

utilitarians, 187

Valentino, Rudolph, 246n26
Vaux, James Hardy, 46; *Vocabulary of the Flash Language*, 22, 72
Venis, Linda, 124–25
Venn, Couze, 247n7
Volney, C. F., 149, 183; *Ruins*, 147

Wade, John, 233
Wallas, Graham, 82, 83
Weber, Eugen: *Peasants into Frenchmen*, 22
Wedderburn, Robert, 281n26
Weir, W., 71, 84, 85; contrast of St. Giles's with developed parts of London, 58–59, 62; identification of open London thor-
oughfares, 80; on idleness in St. Giles's, 68; narrative map of early nineteenth-century London, 45, 46, 52; on Seven Dials, 79; on St. Giles's Rookery, 51, 57, 61–62, 65, 69; view of respectable population toward "dangerous classes," 79
Wells, H. G., 213
Welsh, 26
West: association of modernity with, 190; earliest reference to in cultural-political sense, 247n8; England's struggle to become Western, 13, 20, 237; London's effort to become Western, 39–45, 233; new cultural notion of contrasted with Orientalism, xii–xiii; struggle with Islam, 246n27
Western self, difficulty of locating, 17–18
White, Jerry, 49, 53
Wilberforce, William, 184, 186, 233
Wilkie, David, caricature-like paintings of plebeian characters, 34
Wilkins, Charles, translation of the *Bhagavad-Gita*, 10, 11
Wilson, Ben, 240
Wilson, Kathleen, 253n90
Winstanley, Gerrard, 240
Wollstonecraft, Mary, 14, 149, 183, 231, 238; biological and racial language, 71; on corruption of artificiality and show, 15; critiques of Orientalized femininity, 151; disparagements of Islam, 238; link between aristocracy and Oriental, 14; *Original Stories from Real Life*, 20, 145; *Vindication of the Rights of Woman*, 238
women's rights: contradictory arguments about in first half of nineteenth century, 149; and new imperialist ideology, 150; role of anti-slavery discourse in ideology of, 149
Woolf, Virginia, 238
Wordsworth, Dorothy, 106
Wordsworth, William, 63, 159; concept of magazine about manners and moral instruction for the people, 106–7; desire to turn plebeian consciousness into poetic modernity, 115; engagement with radical politics in 1790s, 122; Fenwick notes, 106; Occidentalizing forces in work, 87; other consciousness, 109–21; plebeian characters like "us" or as "other," 108; references to and treatment of common

people, 35, 87, 106–9; and Ritson, 103;
savage and civilized English characters
in, xx, 25; and Spenserian stanza, 116,
117; turn to the ballad, 87, 92
Wordsworth, William, *Lyrical Ballads*, 33;
1798 Advertisement to, 103, 104, 121,
123; affinities with contemporary poetry,
123; and broadsides, chapbooks, and
popular ballads, 92; and civilization
of savagery, 109–21; crossing of line
between settled and wanderers, 104;
distinction between plebeian experience
and narrativization in poetry, 115–21;
form, 121–24; interventions into popular
culture, 90–91; preface to, 144; project
to redirect politics of common people to
Occidentalized audience, 127–28; racially
inflected tensions between self and other,
87; relationship to contemporary literary
environment, 124–30; translation of disappearing cultural order into a new form,
129; treatment of common people, 88,
104–5, 106; use of politically and racially
charged literary form for new political
and aesthetic uses, 124, 126–27; viewed
by critics as turn from politics to poetry,
122, 124

Wordsworth, William, poetry: "Adventures on
Salisbury Plain," 117; "Animal Tranquillity and Decay, A Sketch," 111, 119;
"The Complaint of a Forsaken Indian
Woman," 121; "Composed upon Westminster Bridge," 66; contrast between
movement, flow, and speed in *The Prelude*, 65–66; "Descriptive Sketches," 97;
An Evening Walk, 97; "The Female Vagrant," 88–89, 115, 116–19, 121; final version of "Old Man Travelling; or, Animal
Tranquillity and Decay, A Sketch," 109–
14, 115, 116, 119, 121; "Guilt and Sorrow; or Incidents Upon Salisbury Plain,"
117, 119; "*Lines Left Upon a Yew-Tree*,"
115; "Michael," 107; "The Old Cumberland Beggar," 106, 113–14, 115, 116, 119,
121, 122; *Prelude*, 93; "Salisbury Plain,"
117–19, 121; Salisbury Plain poems, 87,
106, 117–19; "Simon Lee," 115–16; "The
Thorn," 115; "Tintern Abbey," 122, 128;
"We Are Seven," 115
Wrangham, Francis, 125
Wren, Christopher, 54

Young, Mary (Jenny Diver), 40